THE CHALLENGE OF LIBERTY

The
CHALLENGE *of*
LIBERTY

by Robert V. Jones

THE HERITAGE FOUNDATION, INC.
75 E. Wacker Drive, Chicago, 1, Illinois

LIBRARY OF CONGRESS CATALOG CARD NUMBER 56–7997

PRINTED IN THE UNITED STATES OF AMERICA

Contents

THE CHALLENGE OF LIBERTY

BOOK ONE

THE CHALLENGE TO UNDERSTAND LIBERTY

Chapter 1

THE CHALLENGE TO OUR TIME

To every age comes its own challenge, different from the challenge to any other age. Although the elements of the problem of social existence remain always the same, yet as each generation variously emphasizes or neglects particular elements of that problem, the challenge to the succeeding generation is presented in different form.

The challenge to the Occidental world in our time is to maintain liberty, as individual freedom of action and as the social order providing such freedom. Our generation, the recipient of such a heritage of liberty as few other societies have ever obtained, has become oblivious to its riches by reason of their abundance. Careless of our inheritance, we now face the challenge of maintaining it, and the danger is great that it may be lost.

If the loss occurs, it will come through the growth of collectivism, which continues to increase its influence throughout the western world. We today devote much of our energy and wealth to preparation for possible war with communist nations; nevertheless at the same time we continue to adopt additional collectivistic practices, not seeming to comprehend that by this course the ultimate victory of communism is ensured. This anomalous policy, which opposes communists but receives their teaching, is possible only because we presently fail to understand the nature of liberty and are not resolved upon its practice.

Liberty is the doctrine of the social philosophy which we shall here call individualism. Individualism and collectivism are sharply opposed theories of social organization. The one emphasizes liberty for the individual and the other conformity by the individual. The two theories proceed from diverse philosophical positions and arrive at widely separated ways of life. Their conflicts cannot be resolved. One or the other must therefore predominate in a society, and the choice between them, with its vast consequences, must be continuously made by men as part of the process of life.

The necessity of choice is pressed upon us today with dramatic intensity. The rapid spread of socialism and communism during recent decades makes it necessary vigorously to champion liberty or supinely to watch it decay. Meeting the challenge of liberty cannot therefore be deferred; decision must be made in the time that immediately confronts us.

The challenge is two-fold: first, it is the challenge of understanding liberty; and second, it is the challenge of practicing liberty. The second part of the challenge cannot be met without antecedently meeting the first part; the practice of liberty cannot be realized unless its theory be understood.

It is clear that the knowledge of the nature of liberty obtaining in current thought is not comparable to that which prevailed in the period when modern liberty was being built—the eighteenth and nineteenth centuries. In those strenuous times liberty was an explicit philosophy whose champions were familiar with its basic arguments. We may indeed now find it impossible to accept entirely the analysis which then seemed persuasive; but there is little understanding today either of that analysis or of any other in its place. Despite a present renewal of interest in the theory of individualism, the concern of thought does not extend to tracing down to their roots the fundamental propositions upon which the case for the liberty of individualism must stand or fall. This deficiency in current thought—wherein is revealed a superficiality characteristic of it in many ways—seems assignable to three causes.

First, the philosophy of the liberty of individualism has rarely been presented as a systematized whole. There are writings available on the political aspects of liberty, emphasizing personal freedom and democracy; there are treatises on individualistic economics, centering attention on the free market as social regulator and on the productivity of free enterprise; and there are works on freedom of thought, freedom of expression, and the worth of the individual human being. But these partial aspects of the theory of liberty have seldom been brought together into a philosophic unit. Their interrelation has not been disclosed. The young student seeking to know the world he is entering and the older person studying the philosophy of social organization come upon the tenets of liberty piecemeal, and may proceed a considerable distance before grasping the concept that the view of things emphasizing liberty is not a haphazard collection of unrelated ideas, but an integrated doctrine of how human beings should live together. The writings that purport to give a rounded view of the philosophy of liberty are limited; this book is an attempt to add to that literature.

Second, collectivism presents itself to our age as a reform, whereas the freedom of the individual is felt to be the prevailing principle of the none too satisfactory world we find about us. Therefore collectivism, whether it be embodied in the proposals of communism, socialism, or governmental paternalism, tends to be considered in a visionary mode, unimpaired by the imperfections that always attach themselves to actuality. The assumption accordingly prevails that the liberty of individualism has been tried and found inadequate; in the light of this assumption, study of the principles of liberty seems unrelated to modern social development.

Third, our schools and colleges have for a long time furnished little objective teaching of social philosophy. In part this has been due to the ascendancy of a materialistic viewpoint, whereby ways of making a living rather than ways of living life have seemed important, and pursuant to which nearly all philosophy, individual as well as social, has been left unexamined. In part this has been the result of a desire, shared by many educators during the past few decades, to further the progress of collectivism. A not inconsiderable portion of the educational world has felt the allure of collectivistic promises. Teachers so influenced have regarded their positions as suitable opportunities for propaganda; wherefore objective teaching of economics, political science, and philosophy has declined, being replaced by presentations slanted to induce belief in the tenets of collectivism.

There has thus occurred a culpable neglect of the philosophical principles which have heretofore supported the development of American culture. How many students, even in our colleges, have ever received any instruction in the theory of the limitation of governmental powers, particularly in the doctrine of the limited authority of our national government? On the contrary have they not been led to assume, both by suggestion and by their very proximity to the state-adulation the educators have succumbed to, that the state can do no wrong, and that the cure for every human ill is to be found in political action through government? How many students, again, have ever heard that there is a philosophic argument for private property? Do they not, rather, frequently receive glowing accounts of the Tennessee Valley Authority and similar socialistic enterprises, with direct or oblique indications that collective ownership is ethical while individual ownership is selfish?

I do not suggest that teachers should indoctrinate the principles of individual liberty, for I hold that they should refrain from propaganda of all kinds, confining themselves to explanation and guiding the discipline of learning. But the theories on which our American society has been developed constitute a body of factual material vital to the present task of living, and should therefore be the subject of instruction.

This deficiency in the knowledge of the philosophy of individualism is the occasion for this book; and its purpose is to attempt to contribute to a better understanding of the principles of that philosophy.

This work is not, however, a neutral presentation. I believe in the liberty of individualism as here expounded. I believe that freedom in itself is the greatest good that society can confer upon the individual. I believe further that a social order of liberty results in the greatest good for the greatest number, that it gives culture and morality their chance, and that only under societies granting individual freedom can great ages of history appear. This work is therefore intended to be an argument for liberty, both as individual action and as social form.

My purpose, further, is not simply to explain liberty and its advantages, nor yet to justify the privilege or right of possessing liberty, but rather to present it in its fundamental aspect as duty. Even as individual man is under a duty, imposed by the nature of existence, to lead a good life, so he is duty-bound to preserve his individual freedom, which is at once the essence and the condition of the life of a good human creature. And as men in their social relation, acting as members of society, are obliged in duty to maintain the form of organization that brings the highest good to all, so they are under an obligation to build their social order and its rules on the principles of equal liberty for all, which constitutes the absolute and ultimate criterion of social justice.

If liberty is to be preserved in our society, it must be deeply believed in, and if there is to be belief, there must be understanding. It is not enough simply to like liberty, or to feel that it is a natural right, or to think it useful as an arrangement that assures the largest production of goods. If these are the only convictions our society is going to hold, liberty will surely disappear. Liberty must be clearly seen as the relation between men which the purpose of life itself demands, and as both the condition and the fact of the unfolding of man's spirit. When these basic truths have been learned, then the proper application of the principles of liberty to all areas of human life can be correctly comprehended.

Chapter 2

THE MEANING OF TERMS

1. The semantic difficulty

Discourse presumes the possibility of communicating ideas by language, and such communication can occur, in the case of printed discourse, only if the inked signs on the page are competent to evoke for the reader approximately the same ideas as those conceived by the author.

Although we can never know with precision how nearly this condition is met, we are nevertheless frequently aware that there is failure to satisfy it, occasioned through the use of equivocal words and phrases. But thought can have social significance only as it is communicated; and truth waits on discourse for its influence.

Obscurity, moreover, may serve as the concealing cloak of error as well as of truth. One cannot avoid suspecting that much of the devious and cloudy disputation of recent years in matters of economics, politics, and social philosophy has been at least in part a cover for weakness, prompted by a fear of being caught and questioned in plain language, whereby the frailty of the argument would be disclosed.

Therefore in things deemed worthy of debate men should speak as plainly as they can. The argument of the present book will strive to be clear.

All branches of social study nevertheless labor under a difficulty from which the natural sciences escape, in that the phenomena of human action, both individual and social, do not submit to rigid classification and consequently not to explicit terminology. The sign H_2O always means the same thing, and likewise the thing to which the sign applies always remains approximately the same. Throughout the realm of natural law like phenomena recur, with uniformity of characteristic that allows precise definition and the use of special names for separate phenomena.

It is otherwise with the facts of human action, which occur in infinite variety and change under hand while being examined. If for example we study an isolated phenomenon such as the authority of the presidency under the American constitution, we find that although we may call the object of our study presidential power, yet there is no constant set of facts that can be placed under that designation, for presidential power has changed with each administration, having been one thing under John Adams, another under Lincoln, and yet another under Truman. We cannot employ a separate term for each manifestation of presidential power, both because the resulting vocabulary would be too large for practical use, and because of the difficulty of agreeing on the separateness of the phenomena. Therefore the study must be conducted in terms of presidential power as a generality, and its analysis must be stated in broad principles rather than in particularities.

In similar manner the complex of laws and customs that we call social organization does not submit to precise analysis and rigid classification. Social organization is different for each society and has changed on each page of the society's history, and will continue to change; wherefore if we should attempt a factual description of a particular current society, and should believe we had succeeded in preparing one, it would yet be inaccurate before the ink had dried.

Social analysis must therefore be conducted in terms of principles rather than in terms of precise phenomena. An enumeration of all the laws obtaining today in the United Kingdom would not be of great use in defining a semi-socialist state, because a semi-socialist state may exist under other laws and decrees, and the particular laws and decrees change. But the principles remain constant, and accordingly in order to understand socialism it is necessary to understand the principles underlying it, of which factual details are but transitory manifestations.

Because of this difficulty which social analysis encounters, however, it becomes the more important that terms be carefully selected and used. In natural science a mistaken term is usually detected promptly from its contrast with the factual material it is placed against. But opponents may conduct an extensive debate on socialism the while each is attaching a different meaning to the term, without becoming aware of either the fact or the extent of the difference in terminology that prevents their debate from being meaningful.

In this work basic terms will be employed with consistent significance, which I shall now indicate.

2. The basic terms of our discussion

Liberty is a grand word, of splendid ancestry and still shining in its implications. It has successfully resisted abuse, and unlike its cousin, the adjective liberal, has not been beaten down by collectivists. Of its numerous meanings, it is used in this work in but two: first, it means the privilege, or more precisely the prerogative and duty, of the individual person to make his own decisions concerning his action; and second, it means the social order that confirms this prerogative and duty for all persons.

These two meanings are closely allied, for the first looks at the act of self-determination from the viewpoint of the individual, while the second regards it from the viewpoint of all the people who comprise a society. Liberty in the first meaning can be experienced only where there is liberty in the second; and liberty in the second meaning has for object the maintenance of liberty in the first. The distinction in meaning is a distinction in emphasis. In this work the intended emphasis will be apparent from the context; but regardless of which emphasis is employed, there will always be carried along overtones of the other. It is appropriate and indeed inevitable that liberty be used with these two emphases, including both meanings yet directing thought particularly to one or the other, because all human action occurs as a duality of individual and social experience.

Liberty as used herein never includes the idea of political autonomy; for although self-government is essential to liberty, yet political autonomy is neither a condition of liberty nor a part of it. Who can contend that the liberty of the people of Illinois requires their political independence from their neighbors in surrounding states? Wherefore the usage that has established liberty as a frequent designation for political autonomy is unfortunate, creating confusion of thought, with upon occasion the most tragic consequences. The working of this error we can see at the close of the war in 1918, when it was supposed that the liberties of the people of central Europe demanded that they be split into inoperable political autonomies, as a result of which mistake they soon lost not only their political independence but also their liberty, an outcome involving the more of tragedy as it flowed from decisions intended to produce human happiness.

The word freedom as here employed means much the same as liberty, but always with emphasis upon individual action instead of social arrangement. Freedom is the experience primarily of people as individual beings, and only secondarily does the word call our attention to the social organization that makes the individual manifestation of freedom possible.

It scarcely needs to be observed that freedom as herein used does not mean security, as by distortion it has been made to do in the recently invented slogans "freedom from want" and "freedom from fear." Strange mottoes, these, for a land whose founders deliberately embraced both want and fear for the sake of freedom, a choice that established both their greatness and our heritage. Freedom is not the absence of a disliked fact or condition; rather it is the quality of self-determination. Both want and fear may, it is true, impair the possibility of freedom, and we properly seek to curb their malevolent influence; but their absence is not freedom, which is something far other.

The word collectivism is a newcomer in our language, having made its first appearance less than a hundred years ago. Originally employed to designate the theory of the collective ownership of property, it has expanded rapidly in recent times to become a generic term, covering all forms of social philosophy that subordinate individual to collective action. As a general term, collectivism performs a useful and needed function, and it is as such employed in this study. Collectivism, then, as here used, means the general viewpoint that sees the individual as existing primarily for the benefit of the group, that regards group welfare rather than individual welfare as the unit for the measurement of human values, that therefore finds the good life in programs of collective action in which the individual is required to participate in an allotted role, and that rejects the society of multitudinous programs of individual action worked out by and for individual persons themselves. As we shall see, this viewpoint is basic to a large number of social concepts and practices, joining them by a common characteristic, and therefore it is appropriate that this general position be indicated by a generic term. Collectivism seems the most suitable designation available.

Communism and socialism are also new arrivals in our language, having appeared in the early part of the nineteenth century. They have been used, and are currently used, in various meanings. As herein employed, communism means the general program of the Communist party of Russia and its satellites, and socialism refers to the general program advocated by the Socialist party in England and by similar parties in western Europe. As so used, communism and socialism designate closely allied species of collectivism—a proposition to be demonstrated, however, as we proceed.

At the opposite end of the spectrum from collectivism lies anarchism. As used herein, anarchism is a generic term, referring to the general viewpoint that all government is evil. It runs from the extreme of nihilism to the more moderate view of replacing organized government with voluntary association as far as possible. Because of the present day's emphasis on the importance of the state, anarchism as a philosophical scheme for human relations tends to be overlooked; yet it is a view of life with indubitable roots in man's nature, and from Zeno the Stoic through Proudhon to Kropotkin it has had its philosophic voices. And not long ago anarchism was represented by an organized movement in Europe and America, as the Haymarket riot in Chicago and the Sacco-Vanzetti case in Massachusetts may serve to bring to mind. If, moreover, history were the record of all human conduct, instead of being as it is but the chronicle of those parts that seem more spectacular, it might transpire that anarchism has been about as much honored in practice as collectivism and individualism. For there always have been societies in which some men could and did live with little or no regard to political ties, becoming each man a law unto himself. But this sort of practical anarchism does not reach the history books to much extent, and it is only by reading between the recorded items and contemplating what is not included there that we can gain an idea of the degree to which anarchism has from time to time been found in practice as a mode of human relation in both the Occident and the Orient, particularly perhaps in the latter.

Midway between the opposites of collectivism and anarchism and opposed to each is individualism. Individualism adopts the welfare of the individual human being, since it is the unit of human life, as its unit for the measurement of human values, and accordingly it regards the state as existing only for the welfare of the individual. In this viewpoint individualism is at variance with collectivism. But it nevertheless also sees that the individual person is but a part of a larger body, the social group, that the welfare of each member of this group is to be taken into account, one unit of welfare being as important as another, and that individual activity seeking welfare must be subject to rules of social organization protecting the individual welfare of all. In this recognition of the need for group action individualism differs from anarchism.

The term individualism as herein used thus means the philosophy that supports liberty both as individual experience and as group control, and accordingly it is the liberty of individualism that is the theme of this study.

Individualism includes the concepts of private capitalism and free enterprise, which are the manifestations of liberty in the economic sphere. But liberty includes much more than the private ownership of capital and the maintenance of a free market, and the system of liberty cannot properly be described either as capitalism or as free enterprise, since these terms refer only to limited aspects of the free society. As used herein, therefore, capitalism is not a synonym for individualism, but is a designation only of that part of individualistic theory which calls for the private control of the land and machines that are the tools of economic production, as distinguished from state control. Similarly free enterprise means only the theory of the free market, which although an essential component of individualism and so of liberty, is nevertheless only a part thereof.

All the terms described above are something less than satisfactory, because they have been used in such varying senses that they do not possess the degree of explicitness desirable. But they are the best terms to be had, and neither events nor discussion can wait on adequate terminology.

We are not, however, primarily interested in definitions of terms, but in investigation of the facts themselves. Human action in its individual and social aspects is the field of our inquiry, and terms are but instruments to be used by thought in conducting its research. Basic terms should therefore be kept rather general in their content as initially employed, that they may be adapted to the facts as these are disclosed.

3. The implication of hypothesis by the use of terms

It is nevertheless unavoidable that terms employed in investigating phenomena, no matter how general those terms may be, should constitute a hypothesis of the explanation to be given to the facts. For at the very least terms indicate the classification to be used in arranging the facts, and such classification is itself a hypothesis respecting their nature and relationship. This is true as well in investigations of natural science as in investigations of social phenomena; the terms the scientists take with them into their laboratories necessarily involve a priori assumptions of the nature of the facts to be found there, for at the least the terminology involves the hypotheses of causation and of susceptibility to mathematical measurement.

As the reader is doubtless already aware, the terminology here presented involves a hypothesis concerning the facts of social action. The hypothesis is that those facts can be arranged in a series, that collectivism is an appropriate term, as above described, for the facts at one end of the series, that anarchism is an appropriate term, as above described, for the facts at the other end of the series, and that individualism is likewise an appropriate term, in the meaning given to it, for those facts that group themselves in the middle portion of the series. Whether this is a correct hypothesis will be for the argument of this study to disclose.

But although the *a priori* inferences of terms are unavoidable, there is always great danger that the implications of a term will unwarrantably be read back into the phenomenon to which it is applied. Names count, even with those who think they are discriminating, and accordingly calling a social fact liberal, socialistic, communistic, or progressive tends to cause that fact to be viewed in the light of the appellation.

The term *laissez faire* contains this danger to an extraordinary degree. Originated by the French physiocrats in the eighteenth century, the phrase was picked up by nineteenth century economists who favored free enterprise, and it has continued in use to the present time. It is most unfortunate, however, in that it suggests nonintervention by the state to the point of anarchy. But individualism is not anarchism; on the contrary individualism calls for state intervention in human affairs, but intervention of a particular kind and quality. Consequently, the designation *laissez faire*, with its strong connotation of nonintervention by the state, is never appropriately applied to any aspect of individualism, and it will not be employed in this book.

In this and in all ways we shall strive to avoid argument by appellation. We shall examine facts, describe them as accurately and simply as possible, and from those facts seek to construct a theory of social organization in which we can believe.

Chapter 3

HISTORY OF THE PHILOSOPHY OF LIBERTY

The concepts that form philosophical thought at any time are made up of reformulation and expansion of concepts developed in the past. Present thinking never starts from zero. Therefore in order to understand present thought it is necessary to know something of past thought. This chapter will accordingly sketch briefly the history of the philosophy of liberty. Inasmuch as a comprehensive history, however, would extend far beyond the chapter's limits, it is proposed to relate only certain chief incidents selected from that history.

1. Plato, Aristotle, and the Stoics

The Athenians of the fifth century B.C., to begin with the Greeks, were greatly devoted to the practice of liberty, but strangely they never produced any philosophic support for their way of life, and on the contrary their philosophers seem to have preferred, at least in theory, the collectivism of neighboring Sparta.

In the *Republic* Plato paints his conception of an ideal society, and his design is highly collectivistic. The inhabitant of his imagined community is taken in hand by the state in his earliest years, and thereafter he is molded by education and training, without any choice of his own, for the precise part he is required to fill in the social order. He is prevented from hearing anything that brings in question the wise design of his government, which he is early led to believe is the will of the gods. History, poetry, and music are rigidly censored, the permitted forms being only those that tend to the framing of desirable character. All property is owned in common, and perhaps wives also. The tasks of the community are to be performed by specialized workers, assigned in accordance with their natural aptitudes. "The shoemaker," said Plato, "was not allowed by us to be a husband-man, or a weaver, or a builder— in order that we might have our shoes well made; but to him and to every other worker was assigned one work for which he was by nature fitted, and at that he was to continue working all his life long and at no other; he was not to let opportunities slip, and then he would become a good workman."[1] Others would be selected and carefully reared to be soldiers, the guardians of the state.

How would the assignment of respective tasks be effected; who would make the decisions on natural aptitudes, educational procedures, and permissible poetry, music, and other sorts of expression? Plato recognized the obvious fact of this problem, but he dismissed it with the proposition that "then only will this our State have a possibility of life" when "philosophers are kings, or the kings and princes of this world have the spirit and power of philosophy."[2]

The tragic error of the *Republic*, however, lies not in its depiction of a society difficult or impossible to accomplish, but in its assertion of the desirability of the social order it presents, the possibility of its accomplishment being waived. Does man exist only or primarily "in order that we might have our shoes well made," and for the purpose of enabling a small number of select spirits to experience authority as philosopher-kings? Few indeed will give, or have ever given, an affirmative answer to this question when put directly; yet it is the premise on which the construction of the *Republic* necessarily rests; for its collectivism denies the individual's right to self-expression and gives regard only to his presumed worth as a servitor of the group. No hint appears in the *Republic* that individual liberty may be a human good, either for itself or for what it may accomplish, and indeed it would constitute an element incompatible with Plato's planned economy. Thus western philosophy begins with a paean to the worth of collectivism, and the influence persists strongly to the present time.

Aristotle in his *Politics* attacked the scheme of the *Republic* at various points, but his criticism was superficial and has had little weight in subsequent philosophic history. He expressed, however, the purpose or aim of social organization in terms which are akin to those of present individualistic thought. "A state exists for the sake of a good life," he wrote. "The state is the union of families and villages having for an end a perfect and self-sufficing life, by which we mean a happy and honorable life."[3] Aristotle also noted, although he did not much develop, the distinction between natural and conventional law.

1. *Republic*, II, 374.
2. *Republic*, V, 473.
3. *Politics*, III, 9.

The Stoics, however, shortly thereafter made use of the idea of natural law as the base of their entire structure of concepts. The law of nature as revealed by human reason is the origin of all knowledge and the guide to all conduct, the Stoics taught. Stoicism, however, made little attempt to use the idea of natural law as part of a social philosophy. It was not until centuries later that the concept, modified by European thinkers, gave rise to the theory of natural rights, which has played such an influential role in social thought down to the present time.

2. Jesus and Paul

The Greeks had regarded man primarily as citizen, as an individual related to a particular *polis*; and the Jews had classified him as he belonged or failed to belong to a favored nation. But in the minds of Jesus and Paul political citizenship became unimportant. In its place appeared the concept that all men are children of God, wherefore they should live together in a relation of loving-kindness. Political association was dropped from consideration. One can read through the New Testament without occasion to suspect that Jesus lived and taught in a time of political crisis, when indeed his nation was being destroyed. Even when urged to discuss the foreign tyranny that oppressed his countrymen he refused to do so, avoiding the difficult issue with the famous aphorism "Render to Caesar the things that are Caesar's, and to God the things that are God's."[4] Paul went further, not only indicating the unimportance of political controversy, but admonishing early Christians to be "subject unto the higher powers," to pay tribute, and not to resist political authority, for "the powers that be are ordained by God."[5]

In the place of the political relation there is presented by the New Testament the relation of morality, a morality that is the attribute of individual conduct as it seeks to express the will of God.

Man-made distinctions, as well as the political relation, disappear from the teaching of the New Testament, for all men are equal before God. Perhaps no one point is mentioned more often in Jesus' teaching than the equality of men in God's concern. The parables of the prodigal son, of the lost sheep, and of the servants who were paid equal wages, and the constant references to the meek and lowly, all attest the prominence of the idea of man's essential equality in New Testament thought.

4. Mark, XII, 17.
5. Romans, XIII, 1.

The two emphases thus included in the doctrine of the New Testament have become foundation stones in the philosophy of individualism.

The first is the proposition that the great purpose of human life is not the development of a political state, but the development of human character, as each individual strives to accomplish the will of God. Jesus said, "Thou shalt love the Lord thy God with all thy heart, and with all thy soul, and with all thy mind. This is the first and great commandment. And the second is like unto it, Thou shalt love thy neighbour as thyself. On these two commandments hang all the law and the prophets."[6] The observance of these two commandments, which Jesus thus set as the goal of all human endeavor, and as constituting the will of God which men are to follow, pertains solely to inner human character. No law of any state can compel love, nor any scheme of social organization assure it. It can appear only as an individual development of the human heart and soul and mind. The proposition thus asserted, that the end of human life is character, the building of the good life by the individual through his personal development, is basic to the liberty of individualism.

The second New Testament principle adopted and developed by individualism is the equality of man. Individualism is not a religion, claims no divine revelation, and is attached to no religious creed. But historically it obtained the two concepts of inner character as life's purpose and of the fundamental equality of men from the New Testament. Nor could it readily have obtained them elsewhere. For these two principles, familiar as they may seem to us at the present time, in spite of our want of devotion to them, nevertheless came with difficulty into the world. Jesus, it is true, was not originating when he said that man should love God and his neighbor, but was quoting prior Jewish writers.[7] But the emphasis he gave was all new. For the Jews the good life had consisted in observance of God's rituals and laws. For the Greeks it had consisted in beautiful accomplishment. But the New Testament introduced the concept that the good life consists first in the goodness of character. This had been said before, doubtless many times, as in Plato's splendid parable of the souls appearing naked for judgment,[8] in numerous places in the Old Testament, in Epictetus and other Stoic writers, but it was the New Testament that gave the idea historical momentum in the western world.

6. Matthew, XXII, 37–40.
7. Deuteronomy, VI, 5, and Leviticus, XIX, 18.
8. Gorgias, 523.

The concept of the equality of all men, moreover, was originated as well as promulgated by the New Testament. The Jews had believed that they constituted a select people in whom Jehovah was especially interested, and the Greeks had regarded themselves as rather obviously superior to all other men. But Jesus made a Samaritan, a half-breed whom the Jews disliked and repudiated as an inferior, his model of the good neighbor, whose kindness was pleasing to God. This idea of the equality of men was new. So obvious, furthermore, are the apparent inequalities of men in many respects, as in strength and intellectual capacity, that the concept of essential equality is difficult to come by; and that Jesus succeeded in presenting effectively his theory of the fundamental equality of all men in the concern of God was an accomplishment of the greatest magnitude.

3. Natural law and the Reformation

No writer of the Christian church advanced any ideas destined to become a part of individualistic philosophy until the thirteenth century, when Thomas Aquinas, reviving Aristotle's distinction between natural and conventional law, laid the foundation for the later development of the concepts of natural law and natural right, so important both to the theory and practice of liberty. Natural law, said Aquinas in his *Summa Theologica*, is comprised of those precepts of human conduct that human reason can ascertain and evaluate as right or wrong. God has given man the light of reason to enable him to know natural law, and thereby to participate in the eternal law of God. Human law, on the other hand, is man's own determination of rules of conduct. It may be derived from natural law, and to the extent that it is so derived it has the force of natural law; otherwise it has only the political force of human law. The distinction thus formulated by Aquinas was importantly developed three centuries later by Richard Hooker. But before considering his contribution to the concepts that make up individualism we must turn aside to observe another train of events.

For a long period of time there had been a movement for reform within the Roman Catholic church, and when at last in 1517 Martin Luther posted his famous theses on the church door at Wittenberg most of the points at issue had become rather well defined. But nowhere among these disputed matters was there included a demand for religious liberty, in which neither Luther nor the other early Reformation leaders were interested. Their goal, developed as events unrolled, was to supplant the church of Rome with a regional church, national or municipal, which would be a reformed institution, cleansed of the faults and errors of its predecessor, but which would by no means tolerate dissidence within the area of its coverage. The reformed church, whether Lutheran or Calvinist, was as unkind to opposition as was the Catholic hierarchy, and at times made use of the same ultimate cruelty of burning to extirpate heresy. "God does not command us," said Calvin, "to maintain any religion, but that only which He hath ordained with His own mouth."

To Calvin and all other Protestants what God had "ordained with His own mouth" was to be found in the Holy Scriptures, and it was the repudiation of the divine authority of the church and the elevation in its place of the authority of the Bible, which book was regarded as a precise rule of life for all matters and divinely inspired even to its punctuation marks, that was the prime doctrinal divergence of Protestantism. This denial of Rome's claim to divine authority through apostolic succession, while necessary to the Reformation's revolt, yet contained within itself the force that would in turn destroy the pretensions of the separate Protestant churches to dogmatic certitude.

For if the Catholic church's right to control the spiritual life of men be denied, then with that denial goes necessarily a denial also of its right to effect a conclusive interpretation of scripture; because if the latter be admitted, then scripture can be interpreted to support the former, and this in fact was what the Catholic church had done. The same reasoning, however, which destroyed any divine authority of the Catholic church to promulgate binding interpretations of the Bible destroyed also any like pretended authority in any Protestant church, which in no case could make a better chain of title to an original grant of authority than could its predecessor. Thus all divinely authorized interpretation, whether Catholic or Protestant, was eliminated; and therefore recourse could be had only to human interpretation, which means an appeal to human reason. The sole judgment available to reason, however, is one based on the standard of reasonableness, which is not absolute but relative and contingent. Uniformity of belief cannot therefore be demanded of human reason; diversity is inevitable; and to attempt uniformity by compulsion is a repudiation of the very reasonableness sought for. In the nature of the case, accordingly, religious liberty must be the ultimate solution of the problem presented by different views of the Bible, once appeal has been limited to the judgment of reason. Thus the Protestant denial of divinely granted authority in a church led inevitably in time to the assertion of religious freedom for the individual.

This conclusion was not acquiesced in, however, until much tragic history had been enacted, as both Protestants and Catholics sought to accomplish God's will, and to enforce their own opinions, by sword and fire. Lutherans, Calvinists, Anglicans, Presbyterians, all insisted not only on the error of Catholicism but also on that of every branch of the Reformation except their own. The religious persecutions and wars engendered of this common bigotry wasted Europe for generations, and when at last they subsided, through exhaustion and recognition of their futility, religious freedom was still not accomplished, but only a grudging toleration of particular sects.

Voices had been raised, nevertheless, for liberty. Robert Browne, George Fox, William Chillingworth, Roger Williams, to name only a few of the better known controversialists, had spoken clearly and forcefully for complete freedom of the individual in determining and practicing his religious beliefs. Their argument was that the Bible is God's word to men, that it is the duty of all men to follow it, that since it is intended as the expression of God's will for all men it must be correspondingly within the right of all men to study it, that it cannot be the privilege of one man to bind another in his understanding of the Bible's meaning, and that therefore God must desire that each man should conscientiously interpret the Bible for himself.

Slowly, but only slowly, the principle of religious liberty so enunciated emerged from the turmoil of the seventeenth century. Not until 1689, one hundred and seventy years after Luther had promulgated his theses, did the Parliament of England adopt the Toleration Act granting freedom in religion to all except Papists and Unitarians, and not until a century later were legislative restrictions of all kinds removed, although prior to that time religious freedom had in practice been approximated.

In America, the early colonists were not, for the most part, protagonists of tolerance for any but themselves. The Puritans of Massachusetts sought a rigid theocracy after the pattern of Geneva, and the largest favor that dissenters from the prevailing religious persuasion could expect in most of the colonies was an uncertain indulgence. But by the time of the Revolution freedom in religious activity had been largely attained in fact if not entirely in theory throughout the land. And when in 1789 the first amendment to the new constitution of the United States provided that "Congress shall make no law respecting an establishment of religion, or prohibiting the free exercise thereof," the momentous fact was signalized that religious liberty had at last become established as part of the individualistic way of life in at least this portion of the Occidental world.

Three lines of thought converged to produce the theoretical base for the practice of freedom in religion. The first was a sense of the futility of strife. For centuries the Christian church had been preaching the doctrines of the man who postulated love of God and one's neighbor as the law of life, the while it had been practicing hate and cruelty to the heterodox. To what avail? When the terror of fanatical intolerance had done its work, when Protestants had been strung from trees by the thousands in Holland, when a third of the population of Germany had been destroyed in the Thirty Years' War, when Papists in England had been disfranchised and punished, what had been accomplished? Did not dissension remain? Was not all the hating futile? Europe began to believe that it was, and turning to other interests, lost its appetite for the sharp doctrinal disputation that had theretofore seemed so important. Favor was directed to cynicism, as exemplified in the Restoration court in England, and to Deism, as found in the thinking of Shaftesbury in England and Franklin in America, and neither viewpoint could concern itself with asserting its opinion by force. Increasingly the feeling grew that intolerance was a waste of human effort.

The second line of thought leading to religious liberty was the Protestant argument, which we have already examined, that each man should for himself determine God's will as found in the Bible, and should correspondingly be privileged to follow, without social molestation, the course of action he found there enjoined. From this it was but a short step to the proposition that individuals should be allowed to hold and live their religious convictions even though not found in the Bible; and this step was in theory taken in America and some parts of western Europe, although certainly not fully observed in practice anywhere.

The third influence in effecting religious liberty was the emergence as a powerful factor in western thought of the doctrine of natural rights. Freedom of the individual to worship as he himself should choose became identified as a natural right of man, with which the state could not properly interfere. To the development of this theory of natural rights, which has touched and molded every phase of life for nearly three centuries, we must now turn.

We have seen that Thomas Aquinas promulgated the concept of natural law, which, being a part of the eternal law of God, may be ascertained by man through the exercise of reason. Upon this idea of the

force of natural law Richard Hooker, in the closing years of the sixteenth
century, based much of his argument supporting the position of the
Church of England, as set forth in his *Laws of Ecclesiastical Polity.*
Closely following Aquinas's analysis, Hooker identified natural law as
the immutable will of God, which the divine being itself follows and
which should likewise be followed by men. Human or positive law,
which includes government, should be man's particular application of
principles of natural law to the problems of human existence, the application to be made by reason, which is efficacious to apprehend natural
law. Government, he further suggested, derives its authority from the
consent, or at least the approbation, of the people governed; and thus
was given currency the thought of popular sovereignty.

Other writers, notably Grotius and Pufendorf, took up the idea of
natural law and developed it at length, analyzing particular rights that
inhere in natural law, and giving the theory of natural law and natural
rights a prominent place in the political thinking of the times.

4. John Locke

But it was John Locke who made the doctrine of natural rights a popular and powerful force that greatly influenced history. His second
Treatise on Civil Government (1690), resting directly and avowedly
on propositions asserted by the "judicious Hooker," presented the argument for the natural rights of man in a form that was eagerly appro-
priated by the thought of the eighteenth century.

If we seek, said Locke, to learn the principles of social organization,
we must first examine the condition of man in his original state. This
is a state of nature, which is revealed to us when all social organization
is stripped away. Two prime characteristics mark this natural state. One
is individual freedom. Men possess "perfect freedom to order their
actions, and dispose of their possessions and persons, as they think fit,
within the bounds of the law of nature, without asking leave, or depending upon the will of any man." The second is equality. The state
of nature is "a state also of equality, wherein all the power and jurisdiction is reciprocal, no one having more than another . . ."

In this state of nature all men are governed by natural law, and the
fundamental rule of natural law is that, "being all equal and independent, no one ought to harm another in his life, health, liberty or possessions . . ." Nor has anyone a right, at natural law, to destroy himself,

since his existence should be at the will of his creator rather than of himself. Since no social machinery exists in a state of nature, the enforcement of natural law necessarily is reposed in each human being, who thereby is authorized to redress wrongs done him, both by recouping his loss and by inflicting punishment.

Where do we find persons in this original state of nature? They must everywhere have preceded the institution of society, responds Locke, and all human beings, moreover, are born in such a state and continue in it until they associate themselves with some society.

But this natural state is disadvantageous in that men are compelled to be at war with one another in their several enforcements of natural law, whereby also they are exposed to the biased judgment that results from a man's being judge in his own cause. To avoid these difficulties, men by agreement enter into society, each surrendering certain of his natural rights to the state, and receiving in exchange social rights resulting from the terms of the social contract.

In this process of the formation of the state by compact two principles obtain. The first is that the state can have only those rights and powers that its citizens confer upon it by their agreement, for the social contract alone is the state's source of authority. The second is that the citizens can give to the state only those rights that they themselves possessed under natural law, for "Nobody can give more power than he has himself . . ."

These two propositions are determinative, in Locke's argument, of all questions of the power of the state. Absolute monarchy is wrong because citizens cannot confer absolute authority upon the state, since no one possesses such absolute authority over others in a state of nature. The state's rule being established by the will of its citizens, it has those powers granted by the will of the majority, and must act in accordance with the will of the majority. When men have made a community, that body obviously cannot act in accordance with the wishes of all if they differ, and so must act as the majority wish, and therefore each citizen in adhering to a society agrees to be bound by majority rule.

The people delegate their power of making laws to a legislative body, which possesses no arbitrary power over society, being limited to the enactment of those laws that are necessary for the preservation of the lives, liberties, and properties of the citizens, and which must govern by standing rules of law capable of being known in advance and enforced by impartial tribunals. All enactments must be limited to the good of the whole commonwealth, since it was for this purpose that the social contract was formed.

The authority conferred by the people upon the government of their state is in the nature of a trust, and if and when a breach of the fiduciary relationship occurs on the part of the government, by its failure to observe the terms and limitations of the grant, it is the people's right to remove the government and to supplant it with another, peaceably if possible but by force if necessary.

This composition of political ideas, some original with Locke and many derived, furnished the framework for the social philosophy of the eighteenth and nineteenth centuries. Natural law and natural rights were the basic premises on which were rested much of the thought and most of the action of that period. And if the idea of a social contract was viewed with skepticism in many quarters, still it constituted a useful allegory; men found it helpful to argue and act as if such a contract had been made.

What are the natural rights that men retain in their own keeping, not granting them, nor possessing the capacity to grant them, to the state? Locke and many other writers set them forth. They are primarily the right to be free in the movements of one's person, the right to make one's own decision on religious practices, the right to freedom of expression both by speech and in writing, and the right individually to possess property. Each of these rights can be curbed by the state only to such extent as is required for the preservation of the commonwealth, a restriction not to be broadly construed.

Locke gave considerable prominence to the individual ownership of property, grouping it with the life and liberty of the citizens as demanding the state's protection. Man has a natural right to the goods on which he has bestowed his labor, because such goods are necessary to his preservation, and even as he cannot transfer to the state an arbitrary control over his life, so he cannot give it such a control over the means of sustaining it. But this being so, it follows that he does not have a natural right to more property, said Locke, than is necessary for this purpose.

5. Adam Smith

Locke wrote in an age when it was still a cultural assumption that economic activity should be collectively regulated, even in small details, by the state. Gradually, however, this assumption was disintegrating and falling away, partly under the influence of increasing freedom of the individual in fields other than economic, partly under the influence of a literature which was questioning the reliability of the state as economic mentor, and partly under the influence of a growing industrialism and an expanding commerce whose changing activity made the older regulation seem outmoded. These tendencies were given philosophical support by the publication in 1776 of Adam Smith's *Wealth of Nations*, the influence of which on the western world was revolutionary. Smith's contribution, like Locke's, was more the synthesis of prior thought than the presentation of new ideas; but the brilliant and cogent form of the restatement gave it immediate historical influence.

It is folly, contended Smith, for the state to assume the function of determining what shall and shall not be produced, and at what price sold. The welfare of society will be better served if each individual, having regard to the market, is left free to produce and sell those things that he thinks there is the greatest demand for, and therefore those in which he will make the greatest profit, as indicated by the action of the market place. The state cannot accurately, and should not morally, substitute its judgment for that of the people as expressed in an open market. "What is the species of domestic industry which his capital can employ, and of which the produce is likely to be of the greatest value, every individual, it is evident, can, in his local situation, judge much better than any statesman or lawgiver can do for him. The statesman, who should attempt to direct private people in what manner they ought to employ their capitals, would not only load himself with a most unnecessary attention, but assume an authority which could safely be trusted, not only to no single person, but to no council or senate whatever, and which would nowhere be so dangerous as in the hands of a man who had folly and presumption enough to fancy himself fit to exercise it."[9]

Arguing thus for individual liberty in economic life, Smith contended for a complementary reduction in the concern and activity of government. The language that he used so accurately depicts the thought and assumptions that predominated in England and the United States during the nineteenth century that it seems desirable to quote from it at length.

"All systems either of preference or restraint, therefore, being thus completely taken away, the obvious and simple system of natural liberty

9. *Wealth of Nations*, Bk. IV, Ch. II.

establishes itself of its own accord. Every man, as long as he does not violate the laws of justice, is left perfectly free to pursue his own interest his own way, and to bring both his industry and capital into competition with those of any other man, or order of men. The sovereign is completely discharged from a duty, in the attempting to perform which he must always be exposed to innumerable delusions, and for the proper performance of which no human wisdom or knowledge could ever be sufficient; the duty of superintending the industry of private people, and of directing it towards the employments most suitable to the interest of the society. According to the system of natural liberty, the sovereign has only three duties to attend to; three duties of great importance, indeed, but plain and intelligible to common understandings: first, the duty of protecting the society from the violence and invasion of other independent societies; secondly, the duty of protecting, as far as possible, every member of the society from the injustice or oppression of every other member of it, or the duty of establishing an exact administration of justice; and, thirdly, the duty of erecting and maintaining certain public works and certain public institutions which it can never be for the interest of any individual, or small number of individuals, to erect and maintain; because the profit could never repay the expense to any individual or small number of individuals, though it may frequently do much more than repay it to a great society."[10]

6. The American Revolution

By the time of the American Revolution the Lockian doctrines of natural law and natural rights had become well known, and they furnished the ideological material which the revolutionary leaders made use of. The Revolution was justified as a war to attain liberty as a way of life, to the accomplishment of which end independence from Great Britain was sought as a means.

The two documents produced by the Revolution exercised profound influence both in Europe and in America. Moreover, the Declaration of Independence and the Constitution of 1789 with its Bill of Rights were social deeds, rather than speculations, and they gave the case for liberty the force of historical accomplishment. Neither of these instruments, however, was new in its concepts, for politics waits with but rare exceptions on preceding philosophical speculation for its in-

10. *Wealth of Nations*, Bk. IV, Ch. IX.

ventions. The Declaration was a rearrangement of part of Locke's argument in Jefferson's more brilliant prose, and the Bill of Rights expressed convictions that had already emerged from the turbulence of the seventeenth and eighteenth centuries; while the Constitution's only new political device—the restraint of the activity of the national and state governments by the Supreme Court—was not contained in the document itself but appeared only as the result of subsequent constitutional development.

These two writings, however, constitute history's noblest political embodiment of the theory of liberty as the basis for social organization. Probably they could not have been produced at any other period. Their authors were men of affairs who yet had taken occasion to study history and social philosophy; they were well versed in the doctrine of natural law and natural rights; and they were paced by a sober sincerity for the public good that seems difficult to comprehend as we view it from amidst the deceit and corruption that have come to pervade public affairs in our own generation.

7. The nineteenth and twentieth centuries

The nineteenth century became increasingly an era of the practice of individual liberty, which came to be regarded not simply as a technique to be applied to particular fields of human activity, but as a principle to govern all social relationship. It was this broad concept of personal freedom that John Stuart Mill sought to justify in his essay on *Liberty* (1859). He unfortunately, however, placed his argument on utilitarian grounds, and the discussion being thus watered down, it constitutes somewhat thin fare after the vigorous debates of the preceding two centuries. It nevertheless embodies two noteworthy contributions to individualistic thought. The first is its recognition of liberty as a principle of universal application, to be based on grounds generally valid for all fields of human action. The second is the proposition that the end of life, or at least one of the most important ends of life, is personal development of character, and that the freedom of the individual, whereby is obtained the opportunity for choice, is an indispensable condition for the best personal development. Each of these concepts is important to the theory of liberty, and the reader will find them embodied in much of the argument of the present work.

By the time the twentieth century opened the Liberal Age had flourished for about five decades, and western society, having accomplished at least a notable portion of the liberty for which the political philosophers had contended, had come to suppose that living in freedom was the most natural thing in the world. Under the influence of the tragic myth of evolutionary progress, it was assumed that a return to a less free condition would be, in the dialectic of history, an impossible development that need not be guarded against because it could not occur.

But that which is not challenged does not have a champion, and thus liberty soon lost its advocates precisely because it had won, at least partially, its case. Philosophic consideration therefore began to turn its attention elsewhere, and before long there could be observed in its speculations the shadow of a returning collectivism.

The early socialists, however, were too close to the late tyranny of the governing classes to think in terms of a reimposition of control by those who call themselves the state; and accordingly they were pleased to imagine a society in which, although property would be communally owned and the citizens would follow a pattern of activity set by the group, yet the state itself and its coercion would "wither away," to use a manner of speaking that became classic in communism.

It is always easy to find fault with an existing social order. The frailties of men and their continuing errors see to that. When the twentieth century brought the depressed economic conditions of the 1930's, moreover, they seemed to fit with the criticism advanced by socialism and communism. Marx had said that individual capitalism must destroy itself, as part of the inescapable dialectic of history. Was it not doing so? An age, therefore, which had been too busy enjoying the material benefits of free enterprise to bother about its philosophic foundations, began to accept the proposition that what was needed was more collectivistic control, imagining in its ignorance of history that such a course would constitute an advance into a new area of social experimentation, rather than a turning back to barren fields worked not too long before.

The very concept of liberalism slowly underwent change. The members of the proletariat, said the materialist philosophers, have no freedom; they are wage slaves, whose lives are controlled by those who own the instruments of production. To give freedom to all, ownership must be shared by all, which can be effected only through the state. Therefore the state must seize ownership, and control must be exercised by state officials. When that is done, all will own, all will have economic freedom, and the other freedoms will follow. Under the influence of this viewpoint, "liberal" policies strangely became those that circumscribed individual liberty. For if the poor man has no liberty, then measures to amend his economic condition must give him liberty, and if enhancing the state's direction of his daily life improves his economic condition, as it was represented it would do, then such enhancement of the state's power must be liberal; and through this line of reasoning all measures that looked to the enlargement of the state's control of individual action came to be referred to as liberal. The term was carried back to the communism of Marx and Engels as the forerunners of present-day collective doctrine, and these classic forms being thus denoted liberal, all current derivatives, whether socialism, communism, or new-dealism, have come to be included under the same designation. The appellation "conservative," on the other hand, is now applied to those who seek to restrict the state's intervention in the life of the individual by curbing governmental power. Thus by a strange turn the words liberal and conservative have come to be used in a way precisely opposite to that in which they were originally employed.

For a substantial period of time the attack of the self-styled liberals upon the institution of personal liberty encountered little philosophic opposition. The doctrines of Hegel and Darwin were popular, and upon them the collectivists claimed to base their case of economic evolution through private capitalism to proletarian communism. Within recent years, however, as the reality of the threat to individual liberty has become more and more apparent, a re-examination of the concept of liberty has begun to take place, and friends and advocates of liberty are more prominently being heard.

In keeping with the cultural atmosphere of our time, the current argument for liberty is being presented primarily, although not exclusively, from the economic standpoint. The recent books containing the most effective presentations of the individualistic position have either been written with an economic emphasis or have been treatises on economics.

Apart from economic discussion, contributions to the philosophy of individualism have not been numerous during the past few decades. Recently pamphleteering has appeared in volume, but from the nature of things it is devoted more to exhortation, frequently in terms of the advantages of the American way of life, than to an examination of principles. Except for its economic development, the philosophy of the liberty of individualism continues to rest for the most part on the presentation of its case as terminated about a century ago.

Chapter 4

LIBERTY AND MAN'S NATURE

1. Man's dual career

The problem of social organization flows from the nature of man. Man's nature being given, the form of his problems is established.

If man were a creature who lived an entirely individualized existence, so that each individual had no contact whatsoever with any other individual, then his only problems would arise out of his relations with nature and with God. His relation with nature would present the problems of shelter, food, and so forth; and his relation with God would bring him the problems of worship, salvation, metaphysical speculation, and like matters. But there would be no social problem of any sort, for there would be no social relation to give rise to any question of the proper degree of dependence or independence that should exist between human beings; and thus there could be no concern for liberty.

If on the other hand man were a form of being that experienced only a collectivized existence, living merely as a component of a social organism, then his relations with nature and with God would give rise to problems as before, although now of somewhat different kind, since they would no longer be the separable problems of individuals but the communally borne problems of the social whole; yet there still would be no problem of social relation. Under a wholly collectivized existence all experience would be embedded in a rigidly fixed social relation that would be beyond modification and so beyond any problem of its form.

Man however lives neither completely alone nor completely as social component. His existence is both individual and social, and it is precisely because it is so that the problem of social organization, including the problem of liberty as a form of social organization, arises. Each man's action must remain his own and at the same time be in relation to his fellows. Although the frame of this relation is established for man as a fact of his universe, yet the detailed content of the relation is not fixed but mutable and subject to man's disposition. Thereby is presented the problem of social organization and with it the problem of liberty.

Life occurs for the human individual both as a complete entity in itself and as a fragment of a larger entity. Each person is a contained universe, a microcosm; and concurrently he lives as an infinitesimally small segment of a greater universe, the macrocosm, whose process engulfs his own.

The universe that the individual intimately knows is the universe of himself. For him the outside world is known only through his own consciousness; and as his perception is conditioned, so is his contact with the outside world. Wherefore we are all insulated universes, proceeding on isolated careers.

If however we are thus set apart, passing our lives in separate worlds of consciousness, we are nevertheless also joined together into a totality that is much vaster than ourselves, the totality of the great universe; and the bonds of our union, molding our separate integrities into a universal whole, never fall below the level of our attention. Each individual process is at all times interlocked with other individual processes. Life for each person begins as a part of the lives of two other persons, and the maintenance of life is at first impossible, and later difficult, without the assistance of others. The hermit does not in fact live alone, and Robinson Crusoe is found only in fiction.

Thus each man, cognizant of his own existence and, through his perceptions, of the realm of vital process in which he is contained, knows that he is both a universe himself and yet but a part of another universe. Human experience is accordingly a dual career, a consciousness at once of the respective processes of the microcosm and of the macrocosm.

This involves a difficulty from which man never escapes. For the realm of the self and the realm of the larger universe each possess a set of needs, privileges, and obligations, and the two sets fail to coincide at many points. Since man knows that he belongs to each realm, experiencing each as a daily fact, he passes his existence within this duality, ever finding it necessary to harmonize in some manner the conflicting claims made by the two realms upon his career, as the process of life brings those claims forward.

It is in this opposition that the facts of morality and immorality, as attributes of human conduct, have their origin. For without the social relation as it is, composed of both separateness and cohesion, there could be no problem of the quality of human action in its effect on others. Man's living must amount to a resolution of this problem imposed by the conflict of the self and the not-self; and for this reason his conduct necessarily bears the attribute of moral quality.

Man's experience is thus a dual career, and the social relation, the relation experienced by each individual between the realm of his own self and the realm of the not-self in which he moves, takes its form from the fact of this duality.

2. Conflict in the social relation

The moral difficulty thus presented to man is heightened by the fact that the social relation is composed, on the one hand, of conflict, and, on the other, of cooperation. Each of these elements in the social relation, moreover, is ineradicable; and the solution of the moral problem must consist, therefore, in adjustment to the facts of conflict and cooperation rather than in attempts to disregard or avoid those facts.

An obvious manifestation of the conflict in the social relation is the competition between individuals for the material things that sustain and embellish life. The self of each individual has its economic needs, but so also has the not-self. At any given time the total quantity of economic goods for the satisfaction of these needs is limited. The quantity of food, houses, clothing, furniture, farms, and factories available at any time is a fixed stock. The needs of the members of society however are without assignable limit, for the wants of human nature continuously expand in variety and extend indeterminately into the future. Though a want such as that for food may be satisfied at a given moment of time, yet it is known that the satisfaction is but temporary and that the want will persistently recur. The economic wants of the members of a society being thus limitless, whereas the stock of goods available at any given time to meet those wants is limited, it follows that consumption by the self, i.e., by one member of society, is always a condition of consumption by the not-self, i.e., by all other members of society.

The stock of economic goods is of course only temporarily a fixed quantity; it can be modified by the effort of human persons. But it can never catch up with wants, which in total grow by what they feed on; and therefore it must always remain true both that the existing stock is insufficient to satisfy all wants and that consumption by each individual is one of the conditions of consumption by all other individuals.

The actuality of this conflict of interest between the self and the not-self, and thus between all members of society, has nothing to do with merit or just deserts. That is, the contributions that different individuals have made to the stock of goods may or may not be regarded as being a relevant factor in determining how those individuals should share in the consumption of the stock. But this does not modify or eliminate the basic conflict in consumption, which is factual rather than ideological in nature, arising out of the facts of the universe rather than out of any human attitude toward them. Living involves a resolution of this basic conflict, in which resolution the idea of reward for contribution may become influential or perhaps controlling, but the impact of the idea is on the resolution, not on the conflict itself.

This conflict of the self and the not-self has been pictured for us by the theorists of evolution as a struggle for existence culminating in a survival of the fittest. It is doubtful, however, if the matter goes so far, for not everything is competition in the social relation. But the fact of economic conflict is nevertheless fundamental, and is of the profoundest consequence to social philosophy.

The conflict in the social relation, moreover, extends beyond the economic sphere and affects as well intellectual activity, for intellectual activity unavoidably involves conflict of opinion. It is in the nature of opinions that they vary. Even as the changing experiences of the same individual produce changing opinions, so the different experiences of different individuals produce different opinions. This inevitable variance of opinions as they are held by different persons constitutes intellectual conflict. The conflict touches on every phase of life as it is lived, from the most amiable to the most profound and passionate. It may involve only such pleasant questions as whether the music of Beethoven or Brahms is preferable, whether cubist art is beautiful, or whether family funds should be spent for a new automobile or for new furniture. But on the other hand it may extend to the stuff of which riots, persecutions, and wars are made, as for example whether God is trinitarian or unitarian, whether transubstantiation occurs during the mass, and whether Edward Duke of York was the legitimate heir to the English crown.

It is a myth of the school of historical materialism that intellectual conflict is of no primary significance in human affairs, that it is the competition of economic wants and the method of their satisfaction that determines all. But this hypothesis, vehemently asserted but never proved, is at variance both with the nature of man and with the facts of history. The conflict that human nature experiences, giving rise to the tensions that produce historical movements, is both intellectual and economic. At times one or the other element of the conflict may predominate and be the more apparent; but to insist that either consistently subordinates the other is unrealistic. Again and again it has been demonstrated in history that clashes of opinion can stir up wells of passion far exceeding in bitterness those aroused by any competition for economic goods; and the explanation for this social phenomenon is the intellectual conflict inherent in the social relation.

3. Combination in the social relation

But if conflict is a constant element in the relation of the self to the not-self, so also is combination. Individuals necessarily act in competition, but they also act in cooperation. The two strands are intermingled in the design of existence, and although they can be distinguished they can never be separated.

Thus each realm of self continuously competes with its realm of not-self for the use of the economic goods needed to satisfy economic wants, but it also is all the while cooperating with its realm of not-self in bringing those very goods into existence. Without such cooperative action there would be very few goods to compete for, since the things that could be produced by isolated individual action would be of the smallest quantity. The economic activity that necessarily manifests competition thus is also necessarily dependent on the cooperation that is involved in specialization and exchange.

Likewise in intellectual activity cooperation of the self and the not-self is an integral component of the process. Opinions clash as they come into existence, but they are produced only by cooperative activity. Each person's opinions must be his own, in the sense that they must be the manifestations of his own thinking process; but though his own in this sense, yet they cannot be other than the product in part of all the opinions he has ever heard and read, including those he has most violently rejected. Opinions are formed as complements or opponents to other opinions. They cannot be produced in an insulated arena. Every opinion of the self is conditioned by opinions of the not-self, whereby they are produced in combination.

Most intellectual activity, moreover, occurs in the form of language, the learning and use of which is a social process, impossible outside the social relation. Language is not only employed for communication between the self and the not-self, but is also the medium of the most individualized and secret thoughts of the self, thereby influencing the character of those thoughts. St. Simeon Stylites on his pillar, supposing that he had shut out the world and was in communion only with God, yet presented his petitions in words the world had taught him, and so unwittingly but inevitably dragged the world with its history and associations along with him into his seclusion.

4. The social problem

All human action, accordingly, whether it be intellectual or economic—and for purposes of social philosophy all action is basically comprised of these two categories—occurs at once as both conflict and cooperation. The social relation is compounded of competition and combination, the one manifesting the separateness of the self from the not-self, the other manifesting their union.

Society being composed of persons, it is a complex of relations of self to not-self. To each individual person, however, society is known only as his own realm of not-self. Although the general form of the realm of not-self is the same for all persons, yet the content of the form, as it is experienced, is different for each person. The realm of not-self of one person includes all persons other than himself, and so excludes himself but includes his neighbor; whereas the realm of not-self of the neighbor excludes the neighbor himself but includes the first person.

The unsuspected egotism that leads each of us to identify society with his own particular realm of not-self is therefore error. None of us has objective experience that can be identified with society, and therefore just what society is we can never quite know. It must remain, as we discuss it, an idea that is slightly different for each participant in the discussion.

Not only is the fact of society thus a different fact for each individual, but it must also be examined by each individual from a viewpoint different from the viewpoints of all other individuals. Society presents many similar aspects to you and me, but we are forever barred from viewing it from the same point of examination.

Man's task, therefore, is not only somehow to resolve the continuous dilemma of conflict and cooperation which he experiences in the social relation, but to do so in a social form that he is forever barred from seeing as a whole, from completely understanding. To each man his place in society must remain an obscurity, which he can never view objectively.

These facts, the conflict and cooperation of life and the incomprehensibility of the social form, are not of man's devising, but are cosmic data. They are the material of the social problem. It is useless to inveigh against them. Complaining of the facts can never lead to a solution of the problem they present, but can only divert attention from the problem's true nature. That problem is to find, within the social form, a pattern of accommodation for the competition and combination that constitute the social relation, a pattern competent to permit the satisfaction to the highest degree possible of the intellectual and economic needs of all men.

5. The comparison of the self and the not-self

Given any two facts, it is a further fact that a comparison of them is possible. Our discussion has identified as two basic facts in the experience of each human being the realm of self and the realm of not-self. It is also a fact, therefore, that a comparison exists between these two realms of experience.

This comparison could conceivably be made by using many different standards of measurement, but since social philosophy has as object the preservation and stimulation of the highest human values, the comparison can best be made in terms of these values. Disregarding for the present the question of the exact nature of such values, we may say that the idea of human value and the accompanying idea of human welfare may be summarized under the general term human importance. We shall therefore compare the realm of self and the realm of not-self, as experienced by each human being, in their human importance.

In making such comparison it is apparent, as a beginning point, that the realm of self and the realm of not-self must be either equal or not equal in human importance, since all possibilities of comparison are contained in these alternative modes.

With respect to the mode of inequality, this is a possible theorem if it be applied to only one individual, but an impossible theorem if attempt be made to apply it to all individuals. One individual could conceivably say with correctness, My realm of self is superior in human importance to my realm of not-self. But no more than one individual in the entire universe could possibly say this with correctness, because as applied to more than one person the theory of superiority of the self to the not-self would be self-contradictory. For although one individual in the universe could conceivably be superior in human importance to all other individuals, yet it would be an impossibility for more than one person to be superior to all others. The theory that the self is superior to its not-self is consequently not a proposition capable of universal application.

In like manner, any theory that the realm of self is superior in human importance to a part of its realm of not-self cannot be universally applied. An individual could conceivably say with correctness, My realm of self is superior in human importance to part of my realm of not-self. But again, this could not be said with correctness with respect to all individuals in the universe, for such application of the proposition would involve a contradiction, asserting that each individual in the universe was superior to some other individuals in the universe.

The case is the same if we change from superiority to inferiority. One individual or some individuals could conceivably assert with correctness that they were inferior in human importance to other individuals in the universe, but all individuals could not correctly make such assertion.

The mode of inequality between the realm of self and the realm of not-self therefore cannot be a theory of universal application. As a universal theory, it is an impossibility. The most that can be said, if the mode of inequality be adhered to, is that for some individuals the realm of self is superior to the realm of not-self, and that for all others the realm of self is inferior to its realm of not-self.

But why should the realm of self be superior in human importance for some and inferior for others? Can any logical basis be suggested for the distinction? All human beings have equal need of welfare. Can it be asserted reasonably that some human beings have more need for human welfare than others? Welfare is a universal need; and although the universality of the need is much disregarded by men, yet it is impossible to find any reason for saying that one person has more need of welfare than another, or that one has less need than another. The need for welfare is an attribute of humanity, and even as all human beings share equally in humanity, so they also share equally in the need for human welfare. By the same token they share equally in the need for the recognition of human values. Therefore they share equally in human importance, for we said that the idea of human importance, as we would employ it, would embrace in a broad way the concepts of human welfare and of human values.

For these reasons and for reasons which will be set out in the three succeeding chapters, the philosophy of individualism rejects the mode of inequality as an explanation of the relation between the realm of self and the realm of not-self. It therefore adopts the mode of equality, asserting that for each individual and for all individuals the realm of self and the realm of not-self are equal in human importance. Thus individualism bases its structure of thought on a proposition of universal application. Recognizing that man's nature leads him through a dual career, it deduces from the universality of this experience the universality of the correct explanation of the mode in which the self stands to the not-self. This mode is one of equality in human importance. All individuals in human society are therefore equal in human importance.

Although the mode of equality in the social relation is thus the only logical hypothesis, it nevertheless is not always so recognized. The inequalities of men in their natural endowments are so apparent that it is easy to fall into the assumption that they are unequal also in their human importance. Much individual day to day action, much social action, and much thinking on social organization is in reality based on this erroneous assumption of inequality. Communism and anarchism both are founded upon it, despite their professions of concern in equality. Let us see why this is so.

6. The mode of inequality in the social relation as seen in collectivism

The superiority of the self over the not-self is obviously the premise upon which all forms of absolutism are supported. In tyranny, dictatorship, and absolute monarchy the superiority of the self, as contained in the ruler, over all his realm of not-self, which he controls without accountability, furnishes the basic principle in the regime's apologia. The want of logic in this basic principle is confessed in efforts to bolster it by ideas of divinity; the Roman emperor became one of the gods, and the Christian church later invented the divine right of kings.

As a practical theorem of social organization, however, the mode of the superiority of the self tends to become an affirmation of the superior importance of a few rather than of one, and of the inferior position of the many. The absolute ruler may boast "L'état, c'est moi," but in practice he cannot maintain this conceit. He must have subordinates to assist him in his governing; and thus there originates an officialdom which, exercising delegated authority that spreads downward through the layers of the hierarchy, issues and enforces decrees controlling the life of the society. Within this governing bureaucracy the principle of the superiority of the self over the not-self becomes the superiority of the self over all the not-self except that portion which is located higher in the hierarchical scale. The importance of each individual depends on his place in the bureaucracy. Each person is less important than all those above him and more important than all those below.

All social authority which does not rely on the franchise of the many must find support in the force of a few. Collectivism discards the franchise of the many in its use of central planning, and in consequence it depends on the force of a few and necessarily asserts the superiority of the few to the many. This development can be seen in Russia and in countries of western Europe as they have moved into socialism. It occurs because collectivism and central planning are coordinates, each requiring the other; central planning is an indispensable element in collectivism, and it necessarily involves the assumption of the superiority of the few. This is a matter of first importance, lying at the base of a correct understanding of the distinction between individualism and collectivism. It calls for our further examination at this point.

The emphasis placed by collectivism on the group is of the essence of the collectivistic position. The instant that collectivistic thought begins to emphasize the rights and liberties of the individual against the group it ceases to be collectivistic and becomes individualistic. Nor is the dividing line vague in most of the area of social organization. Human action is by individual human beings, and the action of each such individual rests ultimately, after due allowance for reflexes, instincts, and habits, upon decision. From the nature of things, the decisions that determine an individual's actions must be made either by the individual himself or by someone else for him. There is no middle ground. Individualism believes in decision by the individual for himself, and subject to the principle of equality strives to effect a social order where self-determination predominates. If therefore collectivism begins also to emphasize the position of the individual, it must either allow freedom of decision in a given area, or not allow it, since there is no middle principle, and to the extent that it allows self-decision it abandons the controlled action of group planning and becomes individualistic.

If collectivism, furthermore, appreciating that by granting rights of self-decision to the individual it is *pro tanto* conceding its own position, attempts at the same time to maintain an emphasis on group action, it dissipates the force of its thought in a dilemma of self-contradiction.

This is illustrated by the Marxian tenet of the ultimate disappearance of the state. History, Marx taught, is largely group action. Capitalism will be destroyed by class warfare, and from the conflict will emerge a society where all action will be guided by considerations of group welfare, pursuant to group plans. But Marx was deeply concerned with man's inhumanity to man, and with this concern went a realization that much of that inhumanity was effected through the state. He wished therefore to eliminate this instrument of possible oppression from his utopia (for it is a utopia despite Marx's disclaimers), and he accomplished this result simply by pronouncing the state out. There would be the administration of a few things, such as sanitation and roads, but the state itself would die away.

Both Marx and Engels remained vague about this last development of communism, saying only that there would be group action in producing the things needed by all, yet no state; and it has sometimes been wondered why they did not proceed to a more explicit description of their conception of this ideal communist condition. The answer is that they could not have done so and have remained either intelligible or collectivistic. It cannot be intelligibly argued both that there will be a state and yet no state. If there is organized group action, in which the individual is compelled to join, then a state in effect exists. Accordingly when Marx says that in the ultimate communist society there will be group action in which the individual will be compelled to join, and also that there will be no state, he is simply expressing an unintelligible contradiction. Had he proceeded to an elaboration of his idea, its impossibility would have been made more apparent, both to Marx and to his readers, and he was accordingly impelled to content himself with an oracular pronouncement of the state-yet-stateless nature of the last day.

Or if Marx had persisted in the thought that the state would disappear, then with the abandonment of the state he would have had also to abandon compulsion of the individual to take part in the group plan, and with that abandonment he would also have abandoned communism, and his thought would have become individualistic. For if the individual is free to join or not join in group plans, economic or other, then he is free to make his own decisions on production and other matters, and a society in which the individual is thus free is individualistic, and is, speaking very generally, the kind of society contended for in this book.

It is because collectivism requires the coercion of the state in enforcing group plans that the idea of the state's dying away has been dropped from communist teaching in the past few years. The reality of events has demonstrated the inconsistency of Marx's doctrine and it has been expediently forgotten.

Group action, with the coercion of the state to compel the participation therein of the individual, is therefore essential to collectivistic theory, which ceases to be collectivistic when it no longer calls for such group action.

But group action requires planning and direction. If the group is very small, the entire group may take part in such planning and direction. But in societies as ordinarily found the group is too large. All the people in the United States cannot get together to decide on programs of production. Not even all the members of a single trade, the steelworkers, for example, can get together to decide on a group program of steel production, prices, and working conditions. Even more difficult is the policing of a program once adopted, if the policing be attempted by a group as a whole. From the nature of things, therefore, the planning of group programs, and their enforcement, must be delegated to a few people, whose decisions thus control the action of the many.

Again it should be noted that if this control of the group program by a few is abandoned, collectivism is also abandoned. For if all the individuals in the group are permitted to disregard the group plan and to make their own plans, each for himself, then each individual can plan and produce as he chooses, and this, speaking again generally, becomes the free market in economic affairs for which this work argues.

Collectivism therefore is compelled to assert the superiority of the few over the many. In any collectivistic society, and in any collectivistic area in any society, the decisions by the few must be imposed on the many if a collective plan is to be followed. When Russian communism ceases to do this it will no longer be communism; when British socialism ceases to do this it will cease to be socialism; and when American new-dealism ceases to do this it will no longer be new-dealism.

Thus collectivism is always and necessarily a social form which makes use of the mode of inequality in the social relation, in its assertion of the superiority of the few in making and enforcing programs of action for the many.

Nor is it of consequence, for the present point, how the few planners are set apart from the rest of the group, whether they be elected, appointed, or seize their place by usurpation. The important item, within our present concern, is their function in directing human action, rather than the method by which they are empowered to exercise that function.

But, the reader may protest, does not all government, no matter how democratic and devoted to liberty it may be, involve exactly this same delegation of authority to a few representatives, who thus become superior to the many? Does not all government therefore become a manifestation of the mode of inequality in the social relation? Where does collectivism differ from individualism in this?

The answer to this question is most important. The inability to distinguish between the divergent quality of different forms of governmental control, the inability to see that social controls of the individual may differ radically in their quality though they all constitute group intervention in individual living, is one of the greatest of present-day handicaps to accurate social thought. No error is causing more confusion at the present time than this supposition that all governmental control is essentially the same in nature or quality, and that therefore the difference between individualism on the one hand and socialism and communism on the other is primarily a matter of the quantity of social intervention. The difference between individualism and collectivism is not simply a quantitative one, but a qualitative one. Quantitatively indeed it is in some respects difficult to compare them. Collectivism no doubt involves more numerous and more complete regulatory items than individualism, but its basic principles are few and simple. Individualism on the other hand is a complex scheme of social organization, and contrary to the accepted notion, requires a far more sophisticated and complex set of laws for its operation than does collectivism.

To put the answer concisely to the question presented above, the delegation of authority to the few in the collectivistic state is to enable the few to make decisions for the many, whereas in the individualistic state the delegation is for the purpose of preserving an equal right of decision to all. In the collectivistic state the few make programs for the many to follow, and no theoretical limit exists to the extent or particularity of such programs. In the individualistic state the few make no programs for the many; on the contrary they preserve conditions in which each may make his own program so far as such exercise of decision is consistent with a like exercise by all; and the limit of authority of the few is explicitly set by the nature of this, their function. The exercise of authority in the one case is premised on the superior importance of the few, and in the other on the equal importance of all.

For the present our discussion will content itself with the foregoing

answer. The radical difference, however, between the social control
that constitutes collectivism and the social control that constitutes individualism, though both kinds of control make use of delegation of
authority, is inherently involved in most of the argument of the present
study, and accordingly will constantly be within the orbit of our attention as we proceed.

Collectivism, then, is a manifestation of the mode of inequality in
the social relation, and this explains its close affinity to fascism, which,
not making use of socialistic or collectivistic nomenclature, and not
bothering to concern itself with where legal title to property may reside,
arrives at the same result of placing the planning and direction of group
action, economic and other, in the hands of a few people. Although
socialists and communists have excoriated the recent fascism of Italy
and Germany as the last vile developments of capitalism, yet it has been
apparent that they have been both disturbed and perplexed by the
similarity, once the pretense of words is removed, of what went on in
Rome and Berlin, while they were fascist, with the pattern of events
in Moscow. Why did ideologies avowing themselves to be opposite in
everything yet produce ways of living so much alike in their processes?

The answer is clear. The essential thing in human action is decision,
the determination of the form which action will take, and communism
and fascism, though they employ different phrases in describing their
reasons, reach the same result of placing the power of decision in large
areas of human action in the hands of a few.

It is for this reason that fascism is properly classified as a form of
collectivism. When the position of fascism is stripped of nomenclature,
it amounts to the proposition that, for the asserted welfare of the
group, all members of the group must submit to a common plan in
most areas of human action, and this is precisely the position of socialism
and communism, and, to a less degree, of new-dealism. Nor does fascism
differ from other forms of collectivism in its idea of group welfare, which
it conceives largely in terms of material prosperity. The distinction
between fascism and other forms of collectivism has consisted, in point
of historical fact, for the most part in the terminology employed to
describe aims and methods and in personnel. Both Hitler and Mussolini were socialists. They nationalized industry in Germany and Italy
even as it is nationalized today in Britain, France, and Russia; and
had they not combined their collectivism with dreams of military glory,
to the destruction of their regimes, the social organization today in
Germany and Italy would probably not differ greatly from that of their

collectivistic neighbors. Thus in its aims and modes fascism differs but little from other types of collectivism.

For much the same reasons, all forms of tyranny and despotism are properly catalogued as variants of collectivism. Regardless of the occasion or justification of the result, they all end in a social order in which group action instead of individual action predominates. The state through its bureaucracy determines the avenues of human activity. It does not matter too much what the slogans are that are used to justify this guidance of the many by the few, nor the ideology that is assumed to explain the submergence of the individual in the group. The unabashed tyranny of Damocles and the rationalized communism of Sparta produced much the same result for all citizens high and low, in that their lives were largely required to conform to a group plan, fixed by a favored few.

7. The mode of inequality in the social relation as seen in anarchism

When we turn from collectivism to anarchism, from glorification of the state as a principal good to its denunciation as a principal evil, we find again that the position taken involves necessarily an assertion of inequality in the social relation.

If the individual should be independent of organized relation with his fellows, untrammeled by enforced association with them or obligation to them, it must be because each individual, when he views life from his own point of view, can properly regard himself as superior in importance to those around him. For his independence of others involves the proposition that he can act without regard to them, that others do not possess a human importance which he can properly be compelled by force to recognize. It is this more or less complete independence of the individual which anarchism in its different forms advocates. When it ceases such advocacy and recognizes the propriety of formal relation between individuals, whereby reciprocal obligations are enforced through social organization, it ceases to be anarchistic.

But the superiority of the self to the not-self is not a possible social concept, as we have heretofore noted. Therefore anarchistic thought sooner or later encounters the dilemma of asserting the superiority of individuals each to each; and to conceal this self-cancellation of its thought it becomes vague in its specifications.

Anarchism will not greatly concern us in our present study. Since our purpose is to delineate the liberty of individualism, we shall advert to collectivism and anarchism only by way of comparison. Anarchism, however, advocates little or no social organization; therefore it furnishes few points for instructive comparison with individualism.

8. The mode of equality in the social relation as seen in individualism

The philosophy of individualism, repudiating inequality in the social relation and thereby disavowing both the superiority of the few and the inferiority of the many, asserts the equality of the self and the not-self in human importance and the consequent equal human importance of all persons. For the individual the theory of equality means that his rights and obligations are neither superior nor inferior to those of others but are on a par with them. For society it means that all persons are equal in their rights and obligations.

Certain conclusions, to be fortified later by other parts of the philosophy of individualism, are indicated by this initial principle of basic equality in the social relation. Since all persons are of equal importance in their rights and obligations, the society of individualism must grant to all persons equally the opportunity for decision in the conduct of life's affairs, for if it did not do so it would necessarily become a society in which decision was vested in a few and thus would become a society maintaining the superiority of the few. The society of liberty must therefore maintain, equally for all its members, the opportunity for freedom of intellectual life and the opportunity for freedom of economic life. And since intellectual life consists of thought and communication, intellectual freedom correspondingly is composed of freedom of thought and freedom of communication. And since economic life consists in the production and consumption of goods and in the ownership of property, economic freedom correspondingly becomes freedom to produce and consume goods through the mechanism of the free market and freedom to own property.

The liberty of individualism is thus composed of intellectual and economic freedom maintained equally for all. The substantive principles that establish the content of this freedom and the administrative principles by which it can be maintained we shall seek to identify.

Chapter 5

LIBERTY AS ETHICAL IMPERATIVE

1. The purpose of life

That life has purpose we ordinarily assume. The fact that we plan our daily careers is a recognition of purpose, for planning presupposes purpose.

Intuition tells us, moreover, that everything which exists has a purpose attached to its existence. At the least, that purpose must be a continued manifestation of the process of existence.

Since human life as a form of existence has purpose, social philosophy must be founded on an acknowledgment of that purpose. Social philosophy advocates particular human action, and all human action should rightly be directed to the accomplishment of the purpose of human life rather than to its defeat.

Social philosophy, nevertheless, should limit its consideration of purpose to propositions having universal application, if it finds that such limitation can logically be imposed. The pattern of human action advised by social philosophy is applicable to the entire community, and consequently the purpose of life upon which it is based must encompass the entire community and reach to the entire life of the community's members.

What is the purpose of life, in terms suitable for a philosophy of social application?

Every form of existence, as we have just seen, includes in its purpose the manifesting of the process by which it endures. Human life, then, has within its purpose the manifesting of the process of human living.

Since, further, the character of anything is what it essentially is, everything that exists has its character. Human life, being a form of existence, thus always has its character, and the process of human living necessarily includes the manifestation of character.

But the purpose of human life includes the manifesting of the process of human living. Therefore the purpose of life also includes the manifesting of human character. We may say, then, that included in life's purpose is the manifestation of character.

Human character is of many kinds, as we acknowledge by the adjectives good, bad, kindly, selfish, and so forth. We must consequently inquire what kind of character it is that life includes in its purpose.

In order, however, to answer this question of the kind of character called for by life's purpose, we must first examine the elements entering into the composition of human character.

Human life is a flow of activity. The action which comprises this flow is divisible into two categories, which although closely intertwined are yet capable of separate identification. The first category is that of volitional process, consisting of human action having a cause in a decision of will. The second category is that of non-volitional process, consisting of human action occurring without the accompaniment of a decision of will. We shall have occasion at a later point in the present chapter to examine the nature of volitional and non-volitional process somewhat more fully, but for present needs it is only necessary to point out the essential distinction between these two forms of human action, that is, that the one occurs with, and the other without, the intervention of will.

Non-volitional process, then, takes place pursuant to those principles of cause and effect which constitute physical law. Accordingly it is determined for the future by past and present causes, and the chain of causation thus being fixed, the future course of non-volitional process is not optional but necessary.

Volitional process on the other hand is not subject to necessity, for if it were it would not be volitional. It is directed by human will, and therefore may occur in the future in varying ways. These different ways are presented to the will as optional forms of future action, and among them the will is required to make its choice.

Whenever options or choices are presented to human thought, it is compelled to exercise judgment with respect to them. The function of comparing or judging is ineradicable, and of two things one must be thought better than the other or they must be thought equally good, to the extent that the two things are presented to the mind in knowledge concerning them. The judgments we thus form are represented in general terms by the words good and bad, better and worse, and best and worst. The particular content of these judgments is not here of importance, nor the reasons for reaching them, either in specific cases or generally. What we must note is that judgment is embedded in human action, and that it becomes especially prominent, because more obviously present, when that action consists in selecting one course of future conduct from various courses presented to the mind as options. Volitional process as it occurs is thus accompanied by judgment, and optional modes of conduct, while they are being contemplated as ideas and also while they are being translated into fact by behavior, are judged to be good or bad, better or worse, or best or worst.

Judgment further tells us that of any two courses of possible future action presented to us as ideas it is the better that ought to become the reality of conduct. So clear is the advice of judgment in this regard that we would consider it a self-contradictory proposition to say that the worse of two modes of conduct ought to be realized as actuality. And of all modes of conduct possible at any time it is the best rather than the worst that judgment tells us ought to be. "Best" and "ought to be" are inescapably synonymous in our thought.

We may say, then, that the purpose of life is concerned with the character of both volitional and non-volitional process. In so far as life is composed of volitional process, the course of action, and consequently the character of action, is not immutably fixed for the future, but is always subject to variation as optional forms of action become available. But the purpose of life cannot include all these optional forms, for of the many presented for consideration, only one can be chosen as a way of actual living. The purpose of life must be, therefore, some one of the optional modes available to us from time to time, and of these optional modes it must be the one that ought to be, since it cannot be believed to be the one that ought not to be. The mode which ought to be is the one which is best. Therefore the purpose of life, in so far as life is composed of willed action, is the best mode of willed action, that is, the best volitional character, that is possible for us.

With respect to non-volitional process, no optional modes of action are available. Therefore the purpose of life cannot be concerned with better or worse modes as they may be selected by the will, but only with the one fixed mode which is destined to occur in accordance with physical law. The conditions under which physical law operates can be changed, of course, by the intervention of human will, and indeed all decisions of human will must find their expression in media that operate pursuant to physical law. But physical law itself is immutable. Human will cannot change it, but can influence only its mode of manifestation. Life's purpose is not concerned with better or worse non-volitional process, but only with the continued manifestation of that process in the form destined for it by physical law.

The purpose of life, then, is the non-volitional character that physical law determines, and the best volitional character that the will can choose.

The character which thus is the concern of life's purpose is not an attribute of life in an abstract sense or of life as a generality, but of life as it appears as an actual biological phenomenon. The purpose of life attaches to human life as a fact and not to it as an abstraction. The only form in which human life appears as a fact is the biological organism we call the individual human being. Therefore the life purpose which our analysis has identified is the purpose for individual human life.

The purpose of human life, then, is that the individual human being shall have the non-volitional character which nature decrees and the best volitional character that he can accomplish by his will. And since non-volitional character is immutable and not subject to will's dominion, and since our ultimate concern in this study is what men can do to mold affairs, we may appropriately shorten our statement to the proposition that the purpose of life is the best character that each individual human being by his willed decisions can achieve.

2. The best human character as God's will

Didactic analysis of the nature of human existence is not the only route to an understanding of the best achievable character as life's purpose. It may also be apprehended as the will of God.

Universal spirit, as we shall consider more at length in the following chapter, is believed by us to be a fact of existence. Therefore it has purpose. Universal spirit constitutes the supernatural and omnipotent entity that we know as God, and accordingly the purpose of universal spirit we may refer to as the will of God, thereby making use of familiar and appropriate terminology.

The will of God must include a purpose for human life, because the human process is part of the universal process to which the will of God attaches, and also because the human spirit is part of universal spirit.

When we contemplate what God's will for human life may be, we at once see that his will must include human character, since his will applies to universal process, of which human process is a part, and since human character is what human process essentially is. And when we further consider what kind of character it is that is within the will of God, we know that his will calls for the best character we can build. For judgment, upon which we must entirely rely in this as in all other matters, tells us that God's will calls for human character as it ought to be; and what it ought to be is the best that can be accomplished.

This thought, that God's will demands of us the allegiance of the best character we can create, evokes within us the emotional experience of belief. All the significant part of life is based on belief, and belief, in the last analysis, is a feeling of satisfaction following thought. The thought that the will of God calls for noble living brings this feeling of belief, and it furnishes for men the principal base for noble living, as history continuously testifies.

It may be enquired, however, why—if God's will is the best possible human character—God does not insure the accomplishment of this purpose by maintaining a universe in which human beings have no choice to do anything less than the best. If character other than the best thwarts the will of God, why does God permit his will to be thwarted? And since men can and do create character other than the best, is not this fact a reason for believing that God's will for humanity must be something other than the best character?

The answer to this objection lies in the nature of the best human character. The best character must always be that which possesses the quality of morality. If man were an automaton, living only as fixed response to natural environment, his living would be without moral responsibility for events, and without moral quality. But such a condition of amorality would be vastly inferior to the life of moral responsibility which man in fact experiences. Man chooses, and by the fact of choice his career becomes endued with moral quality; without choice he would be only an amoral event in an amoral universe.

Therefore the best character can only be that which is freely chosen. God's will for men cannot be accomplished by compulsion. Conduct created by willed decision can alone constitute the best character that is God's object.

But if men are thus to accomplish the object of God by choosing the good and rejecting the bad, the freedom to choose or reject must be conferred upon them, and they must be at liberty to choose or reject the good, and to reject or choose the bad. The inescapable condition of the power to choose the right is the power to choose the wrong. Without this freedom, therefore, the will of God cannot be done. Yet with this freedom it may be thwarted. But the freedom must be given.

This is why men can thwart the will of God. In order that the will of God may be accomplished, its accomplishment must be left to human decision, and thus the will of God in human life depends upon the will of man.

3. The best character includes all other purposes.

We may place the concept of the best character as life's purpose against all other conceivable purposes, and when we do so we find that it is inclusive of all concepts of purpose that can make any claim to being acceptable, and is not opposed by any of them.

Salvation, for example, is a purpose of life stressed by nearly all religions, with connotations both for existence within the present life cycle and in a possible existence beyond death. But although salvation as life purpose is presented in varying ways, it is always thought to be dependent on character (subject to a comment made below). Certain Christian factions, it is true, have held that salvation is obtained by reason of divine election, which is believed to display itself in the first instance by the setting apart, without regard to merit, of the souls that are to be saved. But this view has been coupled with an admission, in one form or another, that the divine election must be confirmed by good conduct on the part of those who are thus appointed to salvation, and will be forfeited by bad conduct, God not being indifferent to the character of his predestined saints. Within all these views, therefore, salvation is ultimately conditioned upon human character, and thus salvation as a purpose for life is included within the broader proposition that the best character constitutes life's purpose. Apparently the dogma of predestination has upon occasion been pushed to the extreme of asserting that God's election takes no account of character, the evil man being as likely to be saved as the righteous. But I doubt if this position has ever been adhered to as a tenet for living, because it amounts to an attempt to eliminate from conduct all human judgment of good and bad, which cannot be accomplished; and in any event it repudiates all purpose for the volitional part of life, which is an untenable belief for reasons already examined.

All other purposes for life that can be framed must involve human process during its earthly existence. All such purposes must furthermore assert something about the way human process is to be made manifest or to unfold; and accordingly they must all constitute an assertion of what the character of human process should be. But character that should be is the same thing as the best character, for the best is simply our designation of what judgment tells us should be. And thus all conceivable purposes for life fall within the broad proposition that that purpose is the best character that human beings can attain.

What constitutes the best character that he or she can create is for each individual human being the great problem of personal philosophy, the answer to which must be attempted daily, as life continuously presents the necessity of deciding how it should be lived.

It is not however a problem for social philosophy, whose task is not to direct the development of individual character, but so to protect it in its proper freedom that it may grow to its fullest realization.

We happen to live in an age in which a deliberate attempt has been made to repudiate the need for a concept of life purpose. During the past half century and more, western philosophy and life have been much under the influence of the viewpoint contained in the doctrines of pragmatism and instrumentalism; and if their influence has now perhaps begun to wane, it is still very powerful. The teaching of these philosophies has been the importance of the immediate practicality of human action. The proper inquiry concerning an item of human behavior, we have been told, is not its adherence to some standard set by a goal or purpose for life, but its success as an instrumentality in securing some practical result that is desired. And when we have inquired what standards should be employed in judging the worth or value of different results that may be desired, the response has been given that this is an invalid question, that the ultimate goals of human process are contained in immediate activity, and that human judgment need not look beyond the desirability of the fact that is at hand.

Ideals that can supply standards being thus repudiated, the object of action becomes necessarily the desire of the present, and action tends to become an end in itself. For although action is judged for its pragmatic or instrumental effect, yet this is viewed as being contained within the action, and not as contained in some ideal which can be regarded as ultimate purpose of all action. The result is twofold. First, all action tends to be held in like regard, for standards of ultimate judgment being discarded, one action becomes as good as the next. The proposition that the practicality of each action must be regarded as lying within the particular action can only mean that each action tests itself, and thus there can be no comparison of acts, and hence one act is as good as another. Second, action tends to become materialistic. The desires toward which our attention is most continuously and forcibly directed are economic needs, particularly the material things that sustain and adorn existence. These desires being the needs that are most prominently at hand in daily experience, the pragmatic and instrumental philosophies, by emphasizing practical action to fill needs, encourage the acceptance of material needs as the predominant element in life.

Pragmatism and instrumentalism are muddled doctrines, not capable of logical statement. They tell us in effect that we should judge without standards of judgment, and that we should consider the efficacy of means but not have regard to the worth or propriety of ends. These are impossible injunctions, having no relation to the realities of existence, and they have contributed in no small degree to the confusion of thought which the Occidental world now struggles with. Pragmatism and instrumentalism must be excised completely from our thought. They must be repudiated as the confused product of a way of thinking which abandoned sound concepts of human nature and human destiny and lost itself in a pseudoscientific approach to the problems of life.

We must see that life has purpose, which purpose is the will of God, and that this purpose must therefore dominate all human activity. It is with reference to this purpose that pragmatic quality and instrumentality must be judged. That which contributes to the best character is pragmatic and instrumental, and that which impairs it possesses neither of these qualities.

4. Volitional and non-volitional process

It is now necessary to turn to a further consideration of willed and non-willed activity, in order to examine the import of these fundamental categories of human action for the problem of social organization.

Human action that is willed takes place without the concurrence of any exterior event or events which can be regarded as determinative cause. The essence of a willed act is that it is a choice among optional possibilities of future conduct. If the selection of one of these possible modes of future behavior is fixed, that is, determinatively caused, by any fact or facts exterior to the will of the subject human being, then no choice exists and a willed act does not occur. Only when choice is possible can the will be exercised, and the extent of choice available to the will is a measure of the freedom available to the person.

The will, nevertheless, can by no means ever operate in complete independence of the facts and events which surround it. On the contrary these facts and events constitute an arena within the limits of which all decisions of will must be made; and although the boundaries of this arena are variable, as the factors composing it are changed, yet the boundaries are always present. As those boundaries are expanded or contracted for the individual human being, so his opportunity for volitional process becomes larger or smaller.

But although will must thus always express itself within a limited arena, yet we know that within will's arena we have a power of choosing, a power of deciding upon some one of optional modes of career. This fact of will, of volitional process that is self-directed, we know by intuition, which is the ultimate base of all human knowledge.

We make no doubt of the fact of will in our individual living. We ponder from time to time what our careers shall be, and we make plans for the future. But pondering and plans are futile if we have no possibility of choice. We know however that we have a power of choice, though events may circumscribe it; and the capacity for choice is the power of will.

Nor do we make doubt of volitional process in our social living. Every system of law is based on a belief in volition, for the essence of law is its assumption of optional modes of human behavior, wherefore it prohibits those modes which, out of all the possible modes, are deemed undesirable. But if all human behavior followed fixed laws of cause and effect there would be neither any need for law nor any opportunity for its injunctions to be effective. Likewise all systems of social order have volition as their occasion. If the social relation between human beings were rigid there would be no social problem; it is because the relation is mutable and subject to the direction of will that social organization occurs.

Those few who occasionally affect a denial of human volition are barred by their denial from any interest in social philosophy and also from argument concerning it. For the subject matter of social philosophy is the choice of the best form of social order, and if human choosing does not occur then there is no valid subject matter for social philosophy and consequently no occasion for interest in it. And since the object of argument is to persuade belief in a particular proposition, if all human action is determined beyond its being changed by will, then so too is all belief determined, for it is a form of human action, and argument to persuade a change in belief is accordingly purposeless.

Turning from volitional to non-volitional process, the latter is human action which takes place independently of any act of will. An obvious example is the growth of cells in the body. Another instance is reflex action, such as that which occurs when the hand is jerked from a flame. The neural activity producing this reflex movement takes place without volitional direction, and although we are conscious of the motion of the hand as it is jerked away, we are not conscious of the neural activity that causes the movement. Non-volitional process is also evinced in those patterns or bents of neural activity which result in instinctive behavior. Action designed to self-preservation is instinctive; and although the particular acts of the man who is in danger may (or may not) be directed by will, yet the general direction of his action is established by neural patterns which are innate, and which induce him to employ forms of action that seem to lead away from the danger and toward a condition of safety. Psychoses resulting in psychotic behavior afford another example of non-volitional process, where the neural patterns may not be innate, but acquired as the result of experiences of which the individual may not (or may) be aware. The behavior that flows from these ingrained neural patterns takes place without volitional act, but it may sometimes be blocked by an act of will, in which case the psychiatric behavior may be eliminated. Lastly we may note habits as a species of non-volitional process. Here the neural pattern that secures the habitual conduct is built up through acts which in most instances are initially evoked by will. But as the act is repeated a pattern of causative neural action is established which no longer requires volitional direction, and the performance of the act then becomes habitual, requiring only an initial stimulus to set it in operation. All skills are habits. The acquisition of a habit, and also its discontinuance, may be effected by volition, as may be also its employment on a particular occasion; but once the series of habitual acts is set in motion its continuance can occur without attention from the will. Were this not so, life as we know it, with its speaking, writing, music, customs, and skills, would be impossible.

5. The moral quality of willed action

Although volitional and non-volitional process are both essential parts of human life, yet we appreciate that volitional process is much more important than non-volitional process as a component of character. For example, if a man be endowed by nature with a fine body and an alert brain, we do not ordinarily account these as indicating what we usually call his character; in order to judge his character we would wish to know what use he makes of his strength and intelligence. Indeed unless we deliberately expand the term character to embrace the non-volitional processes of muscular and neural cells we do not usually think of them as being elements of character at all. It is the decisions that a man makes concerning the employment of his natural faculties, whether they be great or small, that we impute to him as the significant designation of his character.

The reason we do this is because moral quality is an attribute of all volitional process but is not an attribute of non-volitional process, and moral quality is the primary measure of human character, constituting the essence of what the human person is.

Moral quality is a judgment on human behavior, which is imputed to the behavior itself so as to become in a sense a part of that behavior. Although we necessarily frame judgments on all phenomena we find around us, including human process, yet we recognize that all human judgments are contingent and tentative, and that only the judgments of God are absolute and final. Moral quality therefore is not so much a particular judgment which is imputed to volitional process as it is the susceptibility of that process to judgment, and since human judgment is inferior to the judgment of God, moral quality is the susceptibility of volitional process to the judgment of God. And although human judgment of moral quality must remain tentative, and although we can never know the absolute judgment of God, yet we know so surely that moral quality is the significant element in the human process that without it that process would be meaningless to us.

Moral quality is an attribute of behavior whenever there exist, first, an available choice of optional modes of behavior, and second, knowledge of the consequences of the selected mode of behavior. Most systems of criminal law, inflicting punishment only where there is moral responsibility, clearly recognize these two elements of choice and knowledge as the conditions of moral quality. No moral responsibility exists, nor any criminal responsibility, for conduct which is non-volitional, nor for consequences with knowledge of which the actor cannot be charged.

Therefore moral quality inheres only in volitional process and is absent from non-volitional process. The growth of cells is amoral, and so too is reflex action and instinctive and psychotic behavior. The use of habitual action may be willed, and thereby its use may become laden with moral quality, but the habitual act itself is amoral. A lack of skill in habitual action is not a fact of bad moral quality, except to the extent that the want of skill has resulted from a volitional failure to try to improve; the unskilled person who is nevertheless doing his best is not an object of blame but only of commiseration.

Process that is willed however can never escape the burden of moral quality. It has choice, and in the very act of choice it always and necessarily possesses a concept of the line of conduct chosen, included within which concept is an understanding of at least some portion of its more removed aspects, that is, of its consequences. The knowledge of consequences may be small, limiting moral responsibility; but some knowledge of consequences of necessity accompanies each act of choice.

All willed activity, then, has moral quality, and since human life includes willed activity it bears the attribute of moral quality; wherefore all living must be judged to be morally good or bad.

6. Moral quality and freedom

As the purpose of life is the best character that each of us can create, so that purpose includes the best moral quality of living that we can accomplish. Character possesses moral quality, and therefore the best character must be that which has the best moral quality.

Inasmuch, then, as we are required by the purpose of life to build the best moral character we can, we must seek to know the principles governing the development of moral quality.

The basic principle which we must recognize is that moral quality demands, as the absolute condition for its appearance, freedom of the human being to choose between optional ways of conduct. To the extent that such freedom is present, moral quality—either good or bad—is not only possible but inevitable. And to the extent that such freedom is not present, moral quality—of any kind—is not only difficult but impossible. The burden of moral responsibility is the occasion for the appearance of moral quality, and moral responsibility arises only when there is choice of conduct.

The existence of choice depends on freedom. The opportunity for choice is, in fact, freedom, and freedom is enlarged or diminished as the opportunity to choose, to make one's own decisions, is granted or taken away.

The accomplishment of life's purpose and of the will of God depends therefore upon freedom. Without freedom there can be no moral character. The presence of freedom does not assure good moral character, for that depends not only upon freedom but upon right human choice. But with freedom good moral character is possible, whereas without freedom all moral character is impossible.

7. Will's arena

Freedom being the opportunity afforded the will for its exercise, what factors determine the extent of this opportunity?

As heretofore suggested, human will manifests itself in an arena determined by certain factors, which by limiting the choices available to will's decision limit the possible range of its exercise. There are four factors thus establishing will's arena of action, which are here denominated the experiential, psychological, material, and social factors.

The experiential factor is composed of the concepts acquired by the brain through experience. The will can only choose among optional modes of conduct that are presented to it as ideas or concepts of possible action. These concepts must be based on past experience, and accordingly are limited by experience. Since we can thus choose only some course of conduct that we can think of, and since we can think of courses of conduct only to the extent that they have been suggested in some way by experience, it follows that past experience comprises an important limitation on will, and a factor in the composition of its arena. The development of the experiential factor is education, as concepts of action are acquired by the study of history, literature, and science. And what we call the advancement of learning, in both science and the humanities, is but the broadening of the experiential factor.

The psychological factor in will's arena is constituted by the neural patterns, whether innate or acquired, that are the neural equipment through which the will must express itself. Self-preservation has already been noted as an instinctive way in which nervous energy is directed as it in turn controls muscular activity. Therefore the search for food and shelter forms an area of action within which the will is compelled to make some of its choices. Supplying ourselves with food and shelter is not a matter of choice, but of instinctive compulsion. It is only the method of supply that can be chosen, and even that must be selected within limits set by other factors restrictive of volitional process. In the same manner that the instinct of self-preservation furnishes some of the palings in the enclosure that surrounds human will, so do all other instincts have the same effect, notably that of sexual attraction. And likewise reflexes, psychoses, and habits restrict the possible scope of will's action, comprising parts of the psychological factor in will's arena.

Human will is restricted furthermore by the material factor, which is composed of the material facts of environment. These facts consist, first, of the facts of geography, and second, of the facts of available economic goods. Geography's restraining influence on will arises from the circumstance that the will is not only compelled by instinct to seek the means of self-preservation, but is also compelled to accomplish that end with the material means which nature supplies. People living north of the Arctic Circle cannot choose to be vegetarians, and those living in treeless areas cannot elect to have their dwellings made of wood. Likewise the material goods that men fashion by their labor, within the permissive facts of geography, constitute limitations on their action. A society whose efforts produce only the bare means of food and shelter is without the material base necessary to cultural development. These limitations of the material factor confront us on every hand.

Lastly, the arena within which human will is constrained to find its opportunities for expression is composed also of a social factor, which is made up of the social relation and of the rules adopted by men to govern it. As we have seen, the social relation, arising from the fact of man's dual career, is composed of conflict and combination among individuals, and calls for rules of social organization. These rules are by their nature limitations on willed conduct, and indeed the furnishing of such limitations is their very function. They set boundaries to volitional action.

Inasmuch as the experiential, psychological, material, and social factors are all restraints on will, they are also restraints on the development of good character. As the arena of action established by these factors is expanded or contracted, so too is the opportunity to build moral character.

8. Will's arena and liberty

The relation between will and its arena is to some degree reciprocal. While the range of activity of will is limited by the factors composing its arena, will in turn can by its activity influence those factors themselves. In particular it can influence the social factor, which indeed is entirely the product of human decision. By its rules, moreover, the social factor establishes a framework for action which must be observed by will as it influences the experiential, psychological, and material factors. That is, human will determines social organization, which in turn bears on the extent to which will can determine its experiences and its psychological and material environment.

Social organization being thus a product of human decision, it is a part of human life, and therefore the conduct of men in framing social organization should be directed toward the accomplishment of life's purpose, rather than toward its defeat.

Since the purpose of life demands freedom, the task of social organization is the creating of freedom. This it can achieve by keeping will's arena large, that the individual may be free to build the best character he can. But not for some one individual only or for some few is freedom so to be maintained, but for all. This freedom for all becomes liberty, which viewed in its social aspect consists in the largest equal freedom for all individuals that is socially attainable.

9. Liberty as ethical imperative

The purpose of life must be absolute and complete, and not conditioned or partial. A life purpose whose application to life was conditioned on other factors, or which covered only a part of the life process, would not be a true life purpose.

The concept of the best character which we can create, as the purpose for our lives, meets this test. It is absolute, for under all conditions it makes its demand upon us, and no circumstance can ever excuse or justify any character other than the best that is possible to us. It is also complete, because there is no part of life that does not have its character, and to which therefore the purpose of character does not apply.

All of human life, in consequence, is subject to the ordinance, imposed on us by life's purpose and by the will of God, requiring that we each produce the best character that is within our abilities. No consideration whatsoever can at any time release us from this command. It is the first objective of every human activity.

Every human act that creates and maintains social organization is therefore subject to this requirement that the best human character be served. Social organization is simply man acting in combination with his fellows, and this is true whatever the form of the society, whether it be good or bad. However much the state be glorified, all state action yet remains the behavior of individual and mortal men and consequently is subject to the purpose of the best possible character. In framing social order, therefore, the goal of the best character for all men must be made the first law, to which all other laws are subordinate, and the first constitutional principle, to which every detail of the constitution must be made subject.

It is sometimes supposed that the pressure of events may justify or at least condone a deviation from the goal of noble human character. Ends justify means, it is said. If the state is to be built, Hitler warned, some heads must roll in the sand. Mendacity and deceit in party platforms and public speeches are proper, the present vogue has it, if they are used as tools to obtain social reform. But all this confusion of ends and means is swept away when we see that the true end of all human action is good character, and that the true end for all social action is the environment for character's best development.

That environment is liberty. Liberty is the necessary condition to the accomplishment of life's purpose and God's will; for although it is not a condition to the fact itself of purpose, nor to the existence itself of God's will (since that purpose and that will are facts beyond modification or condition), yet it is the necessary condition to the attainment of life's purpose and God's will, because it is the environment we must effect before we can possibly proceed to their achievement. And it is more than necessary condition and environment. It is part of the very process by which the goal is reached; and thus the establishment and continuance of liberty is itself a manifestation of that noblest human character which constitutes the end of our existence.

Since the end is an absolute, an imperative command placed upon us, so also is the necessary condition of the achievement of that end, and the process by which alone the command can be obeyed. Therefore the building of a society providing the maximum equal freedom for all is imperatively demanded of us by the nature and end of our existence. The society providing this freedom is the society of liberty, and liberty is thus imperative.

It is, further, an ethical imperative. Social action is ethical, because it includes the willed decisions of human beings. Accordingly liberty as a form of social action is also a mode of conduct involving moral responsibility and therefore ethical quality. Accordingly, since liberty is an imperative placed upon us, it is also an ethical imperative.

Therefore the man who impairs or destroys liberty is guilty of conduct which absolutely and without qualification is evil, being against life's purpose and God's will, and the man who builds liberty does that which is good, absolutely and without qualification, because he performs the purpose of his existence and the design of God for it.

The foregoing considerations furnish the ethical base for the liberty of individualism. Liberty as individual freedom and as social control is ethical imperative, and the observance of that demand is man's duty.

Liberty has not often been seen in its true form as ethical command. It was as a privilege or right that it first became a force in the modern world as presented in the philosophy of natural law and natural rights, and in the striving of the American and French revolutionaries to be freed from despotic government. In more recent times it has been presented as material advantage. Liberty in economic action produces more goods to supply the needs of life, has been a prevalent form of argument, and therefore we should have liberty as free enterprise.

But while it is true that liberty is a right and a privilege under that reasonable view of things which we may call natural law, and while it is also true that liberty can be counted on to produce the best action of men in the economic sphere as in all others, yet liberty is more than a right and more than economic advantage. Liberty is first of all ethical imperative, imposed by the nature of existence and by the will of God.

Chapter 6

LIBERTY AS THE EXPERIENCE OF TRUTH

1. Human spirit and universal spirit

When we examine our experience as microcosm, we find elements we can summarize as substance and endurance. The person has substance and it endures through a period of time. We analyze and classify these physical elements; but no matter how far we may extend our analysis and classification we know that the physical elements do not comprise the whole of human experience. Beyond the physical elements, in addition to the substantial body passing through a cycle of time, there is something more.

This nonphysical something more we may call spirit, soul, psyche, ego, or—if we wish to emphasize its knowing activity—simply mind. Perhaps the most suitable term, all things considered, is human spirit, and this is the name we shall here employ. But it is the fact, not the name, that is important.

A knowledge of the exact nature of human spirit is not essential to our purpose. We intuitively know that human spirit is a part of our experience, that it lives, acquires knowledge, and by directing human action displays character. Further than this our present concern need not go.

Turning to our experience of the macrocosm, the great universe of which we are so small a part, we find again that the physical elements do not furnish us with a complete explanation. We know that the physical elements are not all, that there is a nonphysical something more, whose necessity we recognize in our discussions of first cause and in our pervasive religious beliefs and practices. This something more we call God or universal spirit; in this chapter we shall use the latter term.

We are intuitively advised that the universe is knowable. All scientific activity proceeds on this intuition. From the secrets of atomic structure to the explanations of disease, we are confident that the facts are knowable. Intuition further advises us that knowableness necessarily connotes a knowing entity; we cannot conceive of a fact being knowable unless there is an entity that can know it. We must therefore conclude not only that the universe is completely knowable, but also that there is an entity that can completely know it.

This entity cannot be human spirit. The limited quality of human knowledge can be readily demonstrated. For example, time must either have had a beginning or not have had a beginning. But either concept is unthinkable; if time had a beginning then before that there must have been a time when there was no time—a contradiction; or if time had no beginning then it extends back infinitely; but time is measurable and so past time must be a measurable infinity—again a contradiction. In similar manner every avenue of thought concerning the fundamental aspects of the universe encounters the bar of an antinomy, as has been shown many times. But we cannot believe that time, space, and other segments of the universe are unknowable; we know beyond doubting that they are knowable; and our conclusion must be, rather, that human spirit is limited in its capacity for knowledge of the facts of the universe.

The knowing entity that can know the facts of the universe must consequently be something other than human spirit. But the only other knowing entity we can conceive of is universal spirit. Therefore universal spirit possesses complete knowledge of the universe; the spirit of the universe is all-knowing.

We must believe, further, that the spirit of the universe is all-good. For all-knowing and all-good are so close that the one attribute cannot be conceived without the other.

Intuitive concepts form the base of our conviction of the fact and nature of human spirit and of universal spirit. It is sometimes objected that intuitive knowledge is not trustworthy, because not subject to verification by the sensory organs. But the proposition that only sensory information can be trusted is a paradox; if it is true it cannot be known, for it itself is a proposition that cannot be learned through observation by the sensory organs, since it is a proposition not concerning observation but concerning nonobservation. It attempts to make use of an intuition to deny the validity of intuitive knowledge.

The example instructs us in the basic fact that all human knowledge is founded in intuition. No other resting place is possible. The scientist who enters his laboratory takes with him as part of his conceptual equipment a host of propositions known only intuitively. Causation, for example, can be known as a principle for the future only as an intuition;

the records of the laboratory give sensory information concerning the past alone, and the projection of causation into the future—the use of past observations for future guidance—can be justified only on the ground of intuition.

Examples need not be multiplied. Men have always based their thought on intuitive concepts and they must always do so; there is no alternative. Therefore when we develop our concepts of human and universal spirit from intuitive convictions we are using the same foundation that all human thought employs.

2. The knowledge of truth

What is truth? Many different answers have been given. With their differences we shall not be concerned, but with what they have in common.

They have this in common: that truth is knowledge of the universe, in its smallest part and in its mighty whole. We know the truth when our knowledge corresponds to fact in the universe. Our experience of truth is therefore the experience of concepts that accord with facts in the universe.

The complete knowledge of these facts, however, is the attribute of universal spirit. The growth of the human spirit in its experience of truth is accordingly toward identity with the truth contained in universal spirit. The human spirit's development, as it contains truth, is toward oneness with universal spirit, a oneness which can never be consummated but nevertheless stands always as goal. Human knowledge is the growth of human spirit in identity with universal spirit.

This growth in knowledge is possible only because human spirit is of the same essence as universal spirit. In this sameness of essence lies the explanation of the marvelous congruence of the concepts embedded in intuition with the processes of the physical universe. We spin out intuition by pure ratiocination into theorems of mathematics, and lo! we find the universe proceeding in accordance with the same principles. Only because of this congruence of concept with fact is science a possible human activity. Even as human concepts are a manifestation of human spirit, so the facts of the universe are a manifestation of universal spirit. The identity of concepts and facts must consequently evidence an identity in essence of human spirit with universal spirit, although the identity is limited to an extent we are not competent to define.

Therefore the growth of the human spirit in knowledge, as it seeks to realize its identity with universal spirit, is also human spirit knowing and realizing itself. Human spirit striving to know universal spirit is also human spirit striving to know itself. Knowledge is self-knowledge in inseparable part.

Truth accordingly is of the knower as well as of the known. Truth is subject-object relation, and the relation is not static but dynamic, as the knower, human spirit, increasingly experiences identity with the known, universal spirit.

3. The knowledge of truth is liberty.

Therefore the human experience of truth is always an active process. Truth is not an attribute simply of a knowing mind, nor yet of a known object. Truth, for humanity, is the experience of the subject-object relation. It is the process of effecting a harmony of the knowing mind with some object of contemplation. Essentially it is the process of the unfolding of the human spirit in oneness with the universal spirit in which it is contained.

The essence of this experience is self-direction, for the unfolding of the individual human spirit in harmony with the universal spirit can never be forced. The application of force necessarily destroys the harmony, which can exist only so long as the human spirit presses its search for identity with universal spirit of its own volition. Thus a compelled striving for growth of the human spirit in oneness with the universal spirit would be a contradiction, for a compelled attitude of attunement with universal spirit could not be oneness, which is a matter of essential spiritual nature and not of form. Therefore the harmony of human spirit and of universal spirit can never be compelled.

But this striving for harmony and oneness with universal spirit is humanity's experience of truth, and from the nature of truth it is the only experience of truth that humanity can ever have. Therefore the human spirit's knowledge of truth can arise only out of self-direction, that is, out of its own freedom. The human spirit must be free if it is to know the truth. This freedom is not simply a propitious circumstance for the acquisition of truth, nor yet is it only a condition for truth's acquirement; it is more than these; freedom of the spirit, when directed toward identity with universal spirit, is itself and of itself the experience and acquisition of truth and the only acquaintance with truth the human spirit can ever know.

But the human spirit is attached to a human body, and the body lives in a world of social relation. Were this not so, were this a universe in which each human being lived an insulated existence, the human problem would be simply the unfolding of individual spirits without regard to each other. But since we inhabit a world of social relation, the problem of the freedom of the individual human spirit becomes the problem of liberty for all human spirits, and this, since spirit is part of the human organism, becomes the problem of individual and social liberty of human beings. The human experience of truth is thus the experience of liberty.

This freedom does not of itself assure acquaintance with truth; if it did so the spirit would not in fact be free and this would not be a moral universe. The essence of this freedom is self-direction, and the spirit may direct itself toward or away from identity with universal spirit. That is the very purpose of its freedom. It is only when the self-imposed direction of development is toward identity that truth is experienced.

Thus truth consists in liberty. And liberty is truth; not in the sense that all exercise of liberty leads to truth, because its wrongly directed exercise leads to untruth, but in the sense that liberty directed to self-realization in integration with universal spirit is the sole experience of the knowledge of truth.

Societies therefore that bar liberty bar also the acquisition of truth, and to the extent that they impair liberty, either intellectual or economic, they also impair their knowledge of truth. The past has time and again demonstrated this as a practical tenet. It is not in the Spartas of history that human beings have known or discovered truth. We close the chapters of these collectivistic societies with little profit from our perusing them, save that of warning; for the lives of their citizens usually accomplished nothing beyond a few disciplines. It is in the societies, rather, that have caught something of the free fire of Athens that the truth has grown and been experienced, and it is to their records that we repair for inspiration and instruction.

The lesson is that liberty is not only the social form that facilitates the knowledge of truth, but that liberty is also the very essence of humanity's knowledge of truth, and that without liberty therefore truth cannot enter into human experience.

Chapter 7

THE EQUALITY OF LIBERTY

1. The persistent idea of the equality of men

The idea is persistent in human thought that men are in some important respect equal to each other. But although this concept of equality has at times been most influential in history, yet there has seldom been an attempt to develop its content with care.

Attention has already been called to the fact that the equality of men occupied a prominent place in the teachings of Jesus, who repeatedly said that all men are equal in the concern of God. But how is this concern equal? Certainly the Creator is not concerned for equality in the intellects, bodies, and emotions of human beings, for men are not created equal in these things.

In Locke's second *Treatise on Civil Government*, it was expressly asserted that in a state of nature all men are equal in their rights. This concept as it was developed included the thought that when men move from a state of nature to a state of social order they relinquish something of this natural equality. But just how this in fact occurs and what principles govern the matter of social equality was never worked out in detail by Locke or other liberal thinkers; and the apparent difficulty they experienced is testimony of the initial error of positing a state of nature as the matrix of the principles of social organization.

But the theory of equality in the state of nature led to the concept of equality of legal rights, which is still vigorously useful for us in the proposition that all men are equal before the law. It is currently supposed that this is a foundation stone in the edifice of liberty, and it is indeed true that there could be no society of liberty which did not observe this principle. But it is not basic in its position, but rather an implementation of other basic propositions and a derivative of the nature of liberty. We do not establish liberty because we believe in equality before the law; we establish equality before the law because we believe in liberty. And even as liberty is declining at the present time in the western world, so is equality before the law; for as we activate once again in history the collectivistic principle of the superiority of a few, we necessarily accompany it with the development of a favored position to be accorded to the few in the administration of the law.

2. The equal need for freedom

The need for freedom arises from the purpose of life, the building of good character. This purpose is derived from the nature of human existence, and inasmuch as existence, of itself, is the same for all persons, it follows that life's purpose is the same for all. And since the purpose of life is also the will of God, we see that God's will for each human being is exactly the same, and that the building of the finest characters we can is the equal will of God for us all.

It is here that equality in the concern of God is found. Whatever may be the reason for the variations in the physical and intellectual endowment of human spirits, they nevertheless can know that God's will for them and the concern of God in their characters is equal for them all.

This is the way men stand in equality before God, and the way they are equal by nature. Their equality is in the ultimate purpose fastened upon them.

If therefore all men are equal in purpose, they have equal need for the condition which makes that purpose possible. Men being equally commanded to create the best characters they can achieve, and self-directed conduct being the absolute condition for the accomplishment of that end, they have equal need for the opportunity for self-directed conduct. This opportunity is freedom. Men therefore have an equal need for freedom.

Not only, moreover, do men have equal need for freedom, but they have an equal claim upon their fellows for the maintenance of the social condition which constitutes freedom. This social condition is the society of liberty, whose creation and preservation is man's duty. The right to claim the performance of this duty is equally distributed among men.

The equal need for individual freedom and the equal claim for social liberty is not affected by the circumstance that men make different uses of freedom. One man builds good character and another bad, but the equality of their need for freedom does not change. Their life purpose remains always the same and equal, unmodified by their success or failure in its achievement; and in consequence their equal need for the condition of the purpose continues without alteration.

The liberty of all requires protection from the acts of those who would impair it; hence the evil man may have to be restrained that equal liberty may be preserved. But though this occur, yet his need for freedom continues unchanged; his freedom is decreased not because his need for it has become less but because he himself has made the diminishment of it a condition to the equal freedom of others.

But no man can rightfully interfere with the freedom of another except as interference is necessary to maintain equal freedom. To interfere beyond the requirements of equal freedom is to obstruct life's purpose and God's will.

3. Equal freedom requires social control.

Were each human person an isolated phenomenon, his need would be for the largest self-directed activity he could accomplish, for thereby he could experience the largest knowledge of truth and would have the largest opportunity to develop his character.

But we do not live as isolated phenomena, but as social creatures experiencing the social relation. And because of this social relation the self-directed activity of each individual is a condition of the self-directed activity of all other individuals. The use of freedom by one affects the use of freedom by all. Within a wide range of action, the use of freedom by one person need not lessen the freedom of his fellows, and may on the contrary expand it. But the use of freedom by one may nevertheless upon occasion diminish the freedom of others, whereby equality of freedom is prevented. If some members of a community exercise their freedom of action to make slaves of other members, freedom is thereby made unequal.

To accomplish equal freedom accordingly requires that some manner of restraint be imposed upon any self-directed activity which by expanding beyond the limits of equal freedom would destroy equal freedom. Such restraint must itself be a form of human action, and two possibilities are present. First, restraint may be imposed by each individual upon his own use of freedom; and second, restraint may be imposed by group action through social control.

Without doubt the maintenance of equal freedom must depend much upon self-restraint. In the multitude of interhuman relations that constitute living, group action in many of them to effect equal liberty is impossible because impractical. Society cannot, for example, police the home, where character development for some members of the family is frequently impaired by the domineering interference with their freedom by others. Self-restraint must moreover be counted on as support for social control, for without a recognition of the principle of equal freedom in the individual careers of the influential part of a society its recognition in social rules cannot be expected.

It is upon social control, however, that equal freedom in its larger aspects must depend. All human experience discloses that most men upon some occasions and some men upon most occasions fall into the error of enlarging their own freedom at the cost of diminishing the freedom of others. Men cannot confidently be asked to be judges in their own controversies; and to expect each human being, the young and the old, the wise and the foolish, to discern day by day the limit to action required by the principle of equal freedom would be to trust in that which never can occur. Only by particular rules adopted by men in concert, known in advance of application and socially enforced, can equal freedom be secured.

Liberty is therefore not only equal individual freedom, but also the social control that secures equal freedom. Man's equal need for freedom is thus an occasion for the social control which constitutes social organization.

Although men have equal need for freedom, yet precise equality of will's arena for all human beings, or even close equality, can never be accomplished. For social control affects directly only the social factor in will's arena, and can affect the experiential, psychological, and material factors only indirectly and to but limited degree. These factors must always remain unequal for different human beings. This however furnishes but additional reason for striving to maintain equality in the social factor.

4. The equality of the social factor

Equality in the social factor in will's arena consists in maintaining for each individual, through the rules which constitute social control, the largest freedom that can be given him without making his freedom larger than that of any other person.

This is the general principle. Its application is the science of social engineering for liberty.

A corollary to the general principle is that when the largest equal liberty for all has been delineated by social rules, the rules must not go farther and seek to control the exercise of freedom within the delineated areas. Freedom is self-decision, and therefore social control of the exercise of freedom is a self-contradiction. To direct the use of freedom is to destroy freedom. Social rules accordingly must restrict themselves to establishing the arena for willed activity and must not attempt to direct that activity.

A second corollary is that in delineating equal liberty social rules need be concerned only with points at which infractions of equal liberty occur. At these points restraints must be constructed barring one person from invading the liberty of another. Since social control is not properly concerned with the exercise of liberty, the maintenance of equal liberty is to be achieved primarily by directing social rules to the prevention of those human actions which would impair equal liberty. In this sense the laws of the free society tend to be negative rather than positive in character, to forbid action rather than to command it.

5. Equal liberty and the equal use of force

The relation of liberty to force will furnish the content of a following chapter. Here we shall note only that equal liberty does not call for equal authority to use force on the part of all members of a society, and that on the contrary the maintenance of equal liberty requires an unequal allocation among the members of a society of the authority to use force in their dealings with their fellows.

If there are to be social rules there must be enforcement of them, for observance of rules can be obtained, all experience teaches, only by some method of inflicting a penalty for want of observance. Thus the penalty for stealing is a jail sentence, the penalty for speeding on the highway a fine, and the penalty for misrepresentation in obtaining a contract the refusal of the courts to permit any advantage to be gained by it.

Whatever the form of sanction employed in securing observance of a social rule, it requires the use of force in its application. Such force must not only be exerted against someone but it must also be applied by someone; the application of force is a human activity performed by individual human beings.

Conceivably the enforcement of rules could be effected by all citizens acting together, as is the practice with some tribal peoples. But more developed societies need specialization in law enforcement as in other activities, and accordingly enforcement is placed in the hand of magistrates and police, who are clothed with more authority to exercise force than other members of the community. Since this unequal use of force is the only adequate method of enforcing social rules, and since such rules are necessary to maintain liberty, unequal authority to use force is compatible with equal liberty.

There is much more about the use of force which will require our attention. Here our point is that unequal authority to use force is not of itself a violation of the equality of liberty.

6. Equal liberty is not sameness.

Equal freedom is equal opportunity for willed activity, but it is not the same use of such opportunity. The use of opportunity depends upon the individual, and if opportunity be truly kept equal the uses of it must always be as various as the abilities and characters of the members of society.

A great danger to liberty whenever it has been developed in the past, and a danger which threatens today, is a craving for sameness in human activity. Under a tyranny those whose accomplishments are small can excuse themselves, and indeed perhaps justifiably, by the consideration that the social order restrains them. But as liberty is created this excuse is removed. In order to escape therefore the self-condemnation of want of achievement, the less able and less industrious seek to remove the comparison that discloses their inadequacy, wherefore sameness is sought to be imposed. It is represented that great differences of accomplishment must flow from differences of opportunity, by which argument it is thought also to show that sameness in accomplishment must be a result of equal opportunity.

This tyranny of the many, when it restrains the freedom of the few, is as destructive of liberty and human character as the tyranny of the few when it restrains the freedom of the many. We see it raising its ugly shadow again today in the ill-considered pleas that increasingly are put forth for unity in various fields of action. Unity is never a sign of liberty and growth, but of tyranny and decadence. When people are free they display differences of opinion, of conduct, and of accomplishment; it is only when they lack freedom that their opinions and actions become the same.

The specialization, then, that finds some men in positions of greater responsibility and influence than others is not a denial of liberty. On the contrary, if opportunity for willed action be kept free and equal such specialization is bound to appear, as men respond differently to the challenge of life. Liberty consists not in procuring the same response, but in keeping the rules of opportunity for response free and the same for all.

An opposite sort of error involving sameness sometimes appears. It is occasionally supposed that equal freedom means simply sameness of privilege of conduct. It is imagined that A and B have equal freedom if A be permitted to rob B provided only that B also be permitted to rob A, and so with other undesirable acts. By this method of demonstration it is thought to show the fallacy of the principle of equal liberty.

But equal liberty not being sameness, a mere similarity of privilege to commit depredation is not liberty, and nothing is proved about liberty by supposing such similarity. Liberty bars robbery and like offenses not because to permit such acts by one rather than by all would result in inequality, but because every such act, whether committed by one or by all, impairs the victim's arena for willed activity by depriving him of the goods upon which such activity in part depends. Liberty is always equal; but not all equality is liberty; and sameness is never liberty.

Chapter 8

LIBERTY AS THE PRIMARY FUNCTION OF SOCIAL ORGANIZATION

1. The question of social origin

Men have long speculated on the nature of social organization, and usually their thinking has led them to seek at least a part of the explanation in the circumstances accompanying the supposed origin of society. Why and how, it has been asked, were societies first formed? What motivations prompted men to join in societies? These motivations being present, did societies arise by agreement or compact of the original founders, were they instituted by the divine being, who delegated the right to rule to "the powers that be" and thus placed authority in rulers "ordained of God,"[1] or did social order emerge simply as the imposed might of the strongest? From considerations such as these it has been believed that the nature of society could be derived.

Plato thought that the motivation to social living was contained in the economic needs of men; by dwelling together they were able to specialize in their tasks and exchange the different products of their labor, thereby making possible a higher level of material existence.[2] Aristotle opined that society had its origin in a political instinct which induced men to live together through an inherent need for association.[3]

But while these and similar theories may express reasons why human beings live in propinquity, they do not tell us why social groups adopt rules for the regulation of the behavior of their members. Invariably societies are characterized by some degree of social control over individual conduct. It is this fact of socially enforced rules which requires analysis and explanation as the significant element of social organization. Mere proximity has its complete explanation simply in the nature of the reproductive process, which necessitates the family for the birth and upbringing of the young, and leads to group living in the tribe as

1. Paul, *Epistle to the Romans*, XIII, 1.

2. *Republic*, II, 369.

3. *Politics*, I, 2.

an expansion of the familial experience. Usually, moreover, the facts of geography necessitate human living in nearness one to another; though men should desire to live separately, where could they go to do so?

Being thus compelled to live together in groups, human beings always have recourse to laws and customs constituting social control. The question then is presented, Why and to what purpose is this social regulation employed? It is to this question that we shall direct our attention, in our effort to discover the essential function of social organization. Before doing so, however, we shall find it helpful to dispose of a preliminary matter.

2. The creation of a state as social function

The regulation that a society exercises over its members is not only acknowledged but emphasized in the term "the state," which in its modern connotation indicates a cultural and legal entity of which individual persons are no more than component parts. Investigation of the nature of social organization frequently assumes that a state in this organic sense is the true type of social organization, constituting its form when completely developed, other forms being simply examples of incomplete growth. This assumption being made, the investigation is conducted as an answer to the question, "What is the state?" This method of procedure, however, by suggesting in the question the answer to be obtained, indicates in advance of analysis that society is an organism wherein the group naturally dominates the individual and furnishes in itself the proper measure of value in human affairs. So often indeed has this method of thought been employed that gradually the assumption of western philosophy has become that a society from its very nature is also a state in this organic sense, an assumption which has greatly aided collectivism in its modern resurgence.

Scientific method, however, must abjure all assumptions concerning social phenomena and seek to observe them as they are rather than as seen through an *a priori* conception of their nature. And when we objectively examine the facts of social organization as disclosed in history, we see that social organization has much of the time appeared, perhaps more often than not, in forms that cannot be brought within the category of a state. On the one hand we have a loosely organized society such as that of the Eskimos, who, although possessing a large body of rules of conduct enforced through social pressure as taboos, yet live together without tribes, chiefs, police, or officers of any kind, and whose society certainly does not constitute a state within any accepted connotation of that term. On the other hand we have the highly organized feudal society of the Middle Ages in Europe, a basic principle of whose organization both in theory and practice was *Nul homme sans seigneur*,[4] under which principle no manor, duchy, or kingdom constituted a state, each being only a component part of the whole Christian world, regarded as integrated in a single organization.

It is of importance to note also that the federal system of social organization, as exemplified in the Achaean League and in our United States, discloses that social organization need not take the form of a state in the currently accepted sense of a unitized and closed organization. A resident of Corinth was a citizen both of his *polis*, Corinth, and of the Achaean League, standing in a direct relation of rights and duties to each organization. More significantly, in the United States from its inception until about 1940, a resident of a constituent state, Pennsylvania, for example, was a citizen of each of two separate sovereignties, the government of Pennsylvania and the government of the United States, whose respective powers were carefully distinguished both in theory and in practice, interference of one with the other being prevented by constitutional provisions enforced by judicial decision. Each of these governments was a true sovereignty, whose activities however were restricted by the federal arrangement. Neither of these governments could be said to have constituted a state within the organic sense for the people of Pennsylvania; nor could the people of Pennsylvania in their capacity as citizens of either one or the other sovereignty be said to compose a state. Nor did the two sovereignties together, nor the people in their two capacities, conform to the unitary idea of a state, for the two sovereignties, opposed in their claims and ruling over the same territory and the same people, could not compose the legal entity that the concept of a state connotes. Thus for a long period of time our society operated, and very successfully, under a form of social organization which did not correspond to the organic conception of a state, as that conception has become familiar in western thought. The fact that our federal system has now disappeared, the sovereignty of the component state governments having been destroyed by Supreme Court decisions and presidential usurpations, which have had the effect of reducing the states to mere departments of the national government, does not invalidate the significance of the prior history.

4. No man without an overlord.

That significance lies in the demonstration that the creation of a state is not a necessary function of social organization. It is clear that societies can exist without composing a state in the sense indicated, because such societies have existed in the past. Nor can they be dismissed as transient forms, for they have upon occasion endured through long periods of time, and have been at least as durable as the Prussian state which Hegel imagined was the ultimate state form in social development. Social organization, therefore, may or may not amount to the cultural and legal entity designated a state, and the current assumption that the creation of such an entity is society's basic function is erroneous.

3. Social rules and the social relation

Although the forms of social organization observable in man's history exhibit the greatest variety, yet they all have this in common, that every society has socially enforced rules to regulate the conduct of its members. A society may lack the organization essential to a state, but it never lacks for rules of conduct. The Eskimos have no public officials; nevertheless a vast and intricate system of taboos regulates individual action, and if some member of the society fails to respect the public opinion that calls for the observance of these taboos, he will, if his conduct continues obnoxious, be killed by common consent. Although throughout the feudal period there were no states, yet each manor had its own customs which were enforced as law in the manorial court, and only gradually did these detailed rules merge into a system of national law, becoming in England the common law that is today the base of our American legal system.

This universality of socially enforced rules of conduct, whatever the social form, indicates that such rules are imperatively demanded by some human need. If we say, expressing the obvious, that men need such rules in order to live together amicably, this does no more than point out the question for our consideration, rather than supply an answer. What we need to know, in order to understand the essential function which social organization always performs, is why human beings require socially enforced rules in order to live together in society. Why is it that the experience of human beings demonstrates that they cannot carry on their existences in propinquity without laws?

The answer to this question must be discoverable in human nature, since human nature is the basic fact manifested in social experience. The fundamental fact of human nature bearing on social experience is the duality of man's career, resulting in the social relation. The need for social rules must accordingly arise from some aspect of this relation. Competition and cooperation among human beings constitute the elements of the social relation, as our analysis has heretofore disclosed, and therefore rules constituting social organization must be directed toward either competition or cooperation or toward both. These rules are always controls of the conduct of human beings, and since they are directed toward competition or cooperation or both, we may say that they always constitute social control of competition or social control of cooperation or both. It follows then that the basic need for social organization, and therefore the essential function that the rules of social organization always serve, is to be found within the need of human beings for social control of competition and cooperation.

4. Social control of competition

Our study has already disclosed that the competitive conflict is both intellectual and economic, and that the economic portion results from the fact that human wants always exceed the goods which human labor is able to supply for their satisfaction. In consequence, only part of the economic wants of a society are ever satisfied and some must necessarily remain unsatisfied.

The determination of what wants will be satisfied, and by the same token what ones will be left uncared for, depends upon the course of competitive activity. This in turn is determined by human decision. Whether goods are plentiful or scarce, that is, whether the unsatisfied wants are less or more pressing, depends in part on natural conditions and in part on human effort, as people make decisions varying the amount and effectiveness of their labor. And when productive effort has performed its task, creating goods to meet wants, the distribution of the stock of goods for consumption by particular persons similarly depends upon human decisions. These decisions, then, constitute in their sum, for the society as a whole, a determination of the course of its economic activity; and since economic activity constitutes at once a manifestation and a resolution of the basic economic conflict in the social relation, these economic decisions constitute controls of the conflict inherent in the experience of each human being as the actor in a dual career.

Such decisions are an unavoidable part of the process of living in a social group, simply because the conflict which they resolve is unavoidable. Since a society is composed of people, the decisions must be made by people, and the essential problem of every society therefore is to determine by its rules of organization what particular people will make these decisions, and under what particular circumstances they will be permitted to do so.

The answers to this problem have been as various as the forms of society. In ancient Egypt it was Pharaoh and Joseph and their bureaucracy who decided what citizens would have grain and how much. In Sparta the decision-function was largely monopolized by the soldier-citizen class. In present-day Russia and to a less degree in Great Britain, the deciding of who gets what is largely done by a hierarchical officialdom, acting through price fixing, wage determination, and other economic controls. In free societies, on the other hand, such as Periclean Athens and the United States, the deciding is done by all members of the group, who are permitted to make their own decisions within rather wide bounds on a free market, determining in individual transactions what they will produce and consume. The individual decisions so made become in their total the society's settlement of the basic economic conflict.

Thus within any society the decisions which control the satisfaction of wants may be made by one person, by a few persons, or by many or all persons. For the present we are not concerned with the advantages of one mode over another, but with the fact that even as the competition of wants is inevitable, so the decisions that compromise that competition are inevitable and cannot be eliminated from society.

The fact of economic conflict and the demand which it makes for resolution through human decision is illustrated in Barrie's play, *The Admirable Crichton*. A group of persons cruising on a pleasure yacht become shipwrecked on an island without prospect of rescue. Supplies are limited, and the problem is presented of utilizing the supplies advantageously and of supplementing them as far as possible in order that consumption and living may go on. It soon becomes apparent that this economic problem requires decision on someone's part, and the person to whom the group turns and who gradually becomes their manager and accepted dictator, allotting shares and directing tasks, is not any of the prominent passengers, but the quiet butler, Crichton, who turns out to be the one who best knows how to decide the clashes of interest and to get things done. A set of rules appears, centering on Crichton's authority, and he carries on the deciding function very well, until rescue comes after many months, when he slips back into his role of the unobtrusive servant. Thus the characters in the play epitomize a society, and their experience in discovering that economic conflict requires social organization, which controls the manner in which decisions are made, shows us the function which every social organization must necessarily perform.

The deciding which is thus inherent in all group experience must be done by particular human beings, and since the deciding has the result of determining whose wants are satisfied and to what extent, and whose wants are not satisfied and to what extent, the identity of those who perform this deciding function becomes a matter of first importance to all members of the society.

How are these people pointed out and vested with the deciding function? Always and inevitably by the rules and customs that constitute the social organization of the society. There is no other way they can acquire the power of deciding, for the rules that are dominant in the society constitute the only possible source of the ability to exercise decision. In a tyranny it is the rules of the tyrannous organization, as the tyrant himself imposes them, that permit him to control decision through his subordinates. In collective societies such as Russia and Great Britain it is the collectivistic organization that permits the large officialdom to decide the economic questions determining production and consumption and thus regulating the economic conflict. In societies maintaining a free market it is the rules of the free market that permit deciding to be done by individuals as producers and consumers. But whatever the pattern of the decision process, some pattern is inevitable. It may be effected by the force of a few or by the franchise of the many. Human beings, however, cannot form a group without developing such a pattern, which results as a necessary consequence of the fact of group living and the fact of economic conflict.

Competition embedded in the social relation, furthermore, is intellectual as well as economic. Here too an adjustment of the competitive conflict becomes a necessary accompaniment of group living, and the adjustment, again, must be made by human decision. Someone must decide whether opinions are to be freely expressed or to be subject to restriction, and if restriction be decided upon, the rules and machinery of censorship must be formulated. These social forms for the freedom or limitation of opinion, whether religious, scientific, or other, necessarily arise through human decision, since they cannot spring into existence spontaneously. Patterns of every variety for dealing with the intellectual

conflict are found in history and can be seen about us. They all have
been created by people who decided, either carelessly or thoughtfully,
for selfish or generous reasons, that the rules should be as they became.

An essential function of social organization, therefore, and one which
it always performs, whether it be the most loose association conceivable
or a closely welded state on the Spartan or Prussian model, is to establish
the rules for controlling the decisions made necessary by the economic
and intellectual conflict. Primarily these rules must point out the people
who are empowered to make decisions, and secondarily they may delineate principles to which decisions should conform. Every type of social
organization performs this function and there can be no social organization without this function's being performed.

5. Social control of cooperation

Turning to the control of cooperative activity, we should first note
that much cooperation is intertwined with elements of competition, and
to the extent that competition is present the regulation of cooperation
by society is included within its activity in controlling competition. But
the cooperative elements in human action may also be separately controlled by social rules, in which event such control becomes an additional
function of social organization. This function, however, is not primary
and necessary, as is the case in the control of competition, but secondary
and optional.

An obvious form of control of cooperative activity, and one often
cited as a prime function of society, is organization for military offense
and defense against other groups. Social organization need not, however, be directed to military preparedness, and it is indeed the professed
aim of much human activity to eliminate such preparedness as a social
function. Societies have existed in the past, moreover, and will again exist
in the future, without a military establishment. The maintenance and
direction of armed forces, therefore, is not an inescapable function of
social organization, but is rather an elective function which may be
assumed or discarded as occasion advises.

The case is the same with the maintenance of internal police. Usually
this is a desirable function for social organization to assume, but it is
not an inevitable function. Societies can exist in theory and have been
found in practice without internal police.

Beyond these matters of external and internal policing, the control of cooperative activity is closely linked with the control of intellectual and economic conflict. The rules of the society may, for example, not only permit free expression of religious opinion but also control in greater or lesser degree the doctrines and practices of an officially recognized church, as is the case today in Great Britain. Here the social rules governing conflict of religious opinion are linked with rules which cover an area of enforced religious cooperation. In like manner the rules may permit free expression of opinion on political and economic subjects but may nevertheless attempt cooperative action in molding opinion by official propaganda, as is the case in the United States at the present time, where the citizens through their taxes are compelled to support great numbers of governmental employees whose task it is to mold the opinions of the citizens themselves who maintain them. Here again the control of cooperative intellectual activity is assumed by the state as a function in addition to its primary function of regulating competitive activity.

With respect to the cooperative action that is involved in the production and consumption of goods, the controls that can be effected by social organization may, if deemed advisable, be extended very far. Indeed the basic position of socialism and of communism is that social controls should completely regulate the cooperative action that is included in production and consumption, with the state owning all or nearly all instruments of production and directing workers in their tasks, and allocating goods for consumption. Such regulation has often been regarded in the past as an appropriate function of social organization. It is not, however, a necessary function of social organization which must inevitably be undertaken by all societies, but is one which may be adopted or not as the particular society may deem wise.

6. Control of conflict as primary function

The control of the conflict between individual human beings remains, then, the imperative function of social organization, which always must be performed and always is performed by the rules of any society whatsoever, for the very existence of a society means that somehow this function is being discharged.

The attempt to perform this function constitutes the origin of society. And since the performance of this function may be accomplished in many different ways, rather than by one particular procedure, it follows that the origin of society is not to be found in one special mode of organization as has often been supposed, but in the variable activity of a social group as it adopts some one of the many possible methods for meeting the basic need of resolving competitive conflict. When men first form societies they are not primarily concerned with explicitly observing either any principle of kingship or of social contract or of merging their individualities in a cultural organism. Instead, they adopt whatever method is nearest at hand, by reason of cultural background and current events, or whatever method seems to the dominant members of the group to be the most suitable, for accomplishing the essential task of resolving competitive interference. They need not approach the problem of social organization in terms of this analysis, even as the marooned voyagers in *The Admirable Crichton* did not analyze principles but rather found themselves demonstrating them; analysis, however, is not needed, for the fact of competition is inevitably present, requiring a scheme for its resolution if any social organization is to exist.

7. Varying modes of performing the primary function

Although the origin of society is thus to be found in a basic need, the satisfaction of which becomes society's primary function, and although differing modes of social organization are available for serving this need, yet not all modes are equally efficacious. Societies in their early stages are probably strongly impelled to adopt tribal communism. But as experience increases, other forms of organization—varying degrees of monarchism, despotism, aristocracy, or democracy—may be tried, which constitute in terms of fundamental principles varying degrees of collectivism, individualism, or anarchism. Confronted with these many possibilities, men can and should seek to employ the mode that is best, and as each individual enters the world he should examine the social organization he finds about him to discover if its rules can be modified in order better to serve not only society's basic need but also the ultimate purpose of human life itself.

In this search for ways of improvement in social organization, men have need for great wisdom and great integrity. Great wisdom because social organization is of all things the most difficult to understand and understanding is not easily transferred from one generation to the next. Great integrity because the mode of social organization directly bears upon each person's economic and intellectual welfare, and accordingly there is required a careful moral sense to separate prejudice from persuasion.

The urge moreover to experiment with social organization, to change it simply for the sake of change, is very strong, particularly in the younger portion of a population, and while this urge may truly be the spur to improvement, it is also frequently the occasion of tragic decline. Therefore the nature of the urge needs to be understood and its dangers in practice guarded against, as men experiment with varying modes of performing society's basic function.

The urge for change arises through irritation over unsatisfied wants. Want means psychological and physiological distress. Since unsatisfied want is a permanent factor in human existence, it follows that the psychological and physiological distress attendant thereon is also a permanent factor. As the seriousness of the disparity between goods and wants increases or declines, so does the irritation arising from the psychological and physiological distress. Wants, moreover, are personal, while the availability of goods is regarded, particularly in a complex society, as being under a strong social influence. The rules of the social organization, it is believed, and correctly enough, have something to do both with the quantity and the division of goods. If, therefore, the goods available to satisfy wants are inadequate, is not a case thereby made for trying to improve matters by changing the social organization?

The mode of thought thus occurring, though completely erroneous, is yet so prevalent in its variants as to be perhaps the dominant note in most discussions of social affairs. Typically it appears in a presentation of an argument in the following manner: In Situation X there are many unsatisfied human wants; therefore there must be something wrong with Situation X; therefore there must be something wrong with the social rules that control Situation X; therefore these social rules should be changed. We constantly observe this pattern of thought in current discussions. A problem is presented, consisting essentially, as all human problems do consist, of unsatisfied but worthy human wants. A change in social rules is accordingly called for. A supposed solution in terms of such a change is then advocated.

The logical gap between the distress of unsatisfied want and a need for change in social rules is seldom perceived; yet there is such a gap, and it is important to understand both the logical hiatus and the phenomenal facts upon which it is based. The view that unsatisfied want per se calls for social change must rest on the assumption that a social organization is possible which will not condemn any worthy human want to go unsatisfied, but which will on the contrary satisfy every worthy human want. This is an erroneous proposition, because a form of social organization caring for all worthy human wants is impossible both in theory and in practice. Every form of social organization is inevitably a compromise of worthy human interests, in which some such interests are denied in order that others may be preserved.

8. Social organization as compromise

Man cannot eliminate the basic fact of unsatisfied wants, since it results from man's nature and the nature of the universe. Nor do men change this datum by joining together in a society, for although the character of the wants that must remain unsatisfied can be influenced by social organization, yet the basic discrepancy between goods and wants cannot be done away with.

All human wants, both intellectual and economic, and both satisfied and unsatisfied, represent human interests. The worthiness of these interests is a matter for individual judgment, but many of them are judged by all people to be worthy of being cared for, and each of them is deemed by someone to be worthy, for otherwise such interest would not be attached to a want. Thus the rules of social organization constitute not only controls of the essential conflict between human beings, but also controls of more or less worthy human interests. And since the function of social organization is to adjust and compromise the competitive conflict, so it may also be said that the function of social organization is to adjust and compromise worthy human interests; and this is a proposition which it is of the first importance to comprehend. Human interests conflict even as do the wants by which they are represented, and as wants are or are not satisfied, so interests are cared for or denied. Since some wants must be unsatisfied, some interests must be left uncared for, and thus the adjustment of competing wants is also necessarily a compromise of conflicting interests. Some interests must inevitably be denied by the compromise, and thereby irritation and distress must be occasioned.

This is a hard truth to face. If worthy human interests exist, must it not be possible somehow to satisfy them? We feel impelled to give an affirmative answer to this question, but it is a fatuous and thoughtless optimism, capable of much tragedy, that leads us to such a response. The compromise of worthy interests is an ineradicable element of social organization, and the question is not whether there will be compromise, but whether it will be effected with wisdom; and the art of social ordering is to choose wisely and kindly the interests to be preserved at the expense of others, rather than to rush precipitantly to the gratification of whatever interest presents itself most forcibly at the moment as worthy.

Whatever form a society may take, whether it adopt the principles of collectivism or of individualism, its rules must thus constitute compromises between competing and worthy human interests. Communism and socialism are compromises, and so is liberty. Their differences may be seen, from one point of view, as differences in the particular interests that are respectively served and denied. For although the compromise function of social organization remains the same, the method of accomplishing that function varies, and variously serves human interests.

As an example of the operation of these principles, consider the divergent schemes for land ownership and use found in the United States of Mexico and in the United States of America. Each of these societies is confronted with fundamentally the same problem, that is, man's unlimited need for goods that are produced from land, and the limited supply of land that can be used in their production. A great range of human interests is involved with far-reaching influence on human welfare. Not all these interests can be satisfied. Each system therefore is compelled to adopt compromises, which preserve certain values and satisfy certain preferred needs, while sacrificing other values and denying other needs.

In the United States of America a person is free to own as much land as he chooses to buy and can pay for, subject only to the rules against monopoly, which however but rarely come into operation in connection with land ownership. The general rule is also that the owner of land is free to make such use of it as he desires, the principal limitations on his use being laws respecting nuisances to others and zoning laws.

The human interests that are served by this system are first, liberty in the use of the basic factor of land, a liberty which has value not only for itself but as enabling the individual to secure an economic foundation for other and more important freedoms; and second, the opportunity afforded for the maximum production of material goods. I shall later have occasion to examine each of these matters in detail, and accordingly shall here only mention them, assuming for the argument's sake that they are in fact values and that they are promoted by our land system.

But are these the only values to be considered? What about the desire of the landless man who earnestly wishes to have a stake in the earth's crust, but has not yet obtained it? What about the advantage that one person may secure over others by ever augmented land holdings? What about the man who becomes rich because of the circumstance that oil or mineral is found on his land, or because his land has become the center of a city?

In Mexico values such as these have been thought worthy of large consideration, and the land ownership scheme has been arranged accordingly. All oil and minerals in place are the property of the federal government, which either extracts them itself or licenses their extraction. No person may continue to own, as against the claim of a landless person who wishes to buy, more than a moderate amount of land, about twenty-five acres. He may own more, but he can be compelled at any time to sell excess acreage to any landless person who wishes to work the land. The federal government itself is also the owner of large tracts of land which it licenses to individuals who wish to farm. The plots assigned are small, only a few acres, in order to make land available to all as independent operators, and when assignment has been made the farmer may maintain his possession as long as he continues to cultivate his tract.

This system preserves some values that are sacrificed by the American plan. But it does so at the expense of some other human interests which it denies. It sacrifices liberty and material prosperity. In order to provide land freely for all, the individual holdings are so reduced in size that capital—labor-saving machinery—cannot be employed, for a man with only five acres or so on which to put his labor has no use for a tractor. The result is that the Mexican farmer works very hard, uses oxen, a wooden plow, and hand tools, and produces very little per unit of labor expended. Nor can he afford to improve the land to make it more productive, even though he may succeed in accumulating a substantial acreage to operate, because his possession is uncertain. Nor is his share in the public ownership of oil and minerals of much avail, for not much is produced, the risks of this type of industry, which can be carried on only by assuming the chances of exploration, not being to the liking of public officeholders, who wish to avoid the responsibility for failure. These circumstances add up to dire poverty for the mass of the Mexican people, for which only slight amelioration is in prospect as long as the present land system remains.

It is not difficult to point out the failings of each of these land systems.

In a sense, they each have something wrong with them, for it is obvious that some human values are denied realization whether the plan be our more individualistic one or the more collectivistic one of Mexico.

In the same way that these land systems compromise human interests, so also does every feature of every social organization and every social rule have the same effect. It is indeed of the essence of a socially enforced rule of conduct that it restrains action which someone thinks is desirable but which others think is undesirable or less desirable than something else. Apart from such conflict no rule is needed. Breathing of air in a public park requires no rule, because no conflict of interests is present. Were all man's wants, intellectual and economic, likewise satisfied without labor and without conflict, there would be no occasion for social organization or law of any kind, and anarchism would be not only possible but inevitable.

Thus every rule of law that can be conceived or effected, by which society controls the action of its members, constitutes a compromise between conflicting wants and also between conflicting human interests. The prohibition against driving an automobile above specified speed limits has as objective human safety, which is a worthy interest; but to accomplish its objective it denies the pleasure and time-saving of speeding, which also constitutes a worthwhile interest in the opinion of most people possessing automobiles. The rule of law which bars the admission of hearsay evidence in Anglo-American courts has as objective the prevention of false testimony, an obviously worthy human interest; yet the application of the rule frequently makes the enforcement of a just claim more difficult, and occasionally impossible, thereby operating in derogation of worthy human interests. In similar manner every possible rule of social control, whether individualistic or collectivistic, can be analyzed and demonstrated to amount to a compromise of interests, denying one interest that another may be secured. In this manner every social rule, no matter how desirable it may be, has yet an objectionable side, and by the same token every form of social organization, being but the complex of itemized compromises, has its truly objectionable features. All social organization is compromise.

The failure to comprehend this proposition that social organization is necessarily compromise leads to the most serious consequences.

First, it assures an inaccurate estimate of existing institutions, whatever they may be, because it judges them by an erroneous standard. There is posited as standard a society in which no worthy human interest is prevented from accomplishment, and in the light of this assumed goal existing social rules are judged. But no such society is possible either actually or ideally, and therefore every existing form of social organization when placed against this false standard must necessarily be found wanting.

Included in this false standard of the ideal society is the concept that it should be without competition. Competition is believed to be the source of the denial of worthy human interests, the method by which human selfishness manifests itself. It is proposed, accordingly, to outlaw competition and to build a society without the element of competition, which it is believed can be readily accomplished if only there be the will to do so. But as we have seen, competition is a cosmic fact, not a legal one. Competition is not of man's invention, it is of the nature of the universe. It is one of the two facts—the other being volition—which attach morality to man's career. Man cannot eliminate this fact, and no form of social organization can eliminate it. Socialism and communism do not do away with competition between human beings; what they do is to channel it into forms which enlarge—rather than diminish—the opportunity for selfishness.

But against this superficial standard of a society without competition, all existing societies seem deficient. Those societies nevertheless that present the appearance of trying to destroy competition are thought to make the most favorable showing, for at least, it is supposed, they are moving in the right direction, even if they have not succeeded—as of course they cannot—in eliminating the competitive conflict. Therefore socialism and communism, which delude their followers with the promise of eliminating competition, are judged more worthy than individualism, which treats with it squarely for what it is—a basic fact.

Second, the failure to understand that all social organization is a compromise of basic conflict leads to a confusion of morality with the conditions in which morality must be produced, and this confusion leads in turn to an abandonment of morality for materialism.

Competition is the occasion of morality. If worthy human interests did not compete, in a competition which must condemn some of them to denial, human will would not be charged with moral responsibility, and human conduct would be without moral quality. What those who envisage a society without competition seek in fact, then, is an amoral universe. They do not appreciate this and would deny it. But the aim of their desire is a world in which the turmoil and strain of decision is removed, and in which the moral problems of competitive activity no longer obtrude because competition has been eliminated. Outside the conflict of human interests, however, there are no moral problems, and thus the ideal society becomes an amoral society.

Its content of interest must accordingly become an indefinitely expanding satisfaction of wants, for in this good society there can be no scarcity of any want-satisfactions, as scarcity would again mean competition. No problem of morality remaining, the attention of thought, the focus of action, must become want-satisfaction. This is materialism, and in the good society as thus envisaged, then, materialism replaces morality. The satisfaction of wants becomes the ultimate good.

If, moreover, the ideal society eliminates the moral problems of competition, then those problems are but transitory and need not be too much attended to. The task of the present day, accordingly, is to eliminate competition as rapidly as possible, and to build up that large consumption of material goods which is the virtue of the good society. Materialism thus becomes the first concern of the present as well as of the future.

The prominence of materialism in our day is in part the result of this trend of thought, the elements of which—although they perhaps have seldom presented themselves in their logical connection—have nevertheless been at work as ideological pressures for some time.

Third, the failure to understand that social organization is compromise leads to unsound proposals for change. Programs for modification are measured by the same false standard that is used for the existing social order and with results equally unfortunate. Two tendencies are observable. In the first place, there is a tendency to approve proposals for reform that promise to diminish competition. Competition is never in fact cut down; it can only be removed to different areas for its manifestation. But this is not understood, and proposals are accepted on their promise. In the second place, there is a tendency to support proposals that cure one ill though they bring two other ills in their train. It is supposed that particularities of social organization are possible which have no disadvantages, and accordingly when a proposal having the advantage of eliminating an acknowledged ill appears, those seeking change do not stay to inquire what the disadvantage of the proposal must be, but at once accept it.

9. Liberty as primary social function

Only the philosophy of liberty recognizes that all social organization is compromise of worthy human interests, and that therefore the

morality of life consists in choosing the more worthy interests that are
to be preserved. In its every aspect, the liberty taught by individualism
is an adjustment of conflicting human wants.

The manner of its adjustment of the competition contained in the
social relation is dictated by the principles we have heretofore examined
—that the experience of truth is liberty, that liberty is ethical imperative
for human life, and that liberty is equal individual freedom. From these
postulates it proceeds to frame its compromises.

Its basic compromise is that it denies some freedom of action to all,
and thus prevents some realization of values by all, in order to assure
the largest equal opportunity for freedom of action for all, and thus to
secure the maximum of value for all. It incurs the disadvantage of
placing limits to will's arena for each individual that it may secure the
advantage of the largest equal arena of will for every individual.

That the compromises of the system of liberty constitute the proper
function of social organization follows necessarily from the points thus
far established in our discussion. Since the resolution of the conflict of
the self and the not-self involves a compromise of human values, it follows that the compromise must be selected which conserves the most
important human values and denies the least important. The most important value is human character, for the best human character is the
purpose of life, and liberty is ethical imperative for human life in view
of its purpose. The ultimate in human experience, moreover, is the
knowledge of truth, and the knowledge of truth is liberty. Therefore
liberty conserves the most important human values, and the values which
it denies must accordingly be less than the most important. Liberty therefore is the required form of the social compromise. And since the accomplishment of that compromise is the essential function of social
organization, the proper discharge of that function is the maintenance
of liberty.

The primary function of every society, therefore, is the compromise
of the conflict inherent in social living, and the primary function of the
good society is the compromise of the conflict by the building and preserving of liberty.

Chapter 9

LIBERTY AS EQUAL OPPORTUNITY

1. The material factor in will's arena

The human will must find its exercise, as we have heretofore noted, in an arena composed in part of a material factor. The elements composing this material factor are geographical facts and economic goods.

The geographical facts are climate and land. Climate influences the whole pattern of living; and the land's fertility, its extent relative to the population, and the minerals and oil contained within it are factors limiting the arena of human conduct.

Economic goods, the things and services produced by men's labor for the satisfaction of their wants, also compose the material factor, for as these goods vary in quantity and quality so they condition willed conduct.

Since the human person includes a material body, all human action has a material base. The body must be sustained and protected by economic goods, and action must be limited to that which the constitution of the body permits. Further, most human action is conditioned by the availability of physical accouterments. Writing requires ink and paper, creating music needs musical instruments, and so forth. The possibility of human action being thus limited by material elements, so also is the arena within which the will can choose, since it must manifest itself through human action.

The availability of these material elements accordingly becomes important to liberty, for freedom to choose is made larger or smaller as the material factor in will's arena supports a greater or lesser possibility of action. The man whose economic goods are sufficient only to keep him alive has no freedom to choose to develop himself culturally. The society barely able to supply its needed food and shelter will exhibit a sparse intellectual record.

But although the philosophy of liberty is thus concerned with the material factor in will's arena, it nevertheless does not deal with it directly but only through the social factor in that arena, through the rules and customs developed for the government of human action as men compete and cooperate in the social relation. Individualism does not prescribe the technology of producing goods; it establishes the social rules that human beings should observe as they exercise their technology. It does not indicate the technique of using the land's productiveness; it discloses the principles which should govern men's relations one with another as they make use of that productiveness.

2. Equal opportunity to use the elements of the material factor

Our consideration of life's purpose has shown us that the basic equality fastened upon men is in the responsibility to build the best characters they can. But this does not mean that their characters should be the same, since equality is not sameness; it means that each man's character should be the best that he can choose, since the morality of choice is essential to good character.

Liberty therefore cannot require that all men make the same use of the material factor in will's arena, for such a requirement would destroy liberty by removing the opportunity for choice. Liberty must demand, rather, that all men have an equal opportunity for the use of the elements in the material factor, and it must limit itself to the prescription of this equal opportunity. For if the social rules should go beyond the provision of equal opportunity and seek to dictate use, they would destroy rather than build liberty. Liberty being the largest equal freedom for all individuals, the demand of liberty is the largest equal opportunity to use the elements of the material factor rather than the largest equal use thereof, for the largest equal use could be obtained only by denying the right to choose the extent of use, thereby denying freedom. Even as will's arena is the opportunity for human action rather than particular action itself, so the material factor in will's arena is the opportunity for action with reference to the elements in the material factor rather than the particular action chosen with reference thereto.

3. What constitutes the largest equal opportunity?

Although the principle of the largest equal opportunity to use the elements in the material factor in will's arena is clear, yet its application presents great difficulty. What constitutes the largest equal opportunity?

The nature of the problem may be clarified by turning again to the Mexican land system, which restricts the right of occupancy to a few acres, equal in amount for all persons. At first consideration it might seem that this was the apex of equality of opportunity. Does not everyone have precisely the same chance to use the land? And indeed it is true that this system does assure equal access to the land for all. But there are other elements in the material factor than land. Liberty must have regard to the goods that labor produces on land and to the opportunity to consume such goods. But the Mexican land system greatly limits the opportunity to produce and consume goods, because the units of occupancy are too small to permit efficient operation. The result is that although the opportunity to use land is kept equal, yet it is also kept small; no one has a large opportunity to produce goods, and in consequence the entire community is restricted to the human action that is possible on a low material base. An undue concern for equality in the use of one element in the material factor has limited the size of the material factor as a whole.

The solution presented by individualism to the problem of the largest equal opportunity consists in the maintenance of a free market and in the permission of private property. Each of these institutions must be framed in accordance with the principles of liberty. How this is to be done will furnish the subject matter of much of Book Two of this work.

4. Equal opportunity for intellectual activity

The same reasoning that teaches equality of opportunity in economic activity also teaches equality of opportunity in intellectual activity. The philosophy of liberty must not demand that all persons experience the same intellectual activity; it must limit its prescription to equality of opportunity for intellectual activity. If social rules should go further and attempt to dictate the kind of intellectual activity each human being should have, in an effort to assure that they all had equal intellectual action, it would not increase freedom but diminish it. The largest equal freedom in intellectual action is therefore the largest equal opportunity for such action.

Here again it is the social factor in will's arena that is the concern of individualistic philosophy. Although the experiential and psychological factors are also important determinants of will's arena when considered from the viewpoint of the opportunity for intellectual activity, yet these two elements are amenable to social influence only through the rules that constitute the social factor.

Inasmuch as all intellectual action has a material base, equality of opportunity for intellectual action will have been in part assured when equal opportunity to use the material factor in will's arena has been accomplished. But there are additional social rules necessary to secure equal intellectual opportunity, and these we shall seek to delineate in the following Book Two.

Thus the building of liberty becomes the specification of equal opportunity. And it is the task of specifying equal opportunity that presents the challenge to practice liberty—the subject of Book Two.

Chapter 10

LIBERTY AND FORCE

"Power tends to corrupt," said Lord Acton, "and absolute power corrupts absolutely."

Acton's insight into the nature of power has been more honored by repetition than by understanding. It has been regarded as a broad diatribe against political power, pointing out the danger that such power can become ruthless and corrupt. But the proposition is more than a warning; it is a specification of a social law.

1. Interhuman influence

Each human being is influenced in his living by others. This interhuman influence is of two kinds: influence by force, where force is exerted or threatened; and influence by inspiration, where no force is exerted or threatened.

By force is meant constraint of the physical person. Force is applied, for example, when a human being is placed in jail or in chains; and it is threatened when such constraint is held out as punishment. Since the physical person, moreover, requires material means for its sustenance and protection, force is applied if these material means are taken away or if their removal is threatened. Inasmuch, further, as nearly all wealth has some relation to the sustenance and protection of the body, any diminution or threatened diminution of wealth is a use of force. Accordingly fines for violations of law are a use of force. So are taxes, for the collection of taxes is not only a deprivation of wealth in itself but is also sanctioned by laws providing for fines and imprisonment for disobedience.

When we consider the many kinds of force that daily surround us and observe how much our lives are thereby molded, we see the substantial part played by the interhuman influence of force.

There remains nevertheless a very large area of influence among

human beings where force plays no part. In our day to day living we are
much under the sway of teachers in the classroom, preachers in the
pulpit, editorial writers in the press, and those who expound their views
in books, in magazines, and over the radio and television, and yet none
of these persons exerts any force upon us. Likewise we are influenced
by thinkers of prior generations. Many of the men heretofore mentioned in this work, such as John Locke and Adam Smith, not only
were influential in their own day but have continued to affect history
up to the present time; yet they never wielded any force over others.
And tremendous influence upon the lives of others has been exerted
during many centuries by the careers and teachings of Jesus in the Occident and of Lao-tzu, Buddha, and Confucius in the Orient, all of whom
refrained from the slightest use of force.

What is the explanation of the great influence thus exerted without
the application of force, which we may call the interhuman influence
of inspiration?

The explanation lies in the fact that a concept of conduct is thereby
supplied, which the will may adopt and translate into action. The function of the communication of ideas and of the furnishing of examples
is to inspire concepts. Thus John Locke inspired in his readers the concept of liberty as natural right, Montesquieu the concept of the tripartite
division of government, Adam Smith the concept of the free market,
and Karl Marx the concept of a communistic society.

The influence of inspiration thus acts upon the experiential factor
in will's arena. It expands the scope of that arena by enlarging the store
of concepts which the will must depend upon in making its choices.
Freedom is therefore enhanced by the influence of inspiration, for it
increases the possible area of willed behavior.

The influence of force, on the other hand, operates primarily upon
the social factor in will's arena, and only secondarily upon the experiential factor, and its effect upon each factor is restrictive rather than
expansive. The application of force between human beings is typically
through socially approved modes of conduct. The influence of force
is accordingly exerted as part of the social factor of will's arena.

What, then, is the relation of the influences of inspiration and force
respectively to the development of the best character, which constitutes
the purpose of human life and therefore the standard by which all its
parts should be measured?

Inasmuch as the result of the influence of inspiration is always to
enlarge the possibility of willed conduct, it stimulates the development

of character, increasing the range of its potentiality. But the concepts of conduct furnished by inspiration may be good or bad, and thus may encourage good or bad character. The moral responsibility of him who influences by inspiration is therefore to inspire concepts of high character, and the moral responsibility of him who receives concepts from others is to choose for emulation those that are good and to discard those that are bad.

Thus the influence of inspiration is an ever-present moral challenge. It leads to moral quality in human life, and as the test it supplies is met or failed, so noble character is created or repudiated. If upon occasion it leads to evil, yet it is also a creative element in the highest good, by which alone great human character is possible.

With respect to the influence of force, on the other hand, it always diminishes the opportunity for character development on the part of him against whom the force is exercised. Since force is constraint of the person, either by direct physical means or by direct economic means, its application necessarily diminishes the willed conduct that can take place.

The influence of force, therefore, is always to restrict the opportunity for the development of human character. The significant unfolding of character depends upon the exercise of volitional process, and to the extent that force prevents volitional experience it destroys the occasion for the growth of the best character.

2. The proper function of force is liberty.

We have seen, however, that liberty demands a limitation on the area for willed activity for each individual in order that the areas for willed activity for all persons may attain the largest equal size. We have seen, too, that this limitation must be accomplished by social control, as rules are set for the observance of individuals. Such rules constitute the application of force, for without the use of force, either in actuality or as threatened actuality, the rules of social organization cannot manifest themselves as facts.

Force therefore constitutes a means by which liberty is secured, and without force there can be no liberty. And since liberty is ethical imperative and the true function of social organization, the use of force to the extent necessary to obtain liberty is our duty, and is the instrumentality by which we as citizens discharge our social function.

The maintenance of liberty is therefore the proper function of the interhuman influence of force. It is, moreover, its only proper function. The use of force beyond that required for the maintenance of liberty is always and unconditionally evil.

For since the use of force is always restrictive of the opportunity to build character, its employment to support liberty is justified only as a compromise that sacrifices some human values in order that larger ones may be obtained. When, however, force is employed for any objective other than equal liberty, it cannot be justified as a compromise, since the opportunity for character-building which it sacrifices must necessarily be greater than any value which it can gain in return. For equal liberty is the maximum of opportunity for character-building for all members of the group, and therefore anything other than equal liberty is something less than the maximum. To aim for something other than equal liberty is therefore to sacrifice liberty, and accordingly to use force for an objective other than equal liberty is to destroy liberty two ways, both in the means and in the end, that is, both in the force employed and in the result achieved.

To suppose, furthermore, that a net sacrifice of liberty could ever be justified, which would be the case if force were used for any object other than equal liberty, would be to suppose that liberty were a conditional factor, inferior to some other consideration, and only to be maintained when other conditions were propitious. But as we have seen, equal liberty is an absolute, an ethical imperative, which is superior to all other social elements, and therefore no sacrifice of liberty whatsoever can be morally justified except that which has as objective a larger liberty in exchange. But this larger liberty can only be the largest equal liberty for all, for the largest equal liberty is the largest liberty. Therefore force directed to any other goal is unethical, defeating life's purpose and God's will.

The immorality of force, when it is exercised for any purpose other than the social control constituting equal liberty, is to be imputed primarily to him who exerts it. In seeking an improper authority for himself, he denies to others the opportunity for decision that alone can build good character. Thus he refuses to others the accomplishment of their life purpose, and his action is consequently unethical, a selfish and corrupt aggrandizement of his will as it strives to impose itself on other people.

The immorality may secondarily become that of him against whom the force is exerted, if he does not resist. Liberty is a duty as well as a right, and even as it is my duty to try to respect and maintain your liberty, so it is my duty to try to respect and maintain my own; and if I weakly acquiesce in the impairment of my liberty I am as guilty of moral dereliction as I would be in impairing that of some other person.

3. The use of force tends to corrupt.

We may now understand why absolute power corrupts absolutely. It is because absolute force, asserting complete dominion over others and thereby denying the right of all others to liberty in developing their characters, is of itself absolute and complete corruption. It is the complete destroyer of human character, and in so far as it is within human capacity to do so it completely thwarts the will of God.

But why does force which is less than absolute nevertheless always and necessarily tend to become immoral and corrupt? Seeing that the force which produces liberty is both a benefit and a duty, cannot we trust this good use of force to continue to manifest itself as a beneficent instrumentality in human affairs, without becoming the excess of force that is evil?

In order to restrain itself within its proper bounds, however, force must comprehend its own limitations. It must know the point at which it ceases to be the great good which builds liberty and becomes instead the great evil which destroys it. But how can the human being who is himself engaged in the exercise of force be expected ordinarily to comprehend this point of limitation? To him, as he exerts power over the activities of others in maintaining liberty, his exercise of force must appear as a beneficial influence in society, as indeed it is. His application of force is from its nature an opposition of his own activity to the activity of others, a contest of conflicting wills. As he determines the extent of the force he attempts to apply, he must judge between himself and others. But can a man judge his own case? We have long since learned that he cannot do so fairly, that he is barred by the fact that he necessarily sees only one side of the matter objectively, since he must view his own side of the problem subjectively. Inasmuch as he cannot view both sides with the same objectivity, he tends to prefer the side he knows the better, which, of course, is his own, and thus he tends to resolve the contest in favor of the expansion of his own power over others.

The exercise of power, moreover, tends to become a matter of habit,

even as all repeated human activity inclines to become habitual. But
although the exertion of force thus becomes ingrained as habitual action
tending to be repeated more and more, yet the determination of the
boundary set by liberty can never enter the ranks of habit, because the
circumstances of the boundary must constantly change, always calling
for a new and different act of determination. The use of force, then, is
ever carried forward by habit, while its limitation requires an ever fresh
exercise of judgment and of will, as the limitation set by liberty is sur-
veyed and respected.

By reason of these factors, which are imbedded in the psychological
nature of the human person, the use of force as an influence in interhuman relations must always tend to expand. But as it expands it must
pass from the realm of good to the realm of evil, from the role of builder
of liberty to the role of its destroyer. And when it becomes destroyer
it corrupts both him who wields the force and him against whom it is
asserted. Power tends to corrupt.

How then can we oppose the corruptive effect of social force, and
halt it at the point where it still is our benefactor as the creator of
liberty?

Only by a form of social organization in which the elements of
force, when they reach the limits of their beneficial exercise, are turned
against each other so that they mutually operate as blocks to further
and excessive expansion. Such a scheme of social organization is feasible.
The principle of thus turning elements of force against each other at the
boundary of their proper activity we call the theory of the separation
of powers and of checks and balances, and we can observe it at work
in all societies that have attained any degree of freedom. We shall
consider the technique of checks and balances in Part IV of Book Two.

The society that does not thus restrict the influence of force as represented by the power of its public officials is doomed to lose its liberty
through the operation of Acton's law.

4. Force and the building of good character

Inasmuch as the exercise of force by one human person over
another consists in constraint or threatened constraint of the body,
limiting its action, force can usually compel particular conduct. "Hand
over your money," says the robber to his victim, "or you will be shot."
"Pay this tax bill," says the tax collector to the citizen, "or your property

will be seized." "Drive within the speed limit," says the traffic policeman to the automobilist, "or you will be arrested." In each of these cases force is threatened, and in each case the threat ordinarily succeeds in compelling the desired action.

The person against whom the force is applied has his range of choice greatly restricted. It is true of course that the victim can choose to be shot, the citizen to have his property seized, and the automobilist to be arrested. But in each of these cases, if the choice were so made, the result would be a constraint of action much more severe than that involved in the demanded alternative. The essence of force, indeed, is the excess of bodily constraint threatened over that included in the conduct demanded as alternative. The application of force accordingly consists in reducing the possibilities of action to two or a few available courses, one of which—the course demanded—involves less of bodily constraint than the others.

For ordinary purposes, however, the use of force does not merely restrict choice but eliminates it entirely. A choice between two amounts of bodily constraint, the one larger and the other smaller, is a choice only in name, and is not in reality a choice at all. The human will operates in an arena determined by factors one of which is the psychological factor. This factor, as we have already noted, restricts the will by the instinct (among other properties) of self-preservation; and inasmuch as self-preservation is always to some degree threatened by bodily constraint, the psychological factor prevents the will from choosing a larger amount of bodily constraint in preference to a smaller, if no other considerations intervene. Thus there would be no real choice between the alternatives of one year in prison and two years in prison, or between a fine of $500 and a fine of $1,000. In each instance the instinct of self-preservation bars the will from selecting the course which would involve the greater loss of bodily activity, sustenance, and protection, and leaves no alternative but the course containing the smaller amount of such loss. The method of force as an interhuman influence is thus to eliminate choice, and it succeeds in its object of compelling particular conduct as it is successful in removing the possibility of choice.

In some cases considerations other than preservation from bodily constraint or danger intervene. It may be believed that to submit to the force that is threatened would involve moral degradation. Thus we have young men in prison today who chose the bodily constraint of imprisonment in preference to service as members of a military organization.

On the other hand there have always been great numbers of men who were willing to volunteer to incur the bodily dangers of military service because they believed the comparative safety of remaining behind involved moral turpitude. We are all familiar, further, with the great personages of history who have suffered the ultimate bodily constraint of execution rather than undergo what they believed to be the moral infamy of retracting their principles.

But moral considerations of this sort do not always enter into the influence of force. The victim does not consider it wrong to give up $10 to avoid being shot, and the taxpayer does not think it morally degrading to pay a tax he is opposed to. Upon certain occasions a moral issue may be made of all these and similar applications of force, but much of the time no question of ethics, on the part of him against whom the force is exerted, is believed to be present.

The nature of force, however, is not affected by the presence or absence of a moral question for the person who is the object of the force. For him, force is always and necessarily a restraint or threatened restraint of the body, and a restriction on choice. As such restriction it diminishes the opportunity for the building of good character. This diminishment in opportunity is justified, as we have already seen, to the extent that it is incurred for the sake of liberty, but this justification, again, does not go to the question of force's nature, which always remains, whether justified or not, a bodily restraint that diminishes choice.

Thus it is impossible for force to build good human character. Its ultimate service in human relations is to build liberty, and liberty of itself is not good human character but only the opportunity for good character. Good character is always the product of right choice and never the product of force.

The greatest misunderstanding on this matter has persisted throughout history and is manifest abundantly in the present day. It lies at the base of the demand for laws and ever more laws that will prescribe desirable conduct and thus compel people to be good. But all such laws and social rules are inexorably doomed to failure in the future, even as they have always failed in the past. They attempt the impossible. Goodness is not created by the compulsion of law, but by the free choice of will. Goodness is not of the fist but of the spirit. Law can prevent goodness, or on the other hand it can give it its chance through liberty, but it can never create goodness, which forever is placed beyond its reach.

This is a hard truth for men to learn. They wish to give righteousness the strength of force, and to compel goodness by social rule. If men persist in developing evil character, cannot they be compelled, it is asked, by social formula to turn to the development of character that is good? The answer of the universe is an inexorable No. Good character arises only from decision. Force can protect decision and give it its opportunity, but it cannot control it, and when it attempts to do so it can only destroy it, and with it good character.

Therefore those who wish to accomplish good in the world by influencing the development of good character in others must use the influence of force only to build equal liberty for all men, and beyond this must place their trust in the influence of inspiration. If they disregard this principle of life and of character, seeking to compel good character by formulas and by laws, they condemn not only the objects of their compulsion to a diminished opportunity for character, but themselves to the corruption that works inwardly on the spirit from doing evil.

This is the explanation of Acton's further observation that the powerful men of history have usually been bad men who have done evil. Since force cannot from its nature compel goodness, it can become conspicuously great only by departing from the limited role of permitting goodness and entering upon the limitless role of doing harm and working corruption. The good use of power is necessarily a limited use of power. Great power, being by its nature evil, corrupts its wielder and turns him to doing evil.

This is the explanation, further, of the fact that communism, socialism, and new-dealism tend to become occasions for the exploitation of personal advantage by those who succeed in getting on top. Central planning, which as we have seen is at the core of all collectivistic practice, requires the maintenance of the superior position of the few by the use of force. But this use of force destroys equal liberty. Being thus evil, it grows to further corruption. The advantages of the few become ever greater, as they acquire more wealth and more power. There is no stopping place in the process, for the only logical principle for effecting a halt, the principle of equal liberty, was abandoned when the collectivized program was entered upon. Therefore in the society adhering to collectivism government must always be privilege.

Not only does power thus tend to corrupt those who wield it, but as already suggested, if it succeeds in establishing itself beyond the needs of liberty it works its corruption also in those who are its victims. Since it destroys liberty it destroys character. Therefore those who acquiesce in the destruction of their liberty must suffer the corruption of their character. The people who submit to a regime of excessive force must become well-trained recipients of orders, obediently doing what they are told. The citizens of Sparta and Prussia are their prototypes.

It is a law of the universe that an unused faculty atrophies and withers away. The capacity for self-decision, for deciding one's own course of conduct, can be lost through non-use. The convict who has long been accustomed to the rigid discipline of the prison, where through the repeated course of months and years he seldom makes decisions for himself but only carries out the decisions that others make for him, loses at last most of his capacity to decide, and when he is released shrinks from the necessity of deciding daily problems in the outside world. Likewise the mass of people in whole societies can lose the capacity for self-decision. This happened in Sparta and Prussia. It is happening today in Russia. And it will happen tomorrow—unless the collectivistic tide is turned—in Great Britain. For where the few make the decisions of the many, the capacity of the many to decide must die, pursuant to that cosmic law which discards the unused and useless.

Thus the façade of great unity and discipline in a society, though often mistaken by contemporaries for a show of strength, is always but a screen for weakness. Behind it the character of the people, which requires self-direction for its growth, is rotting away.

When therefore a society, through long acquaintance with the force of the state in bureaucracy and militarism, becomes too well-disciplined, the just sentence of history is that it shall disappear. The purpose of history is character, and a society no longer serving that purpose must die because useless in the universal program. Survival belongs to the free.

Appendix 1

LIBERTY AND COLLECTIVISM IN HISTORY

Collectivism is constantly portrayed to us by its proponents as a progressive improvement over antiquated conditions. It is a new cure, they say, for old ills; and even though the efficacy of the cure may not as yet have been entirely established, yet they urge us nevertheless to try it as a new experiment moving in the right direction.

Is collectivism indeed new? Is liberty old? Are collective ownership of property and collective direction of activity new experiments in human affairs?

Will it not be wise to consult the record of history on these questions? For history is the great social laboratory of the past, and from its completed experiments conclusions of worth can be extracted.

1. Primitive societies

It is sometimes said, by detractors of individualistic philosophy, that progress consists in the emergence of man from the "individualism of the jungle," and in the replacement of "savage competition" with "civilized cooperation." By statements such as these it is sought to imply that early societies are individualistic and that individualism is the typical form of social organization of so-called primitive peoples. This has been repeated so often that many persons, otherwise well informed, accept it unquestioningly.

But as anyone who has made any study of history and anthropology knows, the facts are almost exactly the opposite. The societies of nearly all nonliterate peoples are collectivistic, the unit of importance being not the individual, but the tribe. Land, houses, and even stocks of food are usually owned in common, and private property is typically very limited. Religious and secular conduct is prescribed in detail, and rigidly enforced by the tribal authorities. Among literate peoples, likewise, the early forms are collectivistic. Trace backward whatever civilization cycle you choose; as you approach its earliest stages you will find, in so far as the historical record furnishes information, a collectivistic scheme of society. "In almost every department of life, the corporation at first is everything, and the individual nothing."[1]

The ownership of land and other forms of property usually indicates the essential character of a society. Man's living has a material base, and therefore the ownership of the tools of production tends both to reflect and to influence the prevailing social philosophy. Thus the collective ownership of land and other wealth among primitive societies is consonant with their general collectivistic character.

There seems reason to believe, moreover, that in early social groups the very idea of ownership of things remains undeveloped. The individual belongs to his clan or tribe, with everything that he does subject to its detailed custom. His economic activity, involving the use of property, is included in this tribal discipline, and accordingly the area within which he can exercise economic choice is not large. The essence of ownership, however, consists in choice as to use, and where use is closely prescribed ownership can be little more than an empty form. In societies, therefore, where use is determined by the law or custom of the group the concept of ownership has no occasion to grow.

Why have societies in their first stages of development usually exhibited collectivistic traits? The answer appears not far to seek. The tribe or clan is a kinship group, an extension of the family. The experience of each human being necessarily begins with family life, where the child is completely subject to the control of his elders and where the determination of property's use is entirely beyond his domain. As he approaches adulthood, it is easy for him to transfer to his tribe the same concepts he has already developed with respect to his family. The elders of the tribe, or the chief, take the place of the elders of the family, or the father or mother, and the communal control of the larger group over property and economic activity seems naturally to succeed to the family control exercised over the child in his youthful activities.

This process requires no invention either of ideas or of social forms. Even as the human being has had no control over the facts of his birth and his upbringing in a family group that necessarily is autocratic and communal, so it is simple for him to move out of the family into a tribe organized on the same autocratic and collectivistic principles. The

1. Burnet, *Early Greek Philosophy*, London, 1892, p. 29 (4th ed.).

difficult thing rather, and the thing that historically has been accomplished only occasionally, is for him to invent a culture in which it is possible for him to move from the autocracy and collectivism of the family into a social organization that is characterized by democracy and individualism.

This seems to be the most plausible explanation of the undeniable fact that nearly all so-called primitive societies, whether found in the Congo jungles or on the North American plains, practice communal ownership of land and other property, the sharing of produce, and the close regulation of individual conduct by tribal custom.

2. Mediterranean civilization

Turning to the background of our own western civilization, our starting point is with the fabulous Greeks. Of the early Dorian life on the peninsula, following the disappearance of Mycenaean culture, we know but little. The picture in Homer is one of feudal collectivism. When however we reach the fifth century B.C., we find two societies, the city-states of Athens and Sparta, of whose organization we possess considerable information, and whose antithetical positions on all basic points of social philosophy are highly instructive.

In the prosperous years following the defeat of the Persians, Athens was a community of about a quarter of a million people, composed of citizens, aliens, freedmen, and slaves. It had a democratic form of government. So fearful were the Athenians of concentrated governmental power, as the result of centuries of experience with kings, dictators, and tyrants, that no one public official was permitted to exercise any ample authority, and many positions were filled by lot rather than by vote in order to prevent long continuance in office by one person.

The government so constituted exercised only a limited power. Its functions consisted of (1) maintaining an army and navy, (2) collecting taxes, administering public funds, and minting coins, (3) maintaining public order, (4) building public works, such as the monumental buildings of the Acropolis, the walls connecting Athens with Piraeus, its harbor six miles distant, and the wharves at Piraeus, (5) providing means for the settlement of disputes between citizens, and (6) furnishing official leadership for certain religious ceremonies.

The government did not regulate trade. It collected a two per cent tax on all imports and exports arriving at or leaving Piraeus, but had no protective tariffs. It did not fix prices or wages, and did not seek to encourage or discourage particular forms of economic activity, except for a concern over the importation of grain, as to which however it is not clear that there was ever any formal governmental control. Governmental expenses were met by taxes, annual contributions received from allied city-states dependent on the Athenian fleet for protection, and silver obtained from state-owned silver mines.

The economic life of this society was varied, vigorous, and individualistic. Athens was filled with handicraft shops, whose workmen specialized in everything from swords to ladies' shoes. The small boats of commerce from all the Mediterranean world unloaded in the harbor at Piraeus, and carried away Athenian or other merchandise in exchange. People from everywhere thronged the Athenian streets. The monetary unit was the drachma, minted by the government and universally acceptable. Large banking partnerships financed commerce by loans, and even issued letters of credit that were received as payment in the cities of the eastern Mediterranean. Goods and services were paid for in money, and artisans were employed for a daily wage much the same as now. The market was free and open to all. Athens was the commercial and financial center of the western world. It was prosperous. It was a city of businessmen as well as of dramatists, sculptors, architects, and scholars, an aspect of its existence during this golden age that is too seldom noted.

The free enterprise of Athens was matched by freedom of expression. Politicians, philosophers, dramatists, and citizens spoke out as they pleased on public issues, and if at times they exercised restraint it was not out of fear of the public officials but of the populace, which was always quixotic and sometimes savage. Religious freedom seems to have largely prevailed, and many and diverse religions were practiced. Nevertheless to deride the officially accepted gods of the city was a crime, for which the Assembly of citizens in one of its irresponsible moods punished the great Socrates with death.

There was little that was collectivistic about Athens in the splendid years of the middle fifth century. It was thoroughly individualistic. We are told by Thucydides that before the battle of Syracuse in 413 B.C. the Athenian general Nicias encouraged his troops by reminding them "that they were the inhabitants of the freest country in the world, and how in Athens there was no interference with the daily life of any man." It was true. Neither before nor since has any society granted the individual citizen a much larger freedom than did Athens in its zenith.

What its handful of citizens did with this freedom is one of the marvels, perhaps the greatest marvel, of history.

Even as we have no difficulty in classifying Athens as an example of individualism, so its rival Sparta is the classic specimen of collectivism. Situated south of Athens on the Peloponnesus, Sparta was a smaller city than its northern rival, and its opposite in nearly everything. Its autocratic government was headed by two kings and a board of ephors, and although we are not well informed of its structure, we know that in its operation it closely controlled the citizen in all that he did.

The population was divided into three classes: citizens, perioeci, and slaves. The slaves were the laborers and artisans; the perioeci were the farmers, tradesmen, and business people; and the citizens were the ruling class and skilled soldiers.

At birth a male infant of the citizen class was examined by an official committee and if frail was killed. Those approved by the examiners continued to live in the family home until the age of seven, when they were placed in a state school. In this school the boys lived together in barracks, received a rudimentary education in reading and arithmetic, and spent most of their time in gymnastics and military training. Girls also were sent to public schools, but their training seems to have been neither so rigorous nor so long continued. Upon reaching thirty the young men were expected to marry and establish individual homes. They continued, however, to take at least one meal daily together in communal clubs or barracks until they were sixty, when they were finally freed from the requirement of communal living.

All males of the citizen class were thus organized into a highly trained army, ready at all times for action. They were also expected to exercise the functions of government. But these two activities, the army and governmental office, were the limits set for their careers. To prevent a broadening of interest, they were restrained from entering into business, except as they supervised agriculture and trade in their capacity as the ruling class.

The economic life of this society was collectivistic. We do not know the system of land ownership, but since use of the land was entirely state-controlled, the concept of ownership could not have been much developed. Apparently the land was regarded as owned by members of the citizen class, who in turn were required to see that it was worked by the two lower classes. The communal barracks were undoubtedly regarded as owned by the state. The principal economic activities were agriculture and simple handicraft. There was little trade with surrounding city-states. Since many of the necessities of life were communally distributed, there was not much buying and selling through the medium of money, and to discourage such individualistic activity the state prescribed heavy iron for coin, instead of the silver and gold used elsewhere.

Individual expression was frowned upon. Spartans were expected to live alike and dress alike, anything beyond the accepted mode being regarded as undesirable ostentation. Practically no artistic or literary activity took place. It seems improbable that any extended discussion of public issues could have occurred, for it is inconceivable that any Spartan could have openly opposed the views of the constituted authorities. All was orderly at Sparta. Not self-expression, as in Athens, but self-effacement in the common lot, obedience to the laws and customs of the state, was the ideal held up before Spartans. It was an ideal they adhered to for a long period of history. It produced a people who were warlike, law-abiding, and dull. Its highest point was reached at Thermopylae, and the only poetry it ever produced was the tragically revealing inscription on the stone erected in memory of the four hundred Spartans who fell defending the pass against the Persian thousands: "Go, stranger, and tell the Spartans that we lie here in obedience to their laws." But a better philosophy than this the Spartans never developed, and they are known to history chiefly because of their long struggle with the Athenians, a struggle in which Sparta was the victor but Athens the survivor.

Leaving Greece and moving to the southern shore of the Mediterranean, we find another highly collectivistic society in Egypt under the reign of the Ptolemies. During this period, which occupied the three centuries preceding the Christian era, the land of the Nile valley was owned by the state and was administered by a large bureaucracy. The farmers owned their own houses, but not the land they tilled. This was assigned to them by the public officials, who allotted acreage, designated crops, and collected a portion of the produce for distribution by the state. The irrigation works and canals were of course also owned and operated by the state. Thus the Nile valley was an Egyptian TVA, but without hydroelectric plants. The state did not own land in the cities, but it did nationalize, as we now say, a great many industries. Mines, factories, banks, stores, and transportation systems were owned and operated by the government. In such portion of the economy as was left to private enterprise the state officials fixed prices and wages whenever they deemed it advisable.

The distribution of the wealth produced by this collectivism was controlled by the bureaucracy, who saw to it that most of it reached their hands. Thus the upper strata enjoyed luxurious living, that gave the Egyptian economy an appearance of prosperity. But underneath was unending want, poverty, and drudgery for the masses of farmers and workers. Occasionally they spiced hardship with open revolt, but the governmental classes had the army to sustain them, and the rebellions were always put down. Great plenty and harsh want continued side by side in this collectivistic society as the normal state of affairs for a long period of time.

There was little room for freedom of expression in a society so organized. Religious activity was controlled by the priesthood, which was a dominant class allied in interest to the government officials. Both groups were hierarchies in which instructions flowed from the top down, and even as economic life was planned by the state's officialdom, so religious life was directed by the priesthood. The worship of particular deities was encouraged or discouraged upon occasion by the authorities, but religious innovation without official support seems not to have occurred. A considerable literary activity at times made its appearance, and Alexandria was for a period a center not only of wealth but also of learning. The stimulus of controversy, however, was largely wanting, and when occasionally it showed itself it was closely controlled by the governing class.

On the whole, Ptolemaic Egypt seems to have constituted a somewhat less complete form of collectivism than that found at Sparta. Perhaps a somewhat greater degree of material wealth and a larger cultural emphasis conduced to less rigidity of social structure. At any rate, its governmental planning and control approximated more the program of socialism than that of communism, as we would today use those terms.

The while Ptolemaic Egypt was passing through its zenith, across the Mediterranean another society was rising to power. The city-state of Rome, beginning as a small and insecure kingdom, had passed through varying fortunes in its earlier history, until by 200 B.C. it had become an oligarchic republic, the master of the entire Italian peninsula, and the overlord of the countries of the western Mediterranean.

Rome and its immediate environs comprised at this time about a million people, divided into patricians, knights, plebeians, and slaves. An additional four million or so lived in the rest of the peninsula, the parts of which exercized varying degrees of self-rule, subject to dictation by Rome. The Roman patricians constituted a hereditary aristocracy, rich and devoted to politics and government. The knights were the business people, technically plebeians but united in interest and social feeling to the patricians. The plebeians were farmers, laborers, and the urban idle. The slaves furnished the base of clerks, domestics, workers, and drudges upon which the economy relied.

A three hundred year struggle between patricians and plebeians had resulted in a complex scheme of government in which authority was divided between representatives of the two groups. The Senate, the dominant governmental institution, was in practice largely hereditary and patrician in membership. But consuls, tribunes, and other officials were popularly elected for short terms, and some, such as the powerful tribunes, were chosen exclusively by voters of the plebeian class. On the whole this government met rather well the two needs of authority and responsibility to popular will, and despite its many and obvious imperfections its record entitles it to be classed as one of the more efficient and durable governmental organizations known to history.

At the date mentioned, this government performed approximately the same functions as those of the government of Athens, heretofore enumerated. It did not regulate trade, nor control prices or wages, nor operate any nationalized industries. It did, however, own mines, which it leased to private operators, and it also assumed the ownership of all lands in conquered territories, which it variously sold back to the former owners subject to taxes, leased, donated to veterans of the legions, or retained as public domain.

But apart from this proprietorship of state land, individual ownership of property prevailed. Earlier the typical private landholding had been small. The Roman farmer had tilled only a few acres, and indeed the small landowners had been the backbone of the republic, furnishing taxes to the treasury, conscripts to the legions, and stability to the body of citizenry. But the third century B.C. had been, like the twentieth A.D., an age of war, and as the farmers left their fields for the legions their small holdings tended to be merged into the estates of the more well-to-do. This process was well advanced by 200 B.C. As the veterans returned from the wars they found their way to Rome, instead of to the countryside, and in the metropolis they formed an ever-increasing crowd of idle and discontented, demanding subsistence from the public treasury. To care for their needs, the government began that special concern for the grain trade, by which Rome was supplied with bread, that was later to become a major governmental function.

The Roman shared some of the Spartan's distaste for commerce and industry. Rome in 200 B.C. was a rich city, and in succeeding centuries it became increasingly prosperous; but its wealth was more the product of tribute from conquered territory than of independent economic development. The principal activities were agriculture and handicraft. Only a small amount of shipping, considering the size and importance of the city, passed through the poor harbor at the mouth of the Tiber, and although the great system of roads that later connected Rome with its colonies was beginning to be constructed, yet no large amount of commercial traffic moved over them, for the Romans were never enthusiastic traders.

They did however give business the benefit of a highly developed system of law, which in many respects still dominates the legal codes of western Europe. Freedom of entry into business agreements, and enforcement of agreements once entered into, the legal essentials of free enterprise, were protected by a carefully devised code of substantive rules and judicial procedure.

Although the government itself was not engaged in economic activity, yet the supplying of governmental needs, especially weapons and provender for the armies, and the construction of public works were leading forms of Roman business. To carry on these enterprises, which were too large for the individual entrepreneur, stock companies were formed, and their shares became a common means of investment.

Rather complete freedom of expression was enjoyed at this time. Both plebeians and patricians spoke out freely on all matters, and the revolutionary period that broke out seventy years later was brought on by the open and vigorous agitation of the Gracchi and others for sundry reforms. As to religious freedom, the people seem to have been satisfied with the diverse opportunities supplied by the traditional beliefs, and there is little ground for an opinion concerning the reception that would have been accorded religious innovation had it been sought. Doubtless a repudiation of the accepted gods would have been thought a dangerous social affront meriting punishment, but the mere introduction of additional deities probably would not have met opposition.

There is no difficulty in classifying republican Rome of 200 B.C. as an example of individualism. Its economy employed the principles of free enterprise and private capitalism, and politically its citizens enjoyed the benefits of liberalism. If the life of the individual citizen at Rome was not as free as at Athens, yet it much more nearly approximated the way of living of the Athenians, whom the Romans greatly admired, than that of the Spartans or Egyptians, whom they scarcely noticed except as additional provincials for the empire as it later developed.

But despite the vigorous independence of the individual Roman, he yet possessed a love for his nation and a pride in its accomplishments that was to pave the way for the disappearance of the republic and the advent of the empire and eventually of collectivism. For the idea that the Roman citizen should support and protect the state was so strong in the Roman mind that it first embraced and then exalted to preeminence the seemingly congruous but nevertheless contrary idea that the state should support and protect the citizen.

Events hastened the growth of this view. The poor and dispossessed sought the assistance of the state, through legislation, in breaking up the great landholdings of the rich into more limited parcels. This would have been a desirable move in the direction of a more individualistic society, but it was blocked by the tactics, legal and extra-legal, of the patricians. The demand then arose for the relief of the debtor class through the cancellation or reduction of debts and the lowering of interest rates, and for price controls for basic living commodities, particularly bread, and finally for doles. Civil war broke out, and when out of its long chaos and ruthlessness the dictatorship of the empire emerged under Julius Caesar, it was accepted with relief for its promise of possible return to public order.

The forms of the republic were retained in the empire. The same public officials continued to be elected and to hold office. But their authority was limited. Dictatorial power was vested in the princeps, or emperor; and through the vast bureaucracy and the army, both of which were under his unqualified command, he ruled with a despotism that was constrained only by his inclination or by his fear of rebellion.

If we look at Rome in the second century A.D. we find a society which has moved a substantial distance from the individualism of the former republic, but which nevertheless has not yet attained the advanced collectivism it was later to experience. Because of its median position it is instructive to observe its elements.

Perhaps the outstanding characteristic of this society was the vast hierarchy of government employees, who, organized in descending layers of authority, covered the empire with their activity, maintaining order, administering the judicial system, supervising public works, managing state business enterprises, regulating private trade and industry, and, above all, collecting taxes. The Roman concept of government had by now entirely changed. No longer was it Senatus Populusque Romanus that ruled, although that majestic title still appeared on public buildings, but instead all ultimate authority was reposed in the Caesar, under whose image and superscription all was done. Nor was the area of governmental activity limited by the constitutional restraints that had operated under the republic. Now its concern covered a wide range of matters formerly left to individual enterprise, and the domain of its control was constantly increasing.

The flow of taxes and tribute from the provinces made Rome one of the richest cities of history, the wealth belonging in part to the government and in part to the patrician class. But the poor and the idle comprised a large portion of Italy's population, and to quiet them the government provided a great public works program, which furnished employment to those who would accept it. Supplementing this was a comprehensive system of pensions and doles which assured economic security to those who would not or could not work. This was the period of the great governmental engineering projects, the aqueducts, harbors, temples, baths, amphitheaters, and the magnificent roads that linked the entire Mediterranean world into one community. It was also the period of bread and the circus, when the public treasury assumed responsibility not only for housing and for food, but also for entertainment. Agriculturally Italy was poor, and although the government from time to time took drastic measures to compel the production of grain, dependence had to be placed continually upon shipments from Africa. Therefore the government closely regulated the grain trade, to secure both adequate supplies and low prices. It set the selling price, required that grain be shipped to Italy rather than elsewhere, operated public warehouses, sold to the Roman poor at half of cost, the balance being paid by the public treasury, and eventually gave out doles of grain as a regular governmental function.

The imperial government was also beginning to take over other business activities. It owned and operated or leased mines of various sorts, and it began to supervise closely, and in some instances to assume, the operation of business enterprises engaged in supplying the army. Once begun, this process of turning over the control of industry to the state on the ground of military expediency steadily continued.

Apart however from the governmental activity mentioned, free enterprise and private capitalism were permitted to function without much state interference during the period of the empire's zenith. Private capital was extensive and it was freely employed in whatever enterprises seemed to offer the opportunity of profitable operation. Garrisons of soldiery maintained peace and order throughout western Europe and the lands surrounding the Mediterranean, and goods and persons could and did move more freely and safely throughout this vast territory during these glowing days of the Pax Romana than at any time since.

But the same strong hand that had established domestic tranquillity had also destroyed freedom of thought and expression. Gone were the great debates in the Senate, and although the emperors thought it advisable to maintain the appearance of consulting the senators and securing their approval through the form of legislation, yet everyone knew that the emperor alone ruled, and accordingly no legislation appeared that did not have his sanction. Criticizing the government was a dangerous activity, and criticism of the emperor was tantamount to plotting rebellion.

The government's unquestioned censorship extended as well to literary as to political expression. Both Seneca and Ovid suffered the punishment of exile by imperial decree, and although in each instance factors other than literary were known to have supervened, yet the despotic treatment they received was a warning to all to keep their utterances within approved bounds.

Constitutional religious liberty was unknown. The emperor forbade or permitted alien religions, such as Christianity, as to him seemed from time to time expedient. The wisdom or humanity of his decisions might be subject to question, but not their constitutional authority.

All in all, Roman society at the close of the second century had moved a considerable distance toward collectivism. The dominant factor in influencing its further progression toward that end was the centralization of governmental authority. Everything depended on the emperor. A series of five great rulers in the imperial office gave the vast Roman domain its brilliant history in the second century. But fortune departed with the death of Marcus Aurelius, and in the succeeding century, as poor sense and worse morals characterized one emperor after another, the Roman people, not fortified by any philosophy of individualistic worth, declined from one collectivistic formula to another in their attempt to stave off the threatened collapse of their civilization.

When after long years of civil strife and economic depression Diocletian appeared on the throne, giving the community a strong but rude and cruel despot for its emperor, it was only to be expected that he should complete the work of collectivization. This he accomplished in spectacular fashion. A large portion of the industry of the empire, particularly in Italy, was expropriated by the government and operated by the bureaucracy for the avowed purpose, first, of properly supplying the army, and second, of promoting the general economic welfare; and the remainder of business and agriculture was subjected, for the same ends, to detailed control that had as limitation only the discretion of the vast officialdom. These measures not having secured an appreciable increase in production and prosperity, Diocletian in 301 issued his famous decree fixing prices and wages throughout the empire. Although no complete copy of this edict has come down to us, yet we know from the parts that have been discovered that it prescribed prices for all known commodities in voluminous detail, and fixed wages for every type of occupation. Economically the consequence of this law was exactly what always happens when government tries the age-old device of substituting its concept of a fair price for the price that the people most concerned—those who buy and sell—accept as fair in their dealings in the market; goods and services that were priced in the decree below the market tended to disappear, or were available only in a "black market," and commodities priced above the market tended to be produced in unwieldy quantities that could not be moved. Socially the effects of the price-fixing law were disastrous. Although apprehended violators were severely punished, even by execution, nevertheless the decree could not be effectively enforced, and rioting occurred in parts of the empire.

The while the state was taking control of factories and the marketplace, it was also assuming domination over the trade unions. Associations of workmen, called *collegia*, appeared at an early day in Rome. We do not know much of their activity or influence, but they became numerous and played a prominent part in the lives of the working people and tradesmen. When collectivism began to grow under the later emperors, the government found the collegia ready-made instruments for the imposition of authority. More and more taxes, dues, and obligations were placed on the collegia until at last, to prevent escape, membership had to be made compulsory. Direction of the activities of the collegia grew ever more complete, and finally the bureaucracy took over entire control, the trade unions thus becoming simply channels for state regulation, by which the working and trade classes were kept within the lines planned for them by their governmental overseers.

The events of Diocletian's reign mark a climactic collapse of Rome's efforts to solve its problems. The individualism of the republic had long since been forgotten. Now intense state collectivism, of as complete a sort as the Romans could envisage, had proved unworkable.

The Roman world thereafter reconciled itself to events and hoped only for the benevolence of despots. Its history became a patchwork, temporally and spatially, of alternating chaos and tyranny, as Mediterranean culture more and more rapidly declined. Despite occasional episodes of tranquillity the hand of death was upon the great civilization of the Greeks and the Romans, which thereafter was to be known to the world only through its bequests to its successors.

3. The Middle Ages

After the western empire had succumbed to the invaders from the north, Europe entered upon the long period of death and rebirth that we know as the Dark Ages. It was an era of collective emphasis. For reasons of security the small landowners, either voluntarily or under compulsion, conveyed their farms to larger and more powerful proprietors who offered in exchange the promise of protection from the pillage and banditry that were characteristic of the chaotic times. Out of this process and out of the pressures of a rude society where the human being had slight hope of surviving if he pursued an individualistic existence, grew the feudal system of the Middle Ages.

This form of social organization, which has been a normal stage in many civilization cycles of the past, reached its peak in Europe during the twelfth century. Let us examine it very briefly at that time.

The population was predominantly rural; cities and towns were rare. The principal form of property was land and the structures upon it, and the status and livelihood of nearly all persons was determined by their relationship to some piece of land.

The rules for the use of the land were complex, and although they preserved a general similarity throughout a given realm, and even to some extent throughout Europe, yet they varied in details from one manor to the next.

If we were to enquire who owned the land and the buildings upon it, we should find it difficult to obtain an answer. For the concept of ownership in the sense in which we today employ the term, and in which it would have been understood in classical Athens and Rome, was foreign to the feudal system. In a manner of speaking all the land of a given sovereignty, the kingdom of France for example, was owned by the king; yet what he owned was not the land itself but only certain limited rights with respect to it and with respect to the persons occupying it; and he himself was obligated, and perhaps held his lands in fealty, to the pope and emperor. The great lords holding under the king likewise did not own the land in any modern sense, but held only the right to demand specific feudal duties from those below them, subject in turn to the lords' own obligation to perform their feudal duties to the king. Thus society was organized in a pyramid of classes, broadening toward the base and resting upon the land, with the layers interlaced by reciprocal lines of feudal rights and obligations. The obligations centered around the concept of rent to be paid; the rights grouped themselves about the idea of protection from disorder. Every individual was assigned a place in this feudal structure by the circumstance of his birth, which attached him, by feudal rights and obligations that he could not ordinarily expect to modify substantially in his lifetime, to a particular parcel of land. On some of this land he had the right to make his home; with respect to other portions of it there were rent and additional obligations to be rendered or received; but none of it did he own, and ownership as we understand it would have been a puzzling idea to him. Individual ownership of real estate was wholly incompatible with the feudal scheme.

The hierarchal rights and obligations of this system, moreover, although fundamentally concerned with economic livelihood, embraced directly or indirectly nearly all of life in their regulation. Education and marriage were subject to feudal rules. Particular trades were or could be made a matter of feudal privilege. And tithes, a charge against the land, supported the established church.

This church paralleled the secular organization. Its priests, bishops, cardinals, and pope exercised their religious functions in a hierarchy whose authority was concentrated at the top, and held themselves as a body corporate exercising collective ownership of property.

The towns and cities, in the earlier period of the feudal system, were at least in theory as much a part of the feudal scheme as were the fields and forests. But during the movement for incorporation which swept through western Europe, they acquired charters from their overlords that made them partly independent of the feudal pattern. Typically an incorporated city secured a mayor and city council, with authority to legislate and enforce ordinances for local government, and feudal obligations were integrated and reduced.

Europe experienced very little freedom of thought or expression during the centuries of the feudal system. Permitted religious beliefs were fixed by the church, and heresy was not tolerated, either by the ecclesiastical authority, which hunted out the heterodox and the skeptical, or by the secular arm, which executed them when they had been delivered over by their priestly inquisitors. Nor was liberty of thought in other areas any more a characteristic of the feudal design. We need only think of Roger Bacon, who spent sixteen years in prison for but mild divergence from orthodoxy, to appreciate the little range allowed the human mind for its exercise. In all that he thought, as well as in all that he did, the individual was subject to the control of group custom, as enforced by the ruling classes, ecclesiastical and secular.

It was in the incorporated cities that the stringencies of feudalism began to be broken. With the feudal ties loosed from the land within the municipality, individual ownership of real estate and its free alienation became first a possibility and gradually an accustomed part of life. Greater fluidity of capital brought increased independence in ways of living and wider choice in occupations. The growth of the towns and cities and the concomitant development of more freedom from feudalistic restrictions came gradually and at various times in different parts of Europe. But it was the life in the cities that constituted the individualistic leaven in the mass of collectivism.

Feudalism was collectivistic. It is impossible for us to comprehend the historical record of the feudal centuries if we do not bear in mind that a sense of collective living permeated the assumptions by which people lived in the same way that a sense of individualistic living permeated the assumptions of the nineteenth century. It is in the light of this basic fact that the institutions of the time must be examined and appraised. The auto-da-fé, for example, should not be viewed simply as a demonstration of peculiar cruelty by our ancestors for sadistic satisfaction; rather it was a violent expulsion from the community of one who had violated the code of collective living by being drastically different. Collective life necessarily includes a presumption of the desirability of sameness; and therefore unorthodoxy in such an important matter as religion, which seems to involve the welfare of all members of the group, becomes so abhorrent that little revulsion is felt at the burning of the offender. It was the group rather than the individual that was important in feudal times; and accordingly the sufferings of the few were nothing if they seemed to promote the welfare of the many. The individual human being was but a tiny segment in a vast social pattern, well-ordered and accepted. Only exceptionally, and somewhat more frequently in the cities in the latter part of the period, was the individual regarded as constituting separately an important object of concern.

But the cities grew, and so did the nations, and their growth concurred with the disappearance of feudalism. In the struggle between the king and his great feudal lords, a struggle repeated throughout Europe, the cities usually sided with the king, because his more detached position seemed to promise greater municipal independence. Later the Protestants also found themselves taking the part of the royal crown, both to assist in the destruction of the feudal customs that hampered them and to secure the partisanship of an authority large enough to oppose its power to that of the Roman Catholic church.

4. Modern times

By the end of the sixteenth century feudalism had largely disappeared from western Europe. Vestiges of it remained, but as a social system it had been abandoned. In its place was a scheme of monarchical aristocracy, in which all governmental authority was vested in a national ruler, usually hereditary, who was expected to delegate or permit varying degrees of power to the nobles of the realm, who buttressed their positions with claims of inherited feudal prerogatives.

The centuries that intervened between the zenith of feudalism, which in most of Europe occurred in the twelfth and thirteenth centuries, and the later culmination of western liberalism, which reached its peak of development during the nineteenth century, may be thought of as a long transitional period, during which both philosophical assumptions and historical practice were moving from an emphasis on collectivism to a stress on individualism. There were however many and striking exceptions on both the individualistic and the collectivistic sides. A few small principalities in central Europe remained feudal until the nineteenth century. And on the other hand many cities, those of northern Italy and of the Hanseatic League for example, became at varying times during the Middle Ages self-governing communities with democratic institutions, free private economic enterprise, and customs that assured a considerable degree of cultural liberty to the individual.

But the cities tended to be absorbed into the larger community of the nation, a process that eventually was entirely effected. And within the nation the people, who had built up the power of the king in order to escape from the tyranny of the feudal barons, soon found that government by royal decree was as oppressive as had been the control of feudal custom. The ensuing debate over the limitation of sovereign authority (as distinguished from the preceding quarrel over the division of authority between king and barons) continued to be waged by pen and sword for three centuries, until brought to a termination by the natural rights philosophy and by the English, American, and French revolutions.

Thereafter it was established for the cultural cycle which we call Western Civilization that all government, whether monarchical or otherwise, is constitutional, deriving its just powers from the consent of the governed.

But what are the just powers of sovereignty? Government being admitted to be constitutional, the problem yet remains of its proper area of action, and this question was implicitly involved in all the argument and combat of the revolutionary period. It was a struggle in which collectivism was gradually pushed back, as the principle of individual freedom was slowly recognized as being properly applicable to ever greater segments of human action. The collective concept of control of the group through the machinery of the state was by degrees confined to a more and more restricted sphere.

The first important area to be delivered from collective to individual control was that of religion. Throughout Mediterranean civilization, and continuing into western civilization until the sixteenth century, it had been assumed without serious contest that decisions, at least the more important ones, in so vital a matter as religion should be collective. From the condemnation of Socrates to the burning of John Huss the denial of individual religious liberty had not only prevailed but had actually increased in the scope of its asserted authority. But in the sixteenth and seventeenth centuries the collective principle was successfully challenged by the Reformation, which from various sources developed a philosophy of religious freedom, with the result that church and state were separated in much of the west, and religious activity and belief became areas for individual determination.

It is difficult for us of the present day to grasp the momentous character of this transformation. Because we live in an age in which religious liberty happens to be a cultural heritage, we assume that it constitutes a natural and more or less inevitable mode of human association. Nothing could be further from the historical fact. Much of the Orient, it is true, has permitted considerable religious liberty for a long period of time; but within the Occident freedom of religious activity has existed for less than four centuries—a short time compared with the millennia during which collective dominance of religious belief and worship everywhere obtained.

With the defeat of collectivism in religion came also its expulsion from the field of opinion and expression. Here again it is difficult for us to understand the collectivistic viewpoint that until comparatively recent times prevailed. But a society that concentrates its attention on the group rather than the individual, regarding the individual as secondary, is naturally concerned with opinions that have the approval of the group as a whole and has little tolerance of individual views at variance therewith. The unorthodox view, in science and politics as well as in religion, is a disturbing and unwelcome intrusion in the collective tranquillity, and it must therefore be obliterated if possible. An age that adopts the tenets of collectivism cannot avoid the suppression of individual opinion. But when the collectivism of the feudal ages began to disintegrate, science and philosophy joined with religion in demanding freedom of thought and expression. The movement grew. Individualism triumphed. Collective control was ousted from the domain of intellectual activity, and freedom of speech and press became, by the end of the eighteenth century, well established on the whole in Great Britain and North America, and at least partially recognized in western Europe.

Concurrently with its decline in religion, the collectivism of feudal times was also slowly giving ground in the field of economic activity. As heretofore noted, it is a myth of our day, fostered by the collectivists and accepted by the uninstructed, that economic history is a progress from primitive individualism to enlightened collectivism. But on the contrary the individualism that generally prevailed in western Europe in the nineteenth century and the first third of the twentieth was preceded not only by the collective life of feudal times, but also by a long regime of state regulation of agriculture, industry, and trade, that occupied a most prominent place in European civilization until the end of the eighteenth century.

So unquestioned during this period preceding the nineteenth century was the authority of the governing class to regulate economic life, so complete its control in any sphere it selected for its attention, and so thorough its appropriation, through taxes, of a large share of the product of labor and capital, that there was not much occasion for concern by the rulers over the matter of the ownership of property. Ownership is always a shifting concept, and who owns capital assets is always a question of less practical importance than that of who con-

trols them and benefits from them. As feudalism had declined, the
holders of property had become its owners freed from the obligations
of feudal custom. But in place of feudal custom there had appeared
the control and taxing power of the new state. Property was private,
but all property was affected with a public interest that was regarded
as being without limitation.

Governmental regulation of the most extensive and detailed sort was
therefore the normal thing. Both the humble laborer and the prosperous
merchant found themselves confronted by state-imposed rules at every
turn. The workingman could not freely choose his occupation; he must
work only within the narrow area permitted to his guild, and indeed
within only a specialized portion of that. The guilds, like the Roman
collegia, became devices for state regulation, dominated by bureaucratic
members of the governing class, which upon occasion imposed on
the guilds burdens so onerous that membership had to be made compulsory, even as it had been in Rome a thousand and more years before.

This close control over economic life was not simply the result of
regal caprice or of a desire for interference just for the sake of exercising
authority, although probably those influences played a part. Rather it
was the product of a philosophy of state planning, designed to secure
national prosperity and the common welfare, which was accepted by
all members of society as being natural and in the main desirable, or
at least unavoidable. The regulation of the woolen industry in England
in the sixteenth and seventeenth centuries, for example, had as its goal
the building up of an industry that would supply large employment and
lucrative exports. Granted the desirability of the goal and the propriety of social regulation to achieve it, the means employed were logical.
Farmers were forbidden to export wool, and thus were compelled to
sell at a lower price to the English weavers. To force the domestic
consumption of English woolen cloth, the importation not only of
foreign woolens but also of other textiles was made difficult by high
tariffs. Laws were passed to encourage the use of woolens; corpses, for
example, were required to be placed in woolen shrouds. Workers in
the woolen industry were forbidden to emigrate. To lessen foreign
competition, the English colonies were barred from engaging in woolen
manufacture, while the enlargement of the outside market by securing
lower foreign tariffs was a constant object of English diplomacy. Nor
did the concern of government limit itself to these devices of a compulsory nature; it sought the persuasion of a better product as well, and

consequently promulgated regulations fixing in detail the standards of quality that the trade must adhere to.

In similar fashion, and with varying degrees of control, the hand of the state was placed on nearly every occupation throughout Europe. Prices of goods were established, wages were fixed, terms of employment were determined. Farmers and tradesmen were required to sell only in designated markets and at designated times. Specifications of quality were dictated, and particular products encouraged or forbidden.

The American colonies were settled during this era of social regulation, and their early ordinances exhibited the same unquestioning trust in the advisability of collectivism in economic life. From the price of a cord of wood or of a glass of beer to the wage of a carpenter, all was subject to the control of legislation. We are accustomed to think of the first settlers in this land as seekers after freedom, and in certain most important respects this was true. Various of the colonies were founded by those in search of a freedom—at least for themselves—in religious and cultural life that could not be found in their homeland. But the idea of individual freedom in economic activity was not being as much developed as the concept of similar liberty in religion, expression, and politics, and in the 1600's there were few who were looking for economic freedom as a means to greater prosperity; and consequently the Europeans who migrated here established, upon their arrival, much the same pattern of social control over economic life that they had been accustomed to in the countries whence they came.

This dominance of government in economic affairs reached its greatest development in England and France in the sixteenth and seventeenth centuries. Its theory and practice have come to be known as mercantilism, which is usually explained as the attempt to build national wealth through encouraging the expansion of exports and the diminution of imports, thus causing an inflow of specie paying for the surplus of exported goods. But the practices of western Europe in the centuries preceding the nineteenth went much further than this, embracing the details of purely domestic as well as foreign trade. Rather the period should be regarded as one in which certain of the principles of collectivism were assumed to be correct and were accepted as forming the working rules for the state. It was government that alone was regarded as capable of making decisions on all contested points of procedure in economic development. The individual could not be trusted and his decisions might be wrong, and therefore the correctness of the state must be made use of instead.

But in the eighteenth century the practice of state planning and regulation came under vigorous attack, both from theorists and from events. The writers of the period began to say that human government could not be expected to rule wisely all details of economic life, and that since each man in planning for himself also planned for the common good, the directive control of the state should be lifted from industry and trade. Eventually Adam Smith presented his influential argument for free economic enterprise, reasoning that the market is the most desirable social regulator. Events were spotlighting this debate. Government was growing increasingly in disrepute, the repressive grasp of the ruling class was being challenged in Europe and in America, and the objection to state rule in other fields was spreading also to the field of livelihood. Freedom of individual economic activity was being identified with liberty, and liberty was the rallying cry of the times.

Accompanying this distrust of government was a rather rapid increase in the use of capital in the production of goods. This growth of capital was not appearing because of state regulation, but rather in spite of it, and flourished most as the state interfered least. Gradually the ordinances of the state became more and more disregarded, and at length almost forgotten. By the end of the eighteenth century the relation between the state and economic enterprise had radically changed; freedom of the individual had become the dominant element. The new factories and stock companies made obsolete the mass of regulations governing guilds, and proceeded in disregard of them. Nevertheless the regulatory statutes continued on the law books for a long time. In England the regulation of wages by law was not finally repealed by Parliament until 1813. Other regulatory acts were repealed in 1808, 1814, 1821, 1825, and 1835. In France the power of the guilds to restrict workers in their choice of occupation was not destroyed until the revolution. In the German states regulatory legislation persisted longer; some of it was not repealed until the middle of the nineteenth century.

The result of this broad movement toward liberty in religion, opinion, expression, politics, and economics was the Liberal Age, the latter half of the nineteenth century and the first third of the twentieth, one of history's great eras. We are still too close to it to evaluate properly its worth, its accomplishments and its errors, but it seems probable that it will rank very high in the vacillating annals of humanity. However that may be, there is no difficulty in classifying it as an age of individualism as both its eulogists and its detractors assert it to have been. All factors considered, it seems probable that at no time in history, with the possible

exception of Periclean Athens, were men so free in all their activities as
they were in Great Britain, France, and America during this period. The
individual was free to worship as he pleased, to hold and express such
opinions as he pleased, even to the overthrow of the government giving him protection (or asylum as in the case of Karl Marx), to engage
freely in political endeavor, and to labor in such occupation as he might
choose, selling his work or his product in an open market where competition was encouraged rather than impaired. It is not necessary to dwell
at length on the character of the Liberal Age; it is familiar to us as our
immediate cultural predecessor.

It is important, however, to appreciate with some degree of understanding how different the nineteenth century was from most ages of
history. Through his long career man has usually adhered rather closely
to the assumptions of collectivism, and if he has tried upon occasion to
build the institution of freedom in one area of living he has contem-
poraneously neglected it in another. Individual liberty is difficult of accomplishment, requiring over an extended period of time strength of
hand, kindliness of heart, and thoughtfulness of mind. Rarely have these
been conjoined in a populace throughout the requisite term to produce an
individualistic society. But the Liberal Age, as the result not only of its
own endeavors but also of the wisdom and labor of preceding generations, was able to construct a social organization in which the individual could worship, think, talk, write, vote, work, travel, buy, and sell
largely as he chose, without constraint from the state, and yet with opportunity for cooperation with his fellows. Measured by what man
might ideally accomplish, its shortcomings were glaring enough; but
placed against the reality of history, both of the long antecedent centuries and of the century that is following, the late nineteenth century
and the early twentieth in the Occidental world was a glorious age.

5. The changing present

But men are ever dissatisfied. Thus the individualism of the Liberal
Age very soon came under the attack of defamers, who, forgetful of
the past, called for the adoption of collective control of the tools and
procedures of economic activity as though the reintroduction of the
state as regulator would be something new.

These advocates of a return to state power have had their way in most
of the western world, and in consequence the twentieth century has

witnessed a steady and rather rapid abandonment of the principles and practices of individualism, and the adoption instead of the institutions of collectivism. At first the trend was observable primarily in intellectual activity, as socialism and communism became increasingly popular ideas with literati, educators, and the clergy. But the idea soon became material. In 1917 the Bolshevik Revolution imposed a communist state on Russia, and seven years later England had a socialist government. The movement became more swift during the economic depression of the 1930's and the wars of the 1940's. In the United States the political development which called itself the New Deal looked to the state for the alleviation of human ills. Free economic enterprise, under the general designation of "business," not only was distrusted as an institution by an ever-enlarging share of the population, but was constantly castigated by politicians and intellectuals as the cause variously of too much production, too little production, too high prices, too low prices, cutthroat competition, and monopoly. Gradually but surely the assumption returned that only the state, imposing its regulation through a vast bureaucracy, was competent to make those decisions on prices, wages, production, and distribution that the processes of human existence require.

Thus the present is a time when the assumptions of collectivism are steadily becoming once again the accepted patterns of thought of the western world. The group is receiving greater value-emphasis, in place of the individual, and the state is absorbing to itself a constantly larger control of life. For the present generation the good life involves ever more direction of individual action by social agencies, principally by the machinery of the state. It is an age of movement away from the liberty of individualism and toward collectivism; whether the tendency will be halted or will be continued until western civilization subsides in thoroughgoing collective dullness depends upon the yet unknown human decisions of tomorrow.

6. Conclusion

Our brief historical survey has disclosed a factual truth which, though obvious enough, is yet much neglected and indeed often repudiated by modern thought. It is that both individualism and collectivism, in all their essential features and most of their conceivable variants, have been tried many times in the past, with results that are available for study, as clinical records of concluded experiments in the great social laboratory of history.

There is nothing new, that is to say, about communal control of life, whether much or little, and whether economic or intellectual. Social security, TVA, manipulation of money and credit, the molding of public opinion by government propaganda, the control of prices and wages, the allocation of supplies, government planning, communism—all these things have been tried before, often in forms that were almost precise antecedents of the present manifestations.

Thus communal ownership is not new, but rather a very old form of relationship between men and things. The only new elements in today's experiments with communal ownership are the new names given to it and the newness of our own experience with it. We call it nationalization of industry, municipal ownership, and ownership for service rather than for profit. But whatever the exterior trappings of nomenclature, the interior structure of communal rather than individual ownership remains the same.

The collectivists would have us believe otherwise. They would like us to suppose, even as they themselves usually imagine, that state ownership, state planning, and state control are brightly new devices, whose adoption will constitute at least a splendid experiment. But these things cannot furnish a new adventure for society; for they are as old as history, and their use another time can only constitute the retracking of a very old trail. This, however, I hasten to add, is not in itself a point against collectivism, for the old may also be the good. And individualism likewise only offers a way of social arrangement that has been tried before, even though less frequently.

It is important, nevertheless, to separate from collectivism its false claim to novelty. Men are attracted by the promise of that which is proffered as new. Particularly is this true in a generation that mistakes the idea of biological evolution for an idea of inevitable progress. But however specious may be the grounds for the allurement of novelty, the fact of allurement is real, and indeed, when all is said, it is probably the largest influence in the present vogue of collectivistic belief. Nothing then could be more salutary than to disabuse the modern mind of its persuasion that collectivism is new.

Collectivism indeed, far from being new, has been the dominant emphasis of the past. Liberty has been developed less frequently. The Periclean age of the Athenian city-state, the later years of the Roman republic and the earlier years of the succeeding principate, the Renaissance cities of northern Italy, the Hanseatic cities of northern Europe, and the Liberal Age in western Europe and North America, these are the periods, widely separated in time, of the emergence of strongly individualistic societies. Is it only coincidence that they are also, with all their shortcomings, the finest chapters that Occidental man has yet written in his history?

THE ETHICAL POSITION OF COLLECTIVISM

The liberty of individualism presents itself to us as man's duty, as ethical imperative, and as the will of God. The reasons supporting this large claim have been analyzed in the foregoing discussion of Book One.

As a further aid in judging the validity of these reasons, it will be helpful to contrast them with the ethical position of collectivism, as found in its diverse manifestations at the present time.

1. Historical materialism

The ethical position of modern collectivism is complex, and it is also confused. On the one hand it repudiates ethics in its theory of historical materialism, and on the other hand it relies on ethical considerations in its appeals for justice to the proletariat and to the underprivileged and for the righting of wrongs.

Historical materialism is a theory of necessity in history. Men's acts, it teaches, are determined at least in their significant aspects by the material facts of the universe, to which men react in their efforts to gain a living. Imbued in these facts is the element of continual change, and this change appears in the form of the dialectical triad, that is, in an ever repeated series of thesis, antithesis, and synthesis, or affirmation, negation, and negation of negation. This dialectical movement is supposed to occur in every manifestation of existence, in all physical and chemical phenomena, in all economic phenomena, and in all history.

Under this theory every historical event by the fact of its occurrence builds forces of reaction against itself. The reaction when it occurs is the negation of the prior affirmation. But the negation also by its occurrence creates a further reactionary force, which tends to combine within itself elements of both the prior affirmation and negation. This negation of the negation, or synthesis of the prior thesis and antithesis, when it occurs becomes in its turn an affirmation, somewhat improved over the first affirmation because of the dialectical process which has occurred, and subject to further improvement as the dialectical triad endlessly repeats.

The proletarian revolution will take place, Marx, Engels, and Lenin taught, as the negation or antithesis of capitalism, and communism in its ultimate and perfected stage will later develop out of the proletarian revolution, apparently as the synthesis of the prior thesis and antithesis, although the attainment of ultimate communism is not presented in quite this explicitly dialectical fashion. What will happen when this ultimate stage of communism is reached? Will the dialectical triad continue? Will there be a reaction from communism? Marx, Engels, and Lenin never addressed themselves to this question. But it is quite clear that they regarded communism as the goal of history beyond which no improvement in social form would ever be possible. How is this position harmonized with the dialectic? So far as my information extends no communist writer has ever attempted a harmonization.

It is not my purpose to present a critique of historical materialism, but only to point out its influence upon the ethical position of modern collectivism.

First, it gives collectivism in all its forms a sense of destiny. History is marching inexorably toward the goal of perfected communism, and dialectical materialism is the *modus operandi* of history's progress. All members of the communist party in all countries are schooled in this theory. Socialists too are pervaded by it. Through the influence of these disciples, the concept is inculcated in the thinking of fellow travelers, sympathizers, and of society generally. It is closely allied to the idea of evolutionary progress, and even as Marx and Engels welcomed Darwin and adapted his evolutionary theory to their purposes, so the doctrinaires of communism and socialism have made use of the twentieth century's smug acceptance of the theory of evolutionary progress, teaching that more and more collective living is the line of society's progressive and certain development. The collectivist is thus on the side, not of the gods, for modern collectivism has only incidental use for gods, but of historical materialism, which is truth and the spirit of things, the collectivist believes, and therefore something very like a god.

The sense of destiny thus engendered is fortified by the circumstance that belief in the historical movement of dialectical materialism must be an act of faith, and of rather mystical faith. Hegel, Marx, and Engels never deigned to try to prove the historical dialectic as an induction from the observed facts of history; they asserted it as an insight, a vision, as it were, of the innate and basic principle of universal life, and they used history only as an illustration of the truth they oracularly propounded. Likewise the believer of today does not ask for proof; he accepts historical materialism and the movement of history toward communism or at least toward more communal living as an inspired view in which he has faith.

Second, historical materialism gives to present-day collectivism a strong materialistic emphasis. Material things control men's dealings with them, men's dealings with things constitute economic life, and economic life is the real determinant of all other human activities—this is the theory included in historical materialism. Man's way of making a living, it teaches, determines all the significant aspects of his culture. This view being accepted as premise, it follows logically enough that man should devote his attention principally to what he should eat, what he should wear, and how he should be housed, knowing that all things else will be added unto him.

Third, historical materialism results in a special set of human values, divorced from commonly accepted standards of ethical quality. This special set of values is accepted in varying degrees by all modern forms of collectivistic thought. If the destiny of mankind is communal living, then that destiny is the purpose of the universe, and if one happens to believe in God, it is also, one will believe, the will of God. Whatever, therefore, promotes communal living comes to be regarded as good, whatever impedes it bad. Although Marx taught that society in its broader aspects is governed by "tendencies working with iron necessity toward inevitable results,"[1] yet he also clearly believed that destiny is accomplished by the acts of individual men, whose deeds become good or bad as they speed or retard that destiny. Waiving the question of the inconsistency of these two views (and they cannot be reconciled), they yet represent the position of collectivistic thought today. Collective living is the assured condition of the future, which will arrive regardless of the acts of men, but nevertheless men's acts are desirable or undesirable as they hasten or delay the arrival of the apocalyptic day, as they render less or more uncertain that which is nevertheless certain. Many collectivists, particularly communists, would probably repudiate the thought that the viewpoint so developed should be described as ethical, for a conviction of communism is that its development has brought it beyond the concept of ethical quality. But it seems proper to use the words ethical and moral, at least in a limited sense, in speak-

1. *Capital*, Preface.

ing of action approved by collectivism, for those words connote what ought to be, and the action approved by collectivism is of course what it believes ought to be. Thus the cruel liquidation of kulaks is ethical action because it promotes communal living. To promote strikes in the United States is ethical, but to promote them in Russia and Great Britain is unethical. To compel men to work at specified tasks in Russia and Great Britain is the freedom of group planning and therefore ethical; while to compel them to do so in the United States, as by an injunction against a strike for eighty days under the Taft-Hartley Act, is the slavery of capitalism and therefore unethical. These views can be held and are held by the same people, and within the ethics of collectivism they are not inconsistent. For strikes in Russia and Great Britain are believed to impair collective living;[2] therefore they are immoral. Strikes in the United States are believed to speed the advent of collective living; therefore they are moral. In this manner all ethical judgments based on consideration of individual values apart from the group value of collective living are removed from consideration.

These three influences of the theory of historical materialism have penetrated very deeply into modern thought. Despite the fact that Marx and Engels have never been widely read, their readers nevertheless have been devotees who have spread the gospel assiduously, and today its separate influences have become accepted assumptions in the discourse of the classroom, pulpit, press, and public forum; and are all the more potent as molders of opinion and events because they are not recognized, at least much of the time, as attributes and derivatives of the historical materialism of Marx, Engels, and Lenin.

2. The aspiration for a better world

The theory of collectivism appears in our time in many forms, from a belief in municipal ownership of electric plants, through socialism and certain aspects of new-dealism to communism; but all these degrees and variations of collectivistic belief have a common meeting point in an aspiration for a better world in which to live. Is this not a hard world, with poverty, cruelty, and misery? Should it not therefore be made better?

Dissatisfaction with things as they are has probably been present at most times in the world's history. And with justification enough;

2. This was written during the Socialist administration in Great Britain.

the task of providing for the needs of life is so onerous, the cruelties of men are so severe and their stupidities so tragic, that there usually has been ample cause for bitterness and discontent. Sometimes this un-happiness has manifested itself in the form of the revolts of slaves and peasants, sometimes in the slow decay of the spirit of enterprise, and sometimes in an enthusiasm for a modification in the form of social organization. Examples of this last are numerous; indeed one may say that a very substantial part of all history reflects man's effort to better his condition by modifying the social order in which he lives.

The current manifestation of this desire to create a better world by social adjustment is found in the enthusiasm for more collective living. Here is a program which, its proponents assert, condemns present in-justices and promises to do something about them. And that which it promises to do is directed in specific terms to the ailments of society that are most prominent and the parts of life that are most disliked. Does disease and sickness bring sorrow? The Socialist party in England ex-pressly states that good health is the "right" of every citizen, and that it is the duty of society to provide good health "free" to all. If, there-fore, you wish to improve the health of the world, is not the obviously indicated course the adoption of laws which provide for universal good health by enactment? Or if wages are too low to provide all the goods that are wanted—as they always are—does not socialism offer a system of high wages and low prices, all guaranteed by law? Do economic crises and periods of depression and unemployment occur? Why not adopt collective planning which will arrange the steady production and con-sumption of goods, without periodic overproduction and undercon-sumption?

Thus collectivism has for every ill a purported cure, which through the method of a collective plan enforced by law will, it is promised, at once eliminate selfish and inefficient individual action and compel generous and wise social action. The motive that prompts many of the supporters of collectivism to turn to these promises initially and to continue to have hopeful faith in them is an aspiration for a better world.

I do not suggest that this goal continues as an objective guide to the activities of all collectivists. On the contrary, the application of force in the carrying out of collective plans tends to the corruption of those who have the enforcement in charge, and the result to the collectivist is that his position tends to change from one of seeking a better world to one of trying to exercise power over others. But the starting point for

much of collectivistic argument, and the appeal to ideological acceptance, lies in the concept of a striving for a better world.

3. Fair sharing

The desire for a better world, however, constitutes ethical motivation
only. It does not of itself teach or suggest any methods to be employed
for the attainment of that object. What is the ethical position or base
of collectivistic methodology?

When we examine the methods advocated by collectivists, we find
that they include a diversity of programs, all however united in making
use of a plan collectively decided upon and enforced. As I have heretofore shown, this unanimity in the use of some form of collective decision
is inevitable, because the decisions imperative to existence must be made
either collectively or individually, and collectivism cannot resort to individual decision, for if it did so it would abandon collectivism and become individualistic.

If we seek a common ethical consideration in these diverse collectivistic plans, a ground of moral viewpoint which unites them, we shall
find it in the idea of fair sharing of the good things of life. From Marx
to the present, all collectivistic proposals and arguments have been
founded on the ethical proposition that every man has a right to a fair
share in the goods that support life and make it enjoyable. It was because capitalism, in Marx's view, failed to accomplish this that he condemned it as unjust. The workman, Marx argued, does not obtain the
full value of his production, because surplus value is left above the wages
paid, which surplus value goes to the owners of the factories and machines used in the productive process. This is unfair, Marx contended;
justice requires that the laborer receive the entire value of his production,
that his wage be equal to the value which his effort has created. If he
does not obtain this full value in his wage—and the fact of surplus value
proves that he does not do so, according to Marx—then he has been
robbed. Capitalism therefore deprives him of his fair share in the total
production which he helps to create, and capitalism is therefore unjust
and should be destroyed.

It should be noted however that Marx himself did not propose to
give to each laborer the full value of his production, for he said that
the banner of the communist society would proclaim "From each ac-

cording to his ability, to each according to his need."[3] Accordingly the man who had need for more than he could produce would receive it, and since it could come only out of the production of others, these others would be permitted to receive only something less than their production.

What constitutes fair sharing? Collectivistic literature does not enlighten us with affirmative statements, being devoted to showing that free enterprise does not result in fair shares to the members of society, and should therefore be replaced by collectivistic controls. Will the society of these collectivistic controls accomplish fair sharing? The proponents of collectivism of course assure us that it will. But if we inquire why we can have confidence in the fair sharing of a collective society, and how it will be accomplished, the replies become vague, and amount on the whole to no more than that the members of the bureaucracy who will control prices, wages, and incomes will be fair because they will be told by law to be fair, and that their standard of fairness will be their subjective sense of fairness. Why is it that collectivism, which bases much of its case on the need for fair sharing, yet is thus driven to a position of vagueness with respect to it? Basically it is because collectivism abandons the free market, which alone is capable of estimating objectively the fairness of economic distribution. We shall examine this proposition at length in Book Two, where we shall consider the apparatus of individualism for securing the fair distribution of economic goods.

4. The amoral aspect of collectivism

Present-day collectivism in all its forms purports to be scientific. It represents with more or less explicitness that its advocacy is of principles of social action that operate with the sureness of scientific laws of cause and effect, which have been established by scientific observation.

In this reliance upon a scientific position, whereby the proponents of collectivistic programs contend that they are supporting not only what they themselves like, and not only what is just, but also what is scientific, collectivists reflect and acknowledge their Marxian background. Marx and Engels regarded their teaching as scientific, and lost no occasion to insist on that proposition. Their ideas were developed

3. *Critique of the Gotha Programme.*

in the heyday of the nineteenth century's boundless trust in the method of natural science to solve all human problems, when the study of human action was being promoted in the new sciences of psychology and sociology, which solemnly promised to reduce all human conduct to rules of thumb.

In keeping with this enthusiasm for what was thought to be scientific, Marx and Engels asserted that their program was scientific socialism, and not utopian socialism, which they scorned. They did not preach ideals, they asserted, but explained necessary laws.

These scientific pretensions, however, were not honored by an adherence to scientific method. The writings of Marx and Engels are not objective investigations of facts with dispassionate conclusions; they are fulminations against existing injustices and thunderings for reform. Having taken the idea of the dialectic of history from Hegel, they made no more attempt than he had done to place under it a rational foundation. Their criticism of the system of individualistic capitalism, which they centered on the idea of surplus value, was likewise adapted from a prior theory, in this case Adam Smith's labor theory of value, and again without critical evaluation. In *Capital*, it is true, the criticism of individualistic society adheres to a logical scheme of development in its attempt to show the fatal defects of the capitalistic social order. But this is the case only with the destructive argument against capitalism; the constructive presentation of the argument for socialism and eventual communism abandons the scientific method of rational analysis and becomes only inspirational. Over and over it is stated that the proletarian revolution and succeeding socialism and communism are assured by scientific laws whose operation is certain, but just as often as these theses are pronounced they are left unsupported by rational proof of their existence. There is, for example, not the slightest attempt to show that ultimate communism will in fact bring about production from each according to his ability, and consumption by all according to their needs. Marx and Engels say that this will occur, and its eventual occurrence is the focus of their whole theory, but they have nothing whatsoever to say about the *modus operandi* of this blissful condition, except that it constitutes communism and that communism is going to arrive. To call this method scientific is a wholly erroneous use of terms.

But despite this lack of scientific method in the founders of modern collectivistic thought, and despite the consequence that the present-day adherents of collectivism take their position largely as a matter of faith, the tradition nevertheless persists that somehow the tenets of modern collectivism are scientific. Proposals for collective schemes are brought forward with an aura of scientific approbation, the assumption being that they have as support scientific principles that are beyond question. Dialectical materialism in this modern certitude has become the psychology of environment, and historical materialism has become evolutionary progress. The scientific base of collectivistic proposals when they are presented with the aid of these viewpoints is regarded as not open to question.

This claim of modern collectivism to scientific quality is an amoral position, and is to be distinguished from collectivism's justification of any and all means to the accomplishment of communal living. The latter is based upon an assumption of moral quality in human acts, and seeks to justify collectivism's methods and aims as falling within morality.

But in its asserted scientific position collectivism discards this moral viewpoint and treats human action as being without moral quality. Human persons, it teaches, act pursuant to necessary law in what they do rather than from choice. If this be true, it follows that they are not responsible for their acts, and accordingly have no moral responsibility for their acts' consequences, since they cannot choose to avoid them. The conclusion must be that whatever is, is right. There is much of this viewpoint in Marx and Engels. Slavery, for example, they say was not morally wrong in the ordinary sense, for while a bad institution, it was simply the necessary product of economic conditions as they prevailed during the ages of slavery. When the economic need for slavery disappeared slavery was abandoned. Thus the practice of slavery was not morally bad, nor was the freeing of slaves morally good, but those events were only historical occurrences made necessary by economic facts. Likewise in the writings of modern advocates of socialism such as Laski, the acts of individual capitalists are not condemned as blameworthy, however harsh they may be asserted to be, because they are regarded as simply the necessary product of the capitalistic environment.

The influence of environment on conduct thus comes to be greatly stressed in modern collectivism. Environment it conceives as the determinative cause of conduct, rather than as the arena within which will exercises choice. Therefore through collective action it proposes to mold environment in order to produce character as desired. This proposition that man should mold his environment because his environment determinatively molds him involves a seldom appreciated self-contradiction. For man's acts to change his environment must either be caused by that very environment or be independent of it. But if caused by the environment, change can occur only to the extent that environment causes or permits it, and exhortation to human beings to create change is useless. But the collectivists do exhort, and thereby they admit that man can and does act importantly in independence of his environment. Nevertheless they continue to insist that history is but the play of materialistic forces. They do not see that human will is the noble part of man, and that his environment derives its great importance not from any potency to mold his character, but from the fact that it is the arena within which human will must exercise itself as it builds character.

Collectivism not only assumes that it will mold human character by controlling environment; it also relies rather strongly on the proposition that the changes so effected in character will be transmitted from one generation to the next by inheritance, and that thus there will be brought about a change in human nature. This viewpoint underlies modern collectivistic thought to an important degree. The teaching is that as the features of socialism and collectivism are incorporated in the environment, man will behave differently in reaction to his changed mode of making a living. The self-interest that characterizes human action in a society of individual capitalism will not express itself, but will be replaced by an attitude of generous cooperation, which will keep in mind the equal welfare of all. This change, the collectivists say, cannot be expected to take place at once upon the introduction of communism, but will occur gradually over a period of time, as one generation after another sloughs off more of the selfish attitude and adopts more of the group attitude, and as the improved attitude is passed on from one generation to the next by inheritance. It is thus that the slowness of change in human attitudes in Russia is explained. But this explanation assumes that though the change in human nature will be gradual it will nevertheless be certain through heredity, which is thus relied on to bring the communal millennium. For if each human being, through succeeding generations, were endowed when born with the same basic attitudes, having the same instinct of self-interest and the same likelihood of being selfish as his forebears, then there would be as much reason to expect a change in human attitude in one generation of communism as in ten, since the only force then operating would be the influence of environment. And if environment does not operate through heredity, then it must exert its influence *de novo* on each individual during his life span, and what it cannot accomplish in one life span it cannot accomplish in many repeated ones. Accordingly if collectivism cannot progressively change human nature over succeeding generations, its claim of ability to effect a world without self-interest loses a great deal of its force, for experience clearly shows that communism and socialism where tried do not have that effect at once, or within one generation.

But this need for a cumulative effect of environment on human nature, whereby the new race of men of ultimate communism will be created, must rely on the inheritance of acquired characteristics as its biological means. The cooperative attitude and the diminution of selfishness through the influence of environment are, by the collectivist argument itself, acquired characteristics, and by no means accidental mutations. But can acquired characteristics be inherited? What do the experiments of biological science disclose? Darwin, accepting Lamarckism, believed that acquired characteristics could be inherited, and it was partly for this reason that his evolutionary theory was congenial to the historical creed of communism as it was developed by Marx, Engels, and Lenin. Communism thought it had the backing of science, and accordingly was pleased to regard itself as scientific.

Modern research however does not support the hypothesis of the inheritance of acquired characteristics. Although the last word doubtless is not in, it is nevertheless accurate to say that the overwhelming weight of scientific opinion at the present time favors the view that acquired characteristics are not inherited. The difficulties of the Russian biologist Vavilov and his colleagues, as reported in the press some years ago, arose from their research in this field. Perhaps not appreciating the import of their findings to communist orthodoxy, they published the results of years of experiments, showing no evidence that acquired characteristics were inherited. But the Politburo, better schooled in communist doctrine, at once saw the effect of the research on collectivistic ideology, and the findings were savagely repudiated as unscientific, and the scientists themselves were liquidated. To much of the west this was a quixotic incident, like Hitler's banning of modern art. But the Politburo is hardheaded and has no time for idiosyncrasy. The research and the researchers were eliminated because they did not support the collectivistic faith.

The occurrence exposes the shallowness of the claim of the ideology of collectivism to scientific quality. Collectivism, because of the error of its initial position in emphasizing the group at the expense of the individual, cannot be scientific. But it persists in wishing to think that it is. The result is confusion between collectivistic faith and science. On the one hand collectivism likes to assume that it relies on scientific principles of psychology and biology; on the other hand it insists that science conform to its faith that a better race of men can be created by forcing on them a collectivistic environment.

The world can indeed be made better, but not by attempting to force a predetermined mold of human nature through the pressure of collectivistic environment, but rather by making environment the equal liberty that gives human nature its chance to become its best through self-willed activity.

5. The immoral aspect of collectivism

Present-day collectivistic thought toys with the question of moral responsibility in human conduct, and never treats of it forthrightly. It seeks to obtain advantage both ways, by asserting on the one hand that men are entirely the creatures of their environments, and that thereby the environment of collectivistic institutions is bound to produce good and generous people and the environment of individualistic institutions bad and selfish ones, and by contending on the other hand that individualism is a morally retarded viewpoint whose proponents are for the most part meanly interested in the cruel exploitation of their fellows. I have already mentioned how this double position is found in Marx's writings. It also may be seen in the pages of modern exponents of socialism such as Laski. He tells us[4] that men's actions and history are largely determined by environment, which principally is composed of the "economic factor," of "changes in the material forces of production," and of "economic relationships." But he is also a reformer, who wants the world made better by the adoption of socialism and communism, and his books castigate men for their moral error in continuing the system of private capitalism, tainted as he conceives it to be with unethical qualities.

This indeterminate treatment of the problem of moral responsibility is itself immoral. There either is or is not moral quality in men's acts, or in some of them, and likewise there either is or is not responsibility for the consequences of acts. There is no proper middle ground.

This is not to say that all human acts possess moral quality or that all acts possessing moral quality are freighted with the same moral responsibility. I have heretofore attempted to show that the correct view recognizes volitional process as possessing the attribute of moral quality, while non-volitional process lacks it, and that where moral

4. Harold J. Laski, *The State in Theory and in Practice*, New York, 1935, pp. 95–104.

quality is present the extent of moral responsibility depends upon the actor's real or imputed knowledge of the consequences of his acts.

It is the obligation of a philosophy of human conduct to deal explicitly with the question of the ethical ingredient in action. No philosophy can claim to be logical, or to be scientific in its recognition of realities, until it has done so. Modern collectivism however makes no effort in this direction. Because of its mystical faith in communal living as the ultimate goal of men's endeavors, it regards concepts of morality, as it treats all other things, simply as means to be employed in the promotion of the final object; wherefore it adopts, discards, or twists the idea of morality as it variously may serve the collectivistic end. And if we inquire why ethics is thus subjugated to the politics and economics of collectivism, the only reply we shall find in the teachings of socialism and communism is, as we have seen, that collectivistic living as goal is an insight into the nature of things and into history, and that as such revelation it is beyond all considerations of logic and ethics that do not fall within its conceptual boundaries. It is precisely this viewpoint that is immoral, because it denies morality. Ethical concern ceases to be a matter of rational and independent thought, and becomes merely an adjunct of a mystical and a priori assertion.

Coupled with this failure to understand the nature of ethical quality is the fault of not presenting a moral purpose for human existence. Eventual communism, or that cooperative tranquillity comprising the goal of the collectivists whose thoughts do not venture as far as the vision of Marx, is indeed something to strive for under the collectivistic thesis; but being presented as a certain outcome, independent of the vagaries of human action, it eliminates ethical purpose from life. Men do not have a moral responsibility for the result of history, for that is already determined by the forces of historical materialism. But thus to destroy the ethical purpose of men's actions in their historical setting is to destroy the ethical purpose of human life, and to leave history without a moral goal. A historical design which includes no more than the molding of men by their environment is devoid of ethical purpose. And to remove ethical purpose from life and from history is to deny morality, which denial is itself an immorality. The influence of this denial of moral quality in human behavior has gradually penetrated deeply into the accepted modes of thought of the western world.

The greatest immorality of collectivism, however, is not its repudiation of ethical considerations, but its wrongful use of force in human relations. As we have already seen, collectivism necessarily involves an assertion of the superiority of a few in the making of decisions concerning conduct, and this superiority can be maintained only by the use of force. Such force is immoral, because used for an immoral end, and the corruption of its immorality rots the characters of those who exert the force the while it prevents the development of character by those against whom it is exerted. The principles which produce these results have heretofore been examined in Chapter 10.

Modern collectivism, as we have seen, tends to become a belief accepted on faith. As such, it has little tolerance for the dispassionate study of any competing philosophy, and seeks to prevent such study by inveighing against the intentions of the proponents of all competing theses. Only collectivism, it says, is supported by good intentions, and only collectivists are motivated by a sincere ambition to better the lot of men. Sometimes the collectivists refer benignly to their opponents as the victims of capitalistic environment, who are to be pitied as well as destroyed; sometimes this dismissal of the intentions of individualists is not so urbane, on occasions when it better suits the collectivistic purpose to depict individualistic philosophy as the deliberate promotion of selfishness. This is particularly true where the opponent of collectivism is formidable in the presentation of his case; such a man is dangerous, and not simply to be scorned but to be undermined if possible as a rascal. Thus in reading the violent references to Adam Smith in recent decades, one would suppose that instead of having been a pedagogue and philosopher of most modest means he had been a greedy robber of the poor, whose philosophical writings were a rationalization of his own covetousness. Likewise the lashings at John Locke, including quotations from him about "property" without ever an acknowledgment that he explicitly defined property, as he used the term, to mean life and liberty as well as material things, would lead the uninstructed reader to suppose that Locke had been an acquisitive holder of substantial possessions, whereas he was a poor man whose essays on politics were largely or entirely composed while he was a penniless refugee in Holland.

The immorality of this egotistical point of view, which denies the possibility of good intentions outside the circle of collectivistic action, contaminates the entire position of modern collectivism. The believer in collectivism is early indoctrinated with the conviction that only a collectivist can be sincerely concerned about a better world, where the shares of the good things of life will be fair. Even as he accepts his belief in collective living as a revelation in which he has faith, so he also accepts the fanaticism that all opposition to collectivism presents a façade of sham behind which there can be only greed and self-interested cruelty. But this is a false position, which from its nature cannot be more than assumption. Sincerity is a matter of the innermost recesses of the mind, which cannot be known between man and man, but only between man and God. The collectivist cannot know that the individualist is insincere, any more than the individualist can know the same of the collectivist, and the collectivistic assumption that individualism is insincere, or that it is but the reflection of environment and not an objective conviction, can from its nature never be a rational concept but only a fanaticism.

Social philosophy should be a reasoned program rather than a mystic persuasion, and the error of making it the latter, with an attendant dismissal of all opponents as persons whose motives are evil, is an initial and basic immorality from whose corrupting influence both the theory and practice of collectivism in its varying forms never escapes.

The divergence between the moral quality of individualism and the moral quality of collectivism is much wider and more radical than commonly appreciated. Individualism is based on the morality of decision by the individual; collectivism is based on the amorality of conformance by the individual to the group plan. Individualism uses social control to protect individual decision; collectivism uses social control to assure individual conformance. The one sees the human career as dependent upon the morality of choice; the other sees it as dependent upon the amorality of material influences, operating with dialectical certainty. There is no bridge between these opposed positions; they are radically opposed and must remain so.

BOOK TWO

THE CHALLENGE TO PRACTICE LIBERTY

Part I: Intellectual Liberty

Part II: Economic Liberty

Part III: The Liberty of Children

Part IV: Political Liberty

The Success of Liberty

THE CHALLENGE TO PRACTICE LIBERTY

The theory of liberty defines for us the goal of social action. The argument of individualism, approving the concept of the nature of liberty so presented to us, asserts not only that this concept has existence as a part of the process of our thought but also that it furnishes us with the objective toward which we should direct all our social effort. Our duty, as envisioned by the philosophy of individualism, is to embody the abstract form of the nature of liberty in the practical form of social action creating liberty.

In Book One we sought to understand the nature of liberty. Our study disclosed that liberty is the rational solution of the problem presented by the competition of the social relation, that liberty is ethical imperative because unconditionally required by the purpose of life, that individual freedom is the human spirit's experience of truth as it strives for integration with universal spirit, that all men are equal in their need for liberty and in their right to it, that the maintenance of equal liberty is the chief function of the state, that the maintenance of equal liberty consists in the maintenance of equal opportunity rather than in the attempted enforcement of equal response to opportunity, and that the maintenance of liberty as equal opportunity furnishes the sole justification, and therefore the proper limit, for the use of force in human affairs.

How are the values so delineated by the theory of liberty to be achieved? What are the social forms that constitute the realization of liberty in practice? The challenge of liberty in our time is not only that we have the intellectual acumen to understand it, but that we also have the moral courage to practice it. The practical forms of liberty will constitute our study in Book Two of this work.

To facilitate our study we shall divide human action into categories. A major division will be between intellectual and economic action, a division indicated by the nature of the competition and cooperation found in the social relation, heretofore examined in Chapter 4. Intellectual and economic action will each in turn be further subdivided. We shall also examine political action, in its role as a means for the support of intellectual and economic action.

Although this division of the human process into segments is both necessary and helpful, since close observation requires that subject matter be separated into parts for study, yet it also possesses a serious danger. Life as it is experienced is not split into fragments but is a whole process. All economic activity is at the same time intellectual activity, and all intellectual activity depends upon economic activity. And political activity is both intellectual and economic. Therefore if liberty is to prevail in human relations it must permeate the entire life experience. The denial of freedom of action in intellectual activity means its denial in economic activity, and likewise the denial of freedom in economic or political action necessarily includes its denial in intellectual action. But the itemization that unavoidably occurs in human thought tends to obscure this essential oneness. Because we speak separately of intellectual, economic, and political action we imagine that they are separate things. In the reality of life, however, they are only different descriptions of a single process as seen from different points of view.

Individualism and collectivism are consequently philosophies whose application is to the whole of life. A not inconsiderable body of opinion today supposes that we can have collective control in economic action and individual freedom in intellectual action. Not only, however, is liberty ethical imperative for all of life, but the oneness of life makes such a diversity of application of liberty impossible.

We must therefore take care that our separation of human process into divisions for study does not lead us to suppose that the principles of liberty apply with different degrees of validity to different parts of life. The whole of life, rather, should give expression in practical application to the nature of liberty.

But because the discussion in the following pages will embrace the whole of life, it must refrain for brevity's sake from exhaustive analysis of any of the several elements as they are examined. The attempt will be, instead, to present only the outline of the application of the principles of liberty to human affairs, with no more detail than seems necessary to support the general delineation of the way in which the society of liberty must arrange its rules.

PART I: INTELLECTUAL LIBERTY

The intellectual competition and cooperation occurring in the social relation constitute basic data of human life, as we have seen in Chapter 4. Therefore the problem of social philosophy is not the elimination of either competition or cooperation, which in any event could never be accomplished, but the ordering of human affairs with recognition of such competition and cooperation as part of the material of the problem of social existence.

Individualism therefore never seeks intellectual unity as a goal. On the other hand it does not seek intellectual diversity. The goal of individualism is intellectual liberty, the equal freedom of all persons to form and communicate intellectual concepts which agree or disagree as the particular persons in their freedom decide.

In this Part I we shall speak of religious liberty, cultural liberty, liberty of political thought, and freedom of speech and of press. But religious, cultural, and political thought blend in the intellectual process, and, further, thought and its communication are always joined. Therefore our study will not adhere closely to these indicated divisions, but will find it necessary to move back and forth among them.

Chapter 11

RELIGIOUS LIBERTY

The practice of religion consists in religious thought, the communication of religious thought, and the performance of religious acts. Religious liberty must accordingly extend to each of these elements of religious practice.

1. Liberty of religious thought

The principles of liberty require that each human being be privileged to think such religious thoughts as he chooses, without limitation and without interference by others. Since liberty is the largest equal freedom for all, the liberty of religious thought is the largest freedom of religious thought for each person that can be had without impairing a like freedom on the part of all. But in the area of thought this largest freedom is complete freedom, without limit, for no exercise of thought by one person can itself impair the freedom of thought of another. My thoughts may be ever so much opposed to yours, but my thoughts can never interfere with your freedom to think such thoughts as you choose. Therefore liberty of religious thought is complete freedom of the individual to think such religious concepts and beliefs as he wills.

It might be supposed that in practice this principle must always be effective, regardless of its recognition or nonrecognition in theory, because thoughts are secret and therefore are not subject to interference. And in consequence of this natural freedom from interference of secret thoughts, it might further be imagined that liberty of religious thought was an obvious principle scarcely needing statement or consideration. Such views, however, would overlook both the nature of human thought and the sharpness of the conflict of opinion that permeates human relations.

Although the activity of thinking is the process of the individual person and as such is secret, known only to the self, yet the content of thought is in part the product of the not-self as well as of the self. Thoughts cannot escape the consequences of the duality of man's career, and all thinking by the individual person, as we discussed more fully in Chapter 4, must take place under the influence of other persons. Should anyone suppose that his religious thoughts were entirely his own, he would be quite in error; they are the result not only of his own contemplation but also of the ideas communicated to him by others through books, speech, and example. The influence of others is particularly effective in molding religious thoughts, moreover, because few religious thoughts occur in a form original, or even partly original, with the self that is thinker. Groping for an explanation of the mystery of life, the self is moved to accept the explanations that it finds are traditional in the not-self round about it, believing that the traditional explanations, passed on from generation to generation, have the authority of divine revelation, or at least the support of long-continued acceptance by others. Original religious thoughts, though they may be supremely important, are conceived but rarely. Thus the communication of traditional religious thoughts, and of criticisms, modifications, and rejections of traditional religious thoughts, forms the base upon which nearly all religious thinking is constructed.

But since the secret religious thoughts of the individual are in this manner inseparably joined to the thoughts of others, the liberty of religious thought is a principle applying not simply to the secret thought processes of the individual but also to the communication to the individual of the thoughts of others. If liberty of religious thought be recognized, then liberty of religious communication must also be recognized; or if liberty of religious communication be denied, then the denial must be based on a repudiation of the liberty of religious thought. The liberty of the individual to think such religious thoughts as he wills cannot be dismissed, therefore, as a principle of little practical consequence, whose acceptance or rejection can have no effect upon the course of affairs; but on the contrary it must be recognized as the base for the entire structure of religious liberty.

For the liberty of religious acts also depends upon liberty of religious thought, as well as does the liberty of religious communication. Religious acts are but the outward symbols of religious thoughts, deriving their meaning and efficacy from the thoughts associated with them. If religious thoughts are free, then religious acts also must be free; or if religious acts are not free, religious thoughts are denied their freedom.

Even as the liberty of religious thought thus lies at the base of all religious liberty, so religious liberty in turn is fundamental to the entire cause of liberty in human affairs. For if liberty cannot be supported as a basic principle in the field of religion, it cannot be supported as a basic principle in any other field of human action. If the argument for liberty is not sufficient to require religious liberty, it is not sufficient to require intellectual, economic, or political liberty. If the purpose of life does not call for the largest equal liberty of all human beings in religion, it does not call for it elsewhere. Religion permeates every aspect of life; whatever religious belief is held, its position is one of dominance in the human career, touching and guiding all parts of that career. If therefore liberty is not ethical imperative in religion, it cannot be ethical imperative in any part of life.

But even as religious liberty thus occupies a primary place, so the case for religious liberty is shiningly clear. The purpose of life includes the morality of character, and the morality of character, as we saw in Chapter 5, depends upon the possibility of choice, a possibility which can exist only as liberty prevails. Therefore the will of God is served only by a religious faith freely entered into and by religious thoughts freely chosen. Both the great branches of the Christian church explicitly teach today that faith in God and faith in Christ as a redeemer must be the free act of the will of the individual person. Although minor deviations from this basic position from time to time appear, yet the overwhelming weight of modern Catholic and Protestant teaching, particularly as we observe it in this country, is that a compelled belief in the Christian faith would be a contradiction in terms, and that the only adherence to the Christian faith pleasing to God is that which the human spirit freely embraces.

This free adoption of religious belief can occur only where there is liberty of religious thought, for volitional action requires freedom. And since this liberty is equally the need of all men, to which they are all equally entitled, it follows that the liberty of religious thought, required as well by the Christian faith as by the philosophy of individualism, is the largest equal liberty that can be extended to all human beings. But this largest equal liberty of religious thought is complete liberty of religious thought; for the exercise of the liberty to think religious concepts can never of itself impair the liberty of any other human being to think religious concepts. Therefore complete liberty of religious thought is the first principle of all religious liberty.

But although this principle may be clearly perceived in theory, yet it is easily lost sight of in practice. For differences of religious opinion are a form of intellectual conflict, of competition between the self and the not-self, as we saw in Chapter 4; and they may result in the deepest emotional disturbance. To escape such disturbance, men seek to remove its cause by eliminating difference in religious thought; and in doing so they are prone to disregard the command of equal liberty.

The possibility of exerting influence upon the religious thought of another is twofold, as our discussion in Chapter 10 disclosed. There may be the influence of inspiration or the influence of force. The influence of inspiration, in the field of religion, is exercised by teaching, either by word of mouth or in print, and by example. The influence of force is exercised by attempted compulsion of the avowal of particular religious beliefs, by censorship of speech and the press, and by forcible interference with religious acts.

Equal liberty is never impaired by the influence of inspiration, as we further saw in Chapter 10, since it does not restrict will's arena for any person, but on the contrary always enlarges that arena by increasing the store of available concepts for action, i.e., by expanding the experiential factor. Accordingly the use of inspiration by teaching and example is always permissible within the philosophy of liberty.

But men are seldom content to restrain their efforts to the influence of inspiration; and constantly throughout history they have sought to persuade others to conformity with their own religious thought through the use of force. The more gross methods of employing force for this purpose, such as torture to compel public avowal of a particular creed, probably do not influence religious thought greatly, terrible as they are as violations of liberty. The less gross uses of force, however, as evidenced by censorship of the communication of religious ideas, can be highly efficacious, as long as they can be maintained, in influencing religious thought. For since religious thought depends as well upon communication as upon contemplation, the forcible control of communication is also the forcible control of thought. Such use of force, under principles we have heretofore examined, since it does not build equal liberty but impairs it, is always a violation of liberty and therefore always evil. All forcible interference with freedom of religious thought is consequently wrong, a repudiation of the purpose of life and a bar to the accomplishment of God's will.

2. Liberty of religious communication

Since, therefore, we build our religious thought by religious communication, the same reasons that lead to the principle of complete liberty of religious thought for all persons lead also to complete liberty of religious communication. Liberty accordingly demands that all human beings have complete freedom to transmit or receive such religious communications as they will.

Interference with religious communication is censorship, and censorship depends for its efficacy upon force. All forcible censorship of religious communication is a forcible impairment of equal liberty and is therefore evil.

The attraction of censorship lies in its effectiveness. If I am prevented by the force of censorship from ever hearing of the doctrine of nirvana, an important concept in one of the world's great religions, it is highly improbable that I shall ever develop any thoughts on that doctrine. By the same token, if Asiatics are prevented by force from ever hearing the Christian doctrine that Christ is a redeemer, they will never believe in that doctrine. And similarly if the publication of criticism of an existing religion can be prevented, its common acceptance can be made more secure.

Accordingly throughout history the adherents of particular religious creeds have sought the aid of censorship in support of their position. The assumed propriety of such censorship, accepted without question until recent times, no longer obtains, having retreated before the growth of western liberty. But we will be mistaken indeed if we suppose that the danger of such censorship does not constantly threaten, or if we fail to see evidences of such censorship about us.

A prevalent opinion, for example, is that motion pictures should be censored not only for indecency but also for offensive religious views. Pictures that treat a religious faith or a religious tenet with disrespect or ridicule should not be licensed to be shown, the belief is; and censorship boards in some of our cities have in fact recently refused to license the showing of pictures on the ground that they were offensive in their treatment of religious matters. But would anyone dare in the present age to urge a similar censorship of books? And if not of books, why of motion pictures? Or if censorship of the religious content of pictures be allowed, must not the same censorship be applied to books? Both are forms of communication, and in so far as they treat of religious matters they are forms of religious communication, and the same principles of liberty apply to each. Books may offend the adherents of various religious faiths, and so may motion pictures, but censorship for that reason is no more justified in the one case than in the other. The expression of religious opinion, whether it be by way of praise or ridicule, and whether it be direct or oblique, must be kept free from the evil of censorship if religious liberty is to prevail.

But books and magazines are also beginning to come again under a religious censorship exercised by officials of the state. Pursuant to the urging of various religious groups, it is becoming an accepted principle of some public school boards not to purchase for the school libraries books or magazines which are offensive to the religious views of particular faiths. Some boards of public libraries are taking the same position. This is censorship, not the censorship of complete prohibition but the censorship of effective interference with the communication of religious views. It uses the taxing power of the state to encourage the approval of accepted creeds and to discourage criticism of them. The force of the state is thus employed to influence religious thought by impeding religious communication.

It is true, of course, that school and library boards cannot purchase all the books and magazines published; there must be selection. But the principles upon which selection is made by these public bodies must not include the suitability of the religious opinions expressed. Without attempting to define the principles to be observed in selection, we can assert that religious conformity must never be one of them. The assumption, which seems to be growing at the present time, that religious conformity is in fact a proper criterion in spending public money for literature can become a serious threat to religious liberty, not only by impairing the freedom of communicating religious ideas but also by breaching the structure of logic that supports religious liberty as a whole. For if this mode of censorship of books by the state be accepted, it is not a far step to the acceptance of other censorship and ultimately of all censorship. The force of the state, whether embodied in school boards, library directors, or motion picture censors, is never properly used to obstruct the communication of religious views. Religious communication must be allowed complete freedom in the society of liberty.

What shall we say, however, of the expression of religious views that involve a disobedience to existing law? The problem may be illustrated by two examples. Some Quakers believe that man violates the will of

God by taking part in armed conflict under any circumstances, and that military service is a sin. Should Quakers be permitted to communicate this belief, and to preach the religious duty of avoiding military service, though the laws provide for such service? The Catholic church, as another example, holds that marriage is a sacrament and indissoluble, and that to disregard the relation so created, except as may be authorized by the church, is a sin, an offense against the will of God. But most of our states permit divorce and remarriage on terms which the Catholic church holds to be sinful. Some of the judges of the various state courts, before whom divorce cases must come, are Catholics, and some of the litigants seeking divorces are Catholics. Should Catholics be permitted to communicate to judges the religious concept that it is their duty to refuse to grant divorces though litigants be entitled thereto under state laws? Some Catholics teach this today, even as some Quakers teach pacifism.

The problem thus presented may be stated as follows: Does liberty require that people be free to teach or communicate the concept that there is a religious obligation to disobey an existing law?

We are here confronted with the necessity for compromise in a sharp form. No solution is possible which does not bring with it serious disadvantages. If we deny liberty of communication we bar an important area to the exercise of human will in thought and discourse. If on the other hand we permit the teaching of disobedience as religious duty, we render law enforcement, to which the law itself commits us, the more difficult, and thereby place ourselves in the anomalous position of insisting on one thing—obedience to the law—while permitting advocacy of its opposite—disobedience.

It is sometimes supposed that the solution to the present question is contained in allowing advocacy of a change in law, but prohibiting advocacy of disobedience. But this is a denial of the liberty to communicate the concept of religious disobedience. It does not meet the matter but seeks to avoid it. The question of the privilege of advocating peaceful changes in law presents no great problem; liberty clearly demands it and all societies that have pretended to a liberal constitution have allowed it. The problem of the advocacy of religious disobedience is something else.

The difficulty in the matter must be recognized; nevertheless the principles of liberty seem rather strongly to favor permitting the free advocacy of the duty to disobey a law on religious grounds. In the first place, such communication of ideas does not involve force; no one is deprived of choice to heed or not to heed such teaching. To that extent, then, the growth of human character by self-decision is not impaired but furthered. In the second place, the development of sound laws will be more helped than hindered by such discussion. If some human being feels so strongly that a social rule contravenes the will of God that he is willing to accept the penalty for disobedience, let us hear what he has to say. The time is short enough for us to correct our errors, without willfully impeding the possibility of information. Americans should never forget that their institutions were molded and given their American stamp by men who believed that to preach religious disobedience could be not only a right but a duty, and that no small part of the intellectual ferment in which their culture obtained its great beginning came out of complete freedom of religious communication, even to preaching disobedience.

What then constitute religious grounds for advocating disobedience, or should any limits be placed on the assertion of such grounds? It seems clear that no limits are required. If anyone wishes to make a preposterous claim for a religious reason for disobedience, let him do so. If anyone wishes to teach that it is a sin to observe the speed laws, the thing will fall of its own weight.

Do the principles of liberty accordingly place us in the position of permitting the advocacy of unlawfulness but prohibiting unlawfulness itself? The answer is yes. But does not this make the enforcement of law more difficult? The answer again is—probably—yes. This is a cost of the liberal society. The compromises of liberty must sacrifice the lesser to the greater good and the smaller to the more complete logic.

3. Liberty of religious acts

Religious acts include religious worship and the performance of other deeds believed to possess peculiar religious significance.

The philosophy of liberty calls for the freedom of the individual to perform such religious acts as he chooses, subject only to the general limitation that he refrain from impairing the equal liberty of all. So clear is this principle in its application to religious acts that no serious difficulty arises in applying it once the correctness of the theory of liberty as a basic tenet for society is accepted.

Thus all forms of religious worship, both private and public, must be permitted on equal terms in the liberal society.

It is sometimes thought that the public worship services of an unpopular and minority group, whose rites may be made the occasion of disorder directed against them, can properly be suppressed or required to be conducted privately in the interest of tranquillity. In a few South American cities rioting has recently taken place against minority-group chapels, which have been stoned and damaged. Should religious services of minorities be forbidden, at least in public, in order that the peace may not be disturbed? Is it not clear, however, that the rioting rather than the services constitutes the activity to be prevented by the force of the state? Minority services do not impair the religious liberty of the majority nor their liberty in any other manner. Religious services should always be protected from interference by others, whether the services are those of a minority or majority group.

An opposite error is to suppose that religious services are entitled to an extra indulgence at the hands of others, to greater privileges than are accorded to secular acts. Thus it may be supposed that religious publications should be permitted to be sold on streets and in public places without complying with such rules as society may impose on the sale of secular publications in streets and public places. Or it may be thought that religious meetings are entitled to greater privileges in the use of public buildings and places than are other meetings. But the allowance of this proposition would be the denial of religious liberty rather than its affirmance. Liberty is not extended to religious acts because of any extra regard for human acts that are religious, but because of an equal regard for all human acts when they do not impair the equal liberty of action of others. Religious acts do not stand, therefore, on any higher footing than other human acts, in so far as their claim to freedom is concerned. They must at all times submit to the same limitation of equality of freedom that is applicable to all acts, religious and secular alike. For religious liberty cannot be justified as an isolated principle, but only as a part of the larger theory of liberty for the whole of human life.

4. Separation of church and state

The liberty of religious thought, communication, and acts being as above delineated, a requisite to maintaining that liberty is the separation of church and state.

The word separation as used in this well-established phrase is somewhat unfortunate, although no better word seems available. It suggests a more complete cleavage between religious and political activity than is possible. Not infrequently opponents of religious liberty think to refute the argument for the separation of church and state by showing that separation in the complete sense is impossible, whence it is suggested that the whole aim is false. But the doctrine of the separation of church and state does not call for complete insulation of the two organizations. On the contrary the liberty of the church depends upon the laws of the state, and religious freedom can obtain only where social rules preserve it. Separation of church and state means the use of the force of the state to maintain liberty in religious experience for all, and the abstention from the use of force to compel any form of religious experience. It is in this very important sense, but in this sense alone, that church and state must be kept separate in the liberal society.

When we examine history, we find that religious liberty has appeared only when church and state have been separated; and that when they have not been separated, religious liberty has not been present. Religious liberty, indeed, is hard to find in the historical record. We suppose the religious liberty we today enjoy in the United States of America to be a natural thing, believing it scarcely could be otherwise. But in historical fact it is unique. It exists here because of the first amendment to our federal constitution and similar provisions in our several state constitutions, and because we have been blessed with federal and state supreme courts that have consistently interpreted the constitutional provisions to require a separation of church and state.

Why is the historical record as it is? Why is it that separation of church and state produces religious liberty, while the failure to maintain such separation results in the loss of religious liberty?

The answer is supplied by the principles we examined in Book One, particularly in Chapter 10. The state's intervention in religion must involve the use of force, since it cannot intervene in social affairs in any other way. When, therefore, the state is joined to any religious group, it uses its force to compel support of such religious group and so to use force is a repudiation of religious liberty.

The force of the state over its citizens being usually exerted through punishment and taxes, we find that it is for the most part through these channels that the state may use its force to preserve or destroy religious liberty, and that it is when the state refrains from using either imprisonment or taxes to procure a particular pattern of religious experience that the church and state are separated. For example, a law requiring attendance at a particular religious service, or at any religious service, or prohibiting attendance at a religious service, under pain of punishment for violation, would be use of the state's force to compel a form of religious experience. Likewise a use of taxes to support a church or religious school would be to compel all members of the community to join in the maintenance of a particular religious faith in which some of them might not believe. Each of these exertions of the force of the state would constitute an infraction of the principle that state and church should be kept separate. On the other hand, a law forbidding interference with religious services, under pain of punishment, and the use of taxes to employ police to guard religious services from intrusion by outsiders wishing to prevent it are examples of the use of force to preserve religious liberty by separating the state from the church.

Although we today enjoy separation of church and state to a remarkable degree, yet what shall we say about the ubiquitous laws that seek to enlist the force of the state in compelling observance of the Christian Sunday? There are few communities without ordinances restricting business and regulating amusements on Sunday, and it is probably safe to say that not a week goes by without enforcement of such ordinances somewhere through legal action. Yet in general all these laws are a violation of religious liberty, for Christians and non-Christians alike, compelling them by the force of the state to conduct their affairs in accordance with particular ritualistic tenets. Probably there are some of these laws that can be maintained on grounds apart from religious considerations, but most of them should be repealed, even as in many communities the good sense of the people leads them to disregard them anyway.

The question of the exemption from taxation of property used for religious purposes is interesting because it shows us again the balancing of claims that is involved in all social rules and therefore in liberty. This exemption from property taxes means that the taxes assessed on other parcels of property are that much the larger. If all the members of the community contributed to religious institutions in exactly the same proportions as they paid property taxes, the increased tax burden would be exactly offset by the smaller amount necessary to be contributed to sustain the religious institutions. But obviously this is not the case. Some have no interest in any religious institution, and therefore their increased tax bills constitute a compelled contribution to the maintenance of religious activities which they would choose not to support, did the state give them liberty to refuse. Thus far the argument indicates that religious liberty is being impaired by the exemption. But as always there is another side. Most persons believe that quite apart from their religious function churches serve a charitable function in their care for the poor, a cultural function in their educational activities, and a police function in that their influence is to decrease crime. These are proper concerns of the state. Cannot the state therefore subsidize institutions which assist it in these tasks, even though they are religious institutions? But subsidies are extremely dangerous, particularly when paid to religious institutions, because the criteria for their measurement are necessarily vague, and therefore the state is apt soon to be engaged in supporting one religion in preference to others. Moreover if one subsidy—that of tax exemption—is to be used, why not others, such as direct payments of cash? Yet it should be noted that the tax exemption is self-measuring, requiring no action by a state official for its computation, and roughly corresponds to the extensiveness of the activity of the religious institution.

In this conflict of considerations, it would seem that the balance slightly favors tax exemption of property directly used in religious activity, but that the exemption should be strictly limited to such property. The loss of religious liberty because of the tax exemption is probably more than offset by the liberty gained by the community through the nonreligious functions of the institutions, all such functions serving to enhance the liberty of particular citizens and to some extent of all citizens. The exemption, however, it would also appear, should be closely limited to property immediately utilized in religious work; it should not be extended to other property owned by religious organizations. Not only would this add substantially to the deprivation of the religious and economic freedom of all citizens other than the favored organizations, but it tends to the creation of sheltered groups within the community, who are cut off from many of the problems of the community as a whole and whose views and influence must be developed without immediate knowledge of those problems but with a bias in support of additional services through taxes, services which they share in enjoying but not in paying for.

Throughout history and continuing until the present day, the state has usually supported certain priests and chaplains with public funds. It is clear that under usual living conditions this is a violation of religious liberty, since it compels the citizen through taxes to propagate a creed in which he may or may not believe. We recognize this requirement of religious liberty quite generally today, and only under exceptional circumstances does the state support religious personnel. But what of the chaplains in the army, navy, and marine corps? Is their support by the state a justified exception? Without doubt the support of chaplains through taxes is an impairment of religious liberty. But would the refusal to support chaplains amount to a greater deprivation of religious liberty? Religious liberty involves the right to choose religious experience. But the young men of the armed forces are compelled by society to leave the environment in which such choice is possible and to enter one where religious experience would be largely impossible were not chaplains included in the military establishment. It would be better if the chaplains could be supported at private rather than public expense. But as a practical matter this seems very difficult. Chaplains must move with their troops and be subject to military orders if their services are to be available as they should be, and accordingly it would seem necessary to integrate them into the military establishment. Thus the religious liberty of all citizens is slightly impaired, that a much larger loss of religious liberty by the military personnel may be avoided. Again we see how the maintenance of liberty for all is the balancing of interests—not easy, but not impossible of accomplishment. Chaplains of course must be selected so that their representation of creeds corresponds to the proportions of different faiths in the troops, and the troops must have freedom to choose the creed, if any, to which they will attach themselves.

Perhaps the most important problem of religious liberty at the present time—certainly the most pressing—is presented by religious education. How far, if at all, should the state support or encourage religious education, and how far should the state be entirely separated from the religious activity of teaching religious concepts and creeds?

There is currently a widespread demand for formalized religious education. Many religious groups believe that religious teaching should be presented daily in close conjunction with secular subjects. To accomplish this end the parochial school, operated by religious personnel and explicitly teaching religious subjects and dogma, is an appropriate instrument. Other religious groups do not wish to use parochial schools, but wish to have religious education given in close conjunction with instruction in the public schools. For this purpose there have variously been proposals that the Bible be read or studied in public schools, that religious instruction be offered in public school buildings by teachers not compensated by public funds, and that students be excused from attendance at school during regular school hours to receive religious instruction on private premises and from private teachers.

Proponents of parochial schools do not wish to use the public school system, but from time to time they press for financial support, direct or indirect, for parochial schools from the state. If such support be given, it must come from tax money, which means money collected from all citizens by the force of the state. Many of these citizens, however, will not wish to assist in the spread of the religions thus subsidized. But the force of the state, if used for such purposes, would compel them to do so, would compel them to take part in supporting the activities and expansion of religions they do not believe in. This use of tax money to support any religious enterprise is always an impairment of liberty.

The same observations apply to the use of the public school plant or program in any way for purposes of religious instruction. The plant is constructed and the program maintained by tax money, that is, by the force of the state. Thus to use force to compel participation in religious development would be to destroy liberty.

On the whole the decisions of our courts on the separation of church and state have been admirable. They have been based on the sound proposition that our constitution requires that tax money must never be used to support religion.

5. A present threat to our religious liberty

But although our present separation of church and state is largely accepted by all our major religious groups, despite some voices of dissent, yet a danger of not inconsiderable dimensions is contained within the religious community itself in the sympathy of some of its members for collectivism in its economic application. This leaning toward economic collectivism can be found in branches of the Christian church throughout the western world. Free enterprise is condemned as selfish, and socialistic principles are directly or indirectly extolled as the guide to a better world.

To that portion of the Christian church which has become persuaded of the soundness of collectivistic principles in economic action the following questions should be put: If it is a good thing that the state should guide the economic experience of men, telling them what to do in order that they will be directed to doing that which is beneficial for all, why is it not likewise a good thing that the state should guide men in their religious experience, telling them what to do in order that they will be directed to doing that which is beneficial to all? Is not religious welfare as important to humanity as economic welfare? If therefore economic welfare requires social planning, why also does not religious welfare require social planning? If individual choice is bad in the economic realm, because it permits men to do evil, why is it not also bad in the religious realm, where it must also permit men to do evil? If the best results are achieved for men when they follow the planning of an official hierarchy in the task of making a living, why will not also the best results be achieved by their following the orders of an official hierarchy in the task of saving their souls? If submission to the orders of a few who make group plans is the right principle for human action in that portion of life which is economic, why is it not also the right principle for all of life, including that portion which is religious? In short, if the basic principle for six days in the week is to be that men shall do what they are told, why should it not also be the basic principle for the seventh day?

The answers to these questions are clear. Life is a unity, and the theory that denies liberty in one part of life must end by denying it in all parts.

It is the religious community itself which should examine the trend of its thinking. When it has done so, will it not see that its acceptance of collectivistic theory, to the extent that such acceptance has occurred, is based upon principles whose application must lead to the loss of liberty in religion as well as elsewhere?

Chapter 12

CULTURAL LIBERTY

1. Liberty of scientific thought

"Nevertheless it moves," legend tells us Galileo muttered as he arose from his knees after abjuring his Copernican heresy before the Inquisition in 1633. Perhaps he didn't say this. But the story dramatizes the fact that only a short while ago, subsequent indeed to the first colonies in this country, scientific thought in the western world was assumed to be subject to collective control.

We imagine that we have proceeded far from this intolerance of scientific freedom on the part of the individual, and indeed we have, but not as far as usually supposed. It is not very long since the legislature of one of our states sought to suppress by law the teaching of the theory of evolution; and though this law, since it sought only to supervise the public school curriculum and did not interfere with the right to teach evolution elsewhere, was not as inimicable to the principle of liberty as is often supposed, nevertheless it undoubtedly represented an intent identical with that of Galileo's inquisitors—to control by collective action the individual's scientific belief.

Such control of scientific thought is always a violation of liberty. Here the general principle is the same as elsewhere, that the individual should have the largest area for free action that is compatible with equal freedom for all. With respect to scientific thought, moreover, as with respect to religious thought, the principle involves no limitation whatsoever, and the freedom of the individual to hold such scientific opinions as he chooses should be complete. Science consists of hypotheses concerning the sequence of events in the natural world. The correctness of current hypotheses is always subject to varying degrees of uncertainty. Liberty is not concerned with the degree of uncertainty of a particular theory; and the individual's right to believe as he chooses must not be made dependent upon the contemporary consensus, which almost always is subsequently regarded as having been at least partially in error.

The liberty of scientific thought also includes the liberty of scientific investigation. Subject to such obvious limitations as that a laboratory giving off noxious fumes must not be located among residences, the freedom of the individual to engage in scientific investigation should be complete.

But in the light of this principle, what should we say about investigation and experimentation in the field of atomic energy? Should this be open to individuals or should it be limited to the state bureaucracy as at present? Obviously there are conflicting considerations requiring careful attention. On the one hand there is the demand of liberty that the individual be permitted to engage in such scientific activity as he chooses. On the other hand there is the demand of liberty that the physical well-being of individuals be not impaired or destroyed by the wrongful acts of others, whether those others be individuals within the same community or foreign nations bent on conquest. That is to say, the principles involved are the same as those concerned in the question of the laboratory giving off noxious fumes in a residential neighborhood; and whatever the resolution it must be a compromise denying liberty in one form that it may be achieved more abundantly in another. Perhaps the decision taken a few years ago to confine to the state's bureaucracy all scientific work in atomic fission was correct in the light of the situation as it then existed; but it seems probable that matters have now so changed as to make a continuance of the restriction incompatible with liberty. National safety—which means the safety of the individual citizens of the nation—no longer seems to be served to any appreciable extent, if at all, by the policy of restriction; and indeed it seems doubtful if that policy has been of any real service in the past, for it is now officially admitted that the Russians have obtained all the information necessary to build both A-bombs and H-bombs, which is no less than what they would have obtained had atomic investigation been kept completely open. It seems highly probable that as the situation involving atomic energy develops, it will be necessary, if liberty of science and enterprise is to be preserved, to discard the present state monopoly. The precise form of the relaxation we must leave to the future. The point for us to see is that liberty requires, subject only to the limitations and safeguards which liberty itself calls for to procure the equal liberty of all, the same scientific freedom in the field of atomic energy as in any other area of natural phenomena.

2. Liberty of scientific communication

The dissemination of scientific information stands in general on the same ground as scientific investigation; liberty requires freedom of such dissemination subject only to limitations imposed by countervailing considerations of liberty.

The main limitation arises from the fact that some scientific information is directly and chiefly concerned with substantial harm to others. For example, the knowledge of how to grow marijuana and make marijuana cigarettes can have as its primary object only the addiction to drugs, which by nearly universal consent is a matter of substantial harm, not only to the drug addict but also to others who are subjected to the danger of criminal action by the dope-affected person. The liberty to communicate information is therefore more than offset by the liberty of others to be free from the dangers of narcotic addiction. Accordingly the liberty to communicate such information must be denied, except to the extent, if any, that it is useful for medical purposes. All scientific information, of course, may be used for harmful purposes, for all injury to others and consequent impairment to their liberty is accomplished through physical means. But with respect to most science, this possible harm is a small incident when placed beside the main utility, and consequently the possibility of the harmful incident must be incurred that the liberty of communicating the main utility may be enjoyed. Where, however, harm is the main object to be accomplished, communication can rightfully be barred.

A current problem involving the question of scientific freedom is presented by the communication of scientific information on birth control. In some states giving such information is unlawful, subjecting the violator to criminal punishment. These laws are based on the belief that the practice of contraception is immoral or sinful. Since the object of the scientific communication is a wrongful act, it is believed that the communication itself should be blocked. From the standpoint of liberty, however, this overlooks two important facts: first, the great majority of people do not believe the practice of contraception wrong or harmful; and second, even for the minority who regard contraception as a sin, the communication of contraceptive information in no wise impairs their liberty. Accordingly a law prohibiting the communication of such information seriously impairs the liberty of a large majority of society, for it prevents them from choosing to make use of such information; and on the other hand it does not enhance the liberty of the minority, for they can choose not to use such information as well after it is communicated as before, their freedom of choice remaining unimpaired. The law consequently is an unmitigated violation of liberty, representing the attempt of a minority to impose by force its standard of conduct on the majority, in a matter where liberty requires, rather, freedom of individual choice.

Also illustrative of the principles here involved is the case of the communication of scientific information of a military character. Obviously the freedom of the individual is curtailed when he is forbidden to disclose such information. But the prohibition is based on other and countervailing considerations of liberty. Since individual freedom depends upon the maintenance of proper rules to that purpose by the community, it also depends upon the community's being free from outside interference which would render the maintenance of such rules difficult or impossible. History amply demonstrates how heavy is the task of preserving this essential freedom of the community, and how indispensable military measures are to its accomplishment. If therefore the secrecy of particular scientific information will contribute to group protection, the enforcement of such secrecy, with its limitation on the individual's liberty, is a small and justified price for the larger liberty of all which thereby is bargained for.

Except however for compromises of this nature, genuinely made in liberty's name because liberty itself demands them, the freedom of the individual person to disseminate scientific information, or what he believes to be scientific information, should be complete. The freedom to know is in large part the freedom to transmit and receive communication.

3. Liberty of artistic activity

Modern art, said Hitler, is decadent. And accordingly, since he wished no symptoms of decadence within his state, he forbade those modern artistic forms variously designated as impressionist, cubist, surrealist, and non-objective, and encouraged forms more traditional.

Collectivists of today probably do not for the most part agree with Hitler's artistic preference, for since they suppose their philosophy to be a break with the past, they like to emphasize this imagined newness by favoring art which seems also to represent an innovation. But their philosophy does not permit them to quarrel seriously with his method of guiding artistic activity. Art is important, and if life is to be controlled in its important manifestations by the planning of the state, then art expression should be included.

The logical development of this collectivistic viewpoint is seen in Russia, where it is appreciated that art forms both reflect and influence the ideological assumptions by which a society lives, and where accordingly all art is subject to state control. The stage, ballet, opera, motion pictures, poetry, music, literature, all must conform to the approved state line. The press not so long ago carried the amazing report that a new symphony by Shostakovitch had been officially censured for reflecting bourgeois ideology.

We are disposed to think of this rigorous control as bizarre and as an example of Oriental despotism. In a sense this is correct, but we will delude ourselves if we do not recognize that it is also an entirely logical application of the basic collectivistic principle that social life must conform to a common pattern, devised and enforced by the state. Once liberty as social guide is abandoned, once there is a rejection of the principle that equal individual freedom is the first rule of social organization, there is no logical halting place until art as well as all else is directed by the bureaucracy of a Hitler or a Stalin.

Under liberty, of course, artistic expression is the result of the free choice of the individual. It symbolizes the individual artist's awe when confronted with the mysterious beauty of the universe, and it evokes appreciation in the beholder or listener because he too is made to feel the response of wonder. It is not a production to order, supporting a bureaucratic policy for social art, but a production of unique individual experience striving to span the gap between individual and universal spirit. Yet it is not a completely individualized product, an emanation solely of the artist; for it is a part of life and all life is self and not-self. Great art accordingly can be expected only in ages which by design or happy fortune balance the opposition of the self and not-self in liberty; and thus it is fifth century Athens, the Renaissance cities, and western Europe of the Liberal Age that astound us with their prolific flow of works of highest art.

It is sometimes thought that the artist should not only be free, as other citizens are, in the liberal society, but that he should enjoy a special kind of freedom which would enable him to produce objects of art without regard to the pleasure of others. He should obtain his living by grants from the state, rather than be dependent on sales to customers. It is true that at times in the past princes have been great patrons of all forms of artistic endeavor, and our present world is finer because of such patronage. But usually they have been wise enough to interpose their support as customers rather than as the grantors of pensions. It will be well if the matter remains so. And if the customers sometimes do not appear until too late, until after the time when a Van Gogh, a Gauguin, or a Whitman has need of their purchases, yet it is better to have it so than to submit artistic action to the dominance of the state.

Many artists of the present age suppose that they will enjoy complete artistic freedom in the collectivized society. Although quarrels frequently arise when they execute public commissions, their work being rejected as too modern, bizarre, grotesque, or unpleasant, they attribute this to the fact that it is a bourgeois society they are dealing with, imagining that when it becomes a socialist or communist state the improved taste of the public, agreeing with their own, will permit them to do as they artistically please. But the contrary must be the event. When the position of the state is fortified by the philosophy of collective conformity, it must become a more implacable customer-tyrant than ever before. The artist whose conceptions happen to blend with those who are in authority will imagine he is enjoying artistic freedom; but it will only be that he happens to tread the artistic path to which he was anyway officially assigned. The others will be without hope of patrons or customers and without hope of artistic life.

Nor will the collectivized state be wrong in patronizing only its own conception of art. The patron of art must favor what he believes is more beautiful; and the state, since it must act through its officials, can give effect only to the artistic taste of those officials. All artists creating for the state must satisfy their customer, for they cannot do otherwise, and this is true whether the state is that of the individualized or collectivized society. The error of the collectivistic state is not that it expresses its own tastes in art, but that it forces art completely into its dominion.

Of all forms of human action, art has the greatest need of liberty, for without liberty it cannot live, since its essence is individual emotion.

4. Academic freedom

The gregarious side of cultural activity finds expression in the development of schools. Throughout history schools have appeared, and no age has been more devoted to them than our own. We have schools for every interest of the mind and hand, and think that all problems will submit to schooling if only it be of the right sort.

Partly because of our exaggerated notion of the importance of formal schooling, the issue of academic freedom has currently become prominent. If cultural development through education looms so large, then the content of the educational process must be a considerable matter, it is thought, to be carefully and seriously determined. Accordingly the lodging of ultimate decision on the content and manner of teaching has come to assume large stature, and the question of academic freedom has moved prominently to the fore.

The question is essentially one of the identity of the persons who will decide the nature of the cultural development to be fostered in schools. Who shall settle the curriculum? Who shall decide the manner of teaching? Who shall determine whether the principles of communism, socialism, or individualism shall be expounded, and whether a belief in one or another social philosophy shall be inculcated? These are decisions which must be made by people, and not once for all time, but at recurrent intervals. The identity of these policy-fixing people being established, the matter is terminated so far as social organization is concerned. If the power of decision is delegated exclusively to the teachers and administrators of schools, the freedom of these academicians is very large; if other persons in the community are given a voice in policy determination, the freedom of the academicians assumes a more restrained form. The problem of academic freedom is thus a problem of the freedom of people to decide the course of education, and involves the freedom not only of educators but of other members of the community as well, for these several freedoms are interdependent.

Much of the present discussion of academic freedom, failing to penetrate to fundamental considerations, assumes that a distinctive privilege or status attaches to the teaching profession, authorizing it to exercise a freedom not available to other vocations. Under the principles of liberty this is clearly error. In the free society men and women who gain their livelihood by teaching are subject to precisely the same rules concerning freedom as are all other citizens, and the term academic freedom can properly indicate not any difference in basic principle, but only the application of the basic principle of liberty to particular circumstances. The teacher has no privilege of freedom of thought or action that impairs the equal liberty of others, and his freedom up to this point of limitation, though influenced in its character by the particular circumstances of the teacher's profession, is yet the same in its essence and framework as it is for all other persons.

What are the circumstances which give rise to the questions of liberty peculiar to the academic realm? The answer to this question, when analyzed and considered in the light of the imperative of liberty, will furnish us the correct principles of academic freedom.

The teacher, like all other members of the community, acts in two capacities—in a general capacity as individual citizen and in a specialized capacity as the practitioner of a vocation. The circumstances affecting these two capacities differ, and failure to keep in mind this difference leads to confusion.

As citizen the teacher has the same general problem of the conflict and cooperation embedded in the social relation as have all other citizens. The resolution of the intellectual and economic conflict must be made for the teacher as citizen in the same general way as for all other citizens, and in consequence the liberty of the teacher in his capacity as citizen is the same as the liberty of all other citizens, no less and no more.

In his capacity as teacher, however, he enters into two relations which, while broadly resembling corresponding relations in other walks of life, are nevertheless peculiar to his profession. The first is his relation with the students whom he instructs, and the second is his relation with those who employ him, paying him the money which constitutes his livelihood. Each of these relations involves the interest of the opposite party to the relation, and therefore each relation involves also the liberty of the opposite party.

The teacher-student relation is concerned with the act of instruction, and instructing and learning are its content. The teacher has an interest in instructing, and freedom for the teacher in instructing consists in the act of choice, by the teacher, of the subject matter and method of instruction. The student on the other hand has an interest in learning, and freedom for the student in learning consists in the act of choice, by the student, of the subject matter and method of learning. Passing momentarily the problem presented by the student's possible immaturity, it is obvious that these interests and freedoms may clash. The teacher may wish to teach French while the student wishes to learn Spanish, or the teacher may wish to teach socialism while the student wishes to learn history. Or, not to present the conflict in a simple and unusual form but in a subtle and common one, the teacher may wish to inject into his teaching suggestions and assertions that collectivism

is desirable, whereas the student may wish to learn without the inculcation of collectivistic or any other doctrine.

The educators speaking most insistently today for the academic freedom of the teacher seldom if ever mention or consider the academic
freedom of the student; indeed it is apparent that for the most part they
are oblivious to the existence of such an aspect of academic freedom.
But is the teacher the only person in the teacher-student relation whose
liberty is involved? Since the student as well as the teacher is a human
being sharing in the universal life purpose, is not academic freedom an
important thing for him also? How then shall the freedom of both
teacher and student be accommodated?

It may be accommodated by allowing the teacher-student relation to
be created by mutual agreement. When the teacher and student can
agree on what shall be learned and taught, the educational relation
will be created, but not otherwise. To reach such an agreement one
side or both may make concessions, but these will be chosen in order
to secure the advantage of the relation and will not be compelled.
This method is in fact employed almost exclusively in our colleges
and universities today. No student is compelled to accept the instruction of a particular institution, but he may apply to the one whose
curriculum he prefers, and likewise no institution is compelled to
offer particular instruction which a student may prefer, but it may
offer such subject matter and method of teaching as it chooses. The
student must conform to a school's course of study once he has enrolled;
but if he finds there that which he dislikes he may leave; and in fact
transfers from one college to another are very common. Thus in our
higher institutions of learning the academic freedom of both teacher
and student is well observed by the present system in so far as the
student-teacher relation is concerned.

Before proceeding further with this relation, let us turn to the teacher-
employer relation. Here also there may be conflict of interest and attendant clash in the desire for freedom of action, and indeed it is in
this relation that the sharpest opposition may occur.

Who is the employer? In a private school, college, or university it is
the corporation which owns and operates the institution. In a public
school, college, or university it is the state, acting usually through a
municipal corporation set up by the state for the purpose, such as a
school board or a board of trustees. In either case the teacher has an
employer by whom he is paid and who has an interest in the operation
of the school. In the case of the public institutions, further, the cor-

porate employer includes all those persons who are compelled by taxation to furnish the money for the teacher's compensation.

The teacher and the employer may differ on the desirable method of operation of the institution, and such differences may touch on any phase of the operation from curriculum to teachers' qualifications, and whenever such oppositions arise they involve liberty. If the teachers in a public school wish to use the educational methods frequently designated as progressive education, whereas the citizens in the district wish direct instruction in the three R's instead, freedom on each side is involved. The teachers' freedom concerns their choosing the instructional method and curriculum they themselves shall use; the citizens' freedom concerns their choosing the instructional method and curriculum they themselves shall pay for.

Here again the proponents of the freedom of teachers to do as they themselves choose always speak as though only the freedom of the teachers were involved. Under such an assumption, any attempt on the part of the employer—citizens, school board, or board of trustees—to determine educational questions becomes automatically, of course, an invasion of academic freedom. But the assumption is wrong. Academic freedom includes the freedom of those whose efforts supply educational funds as well as the freedom of those whose efforts supply educational discipline; and if it should be desired for any reason to restrict the term academic freedom to the freedom of teachers, excluding therefrom all other freedoms of the educational process, yet this would be only a matter of semantics, for the freedom of the employers, by whatever name called, still would demand consideration. An appreciation of this fact is imperative to a correct solution of the problem of academic freedom. That solution, then, must be a resolution between the freedom of the teacher and the freedom of the employer whereby each freedom is accommodated in so far as possible without impairing equal liberty. Obviously if the teacher determines all questions the employer is left without freedom, and if the employer determines all questions the teacher is left without freedom.

In the free society the dividing line between the two freedoms must be established by agreement between the teacher and the employer, and where a meeting of the minds cannot be arrived at, the teacher-employer relation should not be established, neither the one party nor the other being pressured by social rules into entering into an arrangement not desired. This solution, in fact, is more honored in practice than in accepted theory. The vaguely accepted theory is that educational institutions should be run by teachers as they choose, the freedom of the employer being to furnish money. The teachers are experts, they say, and employers, when they express views, are castigated as self-appointed and incompetent critics. But although the employers tend to acquiesce in this position in theory, yet in practice they exercise some freedom and influence. The teacher-employer relation is to some extent made dependent on standards not advocated by the teachers themselves, and occasionally the employer refuses to effect or continue the relation because of a failure of the teacher to meet a condition imposed by the employer.

The theory that only the freedom of the teacher is involved, vis-à-vis the employer, is however a complete repudiation of equal liberty in society. The teacher may indeed be an expert in education and frequently is such, but it is not the import of the doctrine of liberty that we should turn the direction of our lives over to experts, never choosing for ourselves. We should seek the advice of experts; that is wisdom on our part. But we should follow that advice only as it persuades us of its reasonableness; that too is wisdom on our part. To abrogate our duty of decision, placing control of our affairs in a few experts, is not the message of liberty but of collectivism, and it destroys human character instead of building it.

The free society must therefore attempt to preserve freedom of entry into the teacher-employer relation. It should be a matter of mutual agreement, and wanting such agreement there should not be an attempt to force the relation. The decision of an employer on an educational problem may be ever so unwise—as indeed may be the decision of a teacher—but such want of wisdom is neither in the one case nor the other a violation of academic freedom, being rather an assertion of it. Academic freedom is violated, in the teacher-employer relation, when either party is compelled by law to enter into the relation unwillingly, when the employer is compelled by law to take a teacher he does not want, or the teacher is compelled by law to accept employment he does not desire.

Let us now return to the teacher-student relation and consider the problem presented by the possible immaturity of the student. Maturity and immaturity are of course relative and thereby sometimes difficult to determine, but they are for all that biological facts with which we are compelled to deal, and we constantly do so. Where the student has reached such maturity as in common practice qualifies him to choose for himself (to be determined by an arbitrary rule of age if no other criterion is consented to) no problem of immaturity is presented, and the conflict of the teacher-student relation becomes simply one of the teacher's choice against the student's choice. But where the student is immature, he is not competent to choose for himself. His conduct in learning must nevertheless be decided by someone. His acts in the process of learning are subject to human decision; he must study one or another subject, under one or another set of conditions. Since he cannot choose for himself, someone must and will choose in his behalf. By a process of elimination, the only proper person to choose for him is his parent or parents, or wanting a parent, someone standing *in loco parentis* by custom or law. The teacher is not a proper person to decide for the child because of the possible conflict between the teacher's convenience and the child's welfare, a conflict which is not only possible, but, life being what it is, probable. If then the teacher represents the student in determining the problems of the teacher-student relation, the student in fact has no representation at all; for the teacher's decision must be the teacher's choice and therefore cannot be the student's choice, the student thus being left without choice and so without an exercise of freedom in his behalf. To preserve, then, the immature student's right to free choice in his interest, he must have representation independent of the teacher, and this is supplied by the parent. Accordingly where the student is immature, the teacher-student relation becomes a teacher-student-parent relation, the student's essential freedom being exercised in his behalf by his parent. The parent thus has an interest in the educational process, in the assertion of which he must exercise freedom. This freedom is a part of academic freedom, to be respected and preserved in the society of liberty equally with the academic freedom of teachers.

It was pointed out above that in private schools, colleges, and universities the teacher-student relation is the product of agreement, and that this process of agreement retains the academic freedom both of the teacher and of the student. To a limited extent this maintenance of freedom through agreement is also possible with respect to the public schools. If the student or his parent is dissatisfied for any reason with the teaching presented in one public school, it is sometimes possible to attend another, and it may also be possible to consider a private school as an option. Catholic students and their parents, for example, who do not like the nonreligious teaching of the public school, can usually find a parochial school where they can effect the teacher-student relation with Catholic teachers who will include religious doctrine in their instruction. This flexibility, offering students and their parents freedom of choice in establishing the teacher-student relation, is as it should be.

But for a large body of students optional modes of education are not possible. Their parents do not have the means to send them to private schools and choice between different public schools is not available. Here the student has no opportunity to express his academic freedom by withdrawing from a disliked teacher-student relation; he must accept the teacher made available to him by the public school system. So far as his status as student is concerned his educational preferences can be expressed only through attempts at persuasion, exerted by himself or his parents. He has, however, another avenue of influence. He or his parents constitute part of the corporate employer, and through the teacher-employer relation may exercise the influence of choice in a manner impossible through the teacher-student relation. Parents who wish their children to have better teachers may not be able, within the public school system, to accomplish this result by withdrawing their children from one teacher and placing them with another; but as employers who have a voice in designating the school board they may nevertheless exercise their freedom of choice by bringing about the employment of desirable and competent teachers.

Turning more particularly to the academic freedom of teachers, this is preserved so long as teachers have choice of the teacher-employer and teacher-student relations which they will enter into. In general this academic freedom is well maintained in our land today, but dangers constantly threaten it, and we need to know what these dangers are in order to guard against them.

One danger is the prescription by law of the content of the teacher-student relation. Most states in the Union, perhaps all, have laws making certain instruction mandatory, such as courses in English, American history, and the like. There are numerous valid points in favor of these laws, and without doubt they have exercised, at least for a time, a salutary effect on many school systems. But over the longer term their influence must be debilitating. They substitute the dead judgment of the past for the living judgment of the present. Though the educational system's direct product is knowledge, yet its ultimate aim is good human character, and this is not promoted by removing the element of decision from the educational process. It is the act of choice in the environment of the present that builds character. Men indeed need standing rules to live by, but only, as we have seen, to the extent that liberty requires; and laws prescribing curricula and methods pass beyond that limitation.

Strangely it is the teachers, whose freedom is most adversely affected, who have usually been the leaders in requesting such legislation. Unduly persuaded of the permanency of their current pedagogical beliefs, representatives of teachers' organizations have sought to have them imbedded in law, that all might be made to conform. Thus the choice of the teacher is removed and he can thereafter only follow the mandate of the statute. But the teacher is the one most concerned about teaching materials and methods, and in practice he usually has the most influence in determining courses of action. Yet by legal prescription he destroys his own academic freedom.

This is not to say that the state cannot properly have a voice in the decisions necessary to determine what shall be taught and how. On the contrary, it is the necessary implication of what has already been said that where the state is the teacher's employer, it can and should, as such employer, take part in determining the educational process. But it should do so only as such employer and only in connection with particular employment. That is, it should participate in the determination of educational policy only in public institutions and not in private ones, and it should undertake such participation only at the level where employment occurs and through the state agency handling the employment. Thus the state's participation in educational policy should be through school boards or other governing bodies of particular schools, and by *ad hoc* decisions attempting to meet changing conditions and needs, rather than through fixed ordinances. Neither the school board nor the teachers can properly claim the right to dominate the decisions necessary to carry on educational activity; they must recognize the theoretical as well as the practical necessity of the give and take of agreement. If the school board cannot persuade particular teachers to accede to its wishes, it must find others, if it can, who will do so, or failing that it must make such practical accommodation as is possible. By the same token, if the teachers cannot persuade the board to accede to their wishes and follow their advice, they must try, if they can, to find other boards more favorably disposed, or failing that they must make such practical accommodation as they can, either within or without the teaching profession.

The collectivists within the educational world, and they are many and vocal, do not like the freedom of individualistic philosophy as it works itself out in academic life. Though they speak much of academic freedom, yet what they have in mind turns out to be, on examination, a rigid state system of education, where a few enjoy a great deal of freedom but the many have no freedom at all. This produces a well-ordered and smoothly operating educational system, where the plans of those who direct the organization are efficiently carried out, but it rots the characters of all who participate, teachers and students alike, and its end is national decay.

A second danger to the academic freedom of the teacher is that the teacher-employer relation will be prescribed by law, in details which should, under liberty, be left to the decisions of the parties directly concerned. Currently the problem here involved is being raised by statutes prohibiting the employment of teachers who teach subversive doctrines or who belong to organizations advocating the overthrow of the existing government by force, and by statutes requiring oaths of loyalty or other tests to determine the fitness of teachers on the basis of their adherence to the present form of social organization.

We must here distinguish, if we are to understand this problem correctly, between the teacher in his capacity as citizen and in his capacity as teacher. As citizen, his freedom of political thought should be governed by precisely the same rules as obtain in the case of all other citizens. This matter of the freedom of political thought for citizens, qua citizens, we shall examine in the next chapter.

It is frequently supposed that this should be the end of the question; that if, for example, citizens generally are not prohibited from being members of the Communist party, then this should not be made a disqualifying circumstance for teachers, and that if citizens generally are not required to take loyalty tests, then neither should teachers. Accordingly all legislation of this character peculiarly for application to teachers is regarded as subject to condemnation without further consideration.

But this view overlooks a fundamental aspect of the matter. The qualifications of a citizen are different from the qualifications of a teacher. That which qualifies one as a citizen does not qualify one as a teacher, and indeed the very exercise of the rights of a citizen may serve to disqualify one as a teacher. For example, it is undoubtedly the privilege of a citizen to be ignorant and habitually to be dirty and unkempt, but the exercise of such privilege, while it would not disqualify him as a citizen, would in all communities disqualify him as a teacher. An analogous problem was presented not long since by two Chicago policemen who refused to testify before a grand jury on the ground that their testimony might serve to incriminate them. Being thereupon discharged from the police force, they sought to compel their reinstatement by court action, alleging that they had done no more than avail themselves of the constitutional privilege of all citizens to refuse to testify against themselves. The Supreme Court of Illinois, however, denying their plea, pointed out that while they undoubtedly had a constitutional right, under our constitutional provisions for the protection of personal liberty, to refuse to testify against themselves, yet they did not have a constitutional right to be policemen. Their employment in that role depended in part on considerations other than their qualifications as citizens, and their very exercise of their privilege as citizens in this particular showed their lack of qualification to be policemen. It is likewise with the employment of teachers. The principles of liberty do not prevent the employer of a teacher from considering the manner in which the teacher has exercised his liberty as a citizen; on the contrary that exercise of liberty is a pertinent fact which may indicate the qualification or disqualification of the teacher for his job, and the consideration of that exercise does not call in question the teacher's academic freedom but only his professional fitness.

The refusal of a school board, therefore, to employ a teacher who is a communist is not a denial of the academic freedom of the teacher, but an assertion of the academic freedom of the board to believe that membership in the Communist party is an undesirable attribute for the person who is to fill a particular teaching position. This does not mean that the teacher cannot continue to be a communist; it means that the board cannot be forced to continue the employment of a communist as teacher, and that the particular teacher cannot establish a teacher-employer relation unless he can find a school board desirous of employing a communist as teacher.

In this freedom of decision by the school board, the question of the wisdom of its choice is not involved. Liberty extends to unwise as well as to wise choice; the privilege of doing only that which is decided to be wisest is not freedom but slavery. Therefore, the problem of academic freedom as it is being raised by current attempts of employers, be they the governing boards of public or private schools, to bar communists as teachers, is not concerned with the wisdom of such acts but only with whether they fall within the area of the employers' proper freedom of action. That they do so is clear. To hold otherwise would be to destroy the academic freedom of the employer. A school board should be no more bound to employ a teacher whose professed intention is to use the schools to propagate communism than it should be bound to employ a teacher whose professed intention is to use the schools to propagate Buddhism or other religious creed.

But if the employer should not be required to accept the communist as a teacher, should he on the other hand be required to reject him? It is such automatic rejection that some state statutes are designed to accomplish, prohibiting the employment of communists as teachers. From the standpoint of academic freedom such statutes are objectionable on principles already discussed. They remove an element of decision from the formation of the teacher-employer relation, instead of leaving that decision with the parties immediately concerned. If a school board wishes to employ a communist as teacher—perhaps only for a special purpose, although not necessarily with such limitation—and if the teacher wishes to accept such employment, academic freedom demands that they be permitted to enter into the teacher-employer relation.

There is, however, an opposed consideration which we must note, attached to political liberty rather than to academic freedom. As we shall see in the next chapter, the problem of attempted revolution permits of only one disposition. The liberal society, as well as any other, must oppose change of its own organization by forcible means, and indeed this doctrine is particularly applicable to the society of liberty, which permits change by peaceful action of the majority, thereby making forcible endeavor automatically the action of a minority. This being so, may the free society properly prohibit the teaching of revolution by force, as well as prohibit such revolution itself? This is a close question, involving risk to liberty whichever way it is answered. My own preference is for resolving the conflict in favor of avoiding a prohibition of such teaching, for reasons which I shall indicate in the succeeding chapter. If this view be adopted, then the employment of communists as teachers should not be prohibited as a matter of law, for the objection to them is that they teach revolution, which teaching law should not bar. But if it be decided that the danger to political liberty from permitting such teaching is greater than the danger from prohibiting it, then the statutory prohibition of employing communist teachers is an appropriate implementation of that decision.

But it is undesirable that other qualifications of teachers should be set by law. The state through its laws is at present violating this principle and restricting the freedom of teachers by setting up obligatory qualifications which must be met before employment can be obtained. Yet the teachers should bear in mind that it is they themselves who have urged the state thus to limit them. Representatives of teachers have usually been the ones who have asked the state to take from teachers and school boards the power of decision in areas of qualification and to fix qualifications by statute. By the same token, if and when teachers decide they and their employers should be free to determine qualifications as the question of employment arises, they can probably obtain without much difficulty the repeal of these laws requiring specific educational and other qualifications. If, however, they prefer the retention of these statutes, they can scarcely object on grounds of academic freedom if the state also decides to include non-communism as a qualification.

It may be said, however, that the state prescribes qualifications for doctors, lawyers, and other professions; why not therefore also for teachers? But the original and proper reason for such statutory qualifications in certain vocations is to protect the public, who deal with the members of these professions and yet have no adequate opportunity, acting individually, to ascertain their qualifications. This proper reason has been supplemented in recent times by certain improper ones, all violations of liberty, which have extended statutory regulation beyond its correct sphere. Among these has been a desire to compel improvement, or what has been thought to be improvement, in the level of vocational performance. This has been the asserted motive for seeking statutory regulation of teachers' qualifications. But it violates liberty by taking from teachers and employers the privilege of decision. And no need for protecting the public exists with respect to teachers. For they do not make their vocational contracts in numerous small dealings with the public, under circumstances which make it difficult for their qualifications to be ascertained, but with school boards or trustees who have ample opportunity to make such ascertainment and who customarily do so. The purpose of these statutes, then, is not to protect the public by a police regulation, but to submit academic activity to the supposed beneficent influence of collective planning.

Our discussion may be summarized by saying that academic freedom is the product of applying the general principles of liberty to the particular circumstances of the teacher-employer relation and of the teacher-student relation. The aim of social rules should be to preserve the largest equal liberty of teachers, employers, students, and parents, without aggrandizing the freedom of any one party at the expense of the freedom of the others. Therefore the formation of the teacher-employer and teacher-student relations should be left to voluntary agreement without the interference of social rules fixing the relations' content. When these basic principles are once understood and adhered to, all aspects of the problem of academic freedom find their correct solution.

5. Cultural liberty and collectivism

A vast gulf separates the respective attitudes of individualism and collectivism toward cultural liberty, and their divergent positions here illuminate, perhaps as well as in any other field, the basic opposition of these philosophies in their programs for human living.

Under individualism, cultural development is regarded as the growth of the individual in ways determined by his own choices, subject always to such restrictions as are necessary to insure a like privilege to others. Individualism is not itself concerned with the manner of cultural development which takes place within the liberty so established; as a philosophy of social organization its directives terminate with the formation of areas of individual freedom; and it is an essential part of its creed that beyond this point the directives of society should not go. The way of cultural growth is primarily a way of individual determination, becoming social only as a composite built under the interhuman influence of inspiration, but never determined by the influence of force.

It is here that collectivism must necessarily and decisively part from individualism. As we have heretofore noted, the essence of collectivism is its insistence on conformity of individual conduct to a group plan, for without such insistence it ceases to be collectivism. If therefore any form of cultural activity seems important to the group, it must be dominated by the group, which means that it must be dominated by the few who originate and enforce the group's program. But all forms of cultural activity, if they possess any importance for human life at all, must seem to have some importance for the group, and therefore must sooner or later come within the dominance of the group and its leaders. Collectivistic advocates may represent that in the societies of socialism and communism the individual will be truly free to pursue cultural development; but in practice this can never be so. Under collectivism the individual can be free to pursue only those lines of cultural development that are permitted by the official program, for if he should be allowed to range beyond this, following his own bents, not collectivism but individualism would be the practiced creed.

This collectivistic approach to cultural activity can be seen in the recent development of official American history and official historians. It seems that we should all think alike concerning the history of the past few years. But if any historian who wishes to concern himself should have access to the official records, how could such uniformity be achieved? We are therefore to have no self-appointed historians prying into the facts, but only officially appointed ones, to whom exclusively the archives are being opened. Accordingly there are appearing official volumes of history, written by official historians, who have an advantage of examination of documents denied to other historical researchers. Viewed from the position of collectivism, this is the desired unity of group cultural action; viewed from the individualistic position, however, it is the debasement of scholarship.

The collectivistic point of view toward culture is also apparent in the reaction of the left wing in American educational circles to current criticism of certain educational practices. Much of this criticism has come from parents and others who are not teachers, and the criticism has questioned the efficacy of so-called progressive educational methods. Within the philosophy of individualism this criticism is not only proper as an exercise of cultural liberty but is to be welcomed as an evidence of wide interest in educational matters. But to the left-wingers this is an impossible viewpoint. Citizens should acquiesce without criticism, they assert, in the educational program designed for the community by the experts. Citizens who presume to raise questions are castigated as "self-appointed critics," who should be silenced, if not by force then by torrents of abuse. The use of this phrase "self-appointed critics" as a term of derogation is revelatory of the entire collectivistic position on culture. In the collectivized society there will be no self-appointed critics.

These recent occurrences in history and education are in accord with the basic viewpoint of collectivism, which must always seek to compel the individual to mold his cultural ways to the group design. There are of course details of cultural expression to which the collectivistic state can afford to be indifferent, but the minute regulation of all aspects of cultural activity in Russia informs us that they are not many or important. However much the collectivist may protest and may indeed sincerely believe that he is interested in accomplishing freedom of cultural development for all people, yet his basic philosophical position, which is as well a basic psychological attitude, prevents him from ever arriving at this result. He knows what is best for others; it is this which he always imagines will be embodied in the group plan; and to this group plan the individual must bow; else there will be no group plan in action. This attitude, from which collectivism can never escape, always erupts into manifestation whenever a practical difficulty is presented. This is why the collectivists in the fields of history and education are currently intolerant of criticism and critics, and why they must always exhibit the same attitude in all areas of culture.

To individualism this entire approach to the problems of cultural life is anathema. Everyone, within the philosophy of individualism, is rightly a self-appointed critic of the entire scene around him; that is an integral part of his very purpose of existence, for his self-development can take place only as he subjects the phenomena within which he moves to comparison and critical analysis. He is divinely appointed, as well as self-appointed, to be a critic. Therefore his uncritical acceptance of a group cultural program, sponsored by the state, which to the collectivist presents the attraction of orderly group activity, to the individualist is surrender of the prerogative and duty of spiritual growth. It is in the free striving of individual persons, the individualist believes, as they each seek to build a culture of the spirit, that is to be found the good, the beautiful, and the true.

Chapter 13

LIBERTY OF POLITICAL THOUGHT

We are concerned in this chapter with the application of the principles of liberty to political thought and its communication. The application of liberty to forms of political action we shall consider later.

1. Freedom of political thought

The same principle applies to political thought as is applicable to the forms of thought examined in the two preceding chapters. Liberty demands that the individual have complete freedom to think such political thoughts as he chooses.

Here, again, the general principle is not only the first step to a clear understanding of the problem involved, but is also the base upon which other forms of political liberty must rest. If freedom of political thought be recognized, then it follows that the citizen has a right to receive political information and the right to be free from officially sponsored propaganda; but if freedom of political thought be denied, then the citizen has no ground upon which to base a claim to these rights.

The basic principle of freedom of political thought has, in fact, seldom been recognized in the past by those in political authority who, on the contrary, have usually conceived it their privilege to use the force of the state to mold the political thought of the people over whom they have ruled. Accordingly throughout history governments have sought to control political thought in order to keep it favorable to their regimes. This they have done by forcibly censoring the political information received by their citizens and by using taxes to support their own propaganda. At no time, moreover, has the practice of governmental guidance of political thought been more extended, at least in its attempt, than today, and not only in Russia and its satellites but also, although to a more restrained extent, in our own country.

2. Freedom to receive political information

Censorship by our national government has been attempted by suppressing information and by issuing false information. A dramatic example of both these methods was furnished in connection with the use of the American navy for convoy duty in shipments to Great Britain, many months before Pearl Harbor. This was an act of war, both under international law and in practical effect, and although we now know the fact of its occurrence, yet at the time all information was suppressed, and not even the members of the Congress were given advice of what was happening. When, moreover, rumors began to circulate, it was denied that convoying was being done, which was untrue. By this method the political thought of the people of the country was molded. Had they received true information, their opinions on the events of those crucial times would have been different from what they were; and the administration, knowing and fearing this, influenced opinion by controlling its base of information.

Another important example is presented by American policy toward Germany after the war. At the time of the Quebec conference during the war it was rumored that a drastic program was under consideration for turning Germany after its defeat into an agrarian economy, to be kept at a level of impoverishment with little manufacturing and no heavy industry. We now know on the authority of participants in the conference that this rumor was correct, and that for many months prior to the close of the war officials in Washington worked on the details of such a plan, which was embodied in order number 1067 of the Joint Chiefs of Staff, issued to the military government in Germany for its instruction in ruling the defeated enemy. But although this was a most important political matter, no information concerning it was permitted to reach the American people, and on the contrary it was denied that such a plan for an iron peace was being prepared. In continuance of this policy of secrecy, the contents of J.C.S. 1067 were not allowed to become publicly known until October, 1945, months after the cessation of hostilities.

It is apparent that in similar fashion we do not as yet have the facts about the dealings of our government with the Nationalist government of China and with the Chinese communists.

All these attempts to guide political thought by withholding and distorting facts are a violation of liberty. Even as the individual has a right under liberty to think such political thoughts as he chooses, so he has a right to the information upon which to base a political belief. He has a right to decide which facts he shall regard as important as well as to decide which opinions he shall hold based on those facts. The liberty to receive correct information is a correlative of the liberty to hold political opinions.

There is, nevertheless, an opposing liberty which may sometimes limit the liberty to receive information. It is the liberty to avoid the harm that may be wrought by a foreign enemy. The publication of information may upon occasion be calculated to induce this harm by furnishing assistance to the enemy; and when the danger of such harm is substantial liberty requires that the information be suppressed.

This suppression is usually justified as being in the interests of national security. This, however, is a mode of reference subject to serious abuse. Since everyone favors national security it is easy to suppose that any practice is justified if it can be said to be required by national security. But national security is not the end of government—liberty is its end. The excuse of national security easily becomes the refuge of a government which does not wish to have its deeds exposed to the light of day. All acts of government can be said to have something to do with national security, and if national security is the only consideration, all governmental action becomes secret. In each of the examples cited above, it has been said in extenuation of the official mendacity that national security was at issue, and indeed those were difficult times in which national security was involved. Whether the American navy should convoy British vessels certainly was a question the answer to which involved our security. But secrecy concerning the fact of convoying, when once undertaken, had no effect upon either foreign danger or national security. The Germans knew we were convoying, for they were the objects of the hostile action. The British knew it, for their ships were being protected. Only the American people were uninformed of the fact. Secrecy served only to deny to the American people the liberty of framing political opinions on a question of substantial moment. Likewise with the other examples given above; they all undoubtedly concerned matters involving national security, but secrecy concerning governmental action contributed nothing to that security. In the larger view, considering that national security is more apt to be furthered by broad and informed discussion than by the secret decisions of cabals, the policy of secrecy in these instances undoubtedly exposed national security to additional dangers instead of safeguarding it, and the principal purpose served was to permit the administration in power to proceed on its way without the deterrent of an informed public opinion.

At the present time controversy has again sprung up over the right of the executive branch of our national government to withhold information from Congress and, by the same token, from the people. The dispute is not a new one; and now as heretofore the argument has focused upon the constitutional right of the executive, as a separate division of our government, to keep its activities secret.

But the basic question is not the constitutional one; for whatever we may decide the present constitutional law to be, the fundamental problem is what the constitutional position ought to be. And is it not clear, in the light both of the pragmatic lessons of history and of the principles of liberty, that the doings of the executive should be entirely open to public gaze and to congressional inspection, save only when considerations of military safety clearly justify secrecy?

It is said, in justification of executive secrecy, that the work of the various departments will be greatly hampered if it cannot be conducted away from public and congressional prying, that efficiency requires protection from the interruptions of publicity, and that diplomacy can best proceed when its maneuvers are decently hidden. Doubtless these contentions have merit. But the problem is only partly stated when attention is called to the disadvantages of open information. Does not experience amply tell us of the opposing and terrible dangers of the denial of public information, of secret executive action? Are not the late scandals in the Bureau of Internal Revenue, the Department of Justice, and the Federal Housing Administration ample evidence that the activity of executive departments needs constant scrutiny? And is not the diplomacy of Yalta, where we betrayed millions of our allies for our own advantage, in an act of perfidy which must forever stain the honorable record of our country, sufficient warning of the tragedies that must attend international dealings conducted in secret? For who can believe that the betrayal of Poland and Manchuria would have been countenanced by the American people had they known of the negotiations as they occurred? The impatience of the executive branch of government with the demand for full information can indeed be understood, but it can never be approved or condoned.

With respect to the legislative and judicial branches, we now take it for granted that their proceedings should be open and available to public observation. But it has not always been so; star chambers, cabals, and secret committees are found in abundance on the pages of history. For the moment, however, the lesson has been learned that secrecy in the legislative and judicial branches, whatever its advantages, could end only in the tragedy of the destruction of liberty.

Viewed in the light of liberty, the proper rule is that citizens are entitled as of right to correct and complete information concerning all acts of their government, that they may have freedom of political thought, save only where a disclosure of facts would contribute substantially to a present threat of a military character to national safety. The government which respects the liberty of its citizens will find few occasions to indulge in secrecy and none in which to mislead.

3. Compulsion of political thought

The second method by which governments may seek to influence political opinion is by the issuance of propaganda. This is the peculiar vice of democratic governments, for being more dependent upon the popular will than are tyrannies and aristocracies, they are more tempted to compel political thought to assume dimensions favorable to them. In modern times particularly is such compulsion attractive as a governmental adjunct. The development of the art of public relations and publicity permits viewpoints to be insinuated into public thought so skillfully that the process avoids most of the appearance of propaganda.

Accordingly we find that our federal government has in its employ today many thousands of persons whose task is to put out propaganda designed to mold public opinion. There is scarcely a bureau which does not have its public relations branch, and such a branch has come to be regarded as a normal feature in all bureaucratic organization. The function of the public relations employees is ostensibly to keep the public advised of governmental activity. But is a bureau to present its acts for public inspection in a bad or a good light? Can it be expected to advertise itself as harmful and incompetent or as beneficial and skillful? In practice, then, the particular departments and bureaus conduct their public relations with the aim of commending themselves, gaining the good opinion of the public, and persuading public thought to run in channels favorable to governmental policies.

The effort expended in this activity is very large. Originally the publications of the federal government were factual in character, but today an enormous stream of printed material comes from the Washington presses which makes only a slight pretense of being informative, and is designed instead to secure acceptance of one or another program being fostered by the federal officialdom. Thus there has appeared propaganda for proposals to regulate agriculture, for a compulsory federal health and medical program, for federal aid to education, for increased gifts to foreign nations, for cooperation with the United Nations, and so forth. Sometimes whole campaigns are organized, including not only the distribution of printed propaganda, but also the bringing of groups of influential citizens to Washington for "briefing" by government employees, the holding of similar briefing meetings around the country, speeches by government officials at strategic points and times, and publicity by supporting citizen groups.

These official propaganda programs are of course supported by tax money. They constitute accordingly a method of compelling the individual to support the dissemination of political views which he may or may not approve. He may not believe in socialized medicine, but he is forced by the state to assist in persuading citizens that it is desirable. Further, he is forced to indoctrinate himself. The typical citizen has no decided view on many of these questions as they are initially presented to him, and his political thoughts with reference to them develop as concepts come to his attention. In a free society these concepts would arise through such investigation and attention as citizens would choose to give to the respective problems. Their political thoughts would develop as the product of investigative activity conducted within a large arena for willed action. Under a regime of governmental propaganda, however, the situation is drastically changed, the extent of the change depending upon the extent of the propaganda. In the first place, the citizens as a group are compelled to finance a program supporting a predetermined side of the question, and their capacity to finance an independent investigation is proportionately reduced. In the second place, the propaganda program they are forced to support is so large that their chances of opposing it successfully become small, simply by reason of the difficulty of making their individual voices heard against the competition of the strident voice of the state.

The propaganda of government accordingly becomes an instrument for stifling free political thought and for subjecting political thought to compulsion. As such it is a violation of liberty. The great public relations and publicity departments of Washington are a serious infraction of the citizens' liberties and a sinister portent. It is not enough to reply, as is sometimes done, that liberty is not endangered because voters are not compelled to vote in accordance with the urgings of the propaganda machine. The act of voting must always follow the act of thinking, for there is nothing else it can follow. When therefore political thought is exposed to the compulsion of government propaganda, voting is necessarily placed in the control of the same instrumentality, whose effectiveness in controlling votes will be limited only by its effectiveness in influencing political thought.

Every government employee has the same right to hold political opinions and, with minor exceptions, the same right to express them as any other citizen. But he has no right to compel me through taxes to assist him in propagating his views and in defeating mine. We recognize, at least in theory, that members of the Congress should not use tax money to disseminate their political opinions. By the same token we should recognize that the bureaus of the executive department likewise should not use tax money to popularize themselves and their favored political theories. Yet this is what is done today under the guise of public relations. The arts of publicity, public relations, and advertising have a useful place, but that place is not in government, where the bills are paid by taxes collected from citizens by the force of law. The public relations departments of Washington should be entirely eliminated, root and branch, as a serious offense against liberty. The facts concerning the operations of the bureaus should be simply presented by the bureau heads, themselves, as a necessary but not complicated or artful task.

It is an unpleasant indication of the collectivistic trend that propaganda by government is not more seriously and spontaneously opposed by citizens at the present time. The prevailing view seems to be that such propaganda is not of itself bad, but becomes good or bad as the object of its promotion is liked or disliked. Thus one citizen may approve of pamphlets by the State Department extolling the advantages of foreign alliances, but disapprove of pamphlets by the Department of Agriculture publicizing an agricultural control program. Another citizen may believe in educating the public, as the phrase is, in the virtues of American aid to backward nations, but not believe in similar education in the virtues of socialized medicine. These attitudes are possible only because the concept of the nature of a free society has become dulled. What we must more adequately understand, if we are to avoid the danger of state control of thought, is that governmental propaganda is not a bad thing only when it is opposed to our side of a question and a good thing when it supports our side, but that the effort of the state to mold political thought, through propaganda financed by taxes, is always and necessarily evil. In the society of liberty it will not occur.

4. Freedom of communication of political thought

The communication of human thought involves the transmitting and the receiving of concepts. As the recipient of political thought, the individual has an interest in such communication because his own thought must in part depend upon the communications he receives. As the transmitter of political thought, he has more varied interests. He wants to develop his own thought by the process of expressing it and subjecting it to criticism, but in addition he wants to influence others, in both their political thoughts and acts, and his motives for wishing thus to influence others may range from the finest altruism down to the meanest selfishness.

The philosophy of liberty is alike concerned with the receiving and the transmitting of political views, for they are both important forms of human activity. The general principle of individual freedom which we have examined in the case of receiving political communications applies also to transmitting them. And here likewise the problem of the limitations to be imposed on individual freedom by the requirement of equal liberty for all is related primarily to the problem of the military security of the community, and similarly presents difficult issues to be resolved.

Military danger to the community may arise by acts of persons either outside the community or within it, that is, as war or as rebellion. When the danger results from war waged by a foreign enemy, the limitation on political expression is the same as the limitation war may require on political information; that is, the limitation on expression is justified in those rare instances when freedom of discussion would involve a present threat to military safety.

With respect to military danger created by rebellion, the problem presented is more difficult because it involves a practical and logical antinomy for which no rational solution is possible. Rebellion or revolution is the illegal use of force by a faction in a community against the remainder of the community. The revolutionaries always protest, of course, that their illegal resort to arms has been made necessary by illegal or at least wrongful acts against them on the part of the rest of the community. The occasion for a revolution having arisen, the decision to join or oppose the revolution must be made on the facts as they have occurred up to that time, and by the same token the justification of the revolution must also be determined by the then prevailing circumstances rather than by subsequent ones. But the practical judgment of politics and history must be otherwise, and can be based only on the outcome of a revolution rather than on its beginning. Thus acts which, in the institution of a rebellion, are illegal and subject to punishment, by the metamorphosis of success are changed to acts which bear the stamp of legality and are subject to adulation and reward. The practical rightness of a revolution, the propriety of its claim to allegiance, depends upon its outcome. Yet a moral judgment of the justification of a rebellion must be made without respect to outcome. Thus the analysis of rebellion leads to two opposed principles; under the one principle the judgment of a rebellion must be based on its outcome and under the other it must not be based on the outcome. This logical dilemma cannot be resolved; yet a practical rule of action must necessarily be adopted. The practical rule which, though scarcely logical, must nevertheless be arrived at is that revolutionaries must be treated by all the world that does not join them as taking up arms at their peril, and must be opposed as outside the law unless and until successful, when they must be obeyed as constituting the force of the law.

This position is particularly clear for the liberal society, for its political structure is determined by the voice of the majority, and revolution in the liberal society is *per se* an admission by the revolutionaries that their program is not approved by a majority. The society of liberty, then, though it may have been founded on revolution, must oppose it and may adopt appropriate laws for that purpose.

If therefore the free society must refuse to recognize the right of revolution, though it may have exercised it, should it also prohibit the privilege of advocating revolution? Should freedom of speech on political matters be limited, in the interests of national security, by denying the right to advocate the overthrow of the existing government by force?

We have already seen the difficulty of this question in the similar problem of the advocacy of religious disobedience to law. It seems to me that the resolution of the conflict of interest should likewise in this instance be in favor of individual freedom of communication.

It is true that the open advocacy of revolution may be dangerous to liberty. The right of members of the Communist party to advocate armed overthrow of the existing American government may to some extent foster the growth of the communist movement here. Communists do not have this right at the present time because of the provisions of the Smith act, which makes such advocacy a crime. But supposing the Smith act were repealed, would we have need to apprehend any danger from the advocacy of armed revolution? Is the practical danger of revolution to be expected from its open advocacy or from concealed planning for its accomplishment? The lesson of history seems to be that only those societies which need revolution have any danger to fear from permitting its open advocacy. If this be true, then the gain in security for the free community by prohibiting advocacy of revolution is very small.

It is at least partially offset, moreover, by the stability that is engendered of open discussion. The allure of revolution is the benefit it promises, and if this can be made the subject of open discussion, the truth or falsity of the promise can be explored; but if discussion be banned, the promise is the more apt to be taken at its own evaluation.

The outlawing of the advocacy of revolution, on the other hand, restricts will's arena at an important point. Revolution has been a vital element in history, and from rebellion significant events, both good and bad, have flowed. Our own political institutions originated in the rebellion of the Revolutionary War and were momentously influenced by the attempted rebellion of the Civil War. It is idle to suppose that there will be neither revolution nor the need for revolution in the long future. The development of human character requires maximum equal freedom here as in all else. That maximum, it seems to me on a weighing of the relevant considerations, should include freedom of the individual to advocate overthrow of the existing government by force, not because such advocacy would always or even usually be a wise use of freedom, but because its prohibition would usually and perhaps always be an unwise denial of freedom.

5. Political opposition

Whether or not political expression should be allowed to extend to the advocacy of revolution, it clearly should be permitted, in the society of liberty, to include all opposition short of revolution.

The contrast between individualism and collectivism is well exposed in this matter of political opposition. The viewpoint of the individualist is reflected in Washington's remark, in the early days of the Revolution when the unhappy course of events was bringing harsh criticism of his leadership, that "free people will judge freely, and I do not condemn

them for it; it is the only way to bring matters to a fair discussion."[1]
The individualist does not enjoy or welcome criticism, but he does not
try to bar it. The collectivist on the other hand always seeks to prevent
it. To the attempt at stifling the expression of opposition he is inevitably
led by the basic assumptions of his creed. Those assumptions include
the concept that the activity of a society should follow the decisions
expressed in a common plan, rather than individual decisions expressed
in day to day living, for if individual decisions are permitted to be
followed, then collectivism is abandoned and individualism is adopted.
The common plan as it is from time to time promulgated being thus
the rule for the community, there is no proper place for opposition to
it. Opposition is wrong because its very existence and expression constitute a doubt upon the obligation to follow the common plan. The
duty of the citizen in the collectivized society is strictly to conform
and not to oppose. It is right, then, once the collectivistic position is
assumed, to prohibit the expression of opposing views, for they interfere
with the operation of the common plan, the prime object of the
society's activity.

The collectivized society therefore always seeks to impede the communication of political thought hostile to the regime; and as collectivization progresses in a society, so does interference with freedom of political
speech. This has always happened in the past, and it can be predicted
that it will always happen in the future.

The devices employed to check political criticism are various and include not only laws but also extra-legal practices. Laws to the purpose
may make use of terms suggesting their concern with public safety, they
may assert that their aim is simply to prevent the government from
being slandered or held in disrespect, but their real aim is to avert
political opposition. The extra-legal methods can be even more efficacious
than laws. As collectivization grows, the bureaucracy acquires the direction of more and more affairs, and it can accordingly turn business to
its friends and divert it from its critics. And harassment through a close
application of the many rules and regulations of the collectivized society
can be turned on and off in order to make criticism expensive and cooperation profitable.

In the philosophy of liberty this entire viewpoint is swept away. The
expression of political thought is not desirable or undesirable as it supports or opposes a group program. It is valuable for its own sake, as the
manifestation of the freedom of the individual to develop and express

1. Freeman, Douglas S., *George Washington*, Vol. 4, p. 93.

his own political concepts. It is not regarded as a means to the success of a group plan, but as a means to the development of good human character—the goal of society and the universe.

Under liberty therefore all restraints on the communication of political thought are removed, except only those limited restraints which may be necessary at times for public safety. All devices for limiting political expression beyond this, whether by laws or by extra-legal pressures, are condemned as illiberal and immoral.

Liberty knows, further, that there is usually social profit rather than harm in considering the views presented by the political opposition. It is only the existing regime that can benefit by smothering criticism. One of the doors to the courtroom of the Supreme Court of Illinois bears the injunction, *Audi alterem partem*—Hear the other side. Liberty understands the social wisdom of this. It knows that since every social rule is a compromise of conflicting human interests, it always has its opposed sides. Liberty seeks the utilitarian advantage of listening to them.

6. Present threats to the liberty of political thought and expression

The threat to liberty of thought and expression at the present time, as at all times, lies in the intellectual favor extended to collectivistic doctrine. For the great majority of men, life is guided by mental attitudes which are not deliberately thought out but which are absorbed from the surrounding ideological atmosphere. As that atmosphere becomes more disposed toward collectivism and the assumptions upon which collectivism is based, so all the attitudes of a people drift toward a collectivistic pattern. It is this which has been happening in the western world in the past half century. Collectivism has been increasing its intellectual acceptance, and measurably with that increase there has occurred a shift in attitude concerning nearly all aspects of human activity.

This change in attitude has slowly taken place as well in the area of political thought and expression as elsewhere. An evidence is the increasing emphasis given to unity as a desirable attribute of a people's political experience. For example, in the field of international relations the popular view has become that our country's policy should be bipartisan, as it is said, in the interests of unity. Diversity of opinion is frowned upon as disturbing national solidarity. Foreign relations are thought too important to permit the luxury of partisanship, which is implied to be a division in the community serving fractional purposes rather than those of the whole group. The prevalence of this attitude, though at present slightly in eclipse, reflects the contemporary collectivistic trend. And if the collectivistic character of this stress on unity as a desirable end in itself is not commonly perceived, it indicates the extent to which collectivistic attitudes can be absorbed into public opinion without their true nature's being apprehended.

Liberty is not directly concerned with unity of opinion regarding foreign relations. On the contrary its first concern is to preserve the conditions under which diversity of opinion is possible; and the liberal view on foreign relations, in almost direct opposition to the presently popular notion, is that international affairs are too important to permit the luxury of bipartisanship and must not be left to drift without the benefit of vigorous partisanship. This does not mean that the philosophy of liberty is blind to the fact that partisanship may be used for very selfish purposes without regard to group welfare; liberty knows that partisanship is frequently so employed. But it also knows that the compact force of bipartisanship can likewise be used for very selfish purposes and frequently is so used. It further knows that the unity of bipartisanship in practice can amount only to a stifling of political opposition, and that the diversity of partisanship is necessary to the continued exercise of freedom in political thought and expression. Partisanship further possesses the utilitarian virtue of subjecting foreign policy to the grilling scrutiny which its admitted importance demands, turning out to the public gaze its weaknesses and its strengths, that they may be openly evaluated.

A further current threat to the liberty of political thought is contained in the assumption that it is both the privilege and the duty of the educational system to inculcate specific political attitudes in the young, as a part of their educational process. There is disagreement concerning the particular political beliefs thus to be stressed, but a rather general view exists that political attitudes of some kind can properly be developed as a part of education. There are accordingly those who contend that the schools should indoctrinate Americanism, by which is usually meant a belief in democracy and possibly also in free economic enterprise. Another view which has been popular especially with educators is that there should be developed in the child an attitude variously referred to as one of social consciousness or social responsibility. While this concept is vague, what usually seems to be meant is the development of an attitude of accepting the superior importance of the group as against the individual, an attitude that is closely related to political belief and action in that it is taught as constituting an essential preparation for the duties of citizenship.

Both these viewpoints accept the propriety of using the educational process to implant in the growing child the mental habit of believing in certain political concepts. But in the free society the purpose of education is instruction rather than indoctrination. The point to be noted, however, is the danger that this idea of the propriety of state indoctrination of political concepts will lead to restrictions on political belief generally. If it is sound for the community, through the educational system, to attempt deliberately to mold the political beliefs of the young, why is it not sound to extend the same purpose to adults? If the inculcation of a particular viewpoint is a proper purpose of the state, that purpose needs to be exercised with reference to all members of the group and not simply with reference to children. By this view, governmental propaganda becomes not only desirable but the duty of the state, and the indoctrination and censorship schemes of fascist Italy, nazi Germany, and communist Russia all must be recognized as proper exercises of state prerogative.

The error in this chain of thought lies in the initial assumption that the state has the privilege, in the free society, of indoctrination. It is the right and duty of all citizens to express their views, that the practice of political thought may thrive, but it is not the privilege of particular citizens, acting as the state and through its machinery, to attempt to compel such thought to take particular forms. And the attempt at such compulsion, whether exercised against children or adults, and no matter how subtly concealed within educational procedures, is a violation of liberty.

Our schools should indeed offer instruction at an appropriate age level in the principles included in the philosophy of individualism and free enterprise, and their failure to do this is a serious present fault. They should also, again at an appropriate level, offer instruction in the principles of socialism and communism, because those theories represent important social trends of our time, and there should accordingly be more rather than less instruction concerning them. But such teaching must, within liberty, be objective, explaining rather than proselyting. Its object should be a fair explanation of the facts, that is, of principles upon which opposing social philosophies are based, and it should not be geared to an attempt to secure an acceptance of one view or another.

It is doubtless difficult to understand this. It is easy to think that if one believes in liberty one should indoctrinate it in the young. But such means would repudiate the end. A forced belief in liberty is a contradiction in terms. It must be freely believed in or it cannot be believed in at all.

It must never be forgotten that belief in liberty depends for its acceptance upon the very process which it advocates—freedom of thought.

Chapter 14

FREEDOM OF SPEECH AND PRESS

Inasmuch as thought and its communication are inseparably related phonemena, the discussion already had of the liberty of religious, cultural, and political thought has necessarily been concerned in large part with the liberty of communication of religious, cultural, and political ideas. Our remaining problem is to examine certain questions relating generally to the exercise of free communication by speech and in the press.

1. The use of public places

A continuing problem for freedom of speech is presented by the use of public places. To what extent should people be permitted to use streets, parks, and public buildings for speech-making and meetings? Religious groups, labor unions, patriotic organizations, fraternal societies, and political parties from time to time seek this use of public facilities.

It is sometimes supposed that the purpose for which private use is sought is a relevant factor. If, for example, a permit is sought for a religious meeting in a park, it is believed that more public inconvenience can rightly be borne than if the meeting is only that of a fraternal organization. But if on the other hand the religious group seeking the meeting is a disliked minority in the community, holding religious views looked at askance by the dominant majority, this may be thought sufficient reason for refusing permission.

It is clear, however, that under the philosophy of liberty the nature of the views to be given currency is not relevant to the question of the use of public places for speech-making or meetings. Liberty is not concerned to direct or encourage particular views, but rather to assure that human thought and opinion shall be given the opportunity of freedom to acquire its own direction, untrammeled by the censorship of the state. To encourage religious meetings and to discourage irreligious meetings in public places, or to prefer one religion to another in making public facilities available, is to impose that censorship. Under liberty one opinion is exactly of the same importance as another in so far as the use of public places is concerned. Equal freedom may indeed permit some statements to be made privately—as for example slanderous statements made to a person having a proper interest in the subject matter—which it cannot allow to be communicated publicly. But subject to this qualification it is always a violation of liberty, and accordingly an immoral act, to impede the use of public places upon consideration of the character of the statements to be made. A religious meeting on a street corner must have exactly the same permission as a meeting at the same place to teach socialism, no more and no less.

What principle then should govern the use of public facilities? Clearly it is the principle of public convenience. Freedom of speech is one part of liberty. Another part is convenience of the public in the use of public places. Neither part can be permitted to indulge in excessive growth at the expense of the other. Freedom of speech does not authorize a religious or political meeting at the intersection of State and Madison streets at the noon hour, nor does convenience of the public forbid every street meeting of the Salvation Army. Here as elsewhere in the organization of the free society the rule to be employed must be one of limitation rather than of specification. That is, the rule should indicate the point at which the freedom of individuals in the use of public places is limited rather than specify the uses which can be made. Accordingly the rule becomes: Individual citizens should be permitted to make such use of public places for speeches and meetings as they choose, subject to the qualification that no use should be permitted which would produce a substantial inconvenience to the public.

What constitutes a substantial inconvenience to the public must remain a matter of judgment applied to particular facts. Judgments may differ. But there can be no help for this. Here again liberty cannot be built by rule of thumb. Yet if there be a desire to adhere to the principle of liberty no great difficulty will be encountered.

2. Utterances tending to public disorder

Most communities possess laws or ordinances forbidding speech which is of a character to incite others to riot or commit acts of public disorder. By these rules freedom of speech is limited in the alleged

208 *The Challenge of Liberty*

interest of public safety. For the most part these rules are accepted today without criticism. They need, however, to be examined.

It should be noted that inciting to riot or disorder depends not only upon what is said, but also upon the manner of the utterance, including the circumstances under which it is made. Necessarily therefore it is an ambiguous rule, and since from its nature it is one enforced largely by police officers, its enforcement depends in most part upon interpretations of events made by police officers on the spot.

The general approval of this rule against speech which incites to riot and disorder seems to be associated with the thought that rioting and disorder are crimes, and that therefore incitement to commit them should be made a crime. But in so far as rioting and perpetrating disorder are crimes there is no need for a special law making it an offense to urge their commitment; general principles of criminal law covering conspiracy to commit crime and accessory before the fact take care of the matter. And in fact the rule against inciting to disorder is seldom invoked in cases where the attendant disorder is clearly criminal. For example, picketing in connection with strikes frequently is accompanied by disorder and violence, as everyone knows, and such disorder and violence is always criminal, resulting from a criminal interference with the freedom of action and persons of other people. Nor does this violence—and it is the principal form of rioting appearing in our country— arise without being incited by leaders. Yet only upon very rare occasions is any such leader ever arrested by the police for inciting to riot.

But if on the other hand a citizen, committing no offense of any kind, makes a derogatory remark concerning police activity which he observes before him, if, for example, he criticizes brutality of police in making an arrest, he will in many of our American cities be promptly arrested himself for inciting to public disorder. Such arrests occur with considerable frequency, and they are the principal application today of statutes and ordinances prohibiting speech that incites to riot or disorder.

This situation should not be tolerated in a free society. We need more criticism of the police, rather than less, for of all necessary institutions in a free society the police themselves are the most difficult to regulate and guard from corruption. And in any event freedom of speech demands freedom to criticize the police without nice regard to the occasion.

These laws and ordinances should be repealed, not because they are intrinsically bad in their statement or object, but because they are intrinsically bad in their application and must remain so within the foreseeable future. Such repeal would in no wise hamper proper law enforcement; what would be accomplished would be the removal of an unwarranted restraint upon the freedom of speech of the individual.

3. Slander

In the interest of completeness of statement, mention must be made of the prohibition of slanderous utterances as a limitation upon freedom of speech. Nothing approaching a full consideration of the rules concerning slander, as they have been developed in Anglo-American law, is appropriate here; but that development nevertheless is extremely interesting from the standpoint of the philosophy of liberty, because it illustrates so well the compromise that is inherent in all social rules and the weighing of one interest against another in order to produce maximum equal liberty.

Anglo-American law on slander may be regarded as starting with the proposition that any individual may say what he chooses about another individual; that is, the initial assumption is one of complete freedom of speech. But immediately there is presented the consideration that each individual not only has an interest in freedom of speech; he also has an interest in maintaining a good reputation. If his reputation is harmed by derogatory statements, his freedom of action in dealing with his fellows will be restricted, resulting in a harm perhaps more severe than that which would be incurred by the prohibition of such derogatory statements. The law therefore makes an exception to the initially assumed complete freedom of speech, and makes slanderous statements grounds for an action at law for damages.

But no sooner is this limitation on liberty of speech recognized than another contravening interest presents itself. The community generally has an interest in knowing the true facts about the conduct of an individual. If X has in fact committed a theft, the community has an interest in knowing the truth concerning that fact, even though it be derogatory to X's reputation, and the harm of forbidding statements reporting the truth would be greater than the harm done to X by telling it. Therefore, the law makes a counter exception to the exception already made. It says that although all slanderous statements are prima facie actionable, yet they will lose their actionable quality if it can be shown in defense that the statements complained of were in fact true. For similar reasons the law makes another counter exception. X may have applied to a firm for employment, and in discussing his application one of the firm's partners may say to another that X is a thief, whereas X has never stolen anything and is not a thief. This then is a slanderous statement and it is not true. But it becomes an exception to the proposition that untrue slanderous statements are wrongful, because it was made to a person who had a proper interest in getting a report on X, and consequently is regarded as a privileged communication, and X has no cause of action for the harm done him by the untrue and slanderous statement. But suppose that in making this untrue remark about X, the partner spoke so loudly that many other people, who had no concern with X's employment, heard him. Is it still a privileged communication, the harm of which X must suffer without redress? No, says the law, this becomes again an exception to the prior exception, and harm done to reputation by communicating the slanderous statement to persons outside the scope of the privilege is actionable.

Thus the rules of Anglo-American law move back and forth in limiting freedom of speech where the utterances are slanderous. The framework of principles, slowly built through a long period of time in the strenuous debates of courtrooms, is admirably constructed to preserve the maximum freedom of speech that can be attained without permitting liberty in other respects to be unduly impaired. What these rules of law do is to set boundaries to will's arena for the individual, defining for him the points of limitation beyond which he cannot exercise his freedom to speak as he chooses. The scheme is rather complicated, but no more so than is required by the complexity of the factual material to which the scheme is addressed. It constitutes an example of social intervention carefully designed to preserve maximum liberty, and in its initial assumptions and balancing of conflicting interests presents a good model for the development of social rules in the liberal society.

4. Freedom of the press

Through books more than through any other single instrumentality men can influence the actions of their fellows, directing them in the events that become history. The printed word is the most effective means of giving currency and endurance to thoughts, whereby they become the ideas that mold affairs.

Recognizing this powerful role of the printed word, men have always been tempted to censor it, that they might control its influence. Milton tells us in the *Areopagitica* that the licensing of books was a recent invention of his time, but in this he erred, as his own argument discloses. While our knowledge of antiquity on this score is not full, yet we know that Sparta enforced a rigid censorship, as did the Roman Empire at various times; and that the concept of censorship was by no means novel at an early date we can see from Plato's familiar treatment of it in the *Republic*, where it is adopted as a basic feature both of education and of politics. It will remain, moreover, an always attractive device to those who are not averse to the use of force to curb ideas, and particularly is this true at the present time when the increasing favor of collectivism makes compulsion of the individual, to secure the adherence of his conduct to a common plan, the seemingly proper and normal pattern of social rules.

In general, the principles which the philosophy of individualism indicates for the censorship of the press have already been delineated. Liberty demands complete freedom for the expression of religious, cultural, and political thought by the printed word, except only as some larger liberty may set points of limitation, and these points of limitation have heretofore been discussed.

Our only remaining task is to consider the contention that, in view of the vast power of the press, some mode of social control should be exercised over it to assure that it will properly discharge its great responsibility.

In recent years this contention has taken the form of an insistence that the press, particularly that portion which publishes newspapers, must report the facts of current history accurately, that society has an interest in seeing that this is done, and that in the event of evidence of failure on the part of the press to perform this its duty to the public, society must adopt suitable regulatory measures to assure that the duty will be discharged. A few years ago a privately financed committee, formed to study the press, issued a widely publicized report, holding in substance that freedom of the press was limited by a responsibility to the public to report facts accurately, and indicating that some form of government regulation of the press would be a proper instrumentality for enforcing this responsibility.

As these lines are being written, the Parliament of Great Britain has just defeated a bill which, conformable to the above viewpoint, would have established a Press Council, whose purpose would have been to exercise a vaguely defined supervision of the press, to the end that its productions would embody reportorial truth. Explicit censorship was not provided for, and apparently the Press Council was expected to accomplish its object by disciplining the profession of reporters and publishers rather than by blue-penciling their copy. The method, however, would have been unimportant in comparison with the object of securing the printing of certain material and not other, for if the propriety of that object be once admitted, the method of direct censorship must in time be resorted to. That this bill received substantial support from the Socialist Party is in one view not surprising, since it conforms to the collectivistic position of group control over the individual to which the Socialist Party is committed; but that it should have been introduced in the Parliament of Great Britain and have received vigorous sponsorship there is unhappy evidence of the extent of the penetration of collectivism in the historical home of our modern free speech and free press.

That there is a duty on the part of the press to accomplish reportorial truth can readily be affirmed, even as it is the duty of the doctor to diagnose skillfully, of the lawyer to represent loyally, of the carpenter to build honestly, and of the teacher to instruct fairly. It can also be acknowledged that society has an interest, within a certain meaning of the phrase, in seeing that these duties are faithfully performed by the persons upon whom the obligation of performance lies. But these premises being established, the question remains of the action, if any, which society should take to encourage the observance of these duties. Collectivists are prone to believe that it follows more or less necessarily from the premises that state police action is called for, which, in the case of the press, should take the form of an agency empowered to supervise publishing sufficiently to see that it is factually honest.

It is inevitable that collectivists take this position. Collectivism abandons at the outset of its theoretical development any primary emphasis upon the value of individual decision in life's affairs, and accordingly whenever it is confronted with a problem involving social relations, it is logically moved to abandon individual decision for group control. Within the collectivistic viewpoint, then, it is unsound to entrust the duty of reportorial truth to individual decision instead of to an agency of the state. Individuals if left alone may not observe their duty, and inasmuch as reporting facts truly is a part of the desirable common program of group activity, it follows, within the frame of collectivistic assumptions, that the performance of the duty should be coerced by the police power of the state. This constitutes state censorship, by whatever machinery it be accomplished and by whatever phrases it be described, since its end is the allowance or prohibition of publications as the state may order. And however much collectivists may still draw back from the idea of endorsing state censorship of the press, it nevertheless is a practice toward which their social philosophy impels them. It can be confidently predicted that if socialism continues to grow in England a Press Council bill in some form will be adopted.

In order to understand the opposition of individualism to state control for the purpose of insuring reportorial truth in publications, it is necessary to begin with basic considerations. The primary function of the state is to maintain liberty, not because liberty will produce the best publications, or the best of any other kind of material goods, but because it will produce the best people. The freedom of the individual, therefore, is never to be curtailed by the force of the state except at points where such curtailment is necessary to procure the largest possible equal liberty for all. Accordingly when a prohibition of individual liberty at any point is proposed, the question to be considered is whether the proposed limitation will enlarge or diminish equal liberty, and usually this can be determined by comparing the liberty which will be lost with that which will be gained. As we have heretofore seen, the freedom of the individual to publish whatever he chooses is properly limited in certain respects to protect group safety and individual welfare, on the ground that the freedom lost—to publish military information, libelous utterances, and information inciting to crime—is substantially less than the freedom gained. The same justification must be found if the press is to be socially controlled in any way in an effort to assure reportorial truth.

In assessing the gain which state control in the interests of reportorial truth might accomplish, we should join completely with the proponents of state control in recognizing the importance of accurate reporting. It has already been pointed out at some length that freedom of thought has, as its correlative, freedom to obtain accurate information. And when thought is turned into action, freedom is possible only if action can be based on factual information that is reliable and not deceptive. There can be no question of the importance of reportorial truth to the exercise of liberty.

This being agreed, individualism asks the question, Is more of reportorial truth to be anticipated under a free press or under one supervised by an agency of the state?

To this question history can be expected to supply at least a partial answer, for both the free and the regulated press have had their exemplars in the social laboratory of the past, and the results of the experiments are available for examination. The clinical verdict so presented, moreover, seems to be unusually clear. It is that the free press has almost always produced a high degree of reportorial truth, and the controlled press a low degree thereof. So universal has been this experience, indeed, that it is difficult to find exceptions. Recently we have seen the experiment of the controlled press in Italy and Germany, and currently in Russia and Argentina, and with what results we all know. It will not do to object that these have been bad regimes, devoted to concealing the truth and making use of press control for that purpose. They have all asserted that they were salutary administrations, operated for the welfare of the people and concerned with the publication of the truth that that welfare might be served. But the obvious fact is that reportorial truth has never been accomplished to any substantial degree. Instead the truth has often been suppressed, to some extent continuously and systematically, and untruth has often been encouraged.

If on the other hand it is sought to find an era in which the press has been characterized on the whole by a high degree of reportorial truth, it can be observed in the British and American press during the past one hundred fifty years, when the publishers of information have been free to publish the facts truthfully or untruthfully as they themselves have chosen. Undoubtedly there have been many instances during this period when the choice has been to falsify the news, and undoubtedly, too, there have been newspapers and magazines which have continually followed a policy of distorting their reports, at least in certain areas of information. But the fact nevertheless is clear that at no other time in history have the people been so completely in possession of correct reports of affairs as during this age of the free press. If reportorial truth has been wanting in some publications, it has nevertheless always been available in others.

If we seek an explanation of these historical lessons, we shall find it in part in the fact that the same reasoning which is used to justify state control of the press in the interest of reportorial truth can also be resorted to in justification of the suppression and distortion of the truth. If state control is justified on the ground of group welfare as that welfare is evaluated by the state, then it follows that if group welfare is adjudged by the state to require the suppression of truth rather than its publication, suppression is justified, and by the same token untruth can be justified also.

The reason that the free press, on the other hand, has in practice accomplished reportorial truth is this: Men wish reportorial truth, and if freedom permits it to be published, they will demand and secure it in substantial measure. Given a free press and a free market, no man needs to support mendacity by buying deceitful publications. How will he know? Simply by experience, which practice proves to be a workable guide. He can demand in the free market, and by demanding he will secure, publications that make a reasonably sincere and consistent effort to report facts accurately. More than this cannot be expected from any system that is conceivable, and less than this is bound to be had under any scheme of state control. The free press successfully works to produce reportorial truth, not because it is under the regulating eye of some officer of the state, but because it is under the regulatory control of all members of society as they express their wishes in the free market, where they can support or refuse to support particular publications.

Nor is this a case where the purchaser needs the assistance of his neighbors, by way of organized social action, to test the merchandise offered for sale. There are some goods whose character is such that convenience is greatly served by group rather than individual testing. But no such consideration applies in the case of reportorial accuracy. Whether reports are factually accurate is largely a matter of opinion, and although one man's opinion is doubtless on occasion better than another's because of better exercise of judgment and better knowledge of facts, yet judgments on accuracy must remain for the most part opinions which one individual is as well entitled to as another. The judgment of the community on a publication, therefore, is best expressed by the combined opinions of the members thereof, as they purchase or refuse to purchase it in the free market. In doing this, they need not divorce themselves from opinion more expert than theirs; indeed they probably will make use of more informed opinion in making their decisions. But their ultimate decisions will remain their own.

These are the reasons why the controlled press must always result in a low order of reportorial truth and the free press in a high degree thereof.

State control therefore can offer no gain in reportorial truth as an inducement to its adoption, but must result, rather, in a loss in the reporting of truth and a corresponding loss in the liberty of thought.

In addition to the decline in reportorial truth, state control means the destruction of the freedom of those who wish to publish. It therefore ends in impairing liberty in every way, save only an unwarranted gain of freedom of action by those in political control.

It is sometimes imagined that a middle ground must exist between state control and freedom, involving enough control to assure fair reporting but not enough to destroy the freedom of the press, and that this middle ground only awaits experimentation for its discovery. But this view fails to take account of basic facts. What is published must be determined by human decision. This deciding function must be exercised either by the individuals who publish or by the state officials who control, and in every instance of publication it must be the decision of someone in one or the other group that determines the fact that publication will occur. There is no other possibility. The one case is the free press, the other is state control. The methods of decision are mutually exclusive. Therefore either the free press or state control must prevail in any given area of publication. Experimentation with methods of state control in any form can accordingly result only in an unrelieved loss of freedom.

The liberty of individualism therefore calls for a free press published in a free market, assured that the people of a free society will demand and receive, in such an environment, publications containing reportorial truth.

PART II: ECONOMIC LIBERTY

It scarcely need be said, in an age that places as much emphasis upon material things as does our own, that the economic part of life has its importance. What is very much needed, nevertheless, is an understanding of the correct role of economic theory in relation to the whole of social philosophy.

As matters are at present, economic considerations are dominant in social thought. Here the dialectical materialism of Marx has had its way, so much so that it has become an assumption of our time, echoed in press, pulpit, and classroom, that every human problem has at its base a more or less determinative economic cause. Human character, we are daily told, is the product of economic conditions; and human character being thus controlled, human history is likewise thought to have only or mainly an economic explanation. This view of the preponderant importance of economics in human affairs has its origin in the writings of Karl Marx, who taught that man's way of making his living determines all his career. This pseudoscientific supposition, which like all the basic points in Marxian collectivism is not susceptible of logical demonstration but must be accepted as an article of faith, has nevertheless had superficial appeal in a scientific era. It purports to simplify the analysis of human action, and to make it subject to measurement and classification in the same manner that natural phenomena are measured and classified. Accordingly a large body of current thought, seeking a quick sureness in dealing with human process, has accepted both the explanations and the purported cures of materialism.

But the theory of materialism is false, without support in logic or experiment and deteriorating in its moral influence. The entire discussion of this work is an argument against it. If the analysis contained in Book One is sound, then not economic goods but human character is the purpose of life and the goal of history. Goods indeed have an important part to play in the development of human character, and economics consequently must occupy an important place in the considerations that influence the form of social organization. But the strange myopia that cannot see beyond the satisfaction of economic wants, and that consequently regards the economic factor as the determinant in human affairs, is as uninstructed in the facts of human existence as it is tragic in its consequences.

The true role of goods in human action consists in the part they play as one of the determinants of the scope of willed activity. Goods comprise a highly significant part of the material factor in will's arena, as we saw in Chapter 9. Our study in that chapter, it will be recalled, disclosed that human will always operates within an arena composed of four factors, which we denominated the psychological, experiential, material, and social factors. As these factors expand or contract, so does the arena within which human will can exert itself. And since the quality of human character is determined by decisions made by human will, the larger the arena for willed conduct becomes so too does the opportunity for developing good character become enlarged.

The things and services that satisfy human wants, which things and services are referred to in this study as goods, exert a strong influence in determining the extent of human action. The man or people who must devote all available energy to obtaining the goods called for by the instinct of self-preservation will not proceed far with intellectual culture. And the society which does not create the material things needed for books, music, painting, and other art forms cannot develop the part of human character that finds expression in artistic creation. We must not make the materialistic error of supposing that the existence of an adequate material base insures cultural development, for advanced human character is not so simply attained; yet we must understand that goods are a limiting factor for the volitional process, and thereby a limiting factor in character-building.

Goods constitute, further, the only element in the material factor subject to human control. In addition to goods, the material factor is composed of the natural world—the sea, sky, earth, and climate. Man can do nothing about these natural facts except by his labor to convert them into goods. He cannot change the seasons, nor the chemical and physical properties of the universe, much as these material facts determine the limits of his willed career. But he can create goods which, by expanding the arena of his conduct, will permit greater nobility to his character.

Therefore it is man's duty to create the goods that give more room to his spirit. But since man does not live by bread alone, the manufacture of goods is but the beginning point in the achievement of character. An economic base nevertheless underlies all of life, and economic meaning is immanent in all that we do.

The form of economic action, therefore, strongly influences other spheres of living. Because the struggle to get the material things which support life is constant and pressing, the attitudes and assumptions which are accepted in economic activity tend to become the attitudes and assumptions which are accepted in other kinds of activity. The society that develops economic collectivism must soon lapse into collectivism in the spiritual and cultural manifestations of social existence. The society, on the other hand, that maintains liberty in economic affairs can hope that the experience of liberty will be transferred to other more important areas. The philosophy of individualism therefore stresses the creation and maintenance of the practical forms of liberty in economic action.

But although the prime reason for economic liberty is ethical rather than materialistic, individualism by no means concedes that liberty is less productive of goods for all than collectivism. On the contrary it asserts that liberty is strikingly superior both in efficiency in the production of goods and in the equity of their distribution. Life is all of a piece, and the scheme which best provides for the development of human character will also best provide for those things which that development has need of.

To secure this economic liberty in its practical form, individualism teaches the need of two institutions, the free market and private property.

Chapter 15

THE NATURE OF THE FREE MARKET

1. The determination of production and consumption

Any method of satisfying human want necessarily involves two stages: first, the production of goods, within which term as used in this work services are always included, and second, their consumption. All economic activity is a part of one or the other of these two general processes.

With respect to the production of goods, the concern which the members of society have in this process may be expressed in the question, What goods will be produced? and in the related question, Who will perform the labor of producing particular goods? With respect to consumption, the concern of the members of society is expressed in the question, Who will consume the goods produced and in what proportions?

The answers to these questions determine the pattern of economic activity of a society. And they determine a great deal of human happiness. When it has been decided what will be produced and who will consume it, a large part of human action and welfare has been fixed for the immediate future, and to some extent for the more remote future.

The answers which are made are necessarily the product of human decision, of human will acting within the arena set for it by factors limiting that arena. Since human will is not an abstraction but manifests itself in the world only as particular acts of willing by particular persons, it follows that the answers to the questions of production and consumption must be made, within any society, by particular persons. A matter of prime importance to all the people in the society becomes, therefore, the identity of the persons who will make the decisions determining production and consumption.

Obviously many patterns of social arrangement are possible for indicating these persons. There can be the freedom of decision by individual citizens that prevailed in the days of Athenian prosperity, the absence of such freedom of individual decision as at Sparta, the control of production and consumption by a bureaucracy as in Egypt under the Ptolemies and in the later Roman Empire, the detailed state regulation of production of the European mercantilist period, the return to individual decision in the nineteenth century, or the direction of production and consumption by bureaus established by legislative enactment as now being attempted in parts of Europe and to some extent in the United States. While we do not ordinarily think of these different patterns as devices for designating the persons who will make economic decisions, yet that is essentially their function. They identify the persons who will have the privilege of deciding in substantial measure who gets what.

The particular pattern used by a society is accordingly of vital relevance to its welfare. First, it affects the liberty of its people and thereby the opportunity afforded them to develop good character. If the production of cotton, for example, be regulated by the Department of Agriculture, which through its agents designates the acreage each farmer may plant, the function of deciding his acreage is taken from each farmer and vested instead in a few officials. To the extent of this deprivation, the farmer has taken from him the uniquely human activity of volitional process, and to that extent he is reduced from man to robot. As a society increases the power of bureaus to determine production, so it necessarily reduces the arena of will for each citizen as producer. Second, the pattern by which decision is made influences the ensuing production and consumption, with the attendant effect upon economic well-being. Collectivists and individualists are agreed that production and consumption will be different as one method of decision or another is made use of. Production in Great Britain today undoubtedly would differ substantially from what it is if it were directed by a free market instead of by state agencies. To procure this difference is indeed the very reason which is asserted as justification for state controls.

2. The two methods of economic decision

When we examine the various patterns of social organization employed to indicate the persons who will make economic decisions, we see that they all comprise in different combinations two basic but opposed methods by which economic decisions can be made. On the one hand is the method whereby individual members of society make their own decisions concerning what they will produce and consume. On the other hand is the method whereby individual members of society are required to follow decisions made for them by others. The first method is that of the free market, the second that of the controlled market.

This dichotomy has its psychological base. Since the experience of each individual moves through a realm of self and a realm of not-self, therefore any decision concerning the individual's conduct must be made either by him or by someone else for him. There is no third possibility.

For any given economic area, accordingly, society must adopt the one method or the other, as the permitted form of economic decision. In the matter of wheat acreage, for example, farmers may either be permitted themselves to determine the acres to be planted, in which case the social program becomes the sum of individual decisions, or they may be required to plant the acres decided upon by some social agency empowered to make the decision for them, in which case individual action becomes conformance to plan. The price of steel, as another example, may either be negotiated by buyers and sellers in a free market, or may be fixed by an authority able to compel compliance by buyers and sellers, who thus are deprived of the privilege of decision. In each example the alternatives are mutually exclusive. Decision by individuals on wheat acreage and steel prices, representing the method of the free market, excludes communal planning; while decision by a state authority, being the method of the controlled market, excludes individual decision.

3. The free market and the controlled market

The free market, then, is the social arrangement by which producers and consumers make their own decisions on what they will produce and consume.

The controlled market is the social arrangement by which producers and consumers are compelled to follow decisions on what they will produce and consume, made by others for them.

Both the free and the controlled markets constitute social regulation of the process by which answers are obtained to the questions of what will be produced and who will consume. Both methods require systems of law to govern their operations. It is sometimes supposed—perhaps under the influence of the misleading term *laissez faire*, which has caused so much confusion and misunderstanding—that the free market operates without rules and is a species of anarchy. Nothing could be further from the fact. On the contrary, the laws needed to maintain a free market, as we shall see as we proceed, are far more complex and sophisticated than those required by a controlled market, whose legal scheme indeed is fundamentally rather simple both in theory and in operation.

4. Free market societies and controlled market societies

Although the use of a free market for a particular commodity precludes a planned or controlled market for it, yet the use of a free or controlled market for one commodity does not preclude the use of the opposite type of market for other commodities. Almost always in the past, in fact, societies have made use of a free market for some areas of economic activity and of a controlled market for others. Very rarely has a society attempted to control the market for all goods, as the Emperor Diocletian tried to do in 301 and as we recently tried to do, as a war measure, in this country; very rarely also have free market conditions obtained for the consumption and production of all the goods used by a society.

But either free or controlled markets may predominate in a society, and it becomes a free market society or a controlled market society as one or the other method of economic decision becomes a paramount characteristic.

A free market society, then, may be described in general terms as one in which for the most part individuals make their own decisions on production and consumption. That is, they produce and offer for sale such goods as they choose at such prices as they choose, and they buy and use such goods as they choose at such prices as they choose; and this pattern of self-decision is the prevailing form of economic action. A controlled market society is one in which, in general terms, individuals do not for the most part make their own decisions on production and consumption, but follow decisions made for them by a comparatively few members of the society who plan production and consumption for all. That is, in a controlled market society production and consumption are planned for the entire group by official planners, and economic activity consists, in its prevailing form, in carrying out the decisions on production and consumption so arrived at.

Thus although the methods of free and controlled markets can be sharply distinguished, societies do not submit to such rigid classification, for their employment of free and controlled markets may occur in endless variety. Many societies cannot be said with certainty to be either free or controlled market societies, because the two methods are so nearly in balance that it is impossible to say that either prevails.

5. Creating a free market

A common mode of thought is that a free market occurs in some wild way simply by leaving things alone, and that a controlled market on the other hand is the product of intelligent ordering of human affairs; wherefore the controlled market is regarded as the institution of higher rank. But as frequently is the case with popularly held opinions, it is the opposite view which corresponds with the facts. A market in which production and consumption can occur pursuant to the free choices of individuals will arise only if deliberately arranged for; and if economic affairs are allowed to drift without thoughtful attention, a controlled market is almost certain to emerge. It is hard to keep a market free. Consequently free market societies have appeared in history only at rare intervals. In the long centuries since the prosperous days of classical Athens, its free markets have seldom been emulated.

The difficulty in creating a free market arises from the complexity of the problem of maintaining equal economic opportunity for all individuals, while at the same time permitting unequal response to the equal opportunities offered. That such equal opportunity is of the essence of economic liberty we saw in Book One. But the accomplishment of such equal opportunity is an intricate and formidable task. It can never be effected simply by leaving things alone. If that course be followed, monopolistic control of the market, with attendant unequal opportunity, is certain to develop.

Monopolistic control may be exercised either by private monopolists or by public officials. Private monopolists through control of the supply of a commodity can control its production and consumption. Public officials can control production and consumption through decrees fixing prices and wages and through a great variety of other forms of regulation. Whether the few who thus dominate economic activity act as private monopolists or as public officials, the ultimate effect of their action is precisely the same: They impose their decisions concerning production and consumption on the rest of the community and thereby destroy pro tanto the area of decision for the rest of the community.

Controls are substituted for freedom, and the controlled market supplants the free market.

Thus the creation of a free market requires the devising of social rules which will effectively set limitations both to private monopoly and to public regulation. Such limitations are established with difficulty. Not only is it impossible as a practical matter to determine precisely where the line should be drawn so as to limit monopolistic practices and official interference, but once the location of a line has been agreed upon, the drafting of laws and constitutional provisions to give effect to this line of limitation is a matter of great art. Even so, the difficulties of a free market are by no means insuperable provided there is a conviction in the community that a free market is desirable. Given this conviction, very bad social tools will do remarkably good work, as witness for example the Sherman Act, which though exhibiting in its provisions an almost incredible want of fair and precise draftmanship, particularly for a criminal statute, has yet had a most salutary influence in preserving a free market society in our country.

Concerning monopolistic control of supply, the problem as it is presented to the free market arises in various ways. It may be presented by a limitation in the source of natural supply of a basic material. If there be only one available source of bauxite, a monopoly of all forms of aluminum may be readily effected. Or the problem may result from technological considerations. Telephone service is best when furnished by one supplier rather than by competing companies, and the cost of more than one distributing system for electricity or gas within the same area renders competition impractical for these utilities, as also is sometimes true of transportation service. Again, the problem of monopoly may be created simply by the agreements of producers, who but for such agreements would be in active competition. As Adam Smith observed, competitors can scarcely meet without their conversation's turning to ways of controlling prices. Such attempts are of little effect so long as they are not coupled with agreements establishing control over supply; but when competitors are successful in reaching an understanding on the supply of a commodity, whether by dividing markets, restricting output, or otherwise, they accomplish monopoly and a controlled market. However the problem of monopolistic control over supply may arise, to the extent that it is presented it must be met by limitations, set by social rules, upon the activity of those in a position to exercise the monopolistic control.

Concerning public interference, the limitations which are necessary in order to create a free market are those which will prevent the force of the officialdom of the state from passing beyond that which is necessary to create equal opportunity. In the area of economic affairs, as in all other parts of life, when state force goes beyond the creation of equal liberty, it results in the aggrandizement of the power of the official few and the destruction of the liberty of the common many. To create the equal opportunity that is essential to a free market, the regulation of the market by the state must be limited to those exercises of force which build equal opportunity.

The social rules necessary to regulate monopolistic control of supply and state interference in the market become very complex in an active society which enjoys a high degree of division of labor, such as our own. We can readily see this when we consider that the maintenance of a free market, with its equal opportunity for all, is the fundamental problem of such controversial matters as the open versus the closed shop, state control of prices and wages, price fixing agreements by competitors, picketing, agreements in restraint of trade, division of markets, the basing point system of prices, union hiring halls, mergers of competing corporations, the reasonableness of union initiation fees, interlocking directorates, the method of determining a fair rate of return for public utilities, and many similar questions, all of which are the subject of constant debate, legislation, and litigation.

The conflict of interest that arises in these situations tends to appear to the contestants simply as a struggle for advantage. Labor problems tend to be seen as a contest over the division of a flow of wealth. When so regarded, however, criteria for the logical settlement of disputes disappear. If a strike is no more than a fight over the division of spoils, no logical base for its settlement is possible. Within the philosophy of the free market, however, more than conflicting advantage is involved. Since the first function of the state is the maintenance of liberty, all aspects of the economic conflict must be kept within the setting of the free market. The creation and maintenance of this free market is the first duty of the state within the economic sphere, and all rules for the resolution of disputes, whether they be labor disputes, price fixing disputes, or of whatever character, must be kept within the specifications of action set by the principles of the free market and its basic element of equal opportunity. When this is done, criteria for the logical settlement of disputes will always be available.

The institution of the free market, then, is the product of a complex set of social rules fixed with the aim of maintaining liberty in economic activity. The myriad decisions of individual persons, freely expressing their choices as producers and consumers within the framework of equal opportunity, establish the economic pattern for the group.

6. Mobility in the free market

In a free market, since consumers are free to buy or not as they choose, producers must offer for sale goods that consumers are desirous of buying, at prices they are willing to pay. The individual producer cannot compel consumers to take his wares, but must rely upon his meeting some need as the consumers themselves believe such need to exist.

In order for the producer to bring to market the goods he believes are wanted, which are those he thinks he can sell, he must be free to direct his labor and capital as he chooses. If he is a businessman employing the labor and capital of others as well as his own, he must be permitted to use his entrepreneurial effort in the creation of the goods he judges he can dispose of profitably, that is, at a price high enough to pay costs, including compensation for his own work and for the use of the capital availed of. If he is a workman employed by others, he must be free to accept such employment as he prefers. If he is an investor with savings, either his own or those of others entrusted to his care, which he seeks to place in capital goods, he must be allowed to finance such plant and equipment as he deems advantageous. And as businessman, laborer, and investor he must have freedom to modify his activity from time to time as he himself decides, whether to meet changes in consumer preferences or for any other reasons he deems persuasive.

This liberty of individuals to alter productive activity, though it constitutes an essential condition for the existence of a free market, functions nevertheless under natural circumstances that tend to retard mobility. A factory once built, for example, cannot readily be removed to another locality, and one equipped with heavy machinery for turning out tractors cannot very well be converted to the manufacture of clocks or typewriters. Even moreover as capital tends to be fixed, so also do human skills when once acquired. Workers trained in one trade are reluctant to start over in another, and find it difficult to do so. In addition, natural aptitudes, health, family ties, and social connections all contribute to a considerable immobility of labor.

It must be remembered, however, that despite the hampering effect of these natural factors, there constantly occurs in society a new inflow of labor and capital, uncommitted as to use, that gives the free market great fluidity and versatility in production. Young men and women steadily enter the ranks of producers with untrained hands and foot-loose careers; as they learn new skills and inhabit new places they furnish the means for continually changing the pattern of productivity. Capital goods too are always being modified as fresh savings seek to earn a return by creating additional plant and new and more varied equipment. Given liberty, man as producer can utilize these variable factors to counteract in large degree the items of the environment that make for immobility.

Each consumer must likewise bid for the merchandise of producers, for he cannot oblige them to sell to him, even as they cannot oblige him to buy. The consumer may bid for what he chooses, but many influences operate to circumscribe the area of his choice.

The necessities of climate and the requirements of sustenance and health may impair—perhaps upon occasion very substantially—the ability of the individual to express in the market a preference for those things which, were the natural facts otherwise, he would wish to select and consume. The amount of income which the consumer has available for expenditure is of course an ever-present limitation on his choice in the free market.

These matters limiting the freedom of activity of producers and consumers are not peculiar however to the free market. They are data which every social scheme, whether individualistic or collectivistic, must cope with. Detractors of free enterprise not infrequently point out these retarding circumstances as though they were distinctive shortcomings of the free market, saying that because of them the market is not actually free, that labor and capital do not possess the mobility which theory supposes, and that consumption, particularly of the poor, is largely dictated by necessity, rather than selected. But neither collectivism nor individualism can change biological and physical facts; they constitute rather the arena within which any form of social organization must operate. The theory of the free market neither assumes nor requires a perfect mobility of labor or capital; and the assertion that it is so premised, and that the theory is unsound because the premise is false, is entirely without merit. The free market, rather, is a social form designed to work within the facts of human and physical nature as they are, not supposing a world different from the one that exists.

7. The unit of enterprise in the free market

It is sometimes asserted that under the logic of individualism the only proper unit of enterprise in the free market is the individual himself, associations of individuals as in partnerships and corporations being applications of the principle of collective action; and that since such associations are obviously required in order to carry on large-scale production, individualism breaks down as a working philosophy and must in practice give way to collectivism. By this line of thought it is believed that the inadequacy of individualism is demonstrated.

What an argument of this sort shows, however, is simply the semantic difficulty inherent in human thinking, and the stupid way we frequently permit our thought to be led astray by the sound of words. Individualism, it is true, emphasizes the individual human being as a unit; not, however, as a unit of economic enterprise but as a unit of value. Individualism is not a philosophy calling on each person to live alone, but a philosophy of how human beings should live together in the social relation that is presented to them as one of the data of existence. Accordingly individualism is a theory of association rather than of atomistic anarchy. It calls on men to act in harmony, and sets the rules by which that harmony is to be obtained. But because it treats each individual as an ultimate and equal unit of value, the detractors of the liberty of individualism like to suppose that every shade of meaning that can be attached to the words individual and individualism must come within the individualistic philosophy. This of course is folly, however much it may be practiced.

In the field of economic activity the philosophy of individualism presents no principle which calls for the restriction of the units of enterprise to individuals. On the contrary, such a restriction would be a violation of the liberty of individuals to associate together upon such terms as they select, subject always to the rules necessary for the maintenance of equal liberty for all. Under liberty, individuals must be free to form partnerships, corporations, and such other forms of association as their ingenuity may devise. But they must likewise be free not to join in such group enterprises if they wish not to do so. It is the freedom of the individual to choose that is the root of the matter for individualism, not the size of the enterprise his choice fixes upon. Production of goods in partnerships and corporations is no more collective than production by individuals, provided that the persons who form such partnerships and corporations are free, within the framework they have set up, to decide upon their production instead of being compelled to adhere to a communal plan.

The free market consequently is not impaired simply by the size of the units of enterprise that produce goods for sale. They may be very large or very small, associations of many people or single individuals. What matters is that the activity of these people as they produce goods and offer them for sale be kept free and within the bounds required for the maintenance of equal opportunity.

The fact, further, that some kinds of production are impossible for the individual and can be carried on only by associations of individuals does not impair the free market. What chance, the opponents of individualism like to ask, does the single individual have to enter the business of producing steel in the vaunted free market? Or the business of running a railroad or any other industry requiring great capital? The answer is, of course, that acting entirely alone he has no chance at all. But the same thing is also true in the controlled market of a collectivistic society, for the inability of the single individual to produce steel results not from any social arrangement but from technological facts. Neither the controlled market nor the free market nor any other social scheme can make it possible for the individual to enter the steel business alone, and the free market of individualism is not open to criticism on that score. What the free market does is to permit the individual to enter the steel business in association with others—as worker or investor—if he chooses to do so; and the difference between the free market and the controlled market lies in the extension or withdrawal of this privilege of choice. The free market does not pretend to grant to the individual choices not within the realm of technological possibility, but only the largest equal area of choice available within that realm.

8. Monopoly and the free market

Although the subject of monopoly in its relation to the free market demands a separate chapter for its consideration, the sketch of the free market contained in the present chapter would not be complete without reference to it.

As we have already seen, private monopoly constitutes one of the two general methods by which controls can be exercised over the market for goods, the other method being public regulation.

What is monopoly? In general terms monopoly may be said to be substantial control over the supply of a particular good. A monopolist is one who can substantially control the quantity of a good which will be placed on the market for sale. But when these general statements have been made, a host of difficulties both of terminology and of concept begin to appear.

These difficulties spring from the fact that the forms of monopoly, as they develop in the conduct of affairs, do not submit to sharp classification. As is the case with so much of social phenomena, the manifestations of monopoly vary from one to the next by small degrees. Every producer exercises some control over the supply of the good which he produces. This control over supply may be very slight. A worker in a furniture factory who quits his job because of dissatisfaction with wages or working conditions exercises a small influence on the supply of furniture. The farmer who decides to cut back his production of hogs because of a drop in prices likewise exercises a very small control over supply. At the other end of the scale is the producer who for some reason can exert complete control over the supply of a good. The producer of an article manufactured under a patent is frequently in this position. The supply of the patented article is entirely within his control. The holder of a copyright similarly can entirely control the supply of the copyrighted work. Likewise the producer of a good based on a natural commodity whose only source is within his ownership has a complete monopoly. Thus some years ago the supply of aluminum was completely controlled because the producer of aluminum also owned the only available bauxite ore bodies. Thus there is no producer, no matter how humble his position in the productive scheme, who does not exercise some control over the supply of some good, and on the other hand there are a few producers who are so situated that they can exert something approaching complete control over supply.

In between these extremes of exceedingly small and exceedingly large influence upon supply many gradations appear. Every producer of a branded good has complete control over the supply of that particular brand, although he may have but very slight control over the supply of the general class of goods to which the branded product belongs. Thus every manufacturer of toothpaste gives his product a brand name, trying to obtain consumer preference for the particular kind of toothpaste he sells under his brand. Of the supply of this branded article he has complete control. But his brand of toothpaste competes with all other brands of toothpaste, and over the supply of toothpaste as a whole he can exercise but slight control. To this form of control over supply economists have given the name of monopolistic competition.

Another form of control over supply occurring with some frequency is oligopoly, where production is in the hands of a few producers. Typically oligopoly appears where capital investment is heavy and there is only slight difference, if any at all, between the products of the various producing companies. The cement industry is an example of oligopoly.

Around these typical examples of complete monopoly, monopolistic competition, and oligopoly cluster multitudinous variants, all exhibiting different degrees of control over the supply of a good. The use of particular names to designate some of the more common forms should not obscure for us the fact that the phenomena of control over supply occur in a graduated series.

What significance do these phenomena have for social philosophy?

There are in general three procedures which society can employ with regard to monopolistic phenomena. First, it can permit private monopoly to develop as it will without social restraint. This is the method which was largely followed in western Europe prior to the second World War. It results in cartels and agreements among producers which allocate markets and restrict production in order to keep prices at monopoly levels. To the extent that such private monopolistic control is allowed to establish itself, the market becomes a controlled one. Second, society can eliminate private monopoly by establishing public or state monopoly. This is the method of collectivism. It displaces the limited control of private monopolists by the larger control of state officials, whose decrees determine production and prices. Under this monopoly of officials the market also becomes a controlled one. Third, society by appropriate rules can restrict control over the supply of a good whenever such control becomes substantial enough to impair equality of opportunity among society's members. This is the method of the free market. Barring both private and public monopoly, it establishes a framework of rules within which the members of society may produce and sell as they choose. It is this method whose details we shall examine in a subsequent chapter.

9. The controlled market of collectivism

In order to comprehend more clearly the nature of the free market, it will be desirable briefly to consider further the controlled market as it is advocated by collectivism.

Although collectivists are by no means entirely averse to the controlled market of private monopoly—as witness the enthusiasm of the so-called liberals of the time for the National Recovery Administration of 1933, which authorized monopolistic controls—yet they greatly prefer the market that is controlled by the state. It is to this that we shall direct our present attention.

This acceptance of the state-controlled market involves a complete rejection of the principle of the free market. If in practice collectivism usually leaves some goods to be bought and sold freely, this is by way of concession to convenience rather than to theory. In theory the condemnation made by collectivism of the free market is entire. It proceeds on two grounds.

The first is that the free market constitutes a "selfish system," which does not produce the goods there is the most need for but those which result in the most profit for the producer. Each individual, compelled to look after himself alone, can give thought only to the profit he can get from production, whereas a good social order would produce goods to meet real human needs. This impulsion to selfishness is aided, collectivism asserts, by the private ownership of property. The owners of the instruments of production—land and capital—can control the product, diverting to the nonowners, the proletariat, not their fair share but only enough to keep them quiescent, the balance of the product being unfairly retained by the owners themselves.

The second ground of collectivism's condemnation is that the free market is haphazard and unplanned; that is, its mechanism is not competent to procure the production of those goods that are really needed, even if it did not induce people to act selfishly. Any given society has need during a designated period of time for a certain number of new houses, a certain quantity of textiles, a certain amount of food, and so on. These needs can be calculated in advance with a tolerable degree of accuracy, and they indicate the goods that the society should produce. But the free market, collectivism says, neither has any method for making this calculation nor any way of compelling individual producers to adhere to such a plan should it be made. The asserted result is unplanned and haphazard production, in which each individual is left free to make his own guess, and which can never be expected to produce the goods required for the society's true welfare.

I do not propose to answer these criticisms at this point, for the answers will be more appropriately presented as our discussion advances. Here I wish only to show the nature of collectivism's objections, that the opposition of collectivism and individual liberty on this important matter may be clearly perceived.

The essence of these objections is to be found in the free choice of the individual to produce and consume as he prefers. It is free choice that makes it possible for him to be selfish and it is likewise free choice that results in the allegedly random pattern of production and consumption. Collectivism must therefore oppose this freedom of the individual, for as long as he is permitted to exercise his own preferences there can be no assurance, as the collectivist sees it, that he will be either unselfish or wise. In order therefore to realize desirable economic activity, collectivism believes that the effort of the members of society must be directed along a common plan, which will unselfishly envisage the true wants of the whole community.

Since this collective planning, in which decisions are made not by individuals but for them, constitutes the only alternative to the free market, as we have already seen, and since collectivism greatly prefers the planning of the state to that of private monopolists, it follows that the controlled market of state planning is the only alternative which collectivism presents once it has rejected the institution of the free market.

For operating a state-controlled market, plans and goals must be formulated. In a small society the persons who make these plans can be the legislature and the top executive officials, if the area of planning is not too large. In England in the fifteenth century, for example, the plans for building up the woolen industry and the controls for enforcing those plans, which were mentioned in Appendix 1 of Book One, were effected by Parliament through enactments. In larger societies, however, and where a controlled market is used for more than one or a few commodities, it is humanly impossible for a few legislators and top executive officials to attend to the multitudinous details involved in planning; wherefore the making of plans is necessarily turned over to people who are organized variously in commissions, boards, and bureaus, the size of which officialdom must be directly proportioned to the extent of the planning attempted.

However much—or little—these planners may seek popular cooperation, the realization of their plans depends ultimately on the application of force to compel the recalcitrant; and accordingly the pattern of organization of the bureaucracy tends to be that of a military hierarchy, wherein instructions flow through layers of authority downward while responsibility runs in an identifiable line to a unit at the top. In Russia we see this machinery of planning in a mature form. In Great Britain and France the confusing arrangement of the bureaus that plan and control various portions of the economy does not testify to any difference from the Russian model in basic principle, for that must remain the same for all collective planning, but only to its less complete development in practice. I do not suggest that the enforcement of plans requires the ruthlessness employed in Russia, but only that Russia's form of organization is logically called for once collective planning on a large scale is adopted.

When plans and targets for the production and consumption of particular goods have been formed by the planning authorities, the principal methods of control used to assure their accomplishment are these: the allocation of materials in such manner as to channel them into certain lines of production and to divert them from others, the fixing of prices and wages, the direction of labor to make sure that it is employed in the desired fields, the control of credit and the interest rate, the manipulation of money, the rationing of goods in accordance with the planned pattern of consumption, and the control of incomes. Of these controls the most important is the fixing of prices. Given an effective control over prices, the entire course of production and consumption within a society can be largely regulated, so thoroughly indeed that if the control over prices be complete, scarcely any other controls will be needed.

It is important always to bear in mind that these controls are an indispensable part of collective planning. The collectivist typically glosses over this. In the society enjoying the benefits of unselfish state planning, he says, men will be truly free. He does not point out, indeed he usually seems not to comprehend, that in his collectivistic society, whether it be organized as a socialist state or as a communist state, planning can be accomplished only by controls, and that controls destroy freedom of action for all except a few.

10. State intervention in the free and controlled markets

The view is very widespread that the difference between free enterprise and collectivism is chiefly to be found in the quantity of state intervention that is variously present. Free enterprise is thought to involve a minimum of state intervention, and new-dealism, socialism, and communism to involve only progressively more.

This viewpoint is almost completely erroneous. It is extremely difficult, if not impossible, to compare the quantities of state intervention respectively involved in individualism and collectivism. The significant difference is not at all to be found in the quantity of state intervention, and only confusion of thought can result from looking for it there, but rather it is to be found in that intervention's quality. State intervention is inherent in any society; it is a way of saying that a society exists. What distinguishes one society from another is primarily the object of its state intervention, that is, its quality. If the intervention is directed toward building and maintaining a free market, then liberty is created. If it is directed toward accomplishing or permitting a controlled market, then liberty is destroyed. Whether the intervention of the state is directed toward the one object or the other will have little connection with the quantity or amount of that intervention. For example, our present social rules designed to restrict monopoly, consisting of the Sherman, Clayton, and related federal acts, the similar state acts, and the mass of rules established by court decisions interpreting and applying these acts, constitute a great quantity of social intervention in economic activity. It touches the conduct of business at a great many points, and is a complex and confused body of law. By its quantity and complexity it renders business management much more difficult than it otherwise would be. Doubtless many regard this as socialistic intervention by the state. Not so. On the contrary it is—as we shall examine further at a later point—intervention designed to keep the market free, and to preserve that equal opportunity for all that becomes impossible when monopolistic controls are permitted to develop. Here then we have state intervention large in quantity but individualistic in effect. As an example of state intervention small in quantity but collectivistic in its purpose and influence consider the federal Employment Act of 1946. This misnamed statute does no more than establish a Council of Economic Advisers to assist the President in the performance of his duties. But in a long preamble the act states, in effect, that it is the privilege and responsibility of our national government to guide our economic activity so as to accomplish full employment and prosperity, and that it is to this purpose that the Economic Advisers are to devote themselves. In other words, government should plan our economic action, and the Council of Economic Advisers is an initial step toward this planned economy. Since the Advisers thus far are empowered to do nothing but talk, the state intervention which they constitute is small in quantity, but it is a substantial development toward the planned activity of collectivism.

All state intervention in economic affairs, then, should be judged on the basis of its quality, as it creates a free or a controlled market, rather than as it seems to be greater or smaller in quantity. The quantity of intervention is always and entirely irrelevant in itself.

Having thus noted the general character of the free market of individualism and its contrast with the controlled market of collectivism, we proceed with a more detailed consideration of how the free market operates to build liberty.

Chapter 16

THE FREE MARKET AS REGULATOR OF PRODUCTION

In the liberal society, the answer to the questions, What will be produced? and Who will produce what? are determined through the mechanism of the free market. The manner of operation of that mechanism is the subject of the instant chapter.

1. Exchange and non-exchange production

In an exchange economy such as that which today prevails, most production is not consumed by the producer himself or his family, but is exchanged for other goods. Conversely most consumers produce only a small portion of the goods which they themselves consume, depending upon the production of others for most of their consumable goods, which they acquire by exchange. The process of this exchange of goods, wherever and however it is accomplished, constitutes in general terms the market of a particular society.

Even in a highly specialized society, however, some goods are produced for direct consumption by the producer or his family, goods which consequently do not enter into the exchange process and do not appear on the market. Farmers grow food for their own use, housewives fashion clothing for their families, and householders do the work of repairing, and sometimes even of building, their residences.

For the free market society, this non-exchange production presents no particular problem. It allows such production to occur as the individual producer-consumer decides, and the sum of these decisions as they are made by all the members of the society is accepted as the desirable community pattern in this regard—desirable because representing the choices of the people.

For the controlled market society, however, production for direct consumption by the producers is the occasion of considerable difficulty, which is usually met by regulating such production. In Russia the food which a farmer can grow for his own use is generally limited, according to such information as we can receive, and we know that in England a man cannot paint or repair his own house without official permission. Why is this regulation over all productive effort, even when it does not directly enter into the common exchange of goods, regarded as necessary in a controlled market society?

It is because of the effect which all productive effort has upon the total program of production and consumption of a community. The land, seed, tools, and labor which a farmer would use for home production, if such production were permitted, would thereby be made unavailable for use in the production of goods for exchange; and the paint, lumber, supplies, and labor which a householder would use in repairing or remodeling his house would thereby be prevented from being used in other production. In a planned economy, accordingly, where production for the society is specified as a group program, the accomplishment of the program could be seriously impaired if individual citizens were permitted to indulge in such production for direct consumption as they might choose. If the program calls for a stipulated amount of public building, it will not do to permit individuals to interfere with that goal by deciding to use building material in private repairs to their homes. Or if targets of grains are specified in the plan, farmers cannot be permitted to divert grain lands to growing food and pasturing animals for home use beyond what the plan itself may contemplate, for such freedom would jeopardize the plan, and the plan is the controlling consideration in the community's activity. Under the theory of controls, one control must always lead to another, and a controlled market for the production which enters into exchange induces controls of non-exchange production.

But most consumption at the present day is of goods which are obtained in the market through exchange and which are produced for exchange, and it is with these that we are principally concerned.

2. Price in a free market

When goods are brought to the market for exchange, they are rarely traded directly for other goods, but are sold for money. The amount of money received by the seller and paid by the buyer for a particular good is its price.

In a free market the prices of goods are fixed by agreement of buyers and sellers, that is, by contract. This important fact is obscured in many transactions by the manner in which the bargaining is carried on. From the nature of things, a contract of purchase and sale is created by an offer, made either by the purchaser or the seller and accepted by the other party. In practice, some offers are typically made by buyers and some by sellers. In the sale of houses, for example, the offer that leads to an agreement is usually made by the buyer. But in the sale of merchandise in stores the offer is ordinarily made by the seller, who sets a price on the goods he has for sale, which may be accepted or rejected by the prospective purchaser. By reason of the method of dealing which may be employed, buyers are sometimes misled into supposing that they have little or no influence on price, that it is fixed by the seller alone. In this they are mistaken. In the free market the price is always reached by agreement. Even in cases of complete private monopoly, the monopoly price is set by agreement. It is customary to say that monopoly price is fixed by the monopolist. But the private monopolist cannot fix price; he can only offer to sell at a price. If a sale results it is by agreement. The monopolist's control over supply simply means that, to the extent his offers are not accepted, he can reduce supply to balance the effective demand at his offering price.

In a free market, then, and in a controlled market where the controls are those of private monopoly, prices are fixed by the decisions of individuals expressed in agreements to purchase and sell. In making these decisions on price, buyers and sellers tend to observe certain patterns of conduct which are customarily summarized under the generic term of the law of supply and demand.

Demand exists by reason of human want. But in the market it appears only as a willingness to pay a price for a good. A willingness to pay involves of course an ability to do so. Demand therefore depends not only upon what the buyer wants but also upon the money which he has available to spend. Since this quantity of money is always finite, while the wants toward which it must be directed are without assignable boundary, the buyer is always compelled to spend his money for those things which he prefers. He cannot have all things and must therefore choose to have only some things.

In choosing the limited things which he will have, the buyer-consumer necessarily gives consideration not only to his preferences among goods but to the prices at which they are offered. If a necktie and a book are each offered for sale at a price of $2.00, a buyer's purchase of one of these items is an expression of his feeling that one will satisfy a greater want than the other. But if two items are offered at different prices, an additional consideration enters. A buyer may like steak better than ground beef, but if steak is $1.00 a pound while ground beef is $.50, his preference, expressed as demand in the market, may be for ground beef. If he buys the latter, his purchase registers his feeling that the differential of $.50 can buy for him something which he will enjoy more than the added satisfaction of steak over ground beef. On the other hand if he buys steak, the fact of the purchase establishes that the added pleasure of the want-satisfaction afforded by the steak seems to him greater than any use he can then contemplate for the $.50 differential in price.

This comparison of want-satisfactions is not made in an abstract or absolute way, but in the relative way that is called for by the particular circumstances then and there obtaining. Viewed abstractly, food supplies far greater want-satisfaction than entertainment. But relatively at any particular time entertainment may furnish greater want-satisfaction than food. The comparison the buyer makes is not between food generally and entertainment generally, but between another meal here and now and another visit to the theater here and now. That is, the buyer always chooses between marginal units of commodities, comparing the want-satisfactions which those marginal units seem to him capable of supplying.

On the demand side, therefore, the price paid on each transaction represents the buyer's belief that that price is obtaining for him more want-satisfaction than is then and there available by any other expenditure of the same amount. He may later change his mind and rue his purchase, and frequently in life he does so. But the purchase as made is absolute proof that at that time he feels he is obtaining maximum want-satisfaction. That is the gist of the decision to purchase. The decision may have been induced by fraud or mistake, or it may have resulted from inadequate deliberation. But these facts do not change the fact of the belief in maximum want-satisfaction at the moment of purchase. However occasioned, that belief was there.

On the supply side, price in the free market represents the effort of the seller to obtain money. Every producer is also a consumer who needs money to buy goods. He obtains this money by selling in the market, and whether he sells his labor, commodities which he has produced, commodities which he has employed others to produce, or commodities which he has purchased, his aim is to obtain money through the price of the good that he sells.

In general the seller seeks to receive the maximum amount of money which he believes can be obtained under circumstances as then existing. If one purchaser is willing to pay more than another he usually, but by no means always, sells for the higher price. Sellers do not always believe they are receiving maximum price, in the way that buyers always believe they are receiving maximum want-satisfaction. The tendency nevertheless is toward maximum possible receipt.

In the free market, then, the price in each transaction as it occurs is fixed by contract, and represents maximum possible want-satisfaction for the buyer and approximates maximum possible receipt of money by the seller.

All units of a particular commodity tend to sell at the same price at a given time. By reason of the principle of maximum want-satisfaction a consumer will not pay $.35 a gallon for gasoline at one service station if he knows it is being sold at another a block away for $.30. He may not discriminate between the two stations if the differential is only half a cent, for the want-satisfaction that can be purchased with this small amount may not seem to him to be large enough to warrant the effort in saving it. The buyer may also be willing to pay a differential if he thinks there is a difference in quality. But subject to these considerations, units of the same commodity, whether offered by the same producer or by different producers, tend to sell at the same price in the free market.

The price which will tend to be arrived at for all units of a given stock will be determined by the amount which will be paid by the purchaser who places the lowest valuation, in terms of money he will pay, on a unit of the stock. That is, if there are a thousand units of a stock to be sold, the sellers will try to find a thousand purchasers who will pay the highest price. Among these thousand purchasers some one is willing to pay less than any other. In order to sell the entire stock the seller must sell one unit of the stock to this purchaser, and this valuation tends to set the price at which the entire stock must be sold. The price of this last or marginal unit becomes the price for all units.

As the stock of a particular good increases, there is a decrease in the want-satisfying capacity of each added unit. This results from the psychological fact that the human being obtains less satisfaction as additional units of a good are consumed. Thus a certain amount of food is desired very much and has high utility, but as additional quantities are consumed, the want at that time becomes progressively less, even though it will recur in the future. This diminishing utility occurs for all types of human consumption; as quantity increases utility per unit declines. This decrease in utility may take place with greater or less rapidity depending on the particular good, but it always occurs. It is for this reason that under given conditions a larger stock of a commodity must always be sold at a lower price per unit than a smaller quantity of the same commodity. Price falls as supply increases and rises as supply decreases, when conditions other than supply remain the same.

The price of a given supply of a good, therefore, as it is offered in the free market at any time, tends to be fixed by the marginal utility of that particular supply. As consumers make their choices between different goods that are offered to them, deciding to buy this in preference to that, what they are really doing is estimating the marginal utilities of different goods and giving their estimates practical expression in terms of the money they are willing to spend. No consumer, of course, ever says to himself, as he makes his purchases, "Now I shall compare the marginal utility of this good with the marginal utility of that one." But what he is in effect doing, when the matter is viewed objectively and stated in careful terms, is making such a comparison. By their decisions so reached consumers make prices, and the composite of all their decisions sets the prices of goods at their respective marginal utilities, not precisely, but at an approximation that becomes closer to the subjective reality as the amount of bargaining and higgling in the market place increases.

But the quantity of a particular good, as it is offered in the market, is fixed only momentarily; typically the quantities of all goods constantly fluctuate, sometimes greatly. What factors determine the quantities of various commodities that producers offer in the market? Prior to the offering of such goods, people must of course produce them; and the question accordingly becomes, What factors determine, in a free market, the goods which people produce and offer for sale?

To answer this question we must place ourselves in the position of the producer for the free market, and observe the considerations to which he gives attention, explicitly or vaguely, as he decides upon production.

3. Free market price as the determinant of production

The money return which the producer obtains by the sale of his product must first of all go toward meeting his expenses of production.

If he is a workman selling his labor, the price he obtains must first cover the expenses attributable to his employment. If he is a manufacturer, the price he receives from his production must be used first to pay his manufacturing costs. If he is a merchant, the price must cover the cost of goods handled and the expenses of operation. Whether he is a laborer, manufacturer, merchant, or producer of other sort, the price of his product constitutes the source of the money income which must be used to pay the costs of production. Any excess of price over money costs gives the producer additional funds with which to procure the satisfaction of his wants. But his price must always cover his costs if he is to continue production.

The price of a good, accordingly, as it is established in current transactions in the market, tends to fix a boundary for production; that is, producers of a good will try to hold its supply to a point where the price is high enough to cover at least the costs of production. If they produce beyond this point, enlarging the supply so that the marginal units have a utility which in money is less than the cost of production of those units, some of the production will be at a loss and will have to be discontinued. The discontinuance will proceed until the supply is brought back to the point where marginal utility covers cost.

As the reader can readily appreciate, many refinements of analysis are possible when dealing with costs. There are conditions of decreasing costs and of increasing costs, and there are marginal costs, average costs, and total costs, all these aspects of cost being dominated by the principle that sooner or later in all production the application of human labor encounters diminishing returns per unit of labor expended. With these intricacies of cost analysis, however, we are not concerned in the present study. It suffices for our purposes to observe that cost of production in general sets a boundary to the quantity of production, in the sense that production is not carried beyond the point where marginal utility, as expressed in money, just covers cost of production. That is, as production makes larger the supply of a good, its marginal utility falls; and therefore producers must always try to keep the quantity of production of each good below the point where cost would exceed marginal utility to consumers.

Market price not only serves to determine production by limiting it in this fashion; it also determines it by guiding it among the various possibilities that exist within the area of profitable operation. Every producer seeks to maximize his money return. If he is a laborer he is interested in the net money return available after expenses peculiar to his occupation, such as transportation and tools. If he is a manufacturer or merchant he is interested in the net money return after the payment of his costs. He will accordingly seek in general to direct his production toward those market prices which are highest in relation to costs. There are many exceptions to this principle. Most persons seek not only a remunerative occupation but also a congenial one, and this type of preference has a very large influence upon total production. Within the pattern of preferences so established, however, the tendency is strong for each producer to seek maximum price relative to attributable cost. It is accordingly a principle of human action, operable wherever the members of a society are free to exercise choice, that they tend as producers to bring to market those commodities and services whose price will constitute the highest monetary return for their productive effort.

In a free market society, then, one of the functions of market price, as it is determined by the agreements of buyers and sellers, is to regulate production. Free market price limits production to those quantities which can be sold at a price high enough to cover cost, and directs productive effort toward those commodities and services which bring the highest price in the market relative to cost; and this means, since price is consumers' monetary expression of marginal utility, that production is directed toward those commodities and services possessing the highest marginal utility relative to cost.

The efficient performance by free market price of this function depends, nevertheless, upon human judgment. Production is carried on in advance of consumption, sometimes very far in advance. The price upon which producers must rely in carrying on production is not the price of today while the production is going on, but the price of tomorrow when production will be completed. Production therefore is carried on not so much in the light of present prices as in the light of estimates of future prices. This estimating of future market conditions is part of the task of the entrepreneur or businessman. It is an art which requires experience, application, and judgment. Upon its successful performance depends the smooth operation of the productive machinery in creating goods which can be disposed of without loss.

A part of the forecast required of entrepreneurs is the estimate of the price which will be paid for a new commodity or service not theretofore marketed. Novel goods always present the question of consumer reception. Although human nature craves change in the goods it uses for want-satisfaction, yet it typically desires that change be made slowly, and estimating the extent to which a new good will be accepted by consumers calls for great skill. Upon the exercise of this skill depends progress in the practical arts and in trade and commerce. Producers are interested in trying to find new goods for production because it is in connection with such goods that the highest market price relative to cost can frequently be found. Despite the greater risk involved, this inducement of high price leads producers in the free market society to experiment with new lines of endeavor, giving the society the vitality and interest of change.

Even though forecasting be badly done, however, market price in the free market society will bend production to its dictates. The producer who persists in creating goods which the free market will not pay for at a price high enough to cover costs of production will be compelled eventually to discontinue such production, since the free market will not sustain him in it. Price in the free market thus serves to limit production to the market demand. Businessmen from time to time misjudge the supply of goods which the market will absorb, but their error cannot long continue.

It is a thesis of Marxism and a mistake in which the Keynesian analysis also indulges that in a free market society there is certain to be overproduction. Viewed from its reverse, this is referred to as underconsumption. This is said to be a vital defect of the free market system, causing recurrent crises. While it is true that businessmen are certain to make mistakes on the supply of a good which the market will take at a price high enough to cover costs, yet in the free market the necessary correction is constantly being performed. For a part of the function of free market price, one which it will surely perform if kept truly free, is always to fall low enough to clear the market of the offered supply. If production piles up and is not being cleared through the market, it is a sign that market price is being interfered with and is not moving freely in response to the forces of supply and demand. In a free market, price will fall to the point where past production will be cleared and where future production will be guided into more suitable endeavors. Overproduction is not, therefore, a chronic and fatal malady of the free enterprise system, but occurs as a more or less temporary imbalance which the free market itself, if allowed to operate, will cure with greater or less dispatch and with minimum social harm. But on this matter of overproduction there is somewhat more to be said in the next chapter.

4. Free market price as consumer preference

As each transaction occurs in the free market, the purchaser obtains a good which will render him the maximum want-satisfaction that is possible for the given expenditure of money, as we have already seen. This being true for one purchaser, it is also true for all purchasers, since there are no offsetting considerations when the total purchases of consumers are considered together. That is, in a free market purchasers obtain the maximum want-satisfaction that is possible within the existing productive arrangements, and not only within those arrangements as then existing, but also within those arrangements as they might conceivably be modified within the near future; for as we have seen, businessmen will change production and bring forward new products if the current pattern of consumption indicates that such new products will be preferred by consumers.

Since, therefore, free market price registers the preferences of consumers as they seek maximum want-satisfaction, and since free market price also determines production, it follows that in the free market the productive effort of the community is dictated by consumers' preferences. In the free market society, accordingly, the answer to the basic question, What will be produced? is made by the members of the community in their capacity as consumers as they individually state their preferences through their purchases.

That consumers should thus be allowed to dictate the course of production follows necessarily from the principles of liberty as heretofore established. Since the exercise of freedom of choice in the consumption of goods furnishes the material base for all human life, the direction of production by consumer preference constitutes a vital part of liberty's manifestation.

It is not infrequently said that in the free market consumers vote with their dollars for the goods which they want produced. This figure of speech calls to our attention the fact that different consumers cast votes which differ in their quantitative influence. Purchasers have different quantities of dollars to spend and therefore have differing votes. Is this compatible with the principles of liberty?

In considering this question we must note that purchasers appear in the market in two distinct capacities: (a) as purchasers of goods for direct personal consumption and (b) as purchasers of goods to be used in the production of other goods which ultimately will be used for personal consumption. The housewife in a grocery store is an example of the first, and the purchasing agent of a corporation is an example of the second. Obviously the latter has much more money to spend in the market than the former. Purchases for production, however, whether they be of coal for energizing machines, raw materials for manufacturing, or construction materials for additional plant, are all directed by the preferences of purchasers for ultimate personal consumption. That this task of purchasing goods for productive purposes should be concentrated in the hands of businessmen and corporate executives is not a violation of the principles of equal liberty, but is only a form of the specialization essential to large production; and since their decisions are dictated by ultimate consumer preference, the inequality of their votes is unimportant except as ultimate consumer preference may itself be unequally expressed.

But purchasers for ultimate personal consumption also differ among themselves in the money they have to spend, and when the free market is criticized because buyers exercise different votes, it is to this fact that reference is more particularly made. As we shall see in the two succeeding chapters, however, the money which consumers in a free market have available for spending depends upon the respective contributions they have previously made to production, subject to certain exceptions called for by the principles of liberty. The differing influences of consumers upon the total pattern of consumer preference therefore result, in general, from their differing contributions to production in the free market. And this—it is the argument of individualism—is as it should be.

The figure of consumers as voters is misleading in that it suggests that some of the preferences voted for may not win in the election. This is incorrect. In the free market each voter's candidate always wins. The market is a series of elections and each election is over when the dollar is spent. The elected candidate may turn out to be a great disappointment, but unless fraud is involved the consumer gets what he voted for. He never gets all that he wants—no social institution can give him that —but within the possibilities of production he obtains, as he casts each vote, that which he prefers.

5. Price in a controlled market

To understand how market price performs its function of regulating production in a free market society, we must observe what becomes its role when the market is subject to controls.

With respect to price in a controlled market, a distinction must be made between markets which are controlled by private monopoly and those which are controlled by public regulation.

As regards the former, market price is not fixed by the monopolist, but is established by agreement of the monopolist and his customer. What the customer will pay depends upon his schedule of preferences. The power of the monopolist lies in the fact that he can prevent production from expanding to the point where price, as determined by consumers' schedules of preferences, will barely cover cost of production, and can restrict supply to a point where customers can be found who will pay—because of their schedules of preferences—a price high enough to cover cost by a substantial margin. If the monopolist tries to obtain a very high price, he will of course have to restrict production to meet the purchases of only a few customers, and such restricted production may leave him with only a small total income. He will, therefore, tend to experiment to find the quantity which will render him the highest net income after costs. As we have seen, every producer, even the humblest laborer, exercises control over quantity of production to some extent. But in most avenues of activity such control cannot affect market price to any appreciable amount. It is when control over supply becomes substantial that a monopoly price and not a free market price results.

It is at this point that society, if it is guided by the principles of equal opportunity, will intervene. If circumstances permit, it will prevent the monopolist's control over supply. If this is not possible because of the absence of competing supply sources, it will as a last resort directly regulate price. The circumstances, however, under which competitive sources of supply are so lacking that direct price regulation should be resorted to are much more rare than is frequently supposed.

In markets which are controlled by public regulation, the market price of commodities and services is no longer the subject of agreement between buyer and seller, but is fixed by official decree. The question for the producer and consumer is not the price at which they shall do business but whether they shall do business at the stipulated price.

For the producer, a price fixed by law is a major regulator of his production. He must consider, first, the quantity whose cost will be covered by the stipulated price, and second, the quantity which he can sell at the stipulated price. His production will be limited to the smaller of these two quantities.

The effect of an officially decreed price on production can be analyzed by comparing the fixed price with the price which would obtain if the market were free. If the fixed price is higher than what the free market price would be, under the prevailing conditions, then the quantity of production and consumption of the particular good for which the price is so fixed will be less than it would be under free market conditions. For although producers could furnish more units of the good at the higher price, consumers will not buy as much of it at the higher price. And since production will not exceed what will be purchased for consumption, production will be less than it would be in a free market. Likewise, if the fixed price is below what the free market price would be, production and consumption of the good again will be less than they would be under free market conditions. For now the consumers would buy more of the good but the producers cannot furnish it. The free market price represents their marginal cost, and since the fixed price is below this cost, they will have to cut back production to a point where marginal costs will be covered by the fixed price, and consequently production at the fixed price will be less than it would be at the free price.

Thus a fixed price for a good always results in lower production and consumption of that good than that which would occur under free market conditions.

This is a very important principle and one which is constantly overlooked. There is no way in which the collectivized society can avoid its operation. The free market price of a good, or what the free market price would be if free market conditions were allowed, always represents the maximum quantity of that good which the society is willing to make the effort to produce. Thus the free market price registers a psychological fact obtaining in the society, and this fact is beyond the reach of the collectivistic legislator. Any price that he can fix, therefore, except as it may coincide with what would have been the free market price anyway, must result in lowered production and consumption of the particular good.

6. Fixed prices and coercion

There is only one avenue of escape from the inexorable operation of the principle that a fixed price must mean lowered production and consumption, and that is the use of coercion. The fixed price must be either above or below the price which would be established by the bargaining of buyers and sellers in the free market, and we shall examine the use of coercion in each case.

If the fixed price is above the free market price, it means that the fixed price is more than consumers are willing to pay for the offered quantity. For example, under the system of price controls for farm products currently used in the United States, the fixed price for wheat, which the federal government guarantees to producers, is about $2.50 per bushel at Chicago. The government stands ready to take at this price (by the mechanism of "loans" that do not have to be repaid) all wheat offered to it by wheat growers. On the Chicago Board of Trade, where the price is not guaranteed by the government, the price for wheat at present is around $2.30, which is about the price a farmer would receive if he shipped wheat to grain buyers in Chicago. Thus the fixed price is above the free market price, and in consequence the government acquires a large quantity of wheat. (The Board of Trade is not really a free market, since it is subject to the influence of many controls, but we may properly regard it as a free market for present purposes.) This wheat the government eventually sells either for export or for domestic use, at such prices as it can obtain. Since these prices are below the fixed price, there is a loss on the operation, which loss constitutes the amount of the subsidy paid by society to wheat growers. This subsidy consists of money taken from the citizenry as taxes, that is, by coercion. The people of the United States are thus compelled to purchase and consume, through transactions conducted by the state, a larger quantity of wheat than that which they would choose to buy, if they were free to choose, at the fixed price.

It is frequently said, by way of criticism of this program, that it perpetuates the very surpluses of crops that it is aimed to take care of. Although this is true, it is important to understand the elements in the program which have this effect. Decreeing prices higher than free market prices would not of itself have this result; such decreed prices, though ever so strictly enforced, would only result in lower consumption, which means that some of the producers would be unable to dispose of their production and would have to turn to some other way of making a living. Undoubtedly also, at least as an interim measure while production was being cut down, a black market would appear in which producers would sell the surplus at prices less than those decreed. But unless the force of the state were used to cause consumers to buy the unwanted surplus, the tendency of the high decreed price would of itself cause the surplus to disappear. It is coercion in support of the high price, compelling the members of society to buy what they do not wish, that continues the surplus of production.

This calls to our attention, moreover, the fact that a government purchase program at a fixed price above the free market price leads to coercion to restrain producers. Although the high fixed price deters consumers from buying as much as they otherwise would, it persuades producers to produce more than they otherwise would. Accordingly, if nothing is done to restrict the production of wheat, the taxpayers must be compelled to buy ever increasing quantities of wheat which they do not want. To reduce this absurdity somewhat, we presently use coercion to prevent the wheat growers from producing as much as they would like to do, by allotting wheat acreage to each farmer. Thus the fixed price leads to coercion of both consumers and producers.

If, on the other hand, the fixed price is below the free market price, it means that the fixed price is less than the cost of producing the added units which consumers would be willing to buy at the low price. In this situation coercion must be used to compel producers to produce and sell the shortage below the quantity they would choose to furnish at the fixed price, or consumers must be coerced by some form of rationing into buying less than they would like to buy.

For the use of coercion in support of a price below that of the free market, consider rent control in Britain. Rents are fixed so low that they do not cover the cost of supplying housing; that is, they are below the free market price. Producers therefore will not produce housing unless they are forced to do so. Accordingly money is taken from the members of the community by force, as taxes, and is used to produce housing, either by paying subsidies to private builders or by constructing public housing. With respect to the maintenance and repair of existing housing the application of force is more direct. Since the fixed price of the housing is below the cost of maintaining it, the owner usually does not wish to incur the additional costs. But the state says he must keep the housing he owns in good repair, regardless of the income from it, and puts him in jail or fines him if he fails to do so.

In this case, where fixed price is below free market price, the fixed price itself perpetuates a shortage of the product. As long as fixed price for housing is below the free market price, housing will not be produced unless coercion be used. The shortage will not only continue but will become worse as old houses become uninhabitable. This is occurring in spectacular fashion in Paris, where rent control for nearly forty years has reduced housing to a deplorable state.

Here again, moreover, the use of a fixed price leads not only to coercion to compel action but also to coercion to restrain it. Not only is force employed to compel the production of housing in Britain, but it is also employed to limit the use of housing. Consumers cannot rent such housing as they choose, but only as much as the state assigns to them. That is, there is rationing of housing, as there must always be rationing of any commodity when its price is controlled at a level below free market price.

Thus whether the price of a good is fixed above or below the free market price, the effect is always to lower the production and consumption of that good unless the coercion of the state be introduced. Only by compelling producers to produce either more or less than they would choose to produce at the fixed price, and by compelling consumers to consume either less or more than they would choose to consume at the fixed price, can production and consumption be kept at the level which would be attained by the free market. Force becomes the essential core of the fixed price system, as it is of all collectivism.

7. Consumer preference in the controlled market

It follows from the foregoing that in the controlled market consumer preference is not permitted to regulate production. While the competitive activity of buyers and sellers in the free market gives rise to a market price which expresses completely the preferences of consumers under given conditions, the controlled market diverts production from the channels indicated by the preferences of consumers and directs it into lines dictated by the controls. The more the controls interfere with the operation of the free market the greater is the diversion from consumer preference.

Indeed it is the very purpose of the controlled market of collectivism to interfere with consumer preference. As we saw in the preceding chapter, a major criticism of the free market made by collectivists is that it moves haphazardly in the production of goods, not producing those goods which people really should have, but only those which their unplanned day-by-day decisions happen to bring about. But as our analysis in the present chapter has shown, the free market produces the goods which people prefer, however wise or unwise their preferences may be. Accordingly the collectivists are necessarily placed in the position of denying that production should follow consumer preference, and of asserting that it should follow the dictates of a few collectivistic planners who prepare the economic program for the whole community. The judgment of the few is substituted for the judgment of the many. The few vote the dollars of all.

Therefore representation of collectivists that their planned economy constitutes industrial and economic democracy is a fraud. To whatever extent the free market may be justly subject to the criticism that it permits production to be directed by some rather than by all, the controlled market is subject to the same criticism to a vastly greater extent. It takes the determination of production almost entirely from the people as consumers and places it in the hands of the autocratic few who constitute the governmental bureaucracy.

8. The concept of fair price

What is a fair price? Men seem always to have discussed this question and to have used the concept of fair price as a point of reference. Aristotle debated the matter; so did Thomas Aquinas. And fair price as a standard is constantly referred to today. Much of our discussion of fair price is in terms of synonyms. Thus in public utility regulation we say that a fair price is one which will produce a reasonable rate of return on capital investment. But what is a reasonable rate of return? It is fixed by various regulatory bodies today at from $5\frac{1}{2}\%$ to $6\frac{1}{4}\%$ on the investment. If we inquire why this is a reasonable rate of return, the only answer we can receive—subject to one exception to which we shall return in a moment—is that this constitutes a fair price for use of the capital devoted to the enterprise. This leaves us still asking, What is a fair price? Likewise in the renegotiation of contracts with the federal government for the supplying of arms and munitions of war, the renegotiators are supposed to settle upon a fair price for the commodities supplied. What is this fair price? It is one which gives a fair profit to the contractor. If we ask what is a fair profit, the only answer we can receive—subject again to one similar exception—is that a fair profit is a fair price for the capital and effort of the contractor; and again we are led around in a circle to the original inquiry of the nature of a fair price.

The only way by which this circuitous chain of thought can be broken is by reference to the free market and the price which would be obtained in such a free market for the particular commodity or service. Thus in the regulation of public utilities 6% constitutes a reasonable rate of return because experience in the free market indicates that approximately 6% per annum on the investment is the free market price for the use of capital in enterprises of similar risk and difficulty. Since the utility in a free market society such as ours can be expected to pay the free market price for the labor which it employs and the supplies which it uses, the allowance to it of prices for its product which are high enough to permit the equivalent of the free market return on its capital results in a fair price for the product which it sells.

This reference to the free market rate of return is the exception referred to above, as the only possible escape from reasoning in a circle about fair price. The reasonable rate of return is simply the free market rate of return for like enterprises. We have learned in recent years in connection with our public utility regulation that to set electric rates, for example, so low that the return on the capital invested falls below the free market rate for the use of capital in similar enterprises simply results in curtailing the production of electricity. Those savers who have money to invest will not place it in an industry where the return is below that available in the free market on other investments of like risk. To obtain the flow of new money into the industry which is constantly needed, public service commissions have found that they must allow a rate of return on investment high enough to meet the competition of the free market for funds. This determines the fair price the utility is allowed to charge. It is likewise with the renegotiation of arms contracts with the federal government. A fair profit on such contracts can be determined only by reference to the free market. A fair price for airplanes sold to the government, for example, must be high enough to cover going market prices for labor and for supplies and to leave a profit or net income equivalent to the return which could be had on the use of capital in free market enterprises of similar risk, difficulty, and volume of sales.

A fair price is thus a free market price. The only content available for the concept of fair price is the free market price which would prevail if free market conditions obtained. This free market price, as we have seen, tends to settle on the point where marginal utility equals marginal cost. Except for this idea of a price, as influenced by marginal utility, just high enough to cover the costs of marginal production, the concept of a fair price does not have and never can have any substance. Prices in the free market may rarely reach this precise point, but the concept of it as the objective of free market forces furnishes the idea of fair price.

When this standard of the free market price is discarded, no other standard of fairness remains. The price of wheat at the present time, to take a concrete case, is approximately $2.30 in the free market. Let us suppose that it is a fact that the marginal wheat farmer cannot obtain as good a living as is available in other occupations at the present time unless he receives $3.00 a bushel for his wheat. Is $2.30 still a fair price for the marginal grower's wheat, indicating that he should change to some other activity, or is $3.00 a fair price, because necessary to constitute a parity return? If we say, "Yes, $3.00 is a fair price for the producer to receive," shall we also say, "Yes, it is a fair price for the consumer to pay"? If so, then for what quantity of wheat is it a fair price? Does it constitute a fair price for present production? Would it also constitute a fair price if wheat farmers increased their production five-fold? If it is a fair price for present production because of costs, it must also be a fair price when production is increased five-fold, for costs then will be higher than they are now. Since consumers do not wish to pay $3.00 per bushel for the present production, they obviously will not wish to pay that price for higher production, and coercion will have to be used, both for present and increased production.

But what becomes of the concept of fairness if purchasers are compelled to buy an unwanted commodity at a price they do not wish to pay? And if this is a fair method of dealing for wheat farmers, why is it not also a fair method of dealing for all other producers? Why should not society fix a fair price for all goods and compel consumers as a whole to buy at such fair price all the goods which producers wish to produce and offer for sale at that price regardless of whether consumers wish to do so? One answer of course is that complete chaos would result. Another answer is that no concept of fairness could apply to such a program. The inescapable conclusion is that apart from the operation of the free market there can be no substance to the concept of fairness in prices.

There are two very important considerations that stem from this fact that only a free market can indicate what a fair price is under given circumstances.

The first is that to the extent that collectivists succeed in imposing their planned economy upon a society, they also render fair prices difficult or impossible. To the extent that the free market is destroyed, the standard of reference for determining fairness is taken away. When free markets are entirely eliminated a fair price is anything which a governmental bureau says it is, and the judgment on fair price must be individual and arbitrary, since the free market in which the judgment of the entire community is expressed is no longer available. The collectivist glibly says that under social planning all prices will be fair since the decree of the state will make them fair. But the fact is that such socially planned prices can never be anything more than the arbitrary guesses of government planners, based upon their individual prejudices in favor of one or another group within the community.

The second result of the fact that the free market alone provides fairness in prices is that only within a free market can producers obtain the information which is necessary in order to make production fair to all members of the community. To carry on production which fairly cares for the needs of all at fair prices, a comprehensive volume of information of the needs of consumers is requisite. This information can never be adequately and promptly supplied by a controlled market. The free market, however, quickly and accurately records this information for the use of producers, through the machinery of free market price.

We may conclude our discussion of the regulation of production by the free market by saying that in the free market society, where the prevailing rule is that producers may produce and sell as they choose and consumers may buy and consume as they choose, and where the state intervenes with its force only to preserve equal opportunity, production is directed through the influence of free market price into those goods, out of all productive possibilities, which consumers prefer sufficiently to pay the costs of production.

Chapter 17

THE FREE MARKET AS REGULATOR OF CONSUMPTION

In a free market society, as we have seen in the preceding chapter, the productive effort of human beings is directed toward the creation of those goods which, as consumers, they prefer. And since production, when had, determines consumption, we may conclude that consumption also, in the free market, is determined by the preferences of the consumers. The purpose of the present chapter is to examine the implications of this last statement and the manner in which it manifests itself in the practice of the free market society.

1. Consumption determined by money income

The distinction between market and non-market transactions, already noted with respect to production, is applicable as well to consumption. The production which occurs outside the market, for consumption directly by the producer and his family, is substantial, and it leads to a corresponding amount of non-market consumption. In the free society, this non-market production and consumption is permitted to occur as individual citizens determine. It is not regulated by the state, nor by the market. The election of an individual to expend the effort to create a good determines the fact that he will later consume it.

Most goods, however, are not produced for direct consumption but for the market, because the advantages of specialization require that the market be made use of for the purpose of distribution. In the market, goods are sold by producers for money, and they are bought by consumers who pay a price in money. What a particular consumer can buy depends on the money he has available.

In a free market, therefore, the consumption of the individual, including the consumption of any other persons whom he may support, depends upon the effort he can and will expend for non-market consumption and on the money he has to spend in the market for market consumption. With the former, non-market consumption, we are no further concerned, and our attention will be directed exclusively to the latter. In the remainder of this chapter, when consumption is spoken of it will refer to market consumption unless the context indicates that both market and non-market consumption are intended. But although our attention is thus concentrated on market consumption, we must not forget that an important part of total consumption is supplied by non-market activity, particularly in the case of those members of society whose money income is low. This furnishes a reason for the unreliability of income statistics; they do not present, and it would be well-nigh impossible for them to present, an accurate picture of non-market consumption, and accordingly they fail to indicate accurately the facts regarding consumption as a whole.

When a consumer enters the market he must have money to spend, and his consumption will be limited by the size of his money stock. At any given moment of time the total money stock of a society is held by its members in varying quantities, and during ensuing time they will more or less quickly spend this money for diverse purposes. Some will be used to pay the wages of employees, some for other costs of production, and some for consumers' goods. As each expenditure of money is made by one person it becomes the receipt of money by another person. Thus from moment to moment the quantity of money for the society remains constant (subject to changes in the community's money stock which do not here concern us), although steadily moving from hand to hand. This movement of money within the society is frequently pictured as a circular flow; but this is a quite misleading representation. The picture, rather, is one of multitudinous crisscross lines, sometimes following established patterns for a while but then sure to depart upon new ways of movement. Within this melange of exchange occasional circular figurations can be seen, some with a degree of permanence, e.g., the movement of tax money; but the circular movement is exceptional.

The experience of the individual during any period of time is of a flow of money, as money is received and in turn expended. The goods he can buy for consumption during this period of time must be limited by his money receipts (disregarding for the moment credit purchases). Some individuals can and do use all their money receipts for the purchase of consumers' goods. But many are obligated to use a portion otherwise, only the residue being available for financing consumption. Thus if the individual is an entrepreneur, his money receipts must first be devoted to paying wages, interest, material costs, and other expenses of production; the remainder, if any, is his net money receipts, i.e., his net income available for consumption. Over any given time the consumption of an individual may not exactly correspond to his net money receipts; he may expand his consumption by credit purchases, and he may restrict his consumption by using some of his money for investment expenditures; but in the one case he must later use some of his money to pay off his indebtedness, and in the other case he will have, or at least expects to have, more money for consumption purposes at a later date than he otherwise would receive. For the long run, consequently, the distribution of net money receipts rather closely determines the distribution of consumption, even as for the short run it determines the limits within which it can occur.

The analytical problem becomes, in consequence, that of examining how the free market determines the distribution of net money receipts. As net money receipts are allocated to the different members of society by the operation of the free market, so consumption is regulated. The question of who will consume and in what proportions consumption will occur is answered by the free market through regulating the distribution of net money receipts.

2. The nature of money receipts

All money received by an individual can be divided into two categories: (1) money received in return for a contribution to the production of goods, and (2) money received not in return for a contribution to the production of goods, but otherwise.

The first category is composed of money received as (a) wages, (b) rent, (c) compensation for the use of capital goods, (d) interest, (e) entrepreneurial profit, and (f) proceeds from the sale of property purchased with money received as wages, rent, interest, or entrepreneurial profit.

The second category is principally composed of money obtained by (a) borrowing, (b) gift or inheritance, (c) the sale of property received through gift or inheritance, and (d) theft or fraud.

With respect to the second category, none of the money received in the enumerated modes enters importantly into the purchase of consumers' goods. Money obtained by borrowing—item (a)—is used rather substantially, it is true, to finance the purchase of goods. But since bor-

rowed money must be repaid, it has no effect on the quantity of money
receipts of an individual over the term of the loan; as his money receipts are augmented when the loan is made, so his net receipts are
diminished as the loan is repaid. Money obtained by borrowing is
therefore without influence upon the distribution of money receipts
among the members of society; it affects only the timing, and not the
amount, of those receipts.

With respect to items (b) and (c) in the second category, each of
these constitutes a form of money receipt which the individual occasionally uses for the purchase of consumers' goods, but rarely to any
great extent. Money transferred by gift or inheritance seldom is of large
amount, and when it is of substantial size it is almost certain to be
used for investment rather than for consumers' goods, and the problem becomes one of the money obtained from investments—which
will require a good deal of attention before we are through—rather than
one of money obtained directly by gift or inheritance. Much the same
comments apply to money received from the sale of property which
has first been obtained by gift or inheritance. Here, however, the
quantity of property passing by gift or inheritance is substantial. But
again, the money received from any sale of such property is rarely used
in the purchase of consumers' goods; it is almost always employed in
some form of reinvestment in capital goods; and consequently the
problem of the distribution of consumption must direct its attention
to the money income received from the use of property obtained by gift
or inheritance rather than to money received through its sale. With respect to item (d), nothing need be said; to the extent it enters into the
distribution of money receipts everyone is agreed it should be stopped in
so far as possible.

We may therefore conclude that the money receipts which are obtained not in return for a contribution to the production of goods, but
otherwise, are not important in financing the purchase of consumers'
goods, and in consequence do not play a part of any significance in
regulating consumption. We must look, accordingly, to the money receipts which individuals obtain in return for contributions to the production of goods, in order to understand the regulation of consumption
which is effected by the free market.

The production of goods is accomplished by the application of human
labor to natural resources with the aid of tools, that is, by labor applied
to land with the use of capital. The term "capital," as used in this work,
always means capital goods. In a meager society, each individual could

own his own tools and work on his own plot of land or on land communally owned. To some extent the combination in one individual of laborer, landowner, and capitalist can still prevail, as we see in small agricultural operations. But the specialization which an advanced standard of living requires necessarily outmodes the simplicity of this arrangement, and demands that many laborers, landowners, and capitalists be brought together in one enterprise; the single individual may still be a laborer, a landowner, and a capitalist (e.g., the employee of a corporation who is also a stockholder), but many such persons must be brought together, as must also the labor, land, and capital which they respectively contribute. This task of bringing together and directing the agents of production is that of the entrepreneur or businessman, and he too is one of the contributors to production.

The goods produced by this cooperative process are sold in the market for money, and the money received is distributed to the human beings who furnish the labor, land, capital, and entrepreneurship that have entered into the particular act of production. The agency for effecting this distribution is the entrepreneur; even as he manages the joining of labor, land, and capital in production, so he supervises the distribution of the money proceeds. Indeed, he does more than merely supervise the distribution; he pays the amount of some of the distributive shares in advance, typically wages, rent (of some kinds), and interest, taking the risk that the receipts from the sale of the product will be sufficient to reimburse him, with an overplus or profit which will constitute compensation for both his risk and effort. The division of the money received from the sale of the product is determined by bargaining in the market; the entrepreneur effects bargains with those who furnish labor, land, and capital, and pursuant to these bargains the distribution is made.

The modern corporation is not a person who either consumes or produces, but a form or mode by which human beings cooperate in entrepreneurship. We say that the corporation is the employer, lessee, borrower, and so forth, but this speech is deceptive; it is the stockholders who are in economic reality the employers, lessees, and borrowers; the corporation is a legalistic fiction, permitted in law to act like a person for purposes of convenience. The corporation does not share in the product of its production; only the persons connected with it by bargains and the stockholders share in the product. The corporation itself, then, does not figure in consumption or in the distribution of goods for consumption, except as an agency for human beings who consume, and as such agency it acts in the place of an entrepreneur.

The money, accordingly, which is received by human beings in return for their contributions to production may be classified as follows: (a) compensation for labor furnished; (b) compensation for land furnished; (c) compensation for capital furnished; (d) compensation for money lent to the entrepreneur to assist him in buying the use of labor, land, or capital; and (e) the residual profit, if any, remaining as compensation for the risk and management of entrepreneurship. Although in analysis these forms of compensation are separate, in practice they are usually combined in varying ways. If the producer is a single person, all forms of money receipts are combined together. Typically profit is combined at least to some extent with compensation for capital furnished, for the entrepreneur usually employs some capital of his own. The entrepreneur is also frequently the owner of some and perhaps all of the land used in production, and the amount he is able to retain after paying the amounts stipulated in his bargains with laborers, etc., constitutes rent as well as profit. Similarly the entrepreneur usually furnishes at least part of the stock of money which is used in making advances to workers and suppliers of materials, and accordingly the residual remuneration which he receives includes also interest.

As the process of production moves along, the product is sold in the market by the entrepreneur. With the money received he reimburses himself for the advances theretofore made in financing production, and retains any balance for compensation for the instruments of production he himself has furnished and for his entrepreneurial compensation. Obviously the moneys which the entrepreneur advances for wages, rent, interest, or materials comes in effect from the sale of the product; the entrepreneur will promptly go out of business if for every $1.00 he advances in costs he receives only $.90 from the sale of the product; the money received by the sale of the product must cover the compensation of the costs of production, and constitutes in effect the money to pay that compensation.

The compensation thus paid to the agents of production is not paid to labor, land, and capital as abstractions, but to particular human beings who by their efforts furnish labor, land, and capital. In the free market it is essential, for reasons we shall examine in a later chapter, that land and capital be the subject of private property. Moreover neither land nor capital creates itself or makes itself available for the productive process. In very rare instances land, i.e., natural resources, is ready for use in production in its natural state. But in most instances some labor must be spent on it before it is available. It matters not whether the results of such labor be regarded as land or capital; the point is that neither land nor capital will or can be furnished to the productive process unless those persons who furnish them are compensated. Clearly, also, the human beings who furnish labor neither can nor will do so unless they are compensated, and the same is true of those who furnish the management of entrepreneurship and assume its risks. Nor will the owners of money lend it to entrepreneurs unless they are paid interest. The productive process, then, furnishes through the sale of its product in the market the money which compensates the persons furnishing the elements of production, and their compensation must occur if the process of production is to go on.

The money so received by the persons furnishing labor, land, capital, money, and entrepreneurship provides the means whereby they purchase consumers' goods.

They need not, however, buy only consumers' goods. They may also buy land or capital or they may lend money upon promise of its repayment. Later they may sell the land or capital and may use the proceeds to buy consumers' goods, or they may use the money received on the repayments of loans to buy consumers' goods. Such use of money to finance consumers' goods purchases is unusual, however; most money obtained from the liquidation of investments is used in reinvestment. To the extent that such money is used for the purchase of consumers' goods, however, it constitutes money that has first been obtained by contributions to production.

Since we have seen that the money received by persons otherwise than through contributions to production is used in the purchase of consumers' goods only to a negligible extent, we may conclude that consumption is regulated in the free market by the compensation received by individuals in return for their contributions of labor, land, capital, money, and entrepreneurship to the productive process. As more or less compensation is received for these contributions, so more or less consumption is possible, and the distribution of consumption in the community is in accordance with the distribution of compensation for the labor, land, capital, money, and entrepreneurship furnished in production.

The problem of the free market's regulation of consumption becomes, therefore, the problem of the free market's regulation of the compensation paid to persons for their respective contributions to production.

3. Money receipts and contribution to production

Our inquiry must consequently become, How does the free market regulate the money receipts that are obtained by individuals in return for the contributions which they respectively make to production?

The individual who operates as a single unit of enterprise, furnishing the labor, land, and capital required for the production of the goods or service which he sells, quite clearly can obtain money receipts only to the extent of the market price of his product. And since the market price of his product is determined by the evaluation which consumers place on it, as they compare the want-satisfying capacity of one good with another, we may say that his money receipts are determined by the value of his productivity as estimated by consumers' preferences. As his productivity, thus measured in the market by consumers, goes up or down, so his money receipts and consequently his consumption go up or down. His consumption is thus determined by his contribution to production.

We should note that the free market, in evaluating a contribution to production, takes no account of the merit of the producer except as it is displayed in the merit of his product. The producer may be a man of bad morals, but unless his morals are reflected in the bad quality of his product—as indeed they frequently will be—the market is not concerned in so far as it operates to regulate consumption. On the other hand, the producer may be a person of the very best morals, but unless he produces a product of market value, the free market will not reward him with the money he needs to finance consumption. Nor is the free market concerned with the effort put forth by the producer; it will pay him just as much for his product if he produces it with ease as if he produces it with the most arduous toil. In fact, if he devises ways of producing with less effort, so that his production is larger with the same or less work, it will usually reward him by giving him larger money receipts, thus allocating to him larger consumption, since he has also increased production. Nor, again, is the market concerned with the ability of the producer, except as his ability is embodied in his product, giving it larger favor with consumers. And, lastly, the free market is not interested in the merit of a producer except as that merit consists in a capacity to satisfy the wants of consumers as they themselves experience them. The free market is not an institution for the improvement of consumers' choices, but for the registering of them as they occur and for transmuting them into economic fact. Critics of the free market always point to the great volume of frivolous purchases which take place, while more worthy needs are left uncared for, and they hold this out as a failure of the free market system. But within the philosophy of the liberty of individualism it is not the function of the state to organize a market in which citizens are compelled to consume the goods they ought to have (in the opinion of critics) instead of those they prefer, any more than it is the function of the state to organize a government in which citizens are compelled to obey the public officers they ought to have (in the opinion of critics) instead of those they choose to elect by an exercise of suffrage. It is the great virtue of the free market—as long as it is kept truly a free market through the maintenance of equal opportunity—that it is not an instrument for the coercion of consumers' preferences, but only gives them effect.

When we turn from the single individual as producer to those forms in which more than one person join—the single entrepreneur with employees, the partnership, and the corporation—we find that the analysis of the distribution of money receipts becomes more difficult. But again we can note that the money receipts allocated by the free market to any one enterprise as a whole are determined by the market evaluation of the product or products which that enterprise produces and sells. Obvious as this proposition may seem, it is nevertheless one that is constantly overlooked. For many years, for example, the tone of union activity in this country has been derogatory toward the plants in which the unions are organized. In some instances this attitude has erupted into express denunciation of the quality of the goods produced by the plant where the union members work, coupled with advice to refrain from purchasing such goods. How workers can suppose that their employment by a company can continue if its goods are not disposed of is beyond comprehension, and yet these things happen.

They happen because those who furnish a particular element in the productive process, such as labor, imagine that, even though the total money receipts of an enterprise may decline, yet the money receipts which they themselves obtain can be made to remain the same or even be enlarged, the necessary reduction being taken by the furnishers of the other elements. The question then is, Will this happen in the free market under the circumstances which ordinarily prevail? And this question necessarily brings us to the problem of how the money receipts obtained on the sale of a good are divided among the furnishers of the labor, land, capital, money, and entrepreneurship which were used in its production.

Fortunately for both the length and difficulty of our study, the purposes of the present analysis do not require us to pursue exhaustively this matter of the distribution of money receipts. Economists are not agreed on how wages, rent, capital compensation, interest, and profits are allocated in the free market; and if it were necessary for us to examine these topics to their end, we would not only face a very large task but our conclusions about the operation of the free market would probably rest on a base of limited appeal. As we shall see, however, the explanation of the free market's regulation of consumption and the case for the free market generally by no means require such far-going analysis, but are to be founded on general propositions concerning the free market's division of income among the elements of production, general propositions which can be accepted although there may be no agreement on the identification of the forces and influences operating to effect the free market's result.

The preponderance of wages, rent, capital earnings, and interest is paid by entrepreneurs who make bargains with the people who respectively furnish labor, land, capital, and money. Thus the typical employer of labor is an entrepreneur, that is, an individual or a corporation engaged in producing goods for sale in the market. There are some employers who are not entrepreneurs, e.g., the employers of household servants, but employment of this kind is of small proportions, and the wages paid tend to be determined by those paid in comparable positions in entrepreneurial enterprises. Likewise the typical purchaser or renter of capital goods, and the typical borrower of money, is an entrepreneur, either individual or corporate. When we come to land, the entrepreneur is not the typical owner or renter, since land is used in all human action and no part of such action can claim to be typical of the whole. But the entrepreneur is the principal party who is interested in acquiring the use of land for productive purposes.

What influences govern the action of the entrepreneur as he enters into bargains promising to pay wages, rent, capital compensation, and interest? (Bargains to pay capital compensation are comparatively rare, since capital compensation is usually lumped with the entrepreneur's profit, but undertakings to make such payments nevertheless occur in a total volume which is rather substantial, e.g., payments for the use of machinery.)

Since the entrepreneur is concerned with securing a livelihood, he too like all other members of society must attempt to obtain net money receipts. He can do this in one way and only one—by making bargains with the suppliers of labor, land, capital, and money which will leave a margin between the price consumers are willing to pay for the product when it is sold and the total amount required to be paid under the bargains with the suppliers of the elements of production. Like Mr. Micawber's margin between income and outgo, which though small yet determined the difference between happiness and misery, so the entrepreneur's margin of profit, though small, determines the difference between the production and nonproduction of particular goods. For it is not simply difficult for the entrepreneur to produce a good without a profit-margin; it is impossible. An unprofitable operation can never be more than a temporary matter in a free market; it supplies its own termination in the fact that the entrepreneur cannot pay his bills.

Entrepreneurship, like everything else which is the subject of trade in the market, has its demand and supply. The demand for entrepreneurship is derived from the inexhaustible demand of human beings for goods. People want goods of the quantity and quality which can be supplied only by combining the labor, land, capital, and money of many individuals. In consequence, there is a demand for persons who will perform the work and assume the risk of engaging in business as entrepreneurs. The supply of entrepreneurship consists in the existence of people who are willing to undertake action as entrepreneurs as and when they believe they can receive compensation therefor. The existence of such people within a society seems to depend on general cultural considerations. In our present society we have large numbers of people who are willing and anxious to become entrepreneurs if they can see any reasonable chance of success; they wish to get into business for themselves. Our relatively high standard of living can be ascribed in no small degree to the existence of a large group of people willing to undertake entrepreneurship; and the low standards of some societies must be directly coupled to the paucity of potential entrepreneurship. But given a substantial class of persons desirous of trying entrepreneurship, a society can be assured that they will organize productive enterprises whenever they think they see a chance to produce a good salable at a price in excess of the costs which will have to be paid to the furnishers of labor, land, capital, and money.

The principle, then, upon which the entrepreneur operates is the comparison of productivity with costs. Productivity is the evaluation placed by consumers on the good produced. Costs are the amounts which the entrepreneur must pay pursuant to his bargains with the suppliers of the elements of production used in producing the good. (The entrepreneur will include, in computing his costs, the money he might expect to receive if he furnished to other entrepreneurs any labor, land, capital, or money of his own which he might employ in the enterprise.) To say that the entrepreneur observes the relation of productivity to costs in determining the production which he will manage is simply to state what we have already concluded in the preceding chapter—that consumers' preferences determine production.

Even as a society possessing a stock of entrepreneurship can confidently expect that that stock will be used whenever a suitable demand appears, so it can confidently expect that entrepreneurs will expand their production, employing additional quantities of labor, land, capital, and money, whenever the resulting increase in productivity, as measured by the evaluation of consumers in the market, will exceed the cost of such additional quantities. The incentive to the entrepreneur to expand production is the same as that which moves him to undertake production in the first place, namely, to obtain net money receipts. If therefore the productivity of an additional laborer is believed by the entrepreneur to be $100 per week, while the bargain which can be made with a laborer will call for the expenditure of $90 per week, the entrepreneur will be induced to add the extra laborer to the staff of his enterprise. It is the same with land, capital, and money. Whenever an entrepreneur is satisfied that an additional parcel of land will increase his productivity above the additional cost, he will seek to secure the use of such additional land. Similarly, he will try to buy or rent additional machinery and plant whenever he believes that its productivity will exceed its cost. And lastly, he will undertake to borrow money, to finance the employment of additional labor, land, or capital, whenever the interest charged on such loans is less than the net cash receipts which he anticipates obtaining from the use of the units of labor, land, or capital proposed to be added to the productive process.

The entrepreneur's activity thus supplies the demand for labor, land, capital, and money as factors in production. And the productivity of marginal units of these factors, as they are added to the productive process, constitutes the maximum which will or can be paid for their use.

This being the general nature of the demand for labor, land, capital, and money, as it appears in the free market, we must make inquiry concerning the nature of the supply.

Since the compensation of labor, land, capital, or money is limited to its productivity as an added increment in the productive process, the supplier of a unit of any such factor will tend to seek the use where its productivity as an added unit will be highest. We have already commented on the mobility of the free market. Through mobility, the suppliers of the factors of production shop around in search of the areas of production where the productivity of the factor which they have to offer is greatest. They do not think of this searching in terms of productivity; their attention is directed rather to the offers of entrepreneurs. And this is sufficient, for the offers of entrepreneurs are based upon estimates of productivity and are consequently an index of comparative productivity.

If therefore the market be kept free, which in this connection means that entrepreneurs are prevented from combining together to control demand, the supplier of labor, land, capital, or money will tend to be able to bargain for a compensation equal in amount to the productivity (after the entrepreneur's profit) of the supplied unit as an added factor in the productive process. For if the existing entrepreneurs do not offer to compensate the supplier at a price equivalent to its productivity (less profit), some new entrepreneur, anxious to supply entrepreneurship, can be counted on to do so. The opportunity of profitable entrepreneurship exists as long as factors of production can be bargained for at prices within their productivity, and accordingly in a society possessing a supply of entrepreneurship there will always be entrepreneurs willing to bid up to the limit of productivity, less a profit.

To some extent all units of the factors of production compete with each other. The labor furnished by different machine operators on some machines within a factory, for example, is the same, and accordingly it is a matter of indifference to the entrepreneur whether he employs one person or another. Different pieces of land may compete for use as factory sites, store sites, or farms. Different machines and tools compete for performing the same operation. And every unit of money offered to an entrepreneur competes completely with every other unit that can possibly be offered. Further, the factors of production compete with each other. The use of additional labor in a given factory is competitive with the possibility of using additional land or capital. The use of additional land is competitive with the use of additional labor and capital on presently held land. And the use of additional capital is competitive with the use of additional labor or land with the present capital. The importance of these ramifications of competition is that the entrepreneur is always seeking alternative methods of production which are cheaper; that is, he is looking for competing units of the factors of production. In consequence, all or nearly all units of the factors of production are in competition to greater or lesser degree.

All presently employed units, further, are in competition with added units as they appear. Thus in practical effect every unit employed in production becomes for competitive purposes a marginal unit, whose productivity must be regarded as that which it can be considered to add to the production which would take place without such unit. Thus it makes no difference whether a particular lathe in a machine shop was the first or last to be installed; in determining its productivity the thing to be calculated is what it adds to the productivity of the shop. It is the same with units of labor; every unit of labor is a marginal unit for the competitive purpose of determining its productivity; and accordingly the problem of the entrepreneur is to estimate the productivity of each laborer by estimating what he adds to the productivity which would otherwise occur. Within this sense, then, every unit of labor, land, capital, and money is an added or marginal unit, and the compensation which the entrepreneur will pay for it is limited by the added productivity which it is estimated to create. When any unit is estimated by the entrepreneur to cost more than the added productivity it supplies, its use will be discontinued, because by such discontinuance the entrepreneur will increase his net money receipts.

It must be emphasized that this operation of the free market, as entrepreneurs join labor, land, capital, and money in the productive process, proceeds in accordance with estimates of future conditions rather than with a precise knowledge of present facts. It has been necessary to speak above of productivity as though it were a known fact throughout the productive process. But it never is and never can be. Productivity in the free market is measured by the price that consumers, freely giving expression to their preferences, are willing to pay for a good when it is offered for sale. But with rare exceptions it must be produced before an agreement can be made for its sale, and the exceptions are more seeming than real, covering only a small fraction of total production. This necessity of production in advance of any assurance of selling price arises both from the nature of production and from the nature of consumption. Production is uncertain, because of the vagaries of weather, natural resources, and human skills. Neither the farmer, the oil producer, nor the manufacturer can predict exactly what he will have available for sale, nor can he predict exactly its cost as it will eventually have to be paid. On the consumption side, consumers do not know and cannot know what they are going to need very far in advance. The chances in life are too great. How many people would care to enter into contracts with producers of food and clothing for, say, three years in advance, or even six months? The result of the uncertainties inherent in both production and consumption is that the entrepreneur must always act on his estimates of future facts as well as on his knowledge of present ones. The same is true of the suppliers of labor, land, capital, and money; none of these suppliers can know precisely the productivity of the units of the factor of production which he has to offer. That productivity depends upon events in the future which at present can be seen only approximately.

When, therefore, the entrepreneur on the one side and the supplier of labor, land, capital, or money on the other negotiate a bargain for the supplying of a factor of production, they do not have and cannot have precise information on the productivity of the particular quantity of the factor of production which is supplied. Nor can any conceivable device give them such information. Even if the consumption of every person in the society were prescribed by law to the last detail, there would still be uncertainty in production resulting from natural factors, e.g., the weather and the availability of raw materials, that man's laws cannot control.

It is one of the great virtues of the free market system, however, and a virtue which no other system can possibly possess, that it induces conduct on the part of producers, both entrepreneurs and the suppliers of the factors of production, which tends to approximate that which would rationally take place if the producers foresaw events as they subsequently unroll. Year after year a great mass of goods is produced and taken by consumers at prices that cover by a margin, but only a very thin one, the costs of production as they are paid to the suppliers of labor, land, capital, and money. All except a small percentage of production finds consumers who will purchase it at prices that cover costs with a slight excess of profit for the entrepreneur, which means that the course of nearly all production, though started long before ultimate consumption, is so well directed that it results in goods whose productivity, as evaluated by consumers themselves, almost exactly equals the wages, rent, capital compensation, and interest paid out in their production, the typically small margin being the entrepreneur's compensation or profit for organizing and directing the process that has this result.

How does the free market accomplish this? The answer is by barring from production the producer, whether entrepreneur or supplier of a factor of production, who does not accurately estimate the ultimate productivity of his contribution. Without knowledge of what that productivity will be, since it is an event in the future depending upon consumers' volitional action, he must nevertheless grope toward it, directing his course by his estimate. If he estimates incorrectly, the free market will inexorably and rather promptly, and even before proof of his inaccuracy by the event, eliminate him from the ranks of producers. The entrepreneur who produces a good at a cost of $10 and then finds that consumers will pay only $9 for it must soon go out of business. The laborer who demands $150 per week, while successful entrepreneurs evaluate the productivity attributable to his effort at no more than $125, must go without a job. The owner of agricultural land who wants $15 per acre rent for his land, whereas successful farmers in the community estimate its productivity as equal to only $10, must see his land unused. The owner of capital who wishes to lease or sell it for more than entrepreneurs think its use will add to production will have his capital remain idle. And the possessor of funds offering to lend them at more than the going interest rate will find no takers. Thus those who cannot estimate with some approximate accuracy the productivity of the addition contributed by them to production are eliminated from the productive process.

The accuracy of estimates is encouraged by the specialization which can and does occur in a free market, breaking down the ultimate market for a good into numerous subsidiary or intermediate markets. Thus the manufacturer of the desk at which I am writing had to estimate the price consumers would pay for it in the market for furniture. But the desk was manufactured from various components—wood, varnish, hinges, a lock, and other metal parts—the producers of which paid no attention at all to the market for desks in making their estimates for production. The producer of the wood looked only to the market for walnut boards; the producer of the varnish looked only to the varnish market; the producer of the lock looked only to the market for locks; and so on.

Had it been necessary for each of these producers to direct his attention to the market for desks, it would have been most difficult for him to estimate the productivity of his production. But he did not need to do so. The markets for particular products which develop within a free market society give each producer information on the productivity of his particular product, regardless of the ultimate good in which it may be incorporated. These innumerable intermediate markets are the guide of the entrepreneur. They are indispensable to production which can produce the goods preferred by consumers, and they can occur only in a free market society, where individuals are permitted to buy and sell goods as they choose.

Not only does the free market thus eliminate from production the producer who does not adjust his action to a reasonably accurate estimate of his productivity, but it supports and encourages those producers who succeed in making an approximate estimate of the productivity of their contributions and who act in accordance with such estimate. Thus the entrepreneur who successfully forecasts consumer preference and engineers production at a price within such consumer preference will make a living and will stay in business. And as he experiences greater or lesser success, so his entrepreneurial activity will expand or contract. The laborer who will offer his services at a wage within the productivity of the contribution which he can make will find entrepreneurs who will employ him. The landowner who will make available natural resources at a rent which does not exceed the addition which these natural resources can make to the productivity of an enterprise will be able to rent them to an entrepreneur. It is likewise with capital and with money; the supplier of these can count on finding entrepreneurs who will employ them if he will offer their use at a cost which comes within their contribution to productivity as estimated by entrepreneurs. The suppliers of labor, land, capital, and money, moreover, can count on obtaining compensation that tends to be equal to the contribution to productivity which their additional labor, land, capital, or money is able to make. For in the free market, where entrepreneurs are permitted to initiate or expand production as they choose, entrepreneurship will always appear whenever the factors of production are furnished at a cost within their productivity, for it is under such conditions that the entrepreneur—who is under the necessity of being a consumer as well as any other member of the community—is able to obtain the net money receipts essential to consumption.

We may summarize the immediately preceding discussion as follows: In the free market society, the consumption of goods by each individual is determined by the net money receipts obtained by such individual in return for the contribution he makes to production, such contribution being measured by the additional productivity which results from the labor, land, capital, money, or entrepreneurship which he furnishes. He may furnish any one or more of these factors. If the individual is a

single unit of enterprise, himself furnishing all the factors necessary
to the production of the good which he sells in the market, the productivity of his contribution to production is measured by the market
price of the good which he sells, and no problem arises of the division
of that productivity among the various factors engaged in production.
If the individual is an entrepreneur, the productivity of his contribution
is measured by the difference between the evaluation which the market
places upon the good he sells and the costs he pays in producing that
good. If the individual supplies to a joint enterprise labor, land, capital,
or money, he must do so through an entrepreneur, and the productivity
of his contribution to production is measured by the amount payable
to him under the bargain he makes with the entrepreneur, which in
turn is determined by the addition to productivity resulting from his
contribution. And inasmuch as the activity of entrepreneurs tends to
expand, within a free market, as long as productivity as measured by
consumer preference covers the costs of production which the entrepreneur is obligated to pay under his bargains with the suppliers of the
factors of production, the amounts payable as wages, rent, capital compensation, and interest tend to expand until they absorb the entire
market price of the good produced except the margin necessary to induce
the entrepreneur to assume the obligations and risks of entrepreneurship.

Who is the entrepreneur, who thus occupies such an important place
in the distribution of the market price of goods? He is the small store-
keeper with a single clerk and a small rented space; he is the operator of
a small shop or factory with a few employees; he is a stockholder in the
smallest or largest corporation. As the operator of a small business he
usually makes his bargains himself; as a stockholder he makes his bargains
with the factors of production through a board of directors and corporate
officers who act as his agents. However the entrepreneurial bargains are
made, they must be geared to the principles discussed above, regulating
the distribution of net money receipts, and therefore of consumption,
in accordance with the respective contributions made to production by
the members of society.

4. Equality in the opportunity to take part in production

In Chapter 9 of Book One we considered the general nature of the
equality of economic opportunity which is required by the theory of

liberty. Our conclusion was that the liberty of individualism requires equal opportunity for all to produce and consume goods, and equal opportunity for all to own property. The society that maintains these qualities is a free market society. We now see that equality of opportunity to produce and equality of opportunity to consume are in substance the same thing, because the consumption of the individual in the free market is regulated by his contribution to production. He who has freedom to take part in production has a corresponding freedom to consume. (To this concept it will be necessary to add in due course certain propositions relative to the assistance to be given by society to him who through misfortune is unable to take advantage of his opportunity to produce; this for the present, however, we shall disregard.)

Equality of opportunity to consume being thus conjoined with equality of opportunity to take part in production, it is necessary to consider the elements which compose equality of opportunity to produce. These appear in their general form readily enough from the nature of production. Since labor, land, and capital are united in the productive process by entrepreneurs, who use money for financing the employment of labor, land, and capital, it follows that equality of opportunity to take part in production is realized as there is equality of opportunity to furnish labor, land, capital, money, and entrepreneurship.

We shall examine equality of opportunity to furnish these elements of production in succeeding chapters. Since land, capital, and money are all objects of property ownership, we shall consider equality of opportunity to furnish these elements of production, which means in practice equality of opportunity to own and control property, in the following chapter. Equality of opportunity to furnish labor in the productive process will be studied in the chapter on liberty and the regulation of labor. Equality of opportunity to furnish entrepreneurship will be dealt with in the chapter on liberty and the regulation of monopoly.

When we shall have examined equality of opportunity with respect to these matters, we shall see that it is possible in practice to maintain equality of opportunity in the furnishing of the elements of production. By doing so, the good society builds and maintains a free market and becomes a free market society. In such a society the consumption of goods is regulated, subject always to such modifications as may be effected by public assistance to the unfortunate, by the contributions made by respective individuals to production.

5. The interrelation of consumption and production

Since production regulates consumption, production and consumption vary together. That the total production of a society must set a limit to its total consumption is obvious. That the total non-market production of an individual likewise sets a limit to his non-market consumption, that is, that the things he produces for his own use set a limit to his consumption of such things, is likewise obvious. It is also clear, as our foregoing analysis has shown, that the individual's contribution to market production sets the limit to his market consumption.

What is not so clear, but what is equally true, is that in the free market consumption will always be large enough to use up all production. It was a favorite theme of Karl Marx that free enterprise must result in over-production, with unconsumed goods glutting the market; and this was, in fact, envisaged as one of the vulnerabilities which would result in the overthrow of the free enterprise system. Keynesianism also teaches that when enterprise is exempt from state guidance it is certain to experience underconsumption and consequent stagnation and unemployment.

But in truth it is only the controlled market, whether it be the market of the monetary and fiscal controls proposed by Keynesianism or the market of complete controls advocated by communism, that is capable of long-term production in excess of consumption. In a market which is kept free, consumption will always keep pace with production when any substantial period of time is considered. For short terms, production of particular goods may exceed consumption, because of miscalculation of the size of the market by entrepreneurs, accidents of weather, or a planned increase in inventories by entrepreneurs; but in a free market all such excessive production must be rather promptly sold, for only through the sale of production can the producers themselves gain a livelihood. If producers simply pile up goods without selling them, they must shortly starve. All such goods must be sold to consumers or to intermediate purchasers who will channel them to ultimate consumption. It is by reason of this necessity of the sale of goods, when once produced, to consumers at whatever price consumers will pay, that producers are driven to the production of those goods which consumers want the most. And this necessity of prompt disposition of produced goods to consumers applies not only to the entrepreneurs who engineer production but also to all units of labor, land, and capital which they employ.

It is only in a controlled market that production can be piled up without consumption; and it is only in controlled markets, accordingly, that overproduction, or underconsumption, can occur. For example, we are experiencing a serious overproduction of agricultural goods in this country at the present time, as evidenced by the fact that vast stores of such goods are being piled up. This could not occur in a free market, but takes place only because the market is controlled by the government of the United States, which compels the citizens of the country as a group, through tax payments, to purchase agricultural commodities of certain kinds which they do not want, at prices which they do not want to pay, and to store them without consumption. Since it was the same government which induced the excessive productive capacity, as a war measure, that is now resulting in excessive production, there would be injustice in any precipitate removal of the existing controls on the agricultural market; but this does not change the fact that the present overproduction is occurring because of governmental controls.

We likewise had overproduction in 1954 in various manufactured products, e.g., textiles and automobiles, because of miscalculation of entrepreneurs of the preferences of consumers. But in each case the free market worked off excessive stocks rather promptly, and production was lowered to the capacity of the market to absorb it.

But the term "underconsumption" is also much used in certain forms of current economic theory to indicate not only consumption that is low relative to production, but consumption that is low because the members of society are saving rather than spending the money income which they receive. That is, even as an individual can have an income, say, of $100, but spend only $75 of it, saving the rest, so it is conceived that society as a whole can do the same thing, saving an excessive portion of its income and thereby causing a decline in production and employment.

This line of thought, however, involves the basic error of failing to recognize the offsetting which occurs when the experiences of individual members of society are lumped together in the experience of the group. Although an individual, for example, can be a creditor of another individual, who is his debtor, yet society as a whole can be neither a net debtor nor a net creditor because the credits and debits of the members of society cancel out when they are added together to state the position of society as a whole. While it is true, in like manner, that there can be non-spending (saving) by an individual in a society, yet for society as a whole there can be no such non-spending, in the sense of not spending a portion of income, i.e., saving, because non-spending for one member of society is non-receiving for another member of society, and all such non-spending and non-receiving items cancel out when the experiences of individual members of society are totaled into the society as a group during a given period of time.

We can see this more clearly if we revert to the proposition that the money receipts from the sale of goods produced constitute the source of funds for paying the costs of production, and the further proposition that the net money receipts remaining after the payment of the costs of production constitute the source of funds to be spent for goods to be consumed. To say that society as a whole is receiving 10x dollars during a given period of time from the sale of goods produced is to say also that society is spending 10x dollars during the same period of time for the purchase of goods produced. The sale and purchase are opposite sides of the same coin, and one cannot be any larger than the other. Therefore, to say that society is receiving an income of 10x dollars from the sale of goods, while it is spending only 5x dollars in the purchase of goods, saving the balance, is to assert the impossible. Society as a whole can never non-spend (save) a portion of its income, for the reason that all income is also spending.

Recognizing this difficulty, Keynesian theorists divide time into segments, saying that the spending of society as a whole during one period of time may be less than the income received by society as a whole during a preceding period of time. If the unit of time selected is, say, one week, the argument is that the amount spent by society as a whole in any one given week may be less than the amount that it received as income in the preceding week. The fallacy in this line of thought, however, can be easily exposed by noting that if a given period of time can be divided for the purpose of analysis it can also be put back together for the same purpose. And therefore, if social income and social expenditure are equal in any one period of time, they are equal in any number of periods of time when they are put together, because such periods of time when put together constitute one period of time. If social income and social expenditure are equal in one week, they are equal in any number of weeks when added together.

The basic error consists in assuming that social income and social expenditure in one week have a necessary relation to social income and social expenditure in another week. But the social income of society in Week 1 is not the money which it expends in Week 2. Social income becomes social expenditure as it occurs. It is financed by the society's present stock of money. That stock of money remains the same in Week 2 as it was in Week 1. The income and expenditure activity during Week 1 may, and almost certainly will, result in a change in the persons holding that stock of money as available funds for spending. If production and employment in Week 2 is less than in Week 1, it tells us nothing at all to say that there is underspending (oversaving) in Week 2. Lowered spending is an integral part, an aspect, of the phenomenon of lowered production and lowered employment. It is like saying that there is sunshine when the sun shines, or (more appropriately) that there is less sunshine when the sun shines less. Lowered production in one period as compared with another, which includes lower employment and lower expenditure of money for production, constitutes the data of the problem. To suppose that a statement of a problem is a solution of it assures the futility of the discussion.

The whole concept of non-spending as a relevant element in the problem of adequate production, consumption, and employment is fruitless. It tells us nothing we do not know initially before the problem is attacked.

Another fallacy, unfortunately growing in acceptance at the present time, is to assume that the distribution of consumption is from a more or less fixed flow of goods. This error is fostered by the concept of a gross national product, consisting of all the goods and services produced by a society during a given period of time. This flow is thought of as being divided among the members of society, and the regulation of consumption comes to be regarded as the distribution of this rather fixed quantity. Thus it comes to be felt that if one member of society consumes more, another member of society must necessarily consume less; and therefore if one member of society succeeds in enlarging his consumption, he must be doing so by taking an unfair and immoral advantage of someone else in the society whose consumption he has depressed.

But although the quantity of goods available for consumption at any one time is a fixed stock which must be divided among the members of the group, giving rise to the competition between the self and the not-self which we have heretofore noted, yet over a period of time consumption is of a flow of goods which can and does vary, both for the individual and for the group. The variations occur as the members of society decide as consumers that they wish to consume more, and consequently decide as producers that they will produce more. In the free market society, where equal opportunity to contribute labor, land, capital, money, and entrepreneurship to production is preserved, the economic competition among human beings is transformed from its first aspect of a competition in consumption to a competition in production. In the free market the individual who wishes to increase his consumption can always do so by increasing his production, if he is capable of such increase. And because human wants are infinite, his activity in increasing his production will not displace, except upon occasion temporarily, the production of any other person. It is true that in expanding his production he may lower costs and offer his product at a price which eliminates other producers. But in the free market the other producers can always find other avenues of production if they will offer their labor, land, capital, money, or entrepreneurship at prices within the market value of the added productivity which they thus furnish. Nevertheless the transition may be difficult and at times tragic. This is one of the debit items of the free market and an element in the price that must be paid for the liberty of the free enterprise system. But subject to this qualification, which is of temporary operation (and which must be experienced also by a collectivist system if it wishes to emulate the efficiency and progress of the free enterprise system), the activity of one member of society in increasing his production and thereby his consumption is not at the expense of any other member of society. This would be clear enough if all production were for immediate consumption by the producer or for exchange with others simply by barter; it is the operation of the market and the corresponding intervention of money that obscure the true fact.

And although the competition among individuals in production certainly has its harsh aspects and can give rise to pride and envy, yet it is a far better form of competition than that which simply quarrels over the division of a fixed flow of goods; and it is a great virtue of the free market that it transmutes the basic economic conflict into a competition in production. In the collectivistic society, on the other hand, where free production cannot occur but only production in accord with state edict, the competition must remain one of consumption.

6. "To each according to his need"

In the communist world, Marx and Engels said, the production and consumption of goods would be governed by the motto, "From each in accordance with his ability, to each in accordance with his need." They failed, however, to indicate the technique by which this result would be obtained except by saying that all property would be owned by the state. Presumably too the direction of the productive process would be vested in the officialdom of the state, although not much specification of these matters can be found in Marx and Engels.

Nor did they discuss whether the need of each citizen, thus to be served by the communist program, was to be determined by each citizen for himself or by the state's officers. Throughout the writings of Marx and Engels appears the naïve assumption that human need is simply an objective fact, readily ascertainable.

But this misses completely one of the basic problems of social theory. Is human need, which social organization has for its concern, to be emphasized in its subjective or its objective aspect? Viewed subjectively, the need of each citizen consists of his wants as he himself experiences them and conceives them. Viewed objectively, the need of each citizen consists of his wants as he and his situation are evaluated by an outside observer. Frequently, perhaps usually, the two aspects of need are in conflict in their prescription; witness the steady complaints of socialists and communists that in a free enterprise society people consume trivialities and wasteful luxuries instead of the wholesome and helpful things they really should have. Collectivists seem either to be unaware of the issue between subjective and objective need or deliberately to evade it.

But the issue cannot be dodged; society must be organized with the aim of supplying the needs of human beings as they themselves think those needs exist, or with the aim of satisfying their needs as persons in authority think those needs exist. The one is the social organization sponsored by the philosophy of individualism, the other that sponsored by collectivism.

It was a tragic error of Marx and Engels that they did not face up to the necessity of distinguishing between objective and subjective need, and of adjusting their thinking to the distinction. They wanted it both ways. They wanted men to be free to satisfy their needs as they might choose; but they also wanted men to be compelled to satisfy their needs as they, Marx and Engels, conceived those needs to exist, and as other wise directors of affairs in the future, holding general views similar to those of Marx and Engels, would conceive those needs to exist. But the world of reality demands the distinction because it contains the distinction, arising from the moral problem presented by the human experience of the social relation.

Starting thus in unreality, the program of collectivism fails to provide for the satisfaction of either subjective or objective need. It cannot provide for subjective need because its planning is that of the state rather than that of the individual. It cannot adequately provide for objective need, unless the standard adopted by the state's supervisors is comparatively low, because the productive process it advocates is inefficient.

It is individualism, rather, that succeeds in giving "to each according to his need." The operative principle of the free market is consumer preference, as we have seen, and consumer preference means the direction of production toward the satisfaction of each person's need as he himself believes it to exist. If the market be kept free, further, the individual can direct his activity toward the satisfaction of his needs by contributing to production to the extent that he chooses to do so and can. And since the free market is an efficient productive mechanism, tending to use all instruments of production to their maximum productivity, it produces a comparatively high standard of living for society as a whole, judged by any objective standards that in the light of human experience are appropriate. That the free market does this is established by the historical fact that the highest standards of living in the past have been found in the rather few areas where free market principles have prevailed in practice. It is true that no system of production can ever satisfy all human wants, but within the available techniques the free market assures the maximum of production of the goods consumers prefer.

The free market not only gives effect to subjective need as expressed in consumer preference but it also tends to allocate the production of any good to those individuals in the community who have the greatest subjective need for it. Although production over any period of time is not fixed but variable, yet at any given time the quantity of a good appearing on the market is fixed, and must be allocated to particular consumers. The free market accomplishes this allocation by distributing it to those who will pay the highest price for it. This tends to be—although it by no means always is—those who have the greatest subjective need. Willingness to part with money tends on the average to measure subjective need. That it does not measure it exactly is quite clear from the consideration that the willingness to part with money in paying a price depends not only on the need for the good to be purchased but also on the quantity of money in the possession of the purchaser. On the other hand is the consideration that, since money to spend on consumption is obtained from contribution to production, the quantity of a consumer's money is in part a reflection of the intensity of his needs, as he views them. Thus the consumers who will pay the highest price tend to be those who have the highest subjective need. And therefore by directing the flow of a product to those who will pay the highest price the free market tends to allocate the supply to those who are experiencing, subjectively considered, the greatest need.

Whatever the criticism, furthermore, on the accuracy of the free market's measurement of subjective need, such criticism is in a sense irrelevant, because the free market is not simply the best instrumentality for measuring subjective need; it is the only instrumentality which can even purport to do so. The controlled market involves an abandonment of subjective need as a criterion in consumption; it has little tolerance for the individualistic choosing that characterizes the free market; and it is precisely because it wishes to eliminate the registering of individualistic choice that it places the market under controls. Subjective need as individuals experience it is replaced, as an influence on production, by objective need as state officials decree it, and it is the purpose of the controlled market of collectivism to accomplish this change. The controlled market cannot give expression to the subjective need of the members of society because its very aim is to block the satisfaction of subjective need except as such need conforms to the pattern of economic action set by the current decisions of the state's planners.

Only the free market, then, can give effect to subjective need as it is established in the preference schedules of individual consumers. It is the liberty of individualism as expressed in the institution of the free market, rather than collectivism, that is competent to supply goods "to each in accordance with his need," in so far as the technology of the time permits the accomplishment of that goal.

7. Assistance

The regulation of consumption which we have thus far examined is accomplished by the free market. But there are members of society who cannot take part in the free market. First, there are children, who are incapable both of contributing to production and of making the decisions which the free market necessitates. What age in years shall be stipulated as separating minority from adulthood may be the subject of debate, but once an age figure—more or less arbitrary—is agreed upon, all those members of the group whose age is below it must be classified as incapable of taking part in the free market. Then there are also adults who are mentally or physically handicapped to an extent rendering it impossible for them to contribute labor to production in the free market, and they may not own land, capital, or money which can be contributed. Here, as in the case of minority, no hard and fast line of demarcation is found in the natural facts, and accordingly an arbitrary line or a series of arbitrary lines must be drawn by social regulation, indicating want of capacity to contribute to production. The aged are to be included in this category of persons incompetent to produce.

Since the free market allocates consumption in accordance with contribution to production, it follows that the free market alone will not supply any goods to those incapable of taking part in it. What then shall be done? Detractors of individualism, referring to it scornfully as a *laissez-faire* philosophy which must leave unfortunates in their misery, say that it has and can have no principle except that of pity applicable to those who cannot produce. But in this they misconceive—and seem frequently to misconceive willfully—the basic position of individualism. As the analysis of Book One has disclosed, the liberty of individualism does not present itself as a privilege of selfishness, but as a duty to exercise equal concern for the welfare of all. Free enterprise is not an end of the philosophy of individualism, but a means toward attaining its end, which is equal liberty. Therefore when the means of free enterprise does not attain the end of equal liberty, the means must be supplemented by assistance, to a consideration of which Chapter 19 will be devoted.

8. Equality of consumption

It is a consequence of the foregoing discussion of the free market that individualism does not teach equality of consumption. It teaches, rather, consumption in accordance with production, supplemented by assistance. An enforced equality of consumption it would regard as unethical, because violative of the principle of equal opportunity; if the production of the man who devoted his energy to the productive process should be taken from him and given to the man who refused to produce, the opportunity of the first man would be impaired and equality of opportunity destroyed.

Collectivism likewise, despite its criticism of unequal consumption as found in the free market and its vague advocacy at times of egalitarianism, does not teach equality of consumption. Collectivism indeed is devoid of any clear theory of the distribution of goods for consumption. Communism formerly gave its endorsement to distribution "to each according to his need." This is necessarily a disavowal of equality, for needs vary greatly, being dependent upon age, health, occupation, geographical surroundings, and other factors. The theory of distribution in accordance with need seems, moreover, to have been abandoned by communism, and one hears little reference to it any more either by communists or by socialists.

Although egalitarianism is thus repudiated by both individualism and collectivism, yet it continues to exercise an influence on social thinking. Lurking in the background of much discussion is the assumption that unequal consumption is wrong and that equal consumption, could it be arranged, would be right. It is indeed true that unequal consumption is wrong when it results from unequal economic opportunity. But the cure, when unequal consumption is thus occasioned by unequal opportunity, is to remove the cause of the wrong by eliminating inequality of economic opportunity and by enforcing in its place equality of economic opportunity. No cure can be effected simply by attempting to enforce an equality of consumption, for equality of consumption is neither right nor wrong in itself, but is right only when it results from equal response to equal opportunity, and is wrong only when it results from unequal opportunity. The wrongfulness consists in permitting inequality of economic opportunity to exist.

It is therefore toward the enforcement of equal opportunity in economic action that the good society should direct its efforts. When such equality is attained, consumption will be directly related, through the operation of the free market, to contribution to production, as measured by free market prices, and will be supplemented by assistance rendered under the principles applicable thereto. It is this result which the individualistic society, through the observance of the directives of liberty, seeks to accomplish.

It should be added that theories of social organization do not finally dispose of the question of what inequality of consumption should occur, and particularly is this true of the theory of individualism, whose thesis is that the rules of social organization should constitute opportunity for decision rather than rigidities preventing decision. The use that should be made of unequal income is a matter of individual decision based upon the individual's philosophy of the good life. Where the proper interest of social philosophy terminates, the burden of determining ethical conduct must be taken over by individual philosophy.

9. Collectivism and rationing

In order to complete our delineation of the regulation of consumption by the free market, it is necessary to note the fact that collective regulation of consumption, as opposed to free market regulation, must always include some form of rationing. The superficiality of collectivistic theory usually glosses over or indeed fails to comprehend the inescapability of this basic proposition.

The free market, as we have seen above, allocates the stock of each kind of good as it is produced to those persons whose subjective need tends to be most pressing, and this in a sense constitutes the rationing of the free market system. Collectivism, seeking a distribution other than that which results from consumers' preference, must allocate the items of the stock of each kind of good by decree, and this is rationing.

The inevitability of rationing in the controlled market of collectivism appears readily enough if we note one of the functions of price in the free market. The price set for a good in the free market by the bargaining of buyers and sellers clears the market of the supply of the good as it exists from time to time; the price will always be just low enough to accomplish this result, since producers always must sell their product, having no use for it except for that purpose. Supply and demand at this free market price are in balance, the entire supply finding purchasers. If, now, society establishes some form of control over the market, such control must have the result of changing the relation between consumers and the goods they buy. Either the quantity of a particular good must be changed or the same quantity must be offered to consumers at a changed price. In either case the quantity offered to consumers must be different from what consumers would be willing to buy at the offering price in a free market, because if not different the control is not really a control at all, since it permits free market conditions to prevail.

But if the quantity offered in a controlled market is different from what consumers would buy at the offering price in a free market, some mode of state action must be taken to direct the consumption of the offered quantity. If the offered quantity is larger than what consumers would freely buy, they must be compelled to purchase the unwanted surplus. This can typically be accomplished by a state purchase program financed by taxes, as we at present have with certain agricultural products. Much more frequently, however, the offered quantity is less than what consumers would like to buy at the offering price. This is the situation which always develops when price controls are adopted, such as those in force in this country with respect to a great variety of goods a short time ago. The ostensible purpose of such price controls is to make it possible for consumers to buy goods at lower prices than would otherwise prevail. But the very fact that the decreed price is below the free market price means that consumers will wish to buy at the lower price a greater quantity than is being offered in the market. Thus at the decreed price the effective demand of consumers exceeds the supply. Some form of dividing up the limited supply among would-be consumers must therefore be adopted. For some less important goods this can simply be the rationing of the queue, where those first in line get the limited supply. But for most goods this will not do, and there must be rationing by coupons or by direct allocation of particular goods to particular individuals by decree of the state. Both these methods are typically used.

Thus controls over the market necessarily involve some form of state direction of consumption, i.e., of rationing. Either consumers must be compelled to take goods they do not wish to buy at the price fixed for them, or they must be kept from buying as large a quantity of goods as they would like to buy at the prices at which they are offered. In either case the process becomes one of rationing under the coercion of the state.

This rationing the collectivized society can in no wise avoid. The price in the free market expresses a fact—the quantity of goods which consumers want at a particular price. Nothing the collectivist society can do can change this fact. It continues as a fact regardless of state action. Therefore the only possible course for the collectivized society, if it is to control the market and not to leave it free, is the coercion of rationing.

This use of the force of the state, whether it be employed to parcel out a limited supply or to compel the taking of an enlarged supply, individualism condemns. It is a grave denial of liberty to the individual and a demoralizing aggrandizement of freedom of action to the bureaucracy of the state.

The free market, which directs consumption in accordance with contributions to production, is the basic institution for the regulation of consumption in the theory of individualism.

Chapter 18

PRIVATE PROPERTY

1. Property is control.

Since the production of goods can occur only with the aid of land and capital, the control of these instruments of production is sought by human beings in order both to influence the course of production and to secure at least a portion of the product attributable to their use. It is this control of land and capital which essentially constitutes the property in them. Property is control. He who exercises control over any article, whether it be land, capital, money, or an item of consumers' goods, is in the reality of affairs the owner of it to the extent of his control.

The identity of the persons authorized under prevailing laws to exercise control over things must be designated by some commonly accepted scheme; and for this purpose societies find it convenient to develop systems of muniments of title. Thus in late feudal times the owner of a property in land was he who had taken part in the ceremony known as livery of seizin. At present the owner of a property in land is he who is named in a deed which has been signed, acknowledged before a public officer, and recorded in the public records. A program of muniments of title having been established, the person thereby identified as the holder of title to any article becomes prima facie the one who has control over it.

Convenience may sometimes be served, however, by having the muniments of title indicate a person to be owner who, although the holder of legal title, is nevertheless under an agreement to permit another person to control the property and enjoy the benefits of it. Thus there may be developed a system of property ownership by which title and beneficial ownership can be separated. It is a common occurrence today to have title in one person with control in another. This distinction between title and control is important. Title is a necessary and useful legalism, but the reality is control.

Control resides in decision. The control of land and capital consists in deciding what use shall be made of them in the productive process and how the benefits flowing from such use shall be enjoyed. Control therefore consists in the activity of deciding, of exercising human will. Property accordingly is correctly to be described as the ability of a human being to exercise his will with respect to particular items of land, capital, money, and consumers' goods. To the extent that a man can exercise his will concerning use and enjoyment he is owner, and where his privilege of exercising his will terminates under existing social rules, there also his ownership terminates.

The language we employ in dealing with ownership is frequently misleading. Consider for example the property of a corporation. We say that the corporation is the owner of its property, and with respect to the designations contained in the title deeds and bills of sale this is correct. But this is only a legalism. In reality the corporation is no more than a fictitious person, which can act only through human beings. These human beings are the stockholders, directors, officers, and agents, who variously are privileged to make decisions concerning the land, capital, and money of the corporation, and who therefore are the real owners of the corporate property.

In like manner we usually commit a self-deception when we speak of the state as the owner of land and capital. In so far as the muniments of title are concerned, the state may indeed be the entity indicated as owner. But with respect to the economic reality of control the state is not an entity which can make decisions, since only people can perform that function, and therefore the owners of property vested in the state are variously the citizens and the public officials, as by the state's constitution they are authorized to exercise control.

But only in the smallest communities, where the procedures of town-meeting democracy prevail, can the citizens exercise any control over state property. We have villages and small school districts where the individual citizen is able to take part in the decisions concerning the use of community property. But for the most part such participation in control is impossible. What control, for example, can the individual citizen exercise with regard to the land and capital of the Tennessee Valley Authority or of the Post Office? What control can the individual British citizen exercise over the land and capital used by the nationalized railways, the nationalized electric utilities, the nationalized coal mines, the nationalized steel mills, and so forth? And what control can the individual Russian citizen exercise over all the state-owned land and capital? The answer to these questions is, none at all. True enough, the citizen may be able to vote for members of the legislature and for a few top executives, but these elected officials only appoint general managers of state enterprises, who in turn appoint and control the subordinates who make decisions. Thus the individual citizen is insulated, and always must remain insulated, from any part in the control of state property.

The real ownership in all such property is in the members of the state's officialdom. They make the decisions concerning the use of the land and capital the title to which is vested in the state. They also determine, by fixing wages, rents, and any other income payments, the enjoyment of the benefits attributable to the use of the state's land and capital. Control and therefore ownership is vested in the public officials as a class; and these, if we will disabuse our minds of the deception induced by legal title, will be seen to constitute the real owners of public property.

2. Private property and the free market

Where title to things is held by the state, the control of the state's bureaucracy is usually quite complete with no interfusion of any private control. Where title is held by private persons, however, the private control is typically not complete but is combined with considerable public control. The owner of land cannot build on it such improvements as he chooses, but must comply with zoning ordinances and building codes. In similar manner nearly all private property in things is combined with some public property in the same things.

Public property is not in itself an indication of collectivism. Whether collectivism is involved in public property depends on the use to which it is put. Public property in a municipal electric plant, in the plants of TVA, and in the nationalized railways of Great Britain are instances of collectivism. But the buildings used by the Federal Trade Commission and similar agencies engaged in preventing unfair and monopolistic trade practices are used for individualistic purposes, since their function is to preserve free market conditions.

The problem of the society of liberty is the extent to which it shall allow, respectively, private and public property. In solving this problem, answers must be given to two questions: 1. What division between private and public property is necessary to preserve the free market?

2. What division between private and public property will best serve intellectual liberty?

The free market is economic liberty in practice. Therefore the property system of the free society must preserve the free market.

But there can be no free market where production is carried on with public property. Land and capital are essential factors in production. Control over these factors means control over the productive process. But property is control, as we have just seen, and public property is public control, which in turn is control by the few who constitute the state's bureaucracy. Public property in the land and capital used in production, therefore, means the control of production by the bureaucracy. Production in such case is not carried on pursuant to the dictates of consumers' preferences but pursuant to the dictates of the state's officials. No free market exists but only a controlled market. The individual in Russia has no freedom to produce because land and capital are public property; the individual can produce only as he is permitted by state officials to use land and capital. Even if there were no other collectivistic practices in Russia, the public property in land and capital would give the state bureaucracy complete control over production, necessitating the adherence of all to the communal plan of production dictated by the state.

Equal opportunity of access to land and capital is an essential characteristic of the free market. But there can be no equal opportunity of access to land and capital where such land and capital are public property, because as public property they are the monopoly of the few who constitute the state's officialdom. Public property is public monopoly, which means monopoly by the bureaucracy, and whether monopoly is public or private, its effect is always to destroy equal opportunity of access to land and capital, for the opportunity of such access is concentrated in the hands of a few.

The free market can exist, therefore, only to the extent that there is private property in land and capital. Such private property does not of itself assure the existence of a free market, but it is the first and indispensable step toward it. Where private property prevails, the individual wishing to enter upon production has the possibility of doing so, for he has the possibility of obtaining control of the necessary land and capital. But where private property is forbidden, there can be no possibility of entering upon production, except through the machinery of the state. Private property can be regulated to assure the existence of a free market, but public property can never be so regulated, because public property in the land and capital used in production of itself bars the existence of a free market.

The regulation of private property in the interests of a free market constitutes public control, and therefore a limited kind of public property. This is the mingling of public property with private property in the same things heretofore referred to. But such public property must be restricted to that which is necessary to preserve equal liberty in the free market. Public property is an exercise of force, and the principles examined in Chapter 10 concerning the use of force apply. Public property that preserves the equal freedom of the free market is ethical because it builds liberty; but public property which passes beyond that necessary to preserve equal freedom, becoming public monopoly, is immoral because it destroys liberty.

Thus public and private property are each to be made use of in the liberal society as they serve the free market, neither variety of property being a good or a bad thing in itself but only as it supports that freedom in the market which liberty requires. And since individual freedom is the basic requirement of the free market, therefore private property becomes its basic institution, with only such public property as is necessary to keep the opportunity of private property equal.

The application of this principle means—to make a summary statement—that in the free society there will be public title-holding only of such things as highways, parks, waterways, the sea, public schools, and office buildings for government officials and their staffs, and public control over private title-holding only to the extent necessary to enforce the rules of equal opportunity, such as the rules concerning monopoly, honesty, labor regulation, and other matters which our study will subsequently note. Beyond this there will be no public property—no public electric plants, no public transportation systems, no municipal or nationalized industries.

We usually assume in our country today that items of public property in excess of this are of no great effect upon liberty. We discuss municipal enterprises solely from the standpoint of efficiency, perhaps with superficial consideration of a supposed elimination of profits in publicly operated activity. But the major concern should always be liberty. Not only does every municipal and state enterprise impair the exercise of economic freedom; it also destroys the understanding of the proper roles of private and public property. Public property beyond the needs of liberty is wrong, and must be understood and opposed as wrong.

The ways of life that ensue upon the use of private or public property in production are radically different. Consider for example the Russian farmer living on publicly owned land, in contrast with the American farmer living on privately owned land. Since the Russian land is public property, its use is controlled by the bureaucracy, who requires the farmer to produce and deliver to the public distribution agencies stipulated quantities of products. The farmer's methods of cultivation are dictated as well as his crops, since he can use, for the most part, only publicly owned machinery. He has but little privilege of decision, and is only slightly better than a serf to the public officials, who control in detail his labor and take from his production what they choose. By contrast, the American farmer living on private property, either his own or land rented from another, is free to make his own decisions. He plants what he thinks best, improves the land as he chooses, directs his own labor, and disposes of the product as he decides. He is, in Wordsworth's phrases,

> Man free, man working for himself, with choice
> Of time, and place, and object.

And the difference between the Russian and the American farmer, though it involves more than the mode of property ownership, yet necessarily follows from the divergency in the two modes. "Man free, man working for himself" is an impossibility on a collectivized farm; but it is a possible and common occurrence on the privately owned farms of America, despite the intrusion of recent public controls on agriculture.

Consider again the difference between the industries of trucking for hire in Britain and America. All motor trucks used in hauling for hire in Britain were publicly owned until the denationalization program was recently started, and accordingly a man wishing to enter this industry could do so only as an employee working under the direction of public officials. In America on the other hand, where private property in such trucks is permitted, any man who will save only a small amount of money can purchase a truck on time payments and enter the business of trucking as an independent operator, directing his own labor and making his own decisions, and there are in fact tens of thousands of such small businessmen in the United States at the present time. Again the difference is a necessary consequence of the use of public or private property. A free market in trucking cannot exist in Britain as long as trucks are public property, as many still are, and a controlled market cannot exist in the United States as long as trucks are private property subject only to free market rules.

Economic freedom, then, demands private property in land and capital, with only such public property as is needed to maintain equal opportunity of private ownership.

3. Intellectual liberty and private property

Intellectual liberty as well as economic liberty requires private control of the instruments of production. Freedom to think, to speak, to worship, and to print has its material base in the consumption of goods. Public control of the instruments of production is public control of consumption, and this control of consumption controls in turn the intellectual activity dependent upon it. Public property in the instruments of production is therefore public control of intellectual activity.

We do not ordinarily see that public property is the destroyer of intellectual freedom. But it is. The self-designated progressives of our time who have been carrying on crusades for more public property, partly in the name of intellectual liberty, have in fact been working for intellectual regimentation.

If a man is to be independent of his fellows in his thoughts, he must have the possibility of an independent economic place on which to stand. This possibility cannot exist within a regime of public property; but it can exist within a regime of private property. Private property does not assure intellectual liberty; other applications of the principles of individualism are essential to that end. But these applications are possible and workable upon a base of private property, which alone can give to intellectual liberty the free material support that it demands.

4. Limitations on private property

Proponents of private property not infrequently picture it as a quasi-sacred privilege. A man has a right, they say, to do what he chooses with his own. But if we seek a rational basis for such a claim, we shall find none.

Locke is sometimes quoted as having said that man has a natural right to property; but the most that Locke developed out of the concept of natural right was that since a man has a natural right to life, he also has a natural right to such property, which he himself has created, as is necessary to maintain life. Beyond this amount, Locke's position was, man has no natural right to property.

And indeed the control which constitutes property can exist only as it is conferred by society. Without the protection of social organization control would reside only in the strongest and in him not for long. It is society that through its rules creates the conditions that make property possible and thereby confers the privilege of property. Even therefore as society grants the privilege of property, so it may limit the extent of its grant, if good reason indicates such limitation, without impairing any natural right.

The question accordingly is not the rightfulness of society's placing any limitations on private property, but whether particular limitations ought to be imposed. For the philosophy of individualism, itself the great proponent of private property, the general principle of limitation is clear. It is that private property should be limited at the point where a further grant would impair rather than build equal liberty for all.

There are two kinds of limitation which the liberal society, in response to this general principle, may consider imposing upon private property: (a) qualitative limitation and (b) quantitative limitation. Qualitative limitation is limitation upon the kind of property that may be privately owned. Thus the state may or may not confer upon individuals the privilege of owning rivers or lakes. If it refuses to permit an individual to own such property, this is a qualitative limitation. Quantitative limitation is limitation upon the amount of a particular property which the individual may own. Thus the individual may be permitted to own land but not in excess of a designated amount.

5. Qualitative limitations on private property

All societies have made use of qualitative limitations on private property in the past and make use of them today. Thus the sea has always been public property and so also have navigable waters. Similarly private property is ordinarily not allowed in roads, public parks, and buildings needed for the exercise of governmental functions.

Individualism believes that the sea, navigable waters, public highways, public parks, and public buildings should not be the subject of private ownership. Why? Because private ownership would impair equality of economic opportunity. A private property in the sea would confer but little additional liberty upon the owner but would greatly restrict the liberties of all others. A society could make use of a system of highways privately owned, and indeed if it did so, the financing of the highways by the collection of tolls from those who used them would be a fairer method than by the collection of taxes from all members of the community. But such a system would involve great inconvenience and cost. It would be well-nigh impossible to collect tolls from all users, and to collect them from even most users would be very costly because of the large personnel required. It is better, therefore, to suffer the small loss of liberty that is sustained because of public property in roads than to suffer the large loss of liberty that would be sustained through the great inconvenience and costliness of private property in roads. The case is the same with public parks. It should be noted, however, that supplying recreational facilities in parks for adults, such as golf courses, amounts to compelling the many, including the poor, to support through their taxes the luxuries of a few. The principle of parks should not be extended to such recreational facilities.

These cases of public property illustrate again that neither public nor private property is desirable per se, but only as contribution is made to the preservation of equal liberty. Where public property serves that purpose better, as in the instances above discussed, public property should be adopted and private property subjected to a corresponding qualitative limitation.

6. Quantitative limitations on private property

Quantitative limitations on private property have two objects in view: 1. the prevention of monopolistic ownership of private property; 2. the prevention of unequal economic opportunity through unequal ownership of property acquired through gift and inheritance.

Monopolistic tendencies are inherent in all production, as we have seen, since every producer tends to exercise control over supply. When such control becomes substantial it impairs the free market. Accordingly at that point it becomes the duty of society to place limitations upon the quantity of the instruments of production that can be subjected to private ownership by those carrying on the monopolistic production. The free market society, that is to say, must place quantitative limitations on private property in order to prevent monopoly. Such limitations are in fact placed upon private property today by our antimonopoly laws.

With respect to property acquired by gift and inheritance, here again the proponents of private property sometimes take a sacrosanct position.

The owner of property, they say, has an absolute right to dispose of it by gift or inheritance as he chooses. As to the basis for this asserted right they are vague, and understandably so, for no rational basis is available. No society in history—our own no more than any other—has ever allowed any such unrestricted privilege of distribution of property by gift or inheritance; and if a plain right were involved, surely some society would have discovered it and would have made an effort to give effect to it. On the contrary every society, restricting the extent to which the present can be controlled by the dead hand of the past, has always limited the transfer of the ownership of property by inheritance or gift and has surrounded such transfer, and accordingly the acquisition of property ownership in that manner, by conditions. At the present time we permit certain transfers of property by inheritance or gift and bar others, and it has always been so.

There being no philosophic or rational right to an unlimited transfer of private property by inheritance or gift, and the common sense of people recognizing that they need not be bound by the wishes of those whom death has removed from the sphere of activity, the question presented is what the principle should be that should guide society in framing quantitative limitations, if any, on transfers by gift and inheritance.

In answering this question only a welter of confused and conflicting arguments is possible unless there is resort to the ethical imperative of liberty and its requirement of equal economic opportunity.

When the principle of liberty is applied to the problem, it encounters two worthy but conflicting interests which are both encompassed within the concern of freedom. The one is the interest in rendering assistance to others by transferring property by gift or inheritance; the other is the interest in preventing unequal opportunity of access to the instruments of production.

Neither of these interests is susceptible of precise measurement. How much property is needed for assistance in a particular case cannot be exactly stated, and how much or how little property each member of one generation can receive from the preceding generation without impairing equality of access to the instruments of production is not open to close determination. But standards in these matters can be roughly approximated, and since liberty requires a working rule based upon a compromise of these conflicting interests, it further requires that the working rule be based upon as good an approximation as the members of society can attain. The necessity for a broad approximation fixing a standard is heightened by the fact that the working rule should be applied generally to all situations and not pursuant to the subjective decisions of public officials.

From the standpoint of assistance, the principles we have heretofore considered and shall consider more fully in the succeeding chapter call for a rule permitting an individual to acquire by inheritance or gift an amount of property the return on which will supply him with the necessities of existence. Many members of society need this much assistance. The old and the young typically need it. Since they either cannot or should not contribute labor to the productive process, they should be permitted to contribute land, capital, or money, if they can. For the purpose of being in a position to make such contribution, they should be permitted to acquire by inheritance or gift property sufficient therefor. By the same token, then, persons possessing property should be privileged to transfer it to others to the extent necessary to supply the needs of life for such others.

But if the transfer of property is to be permitted to some members of society for the purpose of such assistance, it must be permitted to any and all. That is, every person must be allowed by the social rules to receive through inheritance or gift—if someone is willing to make the transfer—a stipulated amount of property for assistance. The quantity of property thus permitted to be received cannot be varied for different persons, based on differences in need for assistance, but must be the same for all. The objective criteria of the need of assistance through ownership of property are too few and vague to justify a flexible rule. Any attempt to evaluate the particular need for assistance in each case of transfer by gift or inheritance would in practice be little more than a program of unrestricted guesses by public officials. To avoid this corruption, the rule permitting such transfers must be fixed in amount and apply alike to all persons.

The amount furthermore should be set high enough to constitute a liberal interpretation of the needs of existence. Otherwise the man who wishes by his labor and savings to provide liberally for his widow, and the couple who wish to do the same for their children, will be prevented from doing so.

From the standpoint of assistance, therefore, we may conclude that social rules should permit any person to receive by gift and inheritance a total of property sufficient to provide, when devoted to production, an income constituting a liberal provision for living.

Turning to a consideration of the need for keeping opportunity of

access to the instruments of production equal, we should note that the
receipt of property by gift or inheritance has no relation to any contribution to production theretofore made by the recipient. But although
the receipt of property by inheritance or gift is not dependent upon
contribution to production, yet such receipt exercises an influence—
upon occasion a most important influence—on the relative economic
opportunity available to the different individual members of society.

Let us suppose, to take an extreme but instructive case, that all the
land and capital in a given society should pass by inheritance to the
ownership of one individual. His opportunity to control the instruments
of production would then be very large and the opportunity of all
others in the society to exercise such control would be very small. By
the same token his opportunity to contribute to production would be
great indeed since he would be the contributor of all land and capital,
while the opportunity of all others would be limited to their labor,
at least until they could acquire control over some land and capital
through their savings. By the permission of such a transfer, therefore,
society would create inequality of opportunity in the economic part
of life, and thereby in the intellectual part of life as well. Now suppose
that the case be changed so that the transfer of all land and capital
by inheritance be limited not to one person but to twenty-five. Inequality of opportunity still remains, not as glaring as before but still
as real, and proceeding from the same source of unequal transfer by
inheritance. We can continue to vary the case by enlarging the number
of recipients, and the result of inequality of opportunity will continue
to obtain, though diminishing in its intensity, until we reach the
case where the amount permitted to be transferred to all persons by
inheritance is the same. When this condition of equality of transfer
is reached, the influence of size of inheritance considered apart from
all other factors will be a maximum contribution toward equality of
economic opportunity.

But if equality of inheritance—and also of gifts, for the same principles apply to gifts—be thus established, it must largely remove the
possibility of assisting others to obtain the means of existence through
inheritance and gift. For as we have noted, the furnishing of such
assistance consists in transferring an amount of land and capital sufficient to supply, through the return attributable to it in the market, the
means of existence without the contribution of labor. But although
many members of society must always live without the contribution
of labor—as must the young, the infirm, and the aged—yet all cannot

do so, for the production of goods without labor is impossible, even as it is impossible without land and capital. In consequence an amount of land and capital sufficient to enable all members of the community to enjoy the means of existence without contributing labor is an impossibility, no matter how large that quantity of land and capital may be; and, further, the equal division of all land and capital can make no difference to the proposition that life without labor is not possible for all. An equal division of all transfers by gift and inheritance would therefore prevent assistance, since it would prevent the receipt of a sufficient amount of property to provide the means of existence without labor.

But assistance is of great importance, for its denial would constitute a very large and frequently tragic deprivation of liberty to many members of society. On the other hand, a limited inequality in the acquisition of property by gift and inheritance produces only a limited inequality in economic opportunity. Labor rather than land and capital is the decisive factor in production and the one to which most of the product is attributed. With labor consumers' goods can be acquired, and with savings from money earned by labor the ownership of land and capital can be obtained. Labor itself is not affected by inheritance or gift, nor by inequality in them. Therefore the man who has labor to expend is not too greatly affected by inequality of gift or inheritance, provided the other conditions of the free market be maintained. And the man without labor to expend is the very one who needs inequality in gifts and inheritances, that he may have the chance of obtaining the means of existence through this form of assistance.

The liberal society should therefore permit transfers by gift and inheritance to the extent indicated by the principle of assistance, but should bar any transfers to any one individual beyond that amount. The amount required for a liberal means of existence would be the maximum permitted so to be transmitted or received. The result would be that this allowed amount would constitute the maximum inequality in gifts and inheritances which could occur. Under this rule, assistance could still be rendered and obtained, but inequality in economic opportunity beyond that justified by the principle of assistance would be prevented.

This restriction in the acquisition of property by gift and inheritance is not based upon any principle of egalitarianism in the ownership of property. Individualism does not believe in egalitarianism either in ownership of property or in incomes. It believes that both income and the ownership of property should depend upon contribution to production in a free market and should be commensurate with that contribution; and it knows that contributions will be different as people make different responses to the economic opportunities presented to them. But it believes that the economic opportunities of all should be equal, since this is required by the principle of equal liberty. The acquisition of property by gift or inheritance makes private property depend upon ancestry, rather than upon contribution to production. Thereby it destroys equal economic opportunity.

To the extent, however, that transfers by gift and inheritance are permitted under the principle of assistance they tend to equalize economic opportunity and thereby are justified.

7. Earned property

All private property acquired in some manner other than by gift or inheritance can properly be regarded as earned property. It is earned in the sense that it is acquired by contributing to the production of goods. Apart from gift and inheritance, property can be acquired only by making things with one's own labor or by buying things with money obtained from contributions of labor, land, capital, money, or entrepreneurship to production. Since everyone starts in life owning no property, except that which he may inherit, his initial acquisition of property—apart from gift or inheritance—must be through money received by contributing labor to production. He may save some of this money and buy land and capital, which he thereafter contributes to production. Such land and capital has its source in his original contribution to production. Apart, therefore, from property obtained by gift or inheritance, all property acquired in a free market must be earned by contributing to production.

The question, then, is presented: Should any quantitative limitation be placed on earned property?

The answer, under the principle of equal economic liberty, is clear. Any deprivation of the opportunity to acquire earned property would be an impairment of equal opportunity to produce goods. Earned property represents the response of its owner to the opportunity to produce goods in the free market. To limit such property would be to limit the opportunity to produce, and so to limit the opportunity to produce would be to deny equal liberty. In order to preserve equal economic opportunity, therefore, the free market must not place any quantitative limitation on earned property.

Thus the society of liberty will limit the quantity of property which the individual can acquire by gift or inheritance, but will not limit that which he can acquire by contributing to production. The result will be unequal holdings of property, as different individuals accumulate different amounts of earned property. But the variance in holdings will not result from unequal opportunity, but from unequal response. The egalitarianism of liberty is the egalitarianism of opportunity, not the egalitarianism of response; and therefore to preserve equality of opportunity the laws of the free society must protect inequality in response. Sameness is not liberty, as we saw in Book One, and this applies as well to the owning of property as to other parts of human experience. It is sameness in the opportunity to own property that must be the concern of the philosophy of liberty, and this sameness is achieved by individualism through applying the rules above considered.

8. The evil of collective property

The evil of collective property is that it concentrates the control of land and capital in the hands of a few. Property being decision, the function of decision must be spread as widely as consistent with equal liberty for all. But when property is held collectively, the function of decision is concentrated as the privilege of a few. Collective property and collective planning go hand in hand; they cannot be separated. And collective planning is the stultification of the many, permitting the selfish aggrandizement of the few.

The evil of collective ownership must attach to all forms of collective property, whether they be large or small. The vogue is to suppose that although the collectivization of farms in Russia is probably wrong, yet municipal electric plants and the Tennessee Valley Authority in this country are probably right. Yet in neither the one case nor the other is the public property involved essential to the liberty of individualism, but on the contrary obstructs it. Therefore the evil of public ownership is exactly the same in kind in each instance, although as observed in Russia the evil may seem to us more obvious. And indeed the harm of collective property has proceeded vastly further in Russia than here. But the nature of the harm, though the quantities of it may differ, remains precisely the same. The small developments of collective property, such as those we now observe in our country, are the incipient forms of the disease of collectivism, whose later effect will be the more disastrous as its early stages are the less guarded against.

It is frequently said with respect to public property that although the official class exercises direct control over public property, yet in a democratic society the people through their votes determine the members of the official class, and thereby exercise indirect control over public property. By this argument it is sought to reconcile public property with freedom, and to justify the constant expansion of public property.

This voting control by the citizens over their officials is indeed something, and it is one of the principal differences between collectivism as we see it today in Russia and as we see it operating in Great Britain. But it is not too much. The evil of concentrated control of the instruments of production remains. The privilege of voting, important as it is, does not constitute the exercise of decision in the control of property, but only the selection of the few who shall exercise decision. The liberty of individualism in its economic part does not consist simply in the choice of a few officials, but in the broad spread of the privilege of economic decision.

Chapter 19

ASSISTANCE

1. The obligation to assist others

The free market system allocates consumption to those who contribute to production, their shares in consumption being determined by the amounts of their respective contributions to production as evaluated by society through the medium of market price.

Some persons, however, are barred by incapacity from contributing to production. This incapacity may be total or only partial, and may be of various kinds. It may occur with or without the fault of the incapacitated person. But the market pays no attention to the form or occasion of the incapacity; its mechanism automatically removes from the incapacitated person, to the extent of his incapacity, the possibility of satisfying his wants through participation in market activity.

The forms of incapacity to contribute to production are related to the forms in which contributions to production are made. Even as contributions are of labor, land, capital, and money, so incapacity may exist with respect to any one or more of these modes of contribution. An incapacitated person, accordingly, is one who is unable to contribute any one or more of the instruments of production in sufficient quantity to obtain, in return, the means of livelihood. And a person who is able to contribute any one or more of the instruments of production in sufficient quantity to obtain the means of livelihood is not an incapacitated person. Thus a person who is physically unable to contribute labor to production, but who, because of ownership, is able to contribute land, capital, or money, is not incapacitated. Our concern in the present chapter is with incapacitated persons.

We who are not incapacitated perhaps need no special reasoning to show us that we should help those who are less fortunate. We know it instinctively. Hume said that a natural function binds us to others and makes us feel their misfortunes. In the language of the present work we should say that the realm of self is inseparably a part of the realm of not-self, and that therefore the misfortunes of the realm of not-self are sensed also to be the misfortunes of the realm of self. Knowing this, perhaps clearly, perhaps dimly, we are moved to attempt the amelioration of the misfortunes of others by giving assistance.

But although the obligation to render assistance may possibly need no urging, yet a clear understanding of the nature of the obligation is necessary if we are to discharge it correctly.

The obligation arises from the purpose of human life. That purpose is human character, and for that purpose equal liberty is ethical imperative. Equal liberty, which thus becomes the first function of the state, demands equality of opportunity of access to the factors composing will's arena. Among these factors is the material factor, consisting in an important part of goods to satisfy human wants. The accomplishment of the purpose of life, therefore, depends significantly upon equality of opportunity of access to goods.

But the institutions of the free market and of private property cannot of themselves maintain this needed equality of opportunity. There are persons who are unable to participate in the activity of the free market, and for whom the free market does not represent opportunity. The free and the controlled markets stand in the same case in this regard, since the incapacity that bars participation in the one must also bar participation in the other. It follows that the society seeking to give reality to the liberty of individualism must supplement the free market and private property with some further institution. And since the occasion of this additional institution is the inability of some persons to obtain goods by contributing to production, the institution must be designed to furnish these persons goods without requiring that they first contribute to production. This institution we shall refer to as social assistance, or simply as assistance; and it consists in supplying goods to persons who are barred by some form of incapacity from participating in the free market.

Since liberty is the duty of us all and since assistance is a necessary part of liberty, it follows that the rendering of assistance is the duty of us all, except those who must be its recipients. The self and the not-self are equal in human importance, and the duty is to maintain equal liberty for the not-self even as for the self, for one's neighbors even as for one's own being. And inasmuch as liberty is ethical imperative, so assistance is an unconditional moral obligation.

It may perhaps be objected to the argument that assistance is an integral part of equal liberty that incapacity to contribute to production is simply a form, albeit perhaps an extreme form, of inequality of response to the equal opportunity afforded by the free market, and that since inequality of response comes within the practice of liberty, so also must the inequality of response resulting from incapacity to respond, and that therefore some theory other than that of liberty must be employed to justify assistance, if it is to be justified.

But this objection makes use of the same phrase, "inequality of response," to refer to things which in the reality of life are quite different. The free market, with the allocation of its produce to those who contribute to production, is an institution only for those who are capable of entering into it by contributing to production. It is not an institution for those who are incapable of taking part in it. Although the dividing line between those who can and those who cannot contribute to production is by no means precise, yet there are some who clearly fall within the class of those who are incapacitated, as for example infants and invalids who are bedridden, and there are others who are clearly capable of contributing, this latter class constituting all normal adults. As to those who are clearly incapable of contributing to production, such as infants and bedridden invalids, it is unrealistic to speak of the inequality of their response. In reality no opportunity is presented to them at all, for an opportunity properly considered must include the possibility of a favorable response, that is, of taking advantage of the opportunity. The free market does not and cannot supply opportunity to those who are thus incapacitated, and their inaction with respect to production is not an inequality of response but an incapacity to respond.

But precise categories are unknown in social phenomena (even as they are rare and perhaps nonexistent in natural phenomena) and in consequence there are many degrees of want of capacity which extend through the interval separating total incapacity to produce and the capacity of the normal adult. For example, children, the aged, and the blind are usually capable of making some minor contributions to production. That some difference should nevertheless be recognized between these persons and those who ordinarily contribute to production is commonly acknowledged. Where should the line of difference be fixed? The answer is indicated by the purpose of the free market as an institution. Its purpose is to produce goods for the satisfaction of human want, and elementally for the maintenance of life. We may distinguish, then, between those who are capable of entering into this purpose in its elemental form and those who are not. That is, those who are capable of contributing sufficiently to production to obtain in return the essentials of living comprise one class, while all those who are not so capable comprise another class, and the dividing line between these classes must be the capacity or want thereof to obtain the needs of existence in the free market. For those who do not possess this capacity, the free market cannot be said to provide economic opportunity.

In more or less vague ways, societies have always recognized that assistance as a regular social institution should be provided. What the philosophy of individualism does is to show how assistance as a social institution is founded on the basic imperative of liberty and thereby to show the nature and interconnection of its principles. The need for social assistance is a repudiation neither of the free market nor of individual freedom. On the contrary it is an integral part of the social arrangement required by individual freedom, and accordingly is intimately related with activity in the free market.

2. The methods of assistance

In general, all forms of assistance can appropriately be divided into two classes: (a) assistance rendered through the machinery of the state, and (b) assistance rendered by individuals not acting through the machinery of the state.

State assistance is accomplished through taxation, that is, through force. By the force of the state money is taken from those who have obtained it by their contributions to production in the free market and is delivered to those who have not contributed to production.

By reason of principles we have heretofore studied, this power in state officials to transfer wealth must end in corruption unless it is limited. Such limitation must consist in definite rules indicating the scope for the exercise of such power. The difficulty here encountered is that the occasions for assistance are as varied as the forms of human distress, and consequently it is easy to suppose that the administrators of social assistance should be accorded wide latitude in determining the amount and kind of assistance to be given. But such a rule would disregard the principles operative when the state's force is invoked. Because power tends to corrupt, wide latitude to administrators must be avoided, and here as elsewhere there must be compromise in the working rules.

The compromise to be effected must look both to adjustment of assistance to particular need and to explicitness and uniformity in the provisions of the state's laws. Since the two objectives are not entirely compatible, neither can be entirely accomplished. The art of legislation is to secure each as far as possible without undue impairment of the other.

But the state is not the only possible social agency, and if the necessary limitations to its laws render it an unsuitable instrument for wide latitude in discretionary assistance, other agencies are available for that purpose. Private philanthropy is not subject to the limitations to be placed on state assistance, because being supported by the donations of individuals rather than the force of the state, it does not fall within the operation of the principle that power always tends to corrupt. In consequence, private philanthropy can frame its assistance in such forms as it deems suitable, adapting its aid to its subjective judgment of need in each particular case as it arises. The principles of liberty make no demand that the assistance of private philanthropy proceed by uniform rule; on the contrary, liberty requires that, since private philanthropy can without danger fit its aid to particular cases, it do so. If therefore state assistance must be limited to the enforcement of specific and uniform rules, it becomes the obligation of individuals to supplement state assistance by giving aid either directly or through institutions of private philanthropy.

Thus tax-supported state programs and private philanthropy should blend as instrumentalities for furnishing assistance in the free society, each complementing the other.

It is objected by the proponents of state action, however, that private philanthropy is mere charity, not sure in its rendition because dependent on the will of the individual donor. The right to assistance, it is said, should entirely be placed upon the more certain foundation of law.

This view, however, embodies two erroneous concepts of the nature of law. The first is the error of supposing that law can enforce the exercise of discretion; the second is the error of assuming that laws can continue to be effective without popular conviction of their need. As to the first error, we should note that an essential element of all law, arising from its nature, is the sanction of force. That which law cannot enforce it cannot effect. Therefore law can permit the exercise of discretion, because it can compel noninterference with its exercise; but it cannot enforce the exercise of discretion, because discretion requires the absence of compulsion. Discretionary assistance accordingly cannot be placed upon the certain foundation of law because it is impossible for law to enforce discretionary assistance. If discretionary assistance is to be enjoyed, it can only be permitted by law, and the question then becomes whether the discretionary assistance thus permitted shall be administered by public officials or by private philanthropy. The reasons why the free society must choose private philanthropy instead of public administration in this regard have already been expressed.

Unless a society, moreover, experiences the exercise of private philanthropy, it will cease to hold a conviction of the need of assistance through law. The fear of those who oppose private philanthropy in favor of public assistance is that the members of society will become disinterested and fail to provide the assistance they ought to give. A society, however, which becomes unwilling to support private philanthropy will soon become unwilling to support social assistance by law, for the want of conviction that prevents the first will soon undermine the second. Human laws come and go, and they remain in effect only while a popular conviction sustains them. And a people who are barred from the exercise of private philanthropy, through usurpation of the field by the state, must cease to have conviction of its need.

If assistance, then, is to be furnished adequately in the liberal society, it must be by a coordinated program of state and individual action, the latter being charged with responsibility in those areas calling for assistance of the more discretionary sort.

3. Persons entitled to assistance

The persons entitled to assistance are those, as has been already said, who are unable to contribute to production, and for whom in consequence the free market cannot provide an equal opportunity of obtaining goods. The identification of these persons must be made with reference to the two methods of assistance; there must be an identification of those who are entitled to state assistance, and an identification of those entitled to assistance through private philanthropy.

With respect to state assistance, the identification must be limited to those whose cases are capable of specific designation; but, on the other hand, state assistance should include all persons whose cases are capable of such designation. All persons whose cases are not capable of such designation fall within the responsibility of private philanthropy.

Children comprise a first division of the class suitable to receive state assistance. Children can be specifically defined by reference to age, and their needs for certain forms of assistance, such as education, housing, food, and medical care, can be specified with a workable degree of precision.

The mentally incompetent comprise another division in the class of those entitled to state assistance. While incompetence is not easily determined in some cases, yet experience indicates that a workable rule is possible, and those adjudged incompetent by appropriate social machinery can be supported by the state.

The aged comprise another group capable of specific designation, and since age itself is frequently the occasion of incapacity to contribute to production, it constitutes an appropriate category for state assistance. The varying need for assistance which different persons in the aged category experience is considered below.

Physical inability to perform labor may also render a person incapacitated for participation in the market. Various kinds of physical handicaps, such as blindness, accordingly furnish additional categories for state assistance. Here again, as in the case of the aged, particular individuals, because of their ability to contribute land, capital, or money to production, may not be incapacitated. The treatment of the problem thus presented will be discussed in the following section.

Unemployment also presents a category suitable for state assistance. As we shall discuss more fully at a later point, a small amount of unemployment is not only a necessary characteristic of a free market but is also desirable for certain purposes of a free society. Some unemployment is deliberately incurred by workers as they move from one employment to another in an effort to better their condition, and as to this unemployment no need for assistance arises. But some unemployment results from causes that have nothing to do with the workers themselves, being occasioned by the contraction or discontinuance of the production of certain goods, or by the use of less labor in particular industries. Such unemployment constitutes, while it continues, an incapacity to contribute labor to production; and the persons so unemployed compose a category or class for whom state assistance properly should be made available.

Thus we can identify the following categories for state assistance: children, the mentally incompetent, the aged, the physically handicapped, and the involuntarily unemployed. As to each of these classifications, reasonably precise specifications are possible, whereby persons falling within the classification can be identified without discretion on the part of public officials.

These being the groups for which the state should make assistance available, who are the persons identifiable as the proper objects of private assistance? They are, broadly speaking, all those persons suffering from a want of capacity to contribute effectively to production, who yet do not come within an identifiable category for public assistance. Typically they are those whose want of capacity is temporary and relievable, as caused, for example, by illness or a lack of training.

4. The extent of assistance

The question is, To what extent should assistance be rendered to incapacitated persons? Following the division already indicated between public and private assistance, we shall first consider the proper extent of assistance rendered by the state. The question then becomes, To what extent should state assistance be made available to those persons for whom state aid is appropriate?

Assistance to others, when rendered by the state, must be conducted through taxation. Thus it involves the use of the force of the state, exercised by state officials, as they take from one citizen money which he has acquired in return for contributions made by him to production and give it to another citizen who is unable to make such contribution. The purpose of this use of force is, as we have seen, to compensate for the assisted person's incapacity to contribute to production, and thus —viewing the matter in its more ultimate aspect—to promote equality of liberty.

Having in mind this purpose of state assistance, we can say that the assistance rendered should at least be sufficient to provide the means of livelihood in accordance with prevailing customs and standards. This conclusion follows from the considerations, first, that the purpose of assistance is to provide goods in lieu of those which would be obtained by the assisted person if he could contribute to production, and, second, that what he could so obtain would be at least the means of livelihood in accordance with prevailing customs and standards. What the means of livelihood so gauged will amount to must vary from place to place and from time to time, as the technology and capital of particular societies enlarge or reduce the standard of living available to their members.

The means of livelihood, thus determined, should be regarded as the norm or standard of state assistance, subject to the deviations hereafter discussed. In order to accomplish its basic function of equal liberty, accordingly, the state should make sufficient assistance available to insure the means of livelihood to children, incompetents, aged persons, the physically handicapped, and those who are involuntarily without employment.

But what is to be said of those persons who, though partially incapacitated, are yet able themselves to supply a portion of their needed means of livelihood through contributions to production? Or of those persons who, though falling within one of the categories mentioned in the preceding section, yet are able entirely to furnish their means of livelihood? This problem arises with respect to all categories of incapacity. An aged person, for example, may possess an income from property, and have only a slight need of assistance or no need at all. Should the state nevertheless use its force to collect money from other members of the community, even from the poor, and give it to the well-to-do aged, simply because they have passed a certain birthday? This is what we do in the United States today. It is true that the matter is confused and the issue clouded by referring to the payments made as insurance. The inaccuracy of this designation we shall examine later. For the present we should note that the use of the state's force to make assistance payments to persons who have no need of assistance, or to make assistance payments beyond what is necessary for the means of livelihood, is always an impairment of equal liberty and therefore unethical.

This same problem arises with respect to all forms of public assistance. Should payments to the blind, for example, be made to all blind persons or only to those who have insufficient means? Should the applicant for unemployment compensation be required to show that he is without other means of livelihood? From time to time this problem is discussed as the desirability of the use of "means tests" in rendering public assistance. Such discussion, however, has incorrectly tended to assume that the only method of adjusting assistance to particular need is through the use of means tests; and to the use of such tests it is properly objected, first, that they are a source of humiliation to the assisted person, and second, that they place undue discretion in the hands of public officers, threatening both corruption and unwise administration. Means tests, in consequence, are for the most part in disfavor.

Fortunately, however, a method of separating needy from unneedy cases, involving no discretion on the part of public officials and capable of being made largely self-executing, is readily at hand. It consists simply in requiring all recipients of public assistance to file with the disbursing agency an income tax return (which could be simply a copy of any state or federal income tax return) and in levying a tax at specific rates, up to 100%, on all public assistance received if other income exceeds certain levels. With this system, the payments of assistance to all persons within a designated category would be equally available to all such persons, but all amounts in excess of those needed as a means of livelihood would be recouped through taxation. By appropriate provisions for the offset of any tax due against assistance payments the program could be made to no small degree self-executing. Because of our long experience with income taxation, the machinery for this method of adjusting public assistance to need is easily available.

Such a system would avoid all the objections urged against the use of means tests; it would involve not the slightest humiliation to the assisted person and would neither leave assistance to discretionary administration nor invite corruption. Yet it would serve to limit public assistance to supplying the means of livelihood to incapacitated persons.

At the present time we not only fail to make use of this device of adjustment to need through taxation, but it is our general practice (without exception so far as I know) to exempt assistance payments from all income taxation. Thus a wealthy person over 72 years of age not only receives monthly largess from the state but enjoys it free of income tax. Similarly the person who is unemployed for a part of a year, though his earnings during the employed portion of the year may constitute an ample income, yet collects money from the state free of income tax. If the income tax is an equitable mode of taxation at all, it should apply to income regardless of its source; and beyond this, it can be used to limit assistance to the need of incapacitated persons for the means of livelihood.

As to private assistance, no social rules are required to define or limit its extent. Even as private assistance has its origin in private conviction rather than in public force, so private conviction alone is sufficient for its guidance, without public direction.

5. The right to a decent standard of living

In recent years we have heard much of the asserted right to a decent standard of living. The Declaration of Human Rights adopted by the United Nations Assembly, indeed, includes a decent standard of living among the rights of all human beings.

If this right be interpreted simply as an aspiration toward which all societies should direct their efforts it can have our complete approval. All human persons should seek a decent standard of living both for themselves and for others; and it is, further, a part of the case for individualism that it furnishes the best social machinery for attaining that ideal. The use of the term right in this connection, as in similar ones, contains a good deal of this connotation of an ideal or goal.

But this is by no means its sole connotation; it connotes, and is intended in this usage to connote, a proper claim which the individual can make against the other members of his community. In this connotation right becomes correlative with duty; if the individual member of the community has a right to a decent standard of living, then the other members of the community have a duty to supply him with it; and if there are some members of the community who are not enjoying a decent standard of living, then it necessarily follows, from the initial premise that a decent standard of living is a right, that other members of the community are not doing their duty, and are wrongfully depriving the substandard portion of the community of what it rightfully should have.

It thus follows, within the lines set by this argument, that all persons who do not have a decent standard of living are being exploited by other members of their society. It is this connotation that the poor are also the exploited that is almost always sought to be suggested when it is said that there is a right to a decent standard of living. The poor being thus identified with the exploited, it follows that something should be done about it, and in our time the suggestion usually is that the thing to be done is some form of collectivistic action by the state.

The good intentions of most of those who thus argue for the recognition of a decent standard of living as a human right can be readily admitted, as can also their sincere interest in human welfare. But the philosophy of individualism, though it enthusiastically joins them in setting a decent standard of living for all as an objective of human action, must point out the error, and consequent danger, in their tenet that a decent standard of living is a right.

A decent standard of living is not a human right but a human achievement. It is not a condition attained simply by passing laws, but rather by producing goods. The human right is to have an equal opportunity of access to the elements of the material factor in will's arena. The human duty is to observe this equality of access and not to infringe upon it. But the right being maintained and the duty performed, there yet is no assurance that a decent standard of living will ensue; for the standard of living, both for the individual and the group, depends not only upon opportunity but also upon response to opportunity. A decent standard of living as we conceive it today requires the use of large quantities of capital in the production of goods; a society which lacks the will to create capital or the inclination to use it cannot achieve a decent standard of living, no matter what form of social organization it may employ. The utmost that social organization can do is to confirm men in their rights; it cannot assure that they will make good use of them. An individual who can but will not exert himself cannot expect to enjoy a decent standard of living in a free market society. And a society which will not restrict its population relative to its natural resources and capital cannot have a decent standard of living regardless of the form of social organization.

A decent standard of living being thus a human accomplishment rather than a human right, the error of regarding it as a right has the tragic effect of dangerously confusing human thought. Human rights are of vital importance—this whole work is concerned with them—and so is a good standard of living. They can be attained, however, even in approximate form only with the utmost difficulty, with the clearest of thinking, and with the most strenuous of endeavor. To assert that a decent standard of living is a right clouds both the nature of right and the objective of endeavor. Human rights always have to do with human opportunity, never with human response. Rights are the arena for human action, but response is the action itself, the manifestation of human character. A decent standard of living depends both upon the rights confirmed by the social organization and upon the response thereto. Therefore the assertion that a decent standard of living is simply a matter of right disregards the element of character, and such a disregard must end in calamitous disaster for the society that indulges in it.

6. Compulsory state insurance

Much of the aid given to incapacitated persons at the present time is called social insurance, and some of the details of the method by which aid is given are sought to be explained on the ground that insurance is involved.

Compulsory state insurance in its modern form is a rather recent development, and has been hailed as a device for ameliorating many of the hazards of existence. When the earlier proposals for state insurance were made, the collectivistic nature of such insurance—in so far as it was truly insurance and not simply a form of state assistance—was generally recognized, but at present long association has induced an attitude of uncritical acceptance. Most compulsory insurance programs, moreover, are too complicated for the average citizen to analyze, and since he from time to time receives benefits from them, he is likely to accept the representations of their proponents that they constitute beneficial insurance programs for all members of society.

The fact is, however, that most of our present compulsory programs, which collectively have come to be known as "social security," are not insurance at all within any proper meaning of that designation, but constitute methods of giving assistance, with certain characteristic features of insurance improperly and unfairly tacked on.

Insurance is a pooling of risk by persons who severally contribute small amounts to a fund, from which fund compensation is paid to any members of the group who suffer loss through the occurrence of the risk insured against. Thus insurance is the acceptance of a small and certain expense in exchange for an assurance against a loss which though uncertain might be large if it occurred. By contract the fund is devoted to the benefit of the participants, and since the several payments made by them into the fund, i.e., their premiums, must be made primarily from money received by them as earned property, it follows that the participation in the fund by any insured suffering a loss is to be regarded as having been obtained through contributions made to production.

Insurance from its nature is possible only for those risks concerning which statistical evidence of average occurrence is available, because the protection furnished by small contributions to a common fund must depend on the adequacy of the contributions, and where it is impossible to compute the adequacy of contributions, by reason of want of knowledge of the incidence of the risk, there can be no insurance fund. People can, of course, pool their resources even against an unknown hazard, but in such case the fund is simply a common reserve against an incalculable calamity and cannot properly be called insurance.

With respect to assistance, on the other hand, it does not have its origin in any contractual pooling of funds, but arises from an obligation based on status. It is the status of the recipient of assistance that entitles him to aid from the rest of the community, rather than any contract he has entered into. Nor is the right to receive assistance in any way dependent on prior contributions to production; indeed it is the fact of inability to contribute to production that furnishes the base of the right to assistance; whereas the right to insurance proceeds must be obtained by a prior payment of money which in turn must typically be obtained by contributing to production.

From these differences between insurance and assistance there results a distinction between the prerequisites to the receipt of payments. In order to entitle an insured person to the receipt of insurance proceeds, it is only necessary that a loss be occasioned by a hazard stipulated in the insurance contract. The need of the insured person, his penury or opulence, has nothing to do with his right to be paid. With respect to assistance, however, need is both the occasion and the measure of the payment to be made, for it is need arising from inability to contribute to production that justifies assistance and determines its extent. Nor is the cause of the inability to contribute to production a relevant factor in considering the right to assistance. The inability may arise with or without fault; it may be due to unforeseeable calamity or to hazards that could have been insured against; but whatever its source the incapacity itself is the proper ground for assistance.

In a free market society, individuals are able to establish insurance funds for insurable risks as they choose to do so. In practice, a very large percentage of the population in a society such as ours take part in one or more of such insurance programs, protecting themselves and their families against losses that may be incurred by fire, accident, sickness, theft, or death.

Thus insurance is distinguished from assistance both by the nature of the risk involved and by the nature of the protection available against such risk. Where the risk is not insurable in the actuarial sense, insurance, either voluntary or compulsory, is impossible and no amount of legislation can make it possible.

The principles of insurance and of assistance thus being different, programs of protection based upon them must also differ. The cost of insurance is properly distributable among the members of the group who are subject to the risk and protected by the insurance. Upon the occurrence of the loss insured against the insured person is entitled to be compensated for his loss without regard to any question of its relation to his capacity to contribute to production. The cost of assistance, on the other hand, is properly to be financed by the entire community through its general program of taxation, and a person suffering any of the perils covered by the assistance program is entitled to receive assistance payments only to the extent that he becomes unable to obtain the means of livelihood by his own contributions to production.

Our present "social security" program, however, has confused insurance and assistance principles, with much resultant unfairness. It applies to unemployment, which is not an insurable risk, some of the principles of insurance, and it applies to old age, which is an insurable risk, some of the principles of assistance, and to each of them it applies some procedures which cannot be justified as either insurance or assistance.

Unemployment is not an insurable risk because it occurs with no observable average regularity. It is not possible, therefore, to operate an insurance program covering unemployment, in which the covered persons each pay into a common fund to be used for compensation for losses. If such a fund be set up, the relation between payments into the fund and payments out of it to cover losses must always be accidental rather than calculated. This however is not insurance. Since the risk, nevertheless, is one which occasions incapacity, society should protect its members from the risk, and this protection must be by way of assistance. But assistance is the duty of the entire community and should be borne by the entire community, rather than by only a portion of it. Our present programs of unemployment compensation, however, disregarding the uninsurable nature of the risk of involuntary unemployment, treat such unemployment as though it were insurable. Thus the cost is assessed by taxation against the employees and employers in those areas of employment covered by the program. Persons in other areas of employment are not protected, which disregards the right of all unemployed persons to assistance, and the community does not share generally in the cost, which disregards the society-wide nature of the obligation. Further, the unemployment compensation payments are made without regard to the capacity of the unemployed person to contribute to production, as though such payments were insurance payments which the unemployed person was entitled to because of his payment of insurance premiums into a common fund. All these deviations from sound principle impair liberty, because money—the means of acquiring goods—is taken by the force of the state from one person and given to another without the justification of its being done for assistance.

With respect to old age benefits, the risk here covered is susceptible of treatment as insurance, yet our present program applies many of the principles of assistance. The hazard protected against is the need incident to old age, and this is subject to actuarial calculation, since life spans are lived out with average regularity. Accordingly private insurance companies can and do offer insurance policies against this risk, which a large percentage of our population avail themselves of. The most, then, that the state can do, if it wishes to expand insurance coverage, is to compel citizens to join in insurance programs, either privately or publicly operated. Such compulsory insurance would violate liberty, but, barring the compulsory feature, it would fairly and completely care for the hazard of old age indigence, for every person would, on reaching a specified age, become entitled to payments actuarially related to his contributions.

Our present federal program of Old Age and Survivors Insurance, however, which is our main governmental program for the aged, adheres to the principles neither of insurance nor of assistance. The program is financed by taxes levied against persons included in the program's coverage, and also against their employers if they are employed. The taxes vary with income. The monthly payments start at age 65 if the included person is then unemployed, or by 72 regardless of his being employed or unemployed. The payments are made without regard to the recipient's need, and therefore do not conform to the principles of assistance. On the other hand, the payments are not actuarially related to the taxes paid by or for the account of the covered person, and thus there is no adherence to the principles of insurance. The payments are made pursuant to provisions in the law which have been changed from time to time, and doubtless will be subject to more or less constant change in the future. In general the amount of monthly payment to a covered person is larger or smaller as his past annual earnings have been larger or smaller. But the amount of payment has no actuarial relation to the total taxes theretofore paid by or for the account of the covered person. Thus a person who has paid taxes under the program for only a few years may obtain as large a monthly payment as another person who has been taxed many more years. There are tens of thousands of persons 65 and over in the United States who, though they have never paid more than a few hundred dollars into the program, are now drawing pensions of $100 to $150 per month, free of income tax, despite the fact that they are not in need. In a few months these pensioners recover all their prior tax contributions and thereafter enjoy largess supplied by other citizens.

This confusion of insurance and assistance in our old age program, and regard for the principles of neither, effects a serious impairment of liberty, as unjust taxation always does. The special taxes collected to finance the program are not adequately related either to the benefits received or to the duty discharged.

The injustice of this taxation is enhanced by the fact that a substantial portion of the special taxes collected are not needed for the current costs of the program, and are spent by the United States Treasury in the payment of its other expenses. In lieu of the money so spent, the Treasury places in a so-called reserve an equivalent amount of its promissory notes payable to itself—as though there could be any reality to an obligation in which the obligor and obligee are identical. The imaginary character of this reserve is certain to become apparent in a few years when it is necessary to resort to it to finance the large increase in old age benefits which will occur. Then it will become obvious that the Treasury will have to raise money either by selling in the open market its bonds from the reserve or by redeeming them with money obtained from general tax revenue; the money, that is to say, will have to be raised either through bonds or taxes. But this is exactly what the Treasury would have to do to meet its future obligations in this regard if there were no reserve at all. The reserve is a nullity, its size is of no practical consequence—any more than the quantity of his own promissory notes payable to himself a man might carry in his pocket—and the special taxes assessed against employed persons for the ostensible purpose of financing old age benefits constitute, to the extent of the reserve, a grossly unjust method of raising general revenue.

This unfortunate result has been reached in part because the federal government, in embarking upon compulsory state insurance schemes, has departed from the dictates of the principles of liberty. Compulsory state insurance is always wrong because it always violates liberty, and therefore, beginning in injustice, it must always end in further injustice.

7. Medical assistance

We hear much of socialized medicine in these days. It is said, as a large inscription on one of the buildings at the British Empire Exposition in 1951 proclaimed, that good health is the right of every citizen. If good health is a right, then it follows that it is the duty of the state to assure that right to all its citizens. And if this be true, then should not the state undertake to perform that duty by adopting a program of state-operated medical care?

But the analysis already had in the present chapter shows the fallacy of this approach to the problem of medical care. Good health is not a human right but a human achievement. It depends, as do all human activities, in part upon the form of social organization in which it must be accomplished, but it also depends upon the response which human beings make to the opportunity for good health as that opportunity is presented to them by nature and by social rules. The man, whether rich or poor, whose indolence stands in the way of his achieving good health cannot be heard to say that he nevertheless has a right to good health which others are obligated to procure for him. The society, likewise, which will not use its own best efforts to supply itself with sanitation and medical care cannot be heard to say that it has a right to call on other societies for these things. The only right which exists with respect to health is the right to an equal opportunity of access to the means of good health. Medical care is no more essential to existence than food and shelter, and so far as social form is concerned precisely the same basic principles apply in the one matter as in the others. The rule of liberty is equality of opportunity, not equality of achievement or of success. Each citizen is entitled to equality of opportunity for good health; so far his right runs. But it does not go farther. Beyond equality of opportunity there is no right of the individual citizen nor obligation of the group.

What, then, does equality of opportunity with respect to health require? It requires, first, the maintenance of equality of economic opportunity generally, for it is through economic action that medical service must be produced and enjoyed, and it is through economic action that the individual citizen must obtain the means by which he can compensate those who assist him in achieving health. This equal liberty in economic opportunity means the creation and maintenance of the basic institutions of the free market and private property and of the supplemental institution of assistance.

Medical care, the means to good health, must therefore be included in the means of livelihood furnished to those requiring assistance. A livelihood includes healthful rather than sickly living. As we have seen, the duty of equal liberty includes the duty of supplying the means of livelihood to all those who are prevented by incapacity from obtaining such means by their own contributions to production. Therefore the duty of equal liberty includes the duty of supplying medical care, through assistance, to those who are unable to obtain it for themselves.

Should medical assistance be rendered through public or private assistance, through state programs or through private philanthropy? Applying the principles which our analysis has heretofore developed, we see that although the persons in need of such assistance are capable of identification with satisfactory exactness—for the need of medical care can be recognized and, further, the extent of financial incapacity of the person needing such care can be determined through income tax returns—yet the amount and kind of medical attention is largely a matter of discretionary judgment applied to each particular case as it presents itself. Prescriptions cannot be made by classes nor can there be treatment in accordance with fixed rules. Medical care must be pursuant to *ad hoc* decisions, for which general rules are only broadly possible. In view of this discretionary and variable nature of medical care, it is much better suited to private than to public assistance, for the reasons already noted in this chapter. Private philanthropy—the hospitals, clinics, and medical programs with which we are familiar in this country—accordingly constitutes a much more efficient and appropriate method of rendering medical assistance than so-called socialized medicine.

As long, therefore, as a society is performing its duty of rendering medical assistance to the incapacitated in reasonably satisfactory fashion through private philanthropy, state assistance should not be resorted to. State assistance, because of the discretionary nature of medical care, must always involve a use of power over others which cannot effectively be subjected to limitation. It must, in consequence, tend to corruption, under the influence of the principles discussed in Chapter 10 of Book One. The corruption which will sooner or later appear will be not simply in money, though some of that must occur, but primarily in the quality of medical care, in its technical and administrative aspects. The very large discretionary control which must be lodged in the state officials— doctors, technicians, and administrators—in charge of the socialized medical program cannot avoid violation of the basic principle that the delegation of the use of power should always be accompanied by effective limitations on that power.

Socialized medical programs purport to do far more, of course, than simply to render medical assistance to incapacitated persons; they intend as well the control of all medical service for all persons. In support of proposals to begin the adoption of collectivistic medical schemes it is constantly suggested that good health is so peculiarly essential to human happiness that it needs more concern than that which can be given it by free enterprise and private philanthropy. But the assumption that individualism is incompetent to care for the more essential needs of existence, which should therefore be entrusted to collectivism, is something calling for proof rather than mere suggestion. And if, indeed, collectivism be thought more competent than individualism in procuring the essentials of life, then the beginning should be made with food rather than medical care, for life may continue without medical care but it cannot continue without food. Medical care is truly of great importance to us, but so also are food, clothing, and shelter. The supplying of all these things is included in economic activity, and they all stand on the same footing in relation to the opposed appeals of individualism and collectivism. Socialized medicine is an aspect of socialism, and thereby a mode of collectivism, based upon the same elementary principles and exerting the same emotional appeal. It must stand or fall as collectivism stands or falls.

Under the aegis of free enterprise and private philanthropy we in this country have built a truly remarkable medical plant and medical program, to which all the world resorts.

The plant consists of doctors' offices, hospitals, medical schools, clinics, clinical laboratories, and the research laboratories and factories of the companies manufacturing pharmaceuticals and other medical supplies. The program consists of the private practice of doctors, the free services rendered through clinics and hospitals, the courses of instruction in medical schools and hospitals, the aid and research programs of the many private organizations devoted to particular areas of medical care, the various insurance plans for paying for medical care, and the large research and manufacturing schedules of the corporations producing medical goods. So well is all this organized and operated that few persons in this country are more than minutes away from a hospital, no one need suffer for want of prompt and efficient medical treatment even though he is unable to pay for it, the skill of our physicians and surgeons draws patients from all over the globe, vast research is constantly in progress, and our production of drugs and other medical supplies not only amply cares for our own needs but also those of much of the rest of the world. All this has been accomplished and today takes place without governmental direction or compulsion, but in accordance, rather, with the principles of the liberty of individualism. Certainly there is room for advancement, and fortunately criticism—both well- and ill-advised—is constantly being presented. But because liberty prevails, improvement is steadily achieved.

Yet there are those who would supplant this present American medi-

cal system with socialized medicine, of which there are so many prototypes in Europe. These advocates of collectivism in health and medicine
should be required, as a preface to their advocacy, to show one such
system which even approaches the American system in its accomplishments. Our medical plant and program are proof of the practical efficacy
of private enterprise and private assistance, carried on in accordance
with the principles of individualism.

Chapter 20

ENFORCING HONESTY IN THE FREE MARKET

1. The need for social enforcement of honesty

All human action contains the possibility of dishonesty. One result of dishonesty when it occurs is to defeat reasonable expectation. Inasmuch as all economic action is forward looking, having little regard to the past except as it indicates the future, expectation is its guide. Fragile enough at best, expectation can be destroyed as a guide by dishonesty. All forms of economic action, whether in a controlled or a free market, are consequently impaired in their utility by dishonesty, which every individual accordingly has an interest to guard against.

The forms of guarding against dishonesty are various, and are to be influenced largely by practical considerations. Many deviations from honesty in the market place, probably most of them, can be prevented or protected against by a moderate alertness on the part of the individual. "Let the buyer beware" is a commercial and legal maxim which reflects the proposition that the individual person can and should himself fend off the more easily detected dishonesties.

But some cannot easily be detected by the individual acting alone, or can be found out only too late for him to take the needed precautions. In such cases the procedure indicated by prudence is the institution of social means of enforcing honesty. The free market society has need of many such means, and as customs and technological methods of production change, new social means of enforcing honesty will become necessary, even as the need for former means will disappear.

This use of social intervention to enforce honesty in the market is not a collectivistic device, but is an appropriate instrumentality for keeping the market free, and thus for promoting the liberty of individualism.

2. Enforcement of contracts

Even as most consumption of goods is individual, so most production is social, carried on by the cooperation of many persons. The arrangements by which production thus takes place are effected by multitudinous agreements upon which producers rely. All but a small percentage of these contracts are performed as made, but when nonperformance occurs it defeats expectation and adversely bears on the operation of the free market. A failure to perform may be due to an honest inability to perform, rather than to a dishonest desire to evade performance. The law of the free market, however, treats all failures as defaults, and in general holds parties to performance of their agreements without regard to their degree of honesty of intent.

Not only would injustice be occasioned if contracts were not enforced, but the free market would function most inadequately and liberty correspondingly would be restricted. The free market is based on individual choice. But coupled with choice is responsibility. He who chooses to employ labor must be responsible for its wages, and he who chooses to borrow money or rent land must be responsible for the agreed interest or rent. Without the enforcement of such responsibility there could be little of that reasonable expectation concerning the future acts of others which is imperative to the free market's successful operation.

In order to supply the enforcement of contracts, the free market society furnishes a system of courts, with procedures and officers appropriate to the task of preventing default of contracts where such prevention is possible, and of allowing redress for default where it has already occurred. Although this function of the courts can be succinctly stated, yet in its operating processes it comprises a vast and complicated system of law, composed of principles of decision as laid down by judges of higher courts and of statutes enacted by legislatures, all aimed at applying to the multitudinous circumstances of economic activity a coherent body of rules enforcing the basic tenets of free choice and responsibility and their derivatives.

We do not ordinarily think of this great mass of contract law, touching economic process at every point, as an instrument of the free market. But so it is. The controlled market, not based upon contract but upon status and decree, has little use for it. As the controlled market grows, the importance of the enforcement of contracts diminishes.

3. Measures of quantity

Consumer preference can be a reality only to the extent that there is knowledge of goods. If the articles of merchandise in a store were all wrapped in identical packages, so that the contents could not be discerned by customers, the buyer who took one package rather than another might be said to exercise a preference in some remote sense. But such uninformed preference is not the consumer's choice sought by the free market, which desires, in order to furnish maximum want-satisfaction, maximum information about goods as they are offered for sale. The information so needed is various, differing with the goods, but in general it concerns quantity and quality.

A housewife making purchases in a grocery store could conceivably take along her own scale to verify the quantity of goods sold her, or she could have a scale at home to check weights when she returned with her purchases. Neither of these methods however would be very satisfactory. The first would be cumbersome and embarrassing; the second would be laborious and would occur after the event of purchase. Either method would be inefficient. An efficient method, however, is available, consisting in having the merchant's scales inspected and adjusted regularly by an independent inspector, who can then attach to the scales his certificate that they are accurate. Conceivably this inspector could be employed by an association of customers, but this would be difficult to arrange and would have so many disadvantages that in practice it would probably never be done. A simpler and more efficient method is possible. It is to have an inspector employed by the whole community, the cost being paid through taxes. This has the disadvantage of sharing the cost unfairly, for taxes will not be apportioned in accordance with purchases, but in practical terms the disadvantage is so slight that it can be regarded as far outbalanced by the advantages.

This method of cooperative action through the state should be employed wherever deception in weights and measures is easily possible and where the number of people having an interest in avoiding the deception is large, so that spreading the cost of policing through taxation is not substantially unfair. The applications of this principle in our communities at the present time are numerous, and for the most part they seem to be well advised.

Further, the state can appropriately fix the standards of weights and measures, defining the quantities to be taken whenever such terms as pound, ton, foot, or bushel are used. The establishment of such standards in no way interferes with individual freedom, for it leaves individuals free to adopt other standards in their dealings if they agree to do so; and it promotes freedom by making economic activity more efficient, thereby causing the production of greater quantities of goods and the expansion of the material factor in will's arena.

4. Measures of quality

The same considerations which apply to the quantity of goods offered for sale apply also to their quality. Individual investigation of quality though possible may be inefficient and wasteful, in which case cooperative investigation through an agent appointed and paid by the state may be advantageous.

Thus the health departments of our cities and states determine the quality of milk and other food products, a task which would be in practice an impossibility for most individuals.

Similarly our state and federal laws require the correct branding of products, in order that the consumer may not be deceived but may intelligently exercise preference. A substantial portion of the activity of the Federal Trade Commission is concerned with enforcing accurate labeling. The advertisement of a product is akin to its label. It too should honestly describe the product, and the state can appropriately regulate such advertising in the interest of accuracy. The Federal Trade Commission has this jurisdiction over advertising which appears in interstate commerce and some of our states have similar policing devices.

Although the purpose of this state intervention is in accord with the principles of the free market, yet it contains the danger that, in purporting simply to determine and certify quality, state officials will pass over into the area of deciding what kind of goods consumers ought to have. Anyone examining the reports of the Federal Trade Commission will find many instances where the real complaint seems to have been not that the product was deceptively branded, labeled, or advertised, but that the commission's staff thought it was a poor product on which people should not be allowed to waste their money. This paternalistic attitude is violative of the principles of the liberal society, whose concern should be with the accuracy of the information which consumers have, but not with the wisdom of their choices.

The state may nevertheless properly forbid the sale of products on which there is widespread agreement that their use is deleterious, and not simply require that their deleterious quality be accurately indicated by their labels. Thus it may properly be assumed that no one wants to purchase contaminated food. No one's freedom to choose to purchase it is destroyed, therefore, by forbidding its sale. This is simply a more efficacious way of policing than to permit the sale but to require an accurate label. It must be recognized, even so, that this power to permit or prohibit the sale of a product is dangerous, subject to abuse, and breeding the false persuasion that it is the proper function of the state through its officials to make wise market decisions for its citizens. The power accordingly must be sparingly granted and its use closely watched.

5. Stocks and bonds

It is a tribute to the widespread property ownership created by our free market system that the question of accurate information on stocks and bonds offered for sale has been presented. A less successful society would have had no such problem.

The need for honesty in the statement of facts concerning offered securities is the same as for any other commodity. The proper operation of the free market requires that investors in capital goods exercise choice under conditions of honest information, even as it makes a similar requirement for the benefit of purchasers of consumers' goods.

The correct application of this principle calls for social intervention which will give the prospective investor an honest and adequate statement of facts. The present securities laws of the United States and of the several states on the whole meet this standard rather well. They fail, however, in one respect. The laws of some of the states give officials the right to decide whether a security can be offered for sale. That is, the laws prescribe certain quality standards which securities must meet, and to secure permission to sell the offerer must satisfy state officials that these standards are met by the proposed offering. This is violative of liberty. It transfers decision on investment from the individual to the state. The ends of the free market, and so of economic liberty, are met when the prospective investor has honest and adequate information made available.

6. The examination of banks and other financial institutions

The examination by public officials of banks, insurance companies, and other financial institutions, together with the publication of their financial statements, is a mode of quality certification by the state which the free market society should utilize.

The individual depositor cannot examine a bank's note case or its investment account, to determine the quality of the assets supporting his deposit. Nor can the individual policyholder examine the mortgages and other investments of funds made by his insurance company. Yet these matters are important to the depositor and policyholder. The desired object can be obtained, however, by periodic investigation by a public official and the publication of reports, principally in the form of balance sheets, which reflect his findings. The removal from the balance sheet of unsound assets, or the setting up of reserves for losses on them, gives the depositor and policyholder the information he needs. The same is true for savings banks, savings and loan associations, and other financial institutions in which there are fairly widespread public holdings. Most depositors, of course, are too careless to examine the statements of their banks, and to make the study needed to understand them, but some do understand and examine them, and their acts tend to be serviceable guides to the community.

The danger here is likewise that the officials charged with inspection will deem it their privilege to become managers, and that public opinion, making the same shift in emphasis, will support them in their pretensions. Public certification of quality indeed has its influence on producers of goods for sale, whether they be producers of banking services or of food, and that it should exercise such influence is a desirable result. But this result is a by-product; within the philosophy of individualism the end is the equal opportunity that is afforded by fair information.

7. The distinction between the individualistic and collectivistic views on enforcing honesty

It is frequently supposed that the various forms of state intervention discussed above are aspects of socialism, and that to the extent of their success they represent triumphs of socialism. There is thus built up the concept that if collectivistic action in this regard works well it is a fair presumption that it may also work well in other regards. But this mode of thought overlooks the rather sharp distinction between the individualistic and collectivistic views on enforcing honesty in economic action. The distinction follows from the difference in object. Individualism wishes honesty in connection with a free market and collectivism wishes it in connection with a controlled market. The devices discussed above are all designed to operate in a free market society. They would have little point or utility in a controlled market society.

Collectivism in fact has no great interest in the type of institutions here under consideration, simply because they cannot play a prominent role in its scheme of things. The program of the Socialist party in England does not devote much attention to enforcing honesty in the sale of securities, because in the society it envisages very little if any private investment will remain, all investment being made by or through the state, which will not want to check on its own honesty. It is the same with all other types of state intervention to prevent dishonesty in free economic dealings. Collectivism is interested not so much in eliminating the dishonesty as in eliminating the dealings themselves.

Further, when the operation of an industry is taken over by the state, any certification by the state of the honesty of its own acts becomes an anomaly. If the state is the producer of milk, of what use is its own certificate that the milk is pure? The value of state investigation and certification in the free market society results from the fact that the investigation and certification are independent of the producer. But if the producer is also the investigator and certifier, as is the case in state operation, the value of the certification disappears.

Since the collectivized society, moreover, has as its prime object the bringing of all economic activity into conformance with a group program, it has no great occasion for concern about honesty in the economic activity of individuals; rather its concern is primarily with their obedience to the dictates of the common plan. Honesty becomes important principally in connection with reports on compliance with orders. It does not have great importance as affecting the information given to consumers and their exercise of choice, because in the collectivized society consumers do not exercise choice, being expected to take and use the goods provided for them by the presumed wisdom of the state's plan.

Therefore the common view which regards as socialistic such institutions as the Securities and Exchange Commission, the Federal Trade Commission, and the departments of weights and measures in various cities and states is completely erroneous. These institutions are the tools of an individualistic society rather than of a collectivistic society. Their purpose is to improve the operation of the free market, which they in fact do; and so little do they constitute devices suitable for a controlled market that their use in a controlled market society would be of small effect.

Presumably it is because these institutions constitute state intervention that they are so commonly thought of as devices of socialism or collectivism. But all social organization is state intervention; and even as social organization is inevitable, so also is state intervention. The difference between individualism and collectivism does not concern the need for state intervention nor even its quantity, but turns rather upon its quality, upon the kind of state intervention which the good society should make use of.

The institutions discussed in this chapter, since they facilitate the exercise of choice in the free market, are forms of state intervention which build and protect individual freedom of economic action. Individualism advocates their use. They have nothing to do with the tenets of collectivism. The uninstructed view which does not distinguish between these institutions and those of collectivism furnishes a serious obstacle to the clear understanding of social forms that is essential to sound social action.

Chapter 21

LIBERTY AND THE REGULATION OF MONOPOLY

1. The nature of monopoly

We have already had occasion to note the nature of monopoly. Its occurrence as an economic phenomenon is made possible by the fact that every producer of goods exercises some control over supply. The amount of this control varies with circumstances; the individual wheat farmer, for example, exerts very little influence over the total supply of wheat, whereas the manufacturer of a patented article can control its supply completely.

As long as the control of an individual producer remains small relative to total supply, the exercise of such control is an essential feature of the free market, for it enables the producer to adjust his production to the wishes of consumers, thereby giving the free market its capacity to be responsive to consumer preference. But if under prevailing circumstances the control of an individual producer is not small but large relative to total supply, then the substantiality of his control may enable the producer to oppose rather than serve consumer preference, by producing and offering in the market a smaller supply than that which consumers would wish to buy at the price free competition among producers would establish. When the control of a producer reaches this point, which though indefinite, like the difference between a child and an adult, is nevertheless real and to be reckoned with, the control ceases to be that which conduces to a free market and becomes instead that which effects a controlled market. The control, that is to say, becomes monopoly, which the free society by its rules should seek to prevent.

We can profitably note at this point the place which monopoly occupies in the conceptual framework of market possibilities. The term market is the designation of the process of producing and exchanging goods. This activity from the nature of things is under the direction of human beings, who either as public officials or as private producers and consumers make the decisions which determine market activity. In the free society, both public and private direction of the market has as goal a free market in which consumer preference directs production; and the laws of the free society are designed to assure that the respective ambits of public and private action in the market will be within this objective. Either public or private direction of the market, however, may assume forms that impair the free market of consumer preference and effect instead the controlled market of dictated consumption. When and in so far as public direction creates a controlled market, through transgression of the principles of liberty, the result is the planned economy of collectivism. When and in so far as private direction fails to conform to the principles of the free market, or is prevented from compliance with those principles by natural conditions, such as scarcity of particular natural resources, the result is monopoly. Monopoly, then, is the manifestation of private market activity in such way as to make some segment of the market controlled rather than free. It is thus the parallel, within the area of private action, of collective planning within the area of public action.

Analysts of economic phenomena frequently attempt to delineate precisely the activity to be covered by the term monopoly, and finding difficulty they add auxiliary or subsidiary terms, such as quasi-monopoly, imperfect competition, and monopolistic competition. But the phenomena not submitting to precise division into categories, these efforts become characterized more by crowding the facts to fit the terminology than by adjustment of the terminology to correspond to the observed facts. The difficulty here arises from a failure to bear in mind two basic aspects of production: First, all production of goods is characterized by some control over supply; and second, this control over supply may occur in infinite variety, depending upon circumstances. Every act of production thus has within it a monopolistic tendency, and the manifestations of this tendency are in a constant process of change, shifting with social as well as technological conditions. Only a general description of these manifestations of the monopolistic tendency is accordingly possible, a definitive statement being both impossible and futile; for even though we should suppose that precise definitions of the forms of the monopolistic tendency could be devised, yet they could apply to but a current instant of history, and would become inaccurate with the changes of succeeding times. The terminology of the monopolistic tendency should, therefore, be limited to the terms necessary to an accurate portrayal of its basic factor, i.e., the inherent control over supply, and to a general description of the ways in which that factor tends to exhibit itself in the market.

Social rules governing this monopolistic tendency are inevitable, because the market itself is a social institution created by social rules, which must govern the monopolistic tendency as well as all other factors in the market process. And since the monopolistic tendency can be developed in ways that impair liberty, the social rules should seek to restrict such developments.

The manifestations of the monopolistic tendency which should be barred by social rules have been referred to above as monopoly, and it is believed that this constitutes the proper use of the term. As thus employed, monopoly designates primarily a judgment on a set of facts; and only secondarily does it designate a description of such facts. It is a judgment that a particular factual situation, involving private control over supply, should be prevented because the control over supply has become so substantial that it impairs the free market. And whenever any factual situation involves such control it is a monopoly which should be checked. As herein used, accordingly, the term monopoly does not indicate a precise factual situation, but a judgment on the social results of undue control over supply, in whatever form it may appear.

It may be wondered why the foregoing statement of monopoly is limited to control over supply. Do not monopolists also attempt to exercise control over price, and may not such monopolistic control of price impair equal economic opportunity? The answer is that influence on price can be exerted, within the range of private action, only through control over supply. It is true that many producers who seek to effect price arrangements among themselves do not appreciate this, and think to accomplish higher prices simply by price-fixing agreements, without establishing controls over supply. The event always proves them wrong. The position of the producer differs as to price and as to supply. The producer's control over supply is in a sense absolute; if he decides not to produce a certain good, that particular production will not appear on the market, and if a sufficient number of the producers of a particular good combine, they can restrict total production by their unilateral action. But in private transactions in the market, price is always bilateral, resulting from concurrence by both buyer and seller. Even in the most complete monopoly the producer cannot compel the consumer to pay any price he, the producer, may set. The most he can do is, by limiting or expanding production, to find levels of consumers willing to pay particular prices, and to select the quantity of production yielding the largest monopolistic profit. It is control over supply that is the monopolist's indispensable tool, to which every other conceivable device can be no more than auxiliary.

The use of the concept of monopoly above suggested is, it is submitted, essentially in accordance with practice. Experience drives the concepts behind words to at least some degree of congruence with reality even though that reality be not perceived; and here the reality is simply the need for curbing too great private control over supply. This is the concept around which all discussion of monopoly must and does concentrate, whether or not the focal point be comprehended. This explains the rather amazing development of thought and consequent application of rules under the Sherman Act. Although that legislative enactment is so badly worded that it cannot possibly be taken to mean what it says and accordingly must be taken to have some other but not clearly identified meaning, nevertheless the pressure of economic reality has been such that, given the purpose of curbing the monopolistic tendency, a fairly coherent though tangled body of law has been slowly developed.

The problem, then, for the practical purposes of social organization, is to identify the point at which the always present tendency to control supply grows into monopoly; it is at this point that social rules should intervene. It is on this point too that much confusion of thought exists, a confusion that is unavoidable here as in all other problems of social organization unless the analysis begins with basic considerations of the nature and object of human existence. But by making use of the concept of liberty as ethical imperative and as the first function of the state, the philosophy of individualism is enabled to indicate the general principles that locate the point of monopoly for the practical application of specific rules.

Monopoly is exercised by people who act singly or in concert. When acting in concert, monopolists must usually resort to deliberate arrangement in order to establish monopolistic control over supply. Occasionally, however, concerted action in establishing monopoly does not require a specific undertaking, but arises simply because conditions—such as land ownership concentrated in the hands of a few, for example—induce a group to act together in exercising monopolistic control without the intervention of any agreement to do so. We shall note examples of modes of concerted action as we proceed.

2. The nature of monopsony

The term monopsony, an uncommon but useful word invented by the economists, means substantial control over the demand for a good, even as monopoly means substantial control over supply.

Every consumer in a free market exercises some control over the demand for particular goods. It is this control, evidenced as consumers decide to buy or not to buy, that makes consumer preference the directive force that it is in the free market. Ordinarily the demand for a particular good is compounded of the wants of many consumers, each of whom exercises only a small influence on total demand. Every consumer thus exercises an influence, but only a very small influence, on the demand for bread, shoes, furniture, and similar items of consumption. With respect to certain other goods, the individual consumer may exercise a larger influence; particularly is this true when we come to heavy capital goods; the buyers of ocean-going vessels, for example, are few, and each of them exercises a rather large influence on total demand. More rarely a single buyer may be so situated that he exercises a very substantial control over demand, and it is this condition which constitutes monopsony.

Two examples of monopsony may be noted. The first is the factory constituting the only or principal employer of factory labor within a fairly extensive area. If the factory's employment is small relative to the nonfactory employment in the area, its exclusive demand for factory labor will not be important; but if its employment is large relative to nonfactory employment in the area, its monopsonic position impairs the operation of the free market for labor. Once a labor supply has been attracted to the area and is resident there, the employer can reduce the price offered for labor, i.e., wages, below the figure which a free market would establish, because labor will have to incur the expense of moving in order to find a competitive demand. We shall return to monopsonic labor demand later in this work.

A second example is furnished by the fruit or vegetable packing factory which is the only one of its kind within a fairly extensive area. Here again many sellers must look to one buyer, and because of his monopsonic position the buyer can offer somewhat less, if the sellers are committed to the production of the good, than the price which would be fixed in a free market with multiple buyers. This is the explanation of the prevalence in some areas of cooperative fruit packing factories, operated by fruit growers who sell their production to the cooperative. The fruit growers are committed to their production through the investment in their groves. Usually only one packing plant can be supported in an area. A private plant would tend to offer only a monopsonic price. The cooperative passes on to its member producers any monopsonic profit, and accordingly will tend to give the growers a higher net return for their product than the private plant. This also shows us why vegetable packing cooperatives are rare. Vegetable growers are not committed to any one product, have no investment in fruit trees, and can usually turn from one vegetable to another or to the growing of grains or other agricultural products. Even though, therefore, a packing plant may be the only buyer for particular vegetables within an area, its position does not assure it against competitive buying; the growers can easily turn to other products. There is accordingly little or no opportunity for monopsonic profit, and a privately owned plant will offer approximately the free market price, which is all the cooperative can offer. The latter usually being a less efficient form of operation, it can accordingly give its members less net return for their product than the private plant, rather than more.

On the whole, monopsony offers little problem to liberty. Its impairment of the free market is not great and tends to be transitory. The advisability of possible regulation of monopsonic labor demand we shall consider hereafter. Monopsony of the kind illustrated by the single fruit packing plant can be taken care of by producers' cooperatives, without state intervention.

3. The harm of monopoly

Why should individualism be concerned with the prevention of monopoly? The liberal societies of western Europe, even in the periods when they have been vigorously devoted to economic freedom, have never taken much interest in laws designed to restrict monopoly and to keep production competitive, but have accepted monopolistic cartels and combinations as normal and perhaps desirable. The development of antimonopoly laws in the United States is a unique social phenomenon, both in the world of today and in history. And although these laws are still in an elementary and unsatisfactory stage, they have nevertheless contributed greatly to our economic welfare; for they have succeeded rather effectively in avoiding the harm that is done by monopoly.

This harm occurs in two ways: first, in the impairment of the equality of economic opportunity, and second, in the impairment of consumer preference.

As to the first harm, the impairment of equal economic opportunity, we have heretofore seen that equality of economic opportunity requires equality of opportunity of access to the instruments of production. But monopoly from its very nature involves unequal opportunity of such access. No matter what the occasion of the monopolist's control over supply, whether based upon control of natural resources, agreement between producers, or exclusive privilege granted by law (these comprise the predominant sources of monopoly), the monopolist's position amounts to an exclusion of others from access to the means of producing the monopolized good. Thus where a few persons own all the land available to a society, or where the owners of all manufacturing facilities for a good agree to restrict production and impede the entrance of new competition, or when the law grants to a common carrier, a public utility, a patentee, or a copyright holder an exclusive privilege, the economic opportunity of the monopolist or monopolists is enlarged, to the diminishment of the economic opportunity of others. Monopoly therefore always involves the harm of inducing unequal economic opportunity. As we shall later see, the free society may in certain instances deliberately accept this harm to liberty, in order that other and larger additions to liberty may be secured; this compromise, however, when it is adopted, does not remove the monopolistic harm to equal economic opportunity, but only acquiesces in it as the necessary price for a different and more valuable accretion to the area of liberty.

As to the second harm of monopoly, the impairment of consumer preference, this likewise is an inevitable element in the monopolist's position. By his control over supply, he is able to usurp the role of consumers in dictating production. In the free market, where competition prevails among producers and equality of opportunity of access to the instruments of production is maintained, consumer preference can exercise its directive influence, causing the production of those goods which consumers prefer, out of all those the society can produce. But when monopoly intervenes, the monopolist's control over supply enables him to disregard consumer preference, producing a smaller quantity which can be sold at a higher price and at a larger profit.

It is ordinarily supposed that this larger profit available to the monopolist is the gist of the complaint against monopoly and the totality of its harm. But this opinion is quite in error. A large profit is never of itself a social harm, but constitutes benefit or harm only as it is obtained in a free or controlled market. When obtained in a free market, it signifies that the producer has placed in the market a good which consumers much prefer to other goods obtainable at like cost, and thus it draws productive effort toward consumer preference. When obtained, however, in a market subject to the control of a monopolist, a large profit exercises no such function; it does not direct productive effort toward consumer preference, but on the contrary arises from the fact that consumer preference is being defeated and will continue to be defeated as long as the monopolist's control over supply can be maintained.

Monopolistic profit, therefore, is not itself the harm of monopoly, but constitutes, rather, the symptom of the harm, which essentially consists in destroying equality of economic opportunity and in thwarting consumer preference.

This frustration of consumer preference, moreover, results not simply in dictated rather than preferred consumption, but also in consumption at a lower rate. To the extent that a market is controlled, whether by private monopoly or public planning, the production of goods is less efficient, which means that the given labor supply can produce only a smaller total of goods for consumption. The very purpose of monopoly, as well as of public planning, is to interfere with consumers' choice; and this interference being established, there occurs necessarily a loss of the competitive drive which seeks to attract more custom by the lower price made possible by greater efficiency. The effect, then, of monopoly upon the material standard of living is the same as the effect of collective planning, and for the same reason, i.e., that it interferes with those forces in the free market which encourage large and efficient production.

4. The general theory of the regulation of monopoly

Since market activity in every society must occur within a framework of social rules, and since the monopolistic tendency is inherent in market activity, it follows that social rules regulate the monopolistic tendency in all societies, whether or not it is perceived that such is the case. The problem for the free market society is the kind of regulation consonant with free market principles.

A basic proposition for the free market, as already noted, is that the monopolistic tendency should be curbed at the point where it would become substantial control over the supply of a good. Unfortunately, however, this principle of itself cannot suffice; for its application in practice would soon indicate some situations in which it would impair rather than augment equal economic opportunity. For example, if no electric company is to be permitted to secure substantial control of the supply of electricity for a community, then there must be many small competing companies supplying electricity. But it happens that the present technology of furnishing electricity places a great penalty on small scale production and on the duplication of distributing systems. If therefore the community wishes to avoid monopoly it must forego the advantage of cheap electricity. But liberty may be more impaired by the want of cheap electricity than by the presence of monopoly. Will's arena, which is the measure of individual freedom, has its material factor. Accordingly the free market society may rightly choose to suffer the restriction of monopoly that it may obtain the freedom of action made possible by cheap electricity.

The basic proposition of curbing monopoly is accordingly subject to an exception. Substantial control over supply is to be accepted rather than curbed when its acceptance clearly results in greater economic freedom than would prevail if it were curbed. We come again, then, to an application of social principle requiring judgment rather than precise measurement; and again we see that the consideration of economic freedom furnishes the basic criterion for all economic problems.

But the matter is not ended by saying that in some situations—depending on particular facts—substantial control over supply is to be accepted. For although substantial control may be permitted, yet this substantial control may itself be subject to social rules, and indeed is bound to be so subject in some degree. The holder of a patent, who is allowed complete control over the supply of the patented article, does not thereby become an economic anarchist, outside the influence of social rules in the exercise of his monopoly. It is likewise with public utilities and common carriers. Substantial control over supply, when permitted, is still subject to social rules.

The proper purpose or object of such rules, moreover, is clear, in so far as they deal specifically with the permitted monopolistic control. They should attempt to simulate the conditions of the free market. Since the free market is prevented from operating by the very permission of substantial control over supply, substitutes for the directive influence of the free market should be created by social rules in so far as feasible. Such substitutes are in fact available in a limited way in devices for the regulation of monopolistic price and for the regulation of monopolistic service.

The general theory, then, is that substantial control over the supply of any good should be prevented by law, except in cases where under the prevailing circumstances it clearly appears that economic liberty will be enhanced rather than diminished by permitting such monopolistic control; and in all such cases of permitted monopoly social rules should simulate the influence of the free market as far as possible.

It is to be noted that a new term—permitted monopoly—has been introduced in the above discussion, and that it is in a sense inconsistent with the prior signification attached to the word monopoly standing alone. But there seems to be no help for this; usage speaks of monopoly as something to be barred, but also as something to be permitted on occasion, and no other terms sanctioned by usage are available. Monopoly, then, is such substantial control over supply as should be barred, and permitted monopoly is substantial control which ought likewise to be prevented were regard extended only to control over supply, but which for other considerations should be allowed, although subject to special restrictions.

5. The prevention of monopoly

Even as monopoly may appear in many forms, constantly varying as conditions of production change, so the means to be employed in preventing monopoly must be mobile rather than fixed and capable of adjustment to meet monopolistic conditions as they arise. Accordingly we shall not attempt to examine the technique of preventing monopoly in its details, but shall observe only basic principles.

The phenomena of monopoly usually appear in one of three general modes: monopolies arising because of scarcity of natural resources, monopolies arising because of concerted action by producers, and monopolies arising because of exclusive privilege granted by the state.

With respect to monopolies arising out of natural scarcity, examples of situations which can easily lead to monopoly are furnished by such minerals as bauxite, molybdenum, and asbestos, which are scarce in the sense that they are found in only a few locations. By reason of this scarcity, a single ownership of most or all of the sources of supply could be established without difficulty if the state did not intervene. To prevent such monopoly, therefore, the laws of the state should prohibit integrated ownership of more than a limited portion of the available supply of any natural resource. It is conceivable, but improbable in practice, that a natural resource could be so limited in supply that divided ownership would result in great inefficiency in production or even in impossibility of production. Should this condition obtain, the monopoly of the resource would have to be permitted, but subject to regulation as in the case of other permitted monopolies.

With this exception, however, the requirement of limited ownership of natural resources is basic to the free market system. Monopoly must be prevented; and the reverse of the prevention of monopoly is the permission of only limited ownership. The laws of the society seeking to preserve the free market must therefore establish limits, in terms of a percentage of available supply, beyond which single ownership of resources cannot go. These limits, moreover, must be set with reference to the market area served by the particular natural resource. Since these and related considerations must have regard to particular and changing conditions, the prescription of such limits can suitably be the responsibility of a governmental commission subject to judicial review.

Fortunately the number of scarce natural resources inviting unitized control is not large. But scarcity is relative, not only to the available market area but also to conditions which make for concerted action by a few owners, even though there be no integrated ownership. In this sense, even agricultural land otherwise plentiful has upon occasion become scarce so that monopolistic control has developed. Thus in the Mexican state of Morelia prior to the revolution some twenty or so families were the owners of all the land. By custom they never offered land for sale; each family had a monopoly within its area of ownership. In some of the American colonies in the eighteenth century a somewhat comparable situation developed, in New York particularly. After American independence was secured the colonists broke up these large holdings, by means legal and extra-legal; and the urge which motivated them was sound, even though some of the methods employed may have left something to be desired. The antimonopoly principle founded in considerations of liberty was their justification, despite its lack of identification as such at the time.

It should be noted that this principle, which calls for limitation on ownership whenever conditions induce monopolistic control, is not expressly recognized in our antimonopoly laws today, but is to be observed there only vaguely and indistinctly. Our statutes began with the conviction that monopolistic control was somehow inimical to economic freedom and welfare; but they were not drafted in the light of any clear understanding of the nature of what they sought to prevent. Fortunately the enforcement of these laws was placed largely in the courts, where under the pressure of particular factual situations, and between the opposed contentions of litigants, it was necessary to develop rules of application. Out of this process there is slowly emerging the concept that the amount of ownership of a resource, relative to the total supply of the resource, is directly pertinent to the question of monopoly and that such ownership should be limited whenever necessary to prevent monopoly. Doubtless the further development of this concept can be expected in court rulings of the future; but it would be better if the statutes themselves were overhauled, a reform desirable on many grounds.

The second occasion of monopoly, mentioned above, is agreement between producers, and it is this sort of monopoly against which our antimonopoly statutes were primarily aimed when they were originally enacted. Not that agreements between producers were a new phenomenon sixty years ago; on the contrary competing producers have probably tried throughout history to assuage the rigors of competition by agreements between themselves. But in the latter part of the nineteenth century a new form was given these restrictive agreements by the development of trusts, whereby competing companies lodged their shares of stock with trustees who then could exercise effective control over all the combining enterprises. Although these trusts depended primarily upon agreement to effect monopolistic control over supply, they also occasionally grew so large as to acquire control over a relatively large portion of an available natural resource. This latter development, however, seldom assumed great importance, and agreement was the principal tool relied on.

Such trusts are no longer attempted (although we still speak of antimonopoly statutes as "antitrust laws"), but agreements between producers restricting supply will always continue to be tried. They take many forms, dealing with price, division of markets, quality of goods, and quantity of production. But their effectiveness and social significance is located in their control over the quantity of supply produced.

Lacking such control they cannot be effective, for reasons already noted; such control being established, they constitute if substantial enough the monopolies which are objectionable.

The task of society, then, is to identify the kinds of agreements between producers which can lead to monopolistic control over supply, and to prohibit such agreements by legislation. It is to this object that our present antimonopoly laws are directed, a legislative effort however which has been inadequately performed. In framing such legislation, its prohibition should run as well against agreements which experience has shown to be ineffective in attaining the end of monopoly as against those that can be expected to secure their goal; for the attempt at monopoly, though ill-conceived, should be barred as well as its successful consummation. Therefore all agreements between competing producers designed to fix prices, divide markets, limit competitive sales efforts, or limit production should be made unlawful.

The third general source of monopoly is special grant from the state. From time immemorial states have granted monopolies to individuals or groups of individuals as a matter of favor, or to obtain revenue, or to encourage the development of enterprises which might lag or be inefficient if monopoly were not allowed. Monopolies of this last category are permitted monopolies, already mentioned, whose regulation we shall discuss below. All other forms of monopoly operating under grant from the state are inimical to economic liberty, and they should be eliminated from all societies.

6. The regulation of permitted monopoly

Patents and copyrights are forms of permitted monopoly deliberately created by the state because, in part, of the advantages that are believed to accrue to society generally. Although this reason is almost universally conceded to be sound, yet it does not necessarily follow, as usually supposed, that patents and copyrights when granted should be devoid of further regulation. The same consideration of economic welfare which justifies the state in conferring the monopoly can also serve as justification for its supervision. What that supervision should be must depend upon conditions; the supervision, if any, which would have been appropriate a century ago would scarcely fit with the complex patterns of patent coverage found today; and whether modern practice requires regulation of the use of patents in order to avoid continuous monopoly, instead of the temporary monopoly contemplated by patent doctrine, is not a question of socialism but a question of the maintenance of free markets through the regulation of monopoly.

Apart from these monopolies deliberately created are the numerous enterprises tolerated by the state though involving monopolistic control, and the remainder of our discussion is devoted to permitted monopolies of this type to the exclusion of patents and copyrights. These permitted monopolies are the electric companies, gas companies, water companies, and transportation systems, to cite typical examples, which are permitted to operate as monopolies, their harm to the free market being suffered because it is recognized that their prohibition would entail harm still more serious. But even as the society of individualism can properly prevent monopoly in the interest of economic liberty, so it can regulate it in that same interest when it is permitted; and this regulation of permitted monopoly is by no means a species of socialistic state activity, as is so often assumed, but is an example of the philosophy of individualism at work in preserving the features of the free market in so far as possible under specific conditions.

There are two general branches of the regulation of permitted monopolies: first, the regulation of the price to be charged for the monopolized good, and second, the regulation of the quality and quantity of its supply. The aim of such regulation should be to effect the same price, quality, and supply of the monopolized good as would have been experienced if a free market had prevailed. The influence of the free market is to cause the production of the quality and quantity of a good preferred by consumers at a price covering the cost of production, including entrepreneurial profit, and no more. It is this quality, quantity, and price which should be sought by public regulation. And although this proper object of regulation is seldom envisaged by our regulatory agencies, yet the pressure of facts and of logic is such that it constitutes the result toward which their regulatory action always tends to be directed.

A prime concern of regulation is the price to be charged for the monopolized good. The rates to be fixed for electricity, telephone service, or transportation are the subject of hearings, investigation, debate, and eventual regulatory decision. A salient consideration in the decision is a fair return, as it is called, on the capital invested in the enterprise. It is worth noting that of the many factors which combine in the production of a good, only the return on the capital involved can ordinarily be affected by regulatory action. In the production of electricity, for example, supplies of coal, copper, oil, skilled and unskilled labor, etc. are required. These things, although used to produce a monopolized good, must be obtained in free markets; and accordingly it would be useless as well as ridiculous for a public commission to rule that a fair return for labor used in producing electricity would be, say, 50¢ an hour, for at that rate no labor would be available. It is the same with other currently needed factors in production. But with respect to capital already committed to the production of electricity, such as the plant, machinery, and distributing system, the case is otherwise; here the ruling of what constitutes a fair return can ordinarily be effective. But capital is always wearing out and must be replaced; and not only so, but consumers' preference for a monopolized good may be growing, as it is today for electricity, requiring additional capital investment. As this need for new capital occurs, it becomes clear that the fair rate of return for capital as well as for labor and supplies is the price set in the free market. Conceivably a public commission could rule that a fair return for future capital to be invested in an electric utility would be three per cent—and doubtless there have been state commissioners in recent years who would have liked to make such a ruling—but it would be useless so to rule, for funds simply would not be forthcoming at that rate.

That the concept of fairness, as applied to the price of a monopolized good, has no meaning except as it is related to free market action, is interestingly shown in the variations in the rate of return held to be fair by our regulatory agencies during the past two decades or so. In the early part of that period six to seven per cent was thought to be fair. But the long decline in interest rates wrought a revision in concept, and about five per cent, or perhaps fractionally higher, was held to be fair. Now, however, that there has occurred an upward swing in interest rates, rulings are again appearing that six or six and a quarter per cent is a fair return. A fair return is thus nothing more than the free market return; it cannot be anything else.

But although a monopoly cannot operate at prices below those of the free market, it can if it chooses operate at higher prices, for this is the gist of the monopolist's position as substantial controller of supply. The function of public regulation, then, the monopoly being permitted, is to see that prices charged do not exceed those which would prevail if there were a free market. In the free market the price of a good tends to settle at cost, which is the sum of wages for labor, rent for land, interest on money borrowed, return on capital invested, and entrepreneurial compensation, all at the going free market rates. Accordingly, the price established for a permitted monopoly should be the estimated equivalent of this free market cost, constituted as above stated.

In practice, this is what our regulatory agencies tend to do today, being impelled thereto however more by the pressure of incontrovertible economic facts than by the logic of theory. They cling to the idea of a fair return with the tenacity of Schoolmen. What must be learned is that the concept of a fair return of itself can have no pragmatic application, because it is meaningless except as it is referred to the experience currently being reflected in free market price.

The same considerations apply to the regulation of the quality and quantity of a monopolized good, more usually referred to as the service which a utility should render. Here again the aim of state regulation should be to procure that quality and quantity which the free market would procure were it operating. The monopoly should not be required to go beyond this nor allowed to fall below it. What this standard calls for in particular cases is a matter of judgment, and disputes and variances in opinion can certainly arise; but in practice this standard must be found more workable than any other, and it is the correct standard.

The foregoing being an outline of the regulation of permitted monopolies which the good society should undertake, the question arises as to the identity of the permitted monopolies so to be regulated. Among the many enterprises we see around us, which ones are permitted monopolies whose activities are not sufficiently directed by the competitive pressures of the free market? For many decades now our courts have been saying, when presented with this question in its constitutional guise, that private property can constitutionally be subjected to regulation of price and service whenever it is used in a "business affected with a public interest." But although this phrase seems never to have done much harm in influencing decision, it has never done much good either; and its limitations as a standard are now quite generally recognized. All business activity is affected with a public interest to a greater or lesser degree, and to say that a business should be regulated if affected with a public interest is only to say that any business should be regulated if certain conditions prevail. But what are these conditions? The principle of being affected with a public interest does not tell us anything of these conditions. Our discussion of the principles of the free market and of monopoly, however, has already in effect shown us what they are. Any business activity which has acquired such control of the supply of a good as substantially to interfere with the operation of a free market therein becomes affected with a public interest and becomes subject to regulation. If permitted, such business activity becomes a permitted monopoly subject to social regulation.

Even therefore as the purpose of regulation is the simulation of free market price and service, so the criterion of the propriety of regulation is the absence of free market price and service. And the practical test of whether free market price and service obtain is whether competition exists. Where there is competition between diverse suppliers of a good, the great social function rendered by such competition is the maintenance of free market conditions, with consumer preference directing production and free market price prevailing. Where competition wanes or is absent, the free market progressively relapses and gives way to market conditions dominated by monopolistic control. The want of competition is thus the visible proof of the absence of free market conditions; and accordingly where such want of competition is evident, but the particular activity should be permitted rather than barred, the activity becomes a permitted monopoly, and whatever its nature, is properly subject to social regulation.

Whether competition exists with respect to a particular good is a matter of observation and judgment, and the determination of the question in particular cases calls for no small amount of skill based on business experience. It is usually supposed that the large difficulty here is in failing to recognize the absence of competition, and indeed this is often the case, particularly in societies which have become accustomed to cartel arrangements. The failure to recognize the want of competition of course precludes the imposition of those preventive or regulatory measures which the free market demands. But in a society which has become conscious of the harm of monopoly, as has our own, there is also danger of supposing competition to be absent where in fact it exists, at least in sufficient degree to call for little social regulation.

It is often assumed that quotation of the same price by producers for a commodity is evidence of a want of competition, indicating monopolistic agreement. But if the commodity is one of uniform quality, as cement (which is frequently cited in this regard), the effect of the free market itself will be to secure a uniform price by all producers at a given point of delivery; for a producer quoting a higher price will make no sales, and unless he can quote a price as low as that quoted by other producers he may as well withdraw from competing within that particular territory, or from the business of supplying the good

entirely. Similarity of price for similar products is not an evidence of
monopolistic agreement, nor for that matter of the absence of such
agreement. Agreement or no agreement, similarity of price will exist.
Indeed dissimilarity of price will of itself be indicative rather of agreement to divide markets, and therefore not to compete, than would be
similarity of price. It is informative to note that in industries producing a good of uniform quality, such as cement or baker's flour,
similar prices are referred to in the trade as competitive prices, whereas
a price either higher or lower than the prevailing price is referred to
as a noncompetitive price. Dissimilarity of quoted price for uniform
goods may also result from insufficient activity within a given area to
establish a prevailing price there; but this want of activity is seldom
if ever the product of monopolistic agreement. All this is not to say
that monopolistic agreement may not be resorted to by suppliers to
effect similar prices for goods of uniform quality; what it does mean is
that similar prices for such goods do not of themselves indicate monopolistic agreement, for such prices are the normal and proper result
of the free market wherever activity is in good volume and competition
is present.

The evidence of monopoly, rather, is to be found in facts indicating
substantial control over supply. It is limitation of supply that alone can
make monopolistic prices possible, and that accordingly furnishes the
test for the existence of monopoly.

7. Socialism and antimonopoly laws

Socialism has fashioned out of our antimonopoly laws an argument
that, although entirely invalid, has nevertheless enjoyed wide success
with both popular and informed opinion. The argument points to the
salutary results of the antimonopoly laws in our society, which has
won for them universal acceptance, and then refers to this state intervention as a form of state management of economic activity. This
is implied to be an application of socialist principles, and therefore
is said to be proof of the efficacy of socialism in practice. If accordingly socialism demonstrates its prosperous issue in this limited application, it can confidently be expected to accomplish like success
when applied on a broader scale. We have really accepted socialist
principles in a limited way, it is suggested, in this sanction of state
intervention in regulating monopoly, and it will only be a question of

time until most of us will progress to an adoption of socialism in its larger applications.

This argument has been highly effective. It has resulted in outright conviction that socialism has a good case, at least to some degree, and where it has failed to produce explicit conviction it has caused bewilderment and indecision. It has resulted in the type of thought which says "The time is past [a favorite cliché of muddled thinking] when anyone can argue for unrestricted free enterprise." Socialistic regulation, it is believed, happily restricts free enterprise by means of the anti-monopoly laws; and thus it is thought that free enterprise as a system is demonstrated to be defective and in need of greater or lesser change, the debate being shifted from the question of the need for modification of the free enterprise system to the question of the extent of modification required—some modification being assumed. Manifestations of this point of view abound in present-day discussion.

Yet it is a point of view which is entirely fallacious, failing completely before analysis.

In the first place antimonopoly regulation is not a socialistic device. The regulation of permitted monopolies by our state and federal agencies assumes the permission of such monopolies as private enterprises, subject to regulation of price and service. But socialism by no means believes in such permission of any private monopolies, but believes instead that all monopolistic enterprises (and others as well) should be owned and operated by the state. It may approve of monopoly regulation as a transitional matter, leading to socialistic ownership and operation, but that is all. Regulation in the form we have developed is an adjunct of private enterprise, a mode within which private enterprise operates, and socialism, either theoretical or applied, has no place for it. The writings of socialists have no chapters lauding the merits of permitted monopoly when regulated; Great Britain's nationalized industries—all monopolies—have no external agencies regulating them; and if we should socialize our railroads, for example, a first institution to disappear would be the Interstate Commerce Commission as at present constituted, which simply would have no function in socialized transportation.

In the second place, the agencies we have developed are not, properly speaking, restrictions or limitations on the free enterprise system; rather they are manifestations of the free enterprise system as it develops tools to enable it to operate in its proper mode. The free market is no more anarchy on the one hand than it is collective planning on the other. The free market is always a complicated structure, difficult to organize and to maintain; it depends on social regulation as the means of its existence, and it must be willing constantly to modify the details of such regulation in order to attain in changing conditions its object of equal opportunity in the market for all individuals.

It is necessary always to keep in mind the basic distinction between individualism and collectivism in their ideals of market activity. The ideal of individualism is a market in which the direction of production and consumption results from the decisions of all members of the community, as they exercise the equal economic opportunity accorded them by the laws. The ideal of collectivism is a market in which the direction of production and consumption results from the decisions of a few officials, who plan and direct economic activity as they think best for all. Monopoly is inimical to the free market of individualism, because it pro *tanto* destroys equal opportunity. It is not inimical to the controlled market of collectivism, because that market is by its very nature monopolistic. Public monopoly is collectivism's ideal; it is only when monopoly is private that collectivism objects to it, and then the objection goes to its private rather than its monopolistic character. We can see this affinity of collectivism for monopoly, even private monopoly, at work in western Europe, where the dominance of socialistic thought has produced an atmosphere in which cartels and monopolistic trade arrangements among businessmen are accepted without objection.

But individualism does not permit monopolistic control of supply, in those cases where it does so, because of any affinity for monopoly, but because it finds, under particular conditions as they obtain, that permitted monopoly is less injurious to liberty than would be its prohibition. Insistence that two or more telephone companies compete within a given area would impair liberty more, through economic loss diminishing the material factor in will's arena, than permission to one company to exercise a monopoly subject to public regulation. Such permission is admittedly a compromise, but so are all social rules and institutions, as we have heretofore seen. The question is not whether a particular social regulation is a compromise of conflicting desirabilities, but whether it is a compromise dictated by the principles of individualism or by those of collectivism, by the ideal of the free market or by the ideal of the controlled market.

The distinction just made is useful, further, in calling attention to a danger inherent in the regulation of permitted monopoly in a free market society. The danger is that regulation will pass beyond its proper function of simulating by decree the price and service which would have been set by competition and will direct the management of the permitted monopoly in additional ways. It is easy for regulatory officials to transgress their proper bound; indeed it is difficult for them to refrain from doing so. The free society will accordingly place careful limitations upon the powers of its regulatory bodies, and provide appropriate means for the enforcement of those limitations. The regulation of monopoly and the effective limitation, in turn, of the means of regulation is a difficult art. It is an art, however, which can be accomplished, as our own efforts prove.

Chapter 22

LIBERTY AND THE REGULATION OF LABOR

1. Liberty as standard of reference

What is the proper objective for the regulation of labor? What should labor laws seek to accomplish?

Many of those interested in the welfare of labor would doubtless reply, High wages, good working conditions, and full employment. These are the aims toward which the proponents of labor legislation usually direct their efforts.

Clearly these are appropriate ends for workers and their representatives to pursue in their economic activity. But do these goals also furnish the standard of reference to be used in judging the soundness of labor regulation? Is labor regulation to be appraised solely by its effect upon wages, working conditions, and employment? A common view is that these objectives do in fact furnish the correct standard of reference and that labor regulation should be measured solely by such standard. Arguments for labor proposals are often presented exclusively in terms of the beneficial effect they will have upon wages, working conditions, and employment.

But Hitler and Mussolini each accomplished higher wages, improved working conditions, and full employment; yet the social arrangements by which these ends were achieved are now acknowledged to have been evil and deserving of destruction. Nor was the improvement in labor conditions experienced under the Nazi and Fascist regimes merely incidental to their programs; on the contrary both the Nazi and Fascist administrations aimed deliberately at higher wages, better working conditions, and full employment, and—what is most important for us to understand—their decrees were effectively designed to accomplish these ends. It is not difficult for a collectivistic government to put everyone to work.

But if we condemn systems of labor regulation that were intended to produce and did produce higher wages, better working conditions, and full employment, then we must recognize that a standard of reference composed only of these objectives is invalid. The correct standard will not reject these elements; but it must be a standard which, though including these elements, will yet be superior to them.

Our condemnation of the Nazi and Fascist regimes is based on the method by which they accomplished better economic conditions for labor. We condemn them because they destroyed liberty; the improvement they effected in economic conditions could not compensate for that destruction.

Liberty therefore must be the ultimate standard of reference in labor regulation as in all other social action. Liberty includes within its concern the economic conditions of labor, because those conditions constitute a part of the material factor of the arena in which human character must be built. But liberty also has regard for all other parts of human freedom, and does not permit the whole to suffer that a segment may flourish. Since liberty is ethical imperative and the first function of the state, all development of labor regulation must find its support within liberty's specifications. Every argument concerning labor regulation must address itself to this ultimate standard, and no argument that disregards it can be heard.

2. The free market for labor

It is sometimes said that labor is not a commodity or article of commerce, and that it is improper to treat of the market for labor. The market, it is argued, considers only property values, whereas labor involves human values. This viewpoint finds expression in some of our laws; in the Clayton Act, for example, it is enacted that "the labor of a human being is not a commodity or article of commerce." The apparent purpose of this legislative pronouncement is to deny the validity of the concept of a market for labor. Yet the market for labor is a fact ineradicably involved in the productive process, and the elements that compose the market for labor are necessarily present wherever goods are produced by workers employed at wages. Legislation cannot escape this fact, and can only work harm by trying to deny or avoid it.

This unfortunate, though common, point of view rests in part on the error of supposing that the market measures property values as distinguished from human values. But although science and art may be interested at times in things simply as things, ascribing to them values, so to speak, simply as items of property, yet this is never true of the market. The market has only one interest in goods and services—their capacity to satisfy human wants. Never does the market ascribe to a good or service a value of any kind other than its human value, its value to human beings. The market has no capacity for registering any other kind of value. This is true whether the market be free or controlled, the defect of the controlled market not being that it registers some value other than human value, but that it registers human value imperfectly. When therefore labor is offered for hire in the free market, the value ascribed to it is a human value, i.e., the value the labor has in satisfying human wants.

Labor is offered for sale in the free market by workers and is purchased by entrepreneurs, that is, by the business people who manage the combining of labor, land, capital, and money in the production of goods. The sale and purchase is always made by agreement between the parties. This buying and selling of labor by contract is the labor market of the free market society. It can be eliminated only by forbidding employment and requiring all labor to be done by independent workers, or by setting wages by decree, as is done under collectivism, prohibiting the determination of wages by contract between entrepreneurs and laborers. Neither of these methods, however, can be adopted under the liberty of individualism, which desires both the large production possible through employment and the freedom contained in bargaining. Accordingly the free labor market is an integral part of the economic process in a free society.

It is precisely this buying and selling of labor pursuant to contract, furthermore, that gives to employment dignity and worth as a builder of human character. The terms of employment, if there is to be employment, must be fixed by someone's decision. If this decision is made both by the employer and the employee, the result is employment pursuant to bargaining in a free labor market. If, however, the decision is made only by the employer or by the state, the employee having no part in it, the result is serfdom. As freedom to bargain is impaired, enforced labor necessarily takes its place. But if, on the other hand, enforced labor is to be avoided, then the freedom to bargain must be retained, which means that there must be a free market in which labor is bought and sold by contracts entered into pursuant to the decisions of entrepreneurs and workers.

The free labor market, therefore, wherein labor is sold and bought on terms fixed by agreement, is indispensable to a free society.

3. Freedom to bargain

The view that labor should be removed from the bargaining of the market place is accordingly erroneous. The proposal sounds humanitarian, but in fact it is the opposite. Bargaining is essential to the humanity of the employment process, because without it some degree of enforced labor must ensue as alternative.

Freedom to bargain is therefore the first element in the freedom of labor, and the maintenance of equal freedom to bargain is the first element in the regulation of labor demanded by individualism.

Two problems concerning the freedom to bargain arise: 1. How will the labor bargain be made? 2. What will the labor bargain provide?

Concerning the manner in which the labor bargain is to be made, the issue is the person who will do the bargaining. Is the bargain to be made by the worker himself or by someone acting in his behalf? In modern practice, the someone acting in behalf of the worker is the spokesman of a union, and the issue becomes: Will the worker make his own bargain, or will the union make it for him?

The answer of liberty is that each worker should be permitted to decide this question for himself, and he should be protected against interference in giving effect to the answer he decides upon. If he chooses to do his own bargaining, the union should be prevented from obstructing his bargaining; if on the other hand he elects to have his bargaining done for him by the union, both the employer and nonunion employees should be prevented from obstructing the representative activity of the union.

The foregoing, however, is not the answer contained in our current laws. The Taft-Hartley Act provides that if the majority of the workers in a plant vote to have a union act as their bargaining agent, then all the workers in the plant must recognize the union as their bargaining agent, and thereafter no worker can bargain directly with the employer, who is forbidden to bargain with anyone except the official representative of the union. This arrangement deprives the worker of his freedom, taking from him the character-building experience of decision in arriving at the terms upon which he will earn his livelihood. The privilege of decision thus taken from the worker is transferred to his union officials, who are empowered to fix the terms of the labor contract.

What is the argument in favor of this compulsory union representation? The argument has two main parts. It is said, first, that better terms can be obtained if the workers bargain as a unit than if they bargain individually; and second, that unless the workers are compelled to bargain exclusively through the union, enough of them will refuse to do so to render the union's efforts ineffective, making collective bargaining impossible.

The first part of the argument brings us to a fundamental cleavage between collectivism and individualism. Collectivism is not much concerned with the manner in which the terms of employment are arrived at, provided that they are satisfactory. It expects to coerce individuals into a pattern of conduct conformable to its group plan, and accordingly does not object to coercion in compelling collective bargaining. Individualism, on the other hand, is as much concerned with the freedom of workers in entering into labor bargains as it is with their terms. The core of the individualistic position is the avoidance of compulsion except to protect equal liberty. Accordingly individualism cannot adopt the compulsion of collective bargaining unless some larger liberty is obtained in exchange for the liberty lost.

But if workers are free to decide to join in collective bargaining, as individualism says they should be, then no additional liberty can be gained by compelling them to join. However great the advantages of collective bargaining may be, they are available to workers who choose to avail themselves of them. Beyond this liberty cannot go. Compulsion, if used, would be directed to the workers who do not believe collective bargaining to be advantageous, and to compel these workers to join in a bargaining process which they are free to join but choose to avoid is an unmitigated deprivation of liberty.

The second part of the argument in favor of compulsory collective bargaining is that compulsion is necessary to make collective bargaining effective. But the verdict of experience is against this proposition. For decades many unions successfully carried on collective bargaining without compulsion of unwilling workers to join in the collective bargaining process. What they have done in the past they can continue to do in the future. But even if it were true that collective bargaining would be ineffective without compulsion, still this would furnish no justification for forcing workers to join in the collective bargaining process. Collective bargaining is not an ethical imperative in human relations; judgments are not to be formed solely on the ground of whether collective bargaining is advanced or retarded. The ethical imperative is liberty and it furnishes the standard of reference. Equal liberty is maintained when each worker can join or refrain from joining in collective bargaining as he decides. Liberty is destroyed when this choice is taken away.

But, it is said, the selection of a union bargaining agent by majority vote is an exercise of democracy, and compelling the minority to follow the decision of the majority is simply enforcing the democratic process. An impairment of liberty, however, is never justified by the fact that it is accomplished by the vote of a majority. The enslavement of a minority by the vote of a majority would always be wrong, though it would be democratic. Democracy is not an end in itself. It is the servitor of liberty, the political means which is most likely to secure liberty. But the vote of the majority can be used to destroy equal liberty as well as to build it, and when it is so used it is evil. Equal liberty, not democracy, is the ultimate standard of judgment. That compulsory collective bargaining is accomplished by majority vote does not save it, therefore, from condemnation for its destruction of liberty.

The worker's right to bargain collectively if he chooses to do so being recognized, it must be protected against interference by either the employer or other workers. That such interference can in practice be avoided is shown by the success of the techniques developed under the Wagner and Taft-Hartley acts.

What terms can the labor bargain be permitted to contain? Can society properly impose any restrictions? Under the principles of liberty, the freedom of workers and employers to enter into bargains of their choosing should be subject only to specific limitations enacted by society. What limitations, if any, should there be? The limitations principally attempted in the past concern hours and wages.

In so far as restrictions on hours of work are designed to preserve health and promote safety, society has a proper interest in specifying limitations to the hours that can be agreed to. The burden of caring for those whose capacity to work is lost may fall on society, under the principle of assistance. Society accordingly may seek to avoid this burden by minimizing its cause. Beyond this, no proper case for restricting hours of work can be made. Workers and employers should accordingly be permitted to agree upon such hours of work as they choose, except as considerations of health or safety indicate restrictions.

Limitations on the wages that can be stipulated in the labor bargain are currently effected by minimum wage laws. We shall defer consideration of these wage restrictions until a later point in this chapter, after

the examination of some other matters having a bearing on the problem
they present.

4. Freedom to work

That every individual should have freedom to work is accepted in
theory as axiomatic at the present time; but when we come to cases the
matter is otherwise. As this is being written, a news item tells of a
strike which has been ordered at a coal mine in southern Illinois. One
hundred men, it is stated, were employed at the mine, and about one
thousand pickets were massed at the mine when the strike was
called. Why? In part, of course, simply to dramatize the strike; but
more importantly to make the strike effective by preventing any of
the employees who might wish to work from doing so. And the fact
that the pickets were necessary is proof that some employees would
have chosen to work if they had had freedom so to do. Similar cases
frequently occur.

What is freedom to work? Is it a freedom to be exercised by any
individual upon his own decision? Or can it be exercised properly only
with the consent of other workers, particularly with the consent of a
union?

The freedom to work is the privilege of furnishing labor in any
employment where the worker can agree with the employer on the
labor bargain.

The right to the freedom to work follows necessarily from the
principle of equal economic opportunity. Since equal economic opportunity includes equal opportunity to produce, it also includes equal
opportunity to contribute labor to production. The opportunity to contribute labor to production is, in turn, freedom to work. All men,
therefore, should have an equal freedom to work, and to deny to any
man his freedom to work is to deny him the equal economic opportunity he is entitled to under liberty.

Strikes frequently present the problem of the right to work in acute
form. Rarely do all the employees in an establishment desire to strike;
usually there are some, occasionally a large percentage, who desire to
continue employment uninterruptedly. If a strike is called, those who
desire the strike have an interest in inducing the reluctant employees
to join the work stoppage. As long as the methods of persuasion are
peaceful no problem of the freedom to work is involved. But the meth-

ods frequently do not remain peaceful. Violence and the threat of violence become the methods, including mass picketing, damage to workers' property, assault, and even upon rare occasions murder.

This violence is directed against other workers. The contest is between strikers and nonstrikers. The nonstrikers wish to exercise their freedom to work; the strikers wish to exercise their freedom not to work. The freedom not to work is an integral part of the freedom to work; for freedom is the right to choose and choice means acceptance or rejection. Each side accordingly is trying to exercise an aspect of the freedom to work. It is when either side attempts to use force to prevent the other from exercising its right that trouble begins. If we say that strikers are justified in using force to prevent nonstrikers from working, then by the same token we must also say that nonstrikers are justified in using force to prevent strikers from striking; the right not to work can stand on no higher footing than the right to work from which it is derived; and if force is justified in support of the one it is also justified in support of the other. If force be thus justified, then each side should arm itself and submit to the arbitrament of fighting. This absurdity is the necessary conclusion from once condoning the use of force.

It is argued, however, in justification of mass picketing and other violence, that strikers have a right to make a strike effective, and that if it is necessary to resort to violent methods for the purpose, such resort is justified. This argument, however, only states the original problem in different terms. Obviously the right to strike includes the right to take all proper action to make a strike effective. The problem is whether violence against other workers is a proper form of action. The answer given by the principle of freedom to work is, No, because violence destroys equal liberty.

It is said, further, that if the majority of the workers in a plant vote for a strike, it is no more than an application of the democratic process to compel all workers to join in the strike, abiding by the vote of the majority. This argument again brings up the question of whether control by the majority or the preservation of liberty is the primary concern of society. But here again, an impairment of liberty is made none the more acceptable by the fact that it is voted by the majority. Society should not authorize procedures where a majority vote can destroy liberty. If the law should authorize the compulsion of nonstrikers to join in a strike by majority vote, or should authorize or condone violence against nonstrikers, it would be destroying the liberty of the minority, and it would be none the less wrongful in that it was accomplished by majority vote.

Another current problem involving the freedom to work is presented by the closed shop, where a worker cannot secure employment unless he is a member of a labor union. Obviously this makes obtaining employment conditional upon the approval of union officials; the worker who is not a member of the union cannot secure employment unless the union will first permit him to join, and the worker who is a member of the union cannot continue in employment if the union expels him from membership. Thus freedom to work becomes conditional upon the permission of a union, which in practice means the permission of union officials.

The union shop, permitted by the Taft-Hartley Act, is a variant of the closed shop in that the worker is not required to belong to the union before obtaining employment, but is required to join it within a designated time after employment is obtained. This has the benefit of making it difficult to maintain a closed union, i.e., a union whose membership is not open on equal terms to all. But otherwise the union shop operates with the same effect upon the worker's freedom as the closed shop. There is the same necessity that the worker continue his membership in the union and the same practical control of the labor officials over the worker by reason of that necessity.

In support of the closed and union shop it is contended, first, that they are necessary to the strength of unions; second, that since strong unions are for the benefit of workers, the compulsion exercised on workers in enforcing closed or union shops is for the workers' own good and accordingly justified; and third, that it is only fair to make all workers share in bearing the cost of maintaining a union, since they all share in its benefits.

With respect to the first point, experience does not show that strong unions depend on the closed or union shop. The railroad unions, among the strongest, attained their position while operating under the open shop principle. Compulsory membership of course eliminates all problems of obtaining members and dues. But by the same token there is also lost the salutary necessity of making unions attractive to workers. Can a union claim to be strong when it cannot sell its services to workers but has to dragoon them into its ranks? And is it not probable that when unions come to depend for their existence on the force of government instead of on the attraction of the benefits they offer, they will become so dependent on the state that the state will take them over (as it has done in Russia and to some extent in Great Britain), or so impotent in serving the interests of the workers that they will revolt and disown them?

With respect to the second point, that workers should be compelled to join unions because unions are good for them, this is a reversion to the philosophy and ethics of collectivism. The state's force is ethically used only to impose the conditions necessary to equal liberty for all; and it is never ethically used in compelling the citizen to do something which the state thinks is for the citizen's benefit, unless the act is also necessary for equal liberty, e.g., the observance of sanitary measures. It is not, therefore, a sufficient reason for compulsory union membership that it is in the interest of the unwilling worker.

With respect to the third point, that it is unfair for a worker in a plant not to support the union from whose activity he obtains benefit with all other workers, the answer is that the point, even though its validity be assumed, is by no means great enough to counterbalance the loss in the individual's freedom to work which the closed and union shops entail. In every aspect of existence the individual benefits from some activity by other persons to which he does not contribute. To compel exact responsibility is for the most part impossible. This does not mean that the burdens of life should not be fairly shared, but it does mean that compulsory sharing is not itself the aim of social organization, and should be had only when compatible with equal liberty. And compulsory union membership, in order to eliminate what the unions call the "free rider," destroys liberty rather than creates it, because it takes from one man a substantial part of his freedom to work and places it within the control of another. Fair sharing is not to be purchased at such a price.

And is it so clear, further, that what is involved is simply fair sharing in the cost of a benefit? In view of the recurring evidences of criminality and racketeering on the part of some union officers, can we say that there is only one possible view on the asserted benefits of unionism? Is the worker who objects to the criminal conduct of his union officers to be permitted no dissent? What effective dissent can he have if he is forced to belong to the union and pay his dues? Is it simply fair sharing to compel him to be a union member when he hears that the officers of the union have solicited and received bribes from the employer? Or have used union funds for themselves? Such union conduct is not typical; but it occurs, and in a volume which obviously is not minimal. Compulsory union membership deprives the worker and society as well

of a wholesome restraint on abuses of unionism. It is not just a matter of
fair sharing.

Freedom to work, therefore, includes the right to work without
regard to union affiliation. The closed and union shops are wrong. They
destroy the worker's liberty, since they make his right to work subject
to the consent of third parties. It is the open shop, where the worker
may join a union but is not compelled to do so, that conforms to the
principle of the freedom to work.

5. Freedom to organize

The freedom to organize follows from the nature of the freedom to
bargain and the freedom to work. Since men have the right to
bargain and to work without interference, save such intervention by
the state as is necessary to preserve equal rights for all, they have also
the right to organize into unions of their own choosing, without interference either from employers or from other workers. Under the principles of liberty, freedom of the individual to act as he chooses is the
beginning point in the consideration of the propriety of all action, and
restraints are imposed only at those points where necessary to maintain
the equal freedom of action of others. No such restraining point is encountered in the voluntary organization of unions. Individualism holds
it to be the right of citizens to associate freely together for any purpose
which would be proper for them as individuals. This principle of voluntary association is the justification of both corporations and unions.

The freedom to organize labor unions is accordingly a right, and
union membership should occur as the exercise of freedom. Freedom
is essentially the privilege of choice. The freedom to organize is consequently as well the freedom not to organize as to organize; the privilege
of joining a union must include the privilege of not joining.

Therefore whenever union membership becomes compulsory, it ceases
to be a right or privilege, and becomes instead an attribute of status.
This occurred in the Roman Empire, where membership in the trade
associations, or collegia, was eventually made compulsory, and it occurred
in many parts of Europe about three centuries ago, when workers were
frequently compelled to join trade guilds. Compulsory union membership has also been adopted more recently in Russia. And we are coming
close to having it here in America. There are many ways of making a
living where union membership is no longer a matter of choice but a

necessary accompaniment of the mode of work. It has become an attribute of status, a burden which the worker is not permitted to put down. The laws and customs that are accomplishing this are wrong. They are leading, and will continue to lead, to a modern kind of thralldom of workers.

To what purposes can a labor union properly direct its action? The answer of individualism is, To any purpose which would be proper for the union members if they were acting together as individuals without union organization. This follows from the basic principle of the permission of voluntary association in a free society. But voluntary association should not confer any rights on union members which they would not otherwise have. Union membership should not expand the privileges of the citizen as against the rest of the community; it should only provide him with a more expeditious means of pursuing the rights which are his whether he joins a union or not. Current assumptions tend to clothe union action with privileges not accorded nonunion action. The violence of union strikers, for example, goes unpunished where it would be prosecuted if committed by other citizens. Intimidation by union leaders is tolerated where it would not be accepted from other members of the community. This grant of special privilege to unions is a violation of equal liberty.

Since unions can rightly direct their activity to any purposes proper for the individual members, they can be used for collective bargaining. But they should be permitted to represent only their members, and no worker should be compelled to accept union representation in collective bargaining.

The freedom to work must include, under principles we have examined, the freedom not to work, not to accept particular employment. This freedom also can properly be exercised through a labor union. Strike votes and the calling of strikes by unions are proper exercise of the freedom to work. But compulsion of workers, whether union members or nonunion workers, to induce their joining in a strike that has been called is always a violation of liberty and is therefore never proper union action.

It is the workers themselves who should be the most jealous to preserve the freedom to work in all its parts. To the extent such freedom is impaired, the controls appropriate to an industrial serfdom begin to set in. If in practice the right to refuse to strike is lost, then the right to strike is lost, leaving only the obligation to strike when ordered to do so. Likewise if in practice the right to work without joining a union is lost, then the right to organize is lost, leaving only the obligation to join in a labor organization as a prerequisite to the privilege of working. When rights become transmuted into obligations, liberty is gone and serfdom enters in.

6. Wages in the free market

What determines the wages that labor can obtain in the free market?

Wages in the free market are always contractual; they are fixed by agreements between employers and employees. By contrast, wages in the controlled market of collectivism are fixed by the decrees of state officials, and necessarily reflect the personal opinions of officials concerning what wages ought to be. In the free market, although wages are fixed by a bargaining process in which personal attitudes must play some part, we can nevertheless identify strong impersonal forces that establish a narrow range for the play of personal opinion.

These forces operate, first, on the employer—the entrepreneur—to set a maximum upon the wage he will consent to pay. They operate, second, on the employee to set a minimum to the wage he will consent to receive.

The maximum is the productivity of the employee in the entrepreneur's enterprise. If that enterprise is producing goods which have a market value of $1,000 per day, and if an additional worker can add $15 per day to the market value of production, the entrepreneur will be willing to pay up to, but not in excess of, $15 per day for an extra laborer's wage. If an additional laborer cannot be found at that wage, production will not be expanded. On the other hand, laborers may be available at $14 per day, in which event the entrepreneur will wish to employ another worker.

Why will a worker accept employment at $14, when his labor will add $15 to the product of his employer? If he is willing to accept employment at $14, it is because in other employment in the community $14 is the going wage for similar labor; he cannot get more than $14 elsewhere. There are other enterprises in the community which could expand the value of their product by $14 by taking on an additional laborer; therefore they will pay $14 in wages but no more. The going wage is accordingly $14.

The maximum that the employer would consent to pay in this situation is $15, the minimum that the employee would consent to receive is $14. The maximum is the productivity of labor in particular employment; the minimum is the going wages prevailing in all employment of like kind. Between this maximum and minimum the wage for particular employment will be set by the labor agreement.

It is not difficult to see how the maximum of $15 is determined, but it is not so easy to see why the going wage is $14. What forces tend to set that figure? The explanation of the going wage is contained in the fact that in the free market employers have to compete for labor, and their competition tends to keep all labor employed at its highest productivity at wages that equal that productivity, as measured through the market value of the goods produced.

In order to understand this statement, let us continue with the illustration used above and see what will happen if a number of entrepreneurs devise improved ways of production, which will get $15 of productivity from an additional day of labor. These entrepreneurs will be able to increase their entrepreneurial profit if they expand production. They will, nevertheless, have to pay something more than $14 a day for labor. For the going wage of $14 in a free market means that substantially all workers willing to accept employment at that wage are hired, for if there were any unemployed willing to work at a lower rate they would bring down the going wage. When the entrepreneurs wishing to expand production seek more labor they will find it necessary, accordingly, to offer a slightly higher wage as an inducement to new employees. But this in turn means that other entrepreneurs must adjust their wage scales and production programs to the changed conditions. There will be a tendency to raise wage scales to keep employees, and a tendency also to drop production whose market value cannot pay the increased labor cost.

In a free market society, where monopoly is not permitted to stand in the way, new enterprises and changed enterprises are constantly being attempted. The business people who try these ventures do so simply because they are under the common necessity of making a living, and entrepreneurship in new and changed enterprises frequently seems to offer the best way of accomplishing that end. It is obvious enough that in presenting a new product entrepreneurs are competing for the preferences of consumers; the competition of course goes on all the time, new product or no, but the new product dramatizes the competition. It is not so obvious, however, that a similar competition goes on continuously among entrepreneurs for the use of the factors of production, including labor; but the advent of a new enterprise makes that fact clearer. For the new enterprise must hire labor, and obviously must pay at least the going scale of wages. Under normal conditions it will have to pay somewhat more. It must induce workers to transfer from their present employment, and the inducement must be better conditions of employment. The new enterprise, however, was entered upon only because it seemed to promise a better profit than existing enterprises, and consequently it can afford to try a slightly higher wage scale. A new enterprise or an expanded enterprise thus serves to increase wages and to push the going wage toward the productivity of labor in its best use.

This competition among employers in the free market is always going on, whether or not new enterprises are being established, and its tendency is always to bring going wages up to productivity. For the entrepreneur, to increase his profit, looks for ways to increase the productivity of the labor employed in his enterprise. He may do so by building increased consumer acceptance, by using new capital, or by devising better production methods. If he can succeed in effecting such an increase in productivity, there will be a period of time during which he will accomplish larger profits. But other entrepreneurs, attracted by his larger profits, will seek to emulate them, and in trying to expand into the same field will raise wages to obtain the needed labor. Thus the period of unusually large entrepreneurial profit must always be temporary in the free market, being longer or shorter as particular circumstances determine. Higher profit in the free market is always followed by higher wages, for competition among entrepreneurs keeps entrepreneurial profit only high enough to induce entrepreneurs to take the risks involved, and brings wages up to the level of the productivity attributable to labor, thereby passing on to labor the benefit of improvements effected in productivity.

In the free market the entrepreneur pays the owners of land, capital, and money enough to induce them to contribute to production. The owner of money is able to obtain from the entrepreneur the going rate of interest, as fixed by the demand for and supply of funds. The owner of capital is able to obtain, on average, a return based on the going rate of interest adjusted to the risk in the particular business. The owner of land is able to obtain its economic rent, that is, the difference between its productivity and the productivity of marginal land. The payments to the owners of money and capital are necessary because without them the money would not be saved for lending and the capital could not be produced. The payment of rent to the owner of land is necessary because, first, private ownership of land is essential to the free market, and second, in the free market the competition of entrepreneurs will enable the owners of land to obtain on average an amount equal to its economic rent. Payments of rent to the owners of land are not justified on the ground that the owners have caused the land to be produced, as is the case with money and capital, but on the ground that private ownership in land is necessary and can be obtained, in the free market society, only by the investment of savings procured through contributions to production.

The amounts thus paid by the entrepreneur constitute a distribution to the owners of land, capital, and money of part of the productivity of the enterprise. To the extent that the entrepreneur is himself the owner of any land, capital, and money used in the business—as is typically the case with both individual and corporate enterprises—income should be attributed to such ownership in an amount equal to what would have been paid for the use of the land, capital, and money if it had been obtained by bargaining in the free market. The entrepreneur in effect distributes some of the productivity of his enterprise to himself as owner of some of the land, capital, and money used therein.

The remainder of the productivity of the enterprise is shared between labor and the entrepreneur. But competition among entrepreneurs has the effect of raising the share of labor until wages equal its productivity, computed after allowing to the entrepreneur only the average entrepreneurial profit necessary to induce him to assume the risks of entrepreneurship.

We may summarize by saying that in the free market society wages tend to equal the entire productivity of the productive process, less the amounts necessary to induce people to save money and produce capital, less the amounts necessary to be paid the private owners of land, and less the amounts necessary to induce entrepreneurs to assume the risks of entrepreneurship.

Individualism asserts that the wages so fixed by the operation of the free market are fair and proper, and that any deviation from them by controls placed on the operation of the market results in an unfair distribution of production and a lowering in human welfare.

7. Wages and freedom

The maintenance of wages at the level of productivity, as analyzed in the preceding section, depends primarily upon the maintenance of two elements or parts of the freedom of action of the free market. The first is the freedom of entrepreneurs to enter upon business activity, and the second is the freedom of workers to move from one employment to another. The former constitutes freedom in the demand for labor and the latter freedom in its supply. We have already discussed each of these freedoms, but it will be well to examine them somewhat more fully at this point in the light of their bearing on wages.

Entrepreneurs supply employment by entering upon the production of goods. Accordingly the volume of employment depends upon the activity of entrepreneurs in undertaking production, and any factor which impedes the entry of entrepreneurs into production tends to lower the competition of entrepreneurs for labor. This competition of entrepreneurs, however, is a vital element in the free market's impulsion of wages toward equality with productivity; and it is only through such competition, occasioned by the entry of entrepreneurs into new or expanded business ventures, that workers can find the opportunity of continually turning their labor to more productive forms of employment. If, therefore, the freedom of entrepreneurs to engage in business is in any way impaired, the result must be lower wages than would otherwise prevail, resulting both from the inability of labor to push its efforts into more productive lines and from the attendant difficulty of compelling present employers to pay a wage equivalent to productivity.

The principal threat to free competition among entrepreneurs arises from monopoly in its various forms. As we have had occasion to note many times, the essential feature of monopoly is substantial control over the supply of a good, which means that the monopolist is in a position to limit its production. The monopolist, therefore, whether his position arises from exclusive possession of natural resources, restrictive agreements with others, or a grant from the state, can bar new entrepreneurs from entering the field, either with familiar production techniques or with improved ones. This ability of the monopolist to prevent the entry of competing entrepreneurs is the essence of his monopoly; when he can no longer prevent competition his monopoly disappears. While the monopoly continues, therefore, it not only defeats consumer preference and permits a monopolistic profit, as we have heretofore seen, but it also impairs the demand for labor by competing entrepreneurs, thereby making it more difficult for workers to obtain wages equivalent to the productivity of their work.

This influence of monopoly upon wages is frequently overlooked, the chief objection to monopoly being supposed to reside in the higher prices the monopoly makes possible. It would seem, however, that the effect on wages is a serious consequence of the monopolistic barring of competition; and it may well be that the lower wages of Europe, where cartels and monopolistic trade agreements are permitted, as compared with the wages of America, where antimonopoly laws have been substantially successful in maintaining freedom of entry by entrepreneurs into business, is due in important part to the adverse influence of monopoly.

The second freedom essential to the maintenance of free market wages is the freedom of workers to change employment. If entrepreneurs are to open new or expanded lines of production with increased productivity of labor, they obviously must find new employees. And this process of changing production by new ventures means that there must be a movement of workers from one employment to another. Some of this change in employment may occur within the same plant and some between different plants, and some may take place between different localities. But unless workers can and do move from one employment to another, always seeking a more productive occupation and always threatening to leave a present employer for a new one paying a higher wage, it will be impossible for them to secure free market wages equating productivity with wage payment.

It is this threat of terminating employment that supplies the pressure on the entrepreneur to keep up both productivity and wages. He cannot stay in business without employees; he cannot keep employees without paying competitive wages; and he cannot continue to pay competitive wages in a free market society without constantly increasing labor's productivity, in order to match the wage-bids of new entrepreneurs who enter the market with improved production.

Compared with this changing of employment by workers, acting one by one, the strike is a futile instrument for increasing wages. It does not increase labor's productivity and it cannot compel a wage higher than labor's productivity. There are doubtless occasions when a strike secures an increase in wages at an earlier date than otherwise would occur, and doubtless too strikes can be effective in monopolistic or monopsonic situations, where the competition of other entrepreneurs is not present; but where free market conditions obtain, the strike cannot force a wage higher than the competitive wage-scale, which the free market will deliver in any event; or if a strike should succeed in effecting a wage-scale higher than the competitive wage-scale, it would do so only at the cost of lowered employment in the particular plant or industry, as production was cut back to bring marginal productivity up to the higher wage cost.

Thus, it is freedom of labor to work where it chooses that supplies one of the two great pressures for keeping wages up to productivity. Anything, therefore, which impairs labor's mobility impairs its wage. In the light of this principle workers might well take a second look at some of the fringe benefits, as they are called, that are being offered by employers today. Many of these benefits are of current use to the worker and do not require his continuance at his job to obtain their value. But some are so designed that the worker loses the benefit if he changes employment, and thus he becomes tied to his job. If benefits of the type impeding mobility should become substantial, the effect on wages would be adverse.

But if mobility is thus essential to labor's obtaining wages equal to its productivity, yet mobility also has its other side. For mobility necessarily involves some unemployment. A worker cannot ordinarily leave one employment and accept another without an intervening period of unemployment. It is through temporary unemployment, therefore, that workers better their lot and increase their wages. If such unemployment were impossible, mobility would be greatly restricted. A certain amount of unemployment accordingly is an unavoidable feature of a free market society, and is essential to the maintenance of free market wages. The amount of unemployment necessary to the free market is difficult to estimate, and it will become less, as a proportion of the whole working force, as methods of transportation and communication improve. Viewing the current scene, one might hazard a guess that two or three per cent unemployment is the normal consequence of mobility in labor at the present time.

Thus full employment, in the sense of a total absence of unemployment, is not compatible with a free market. Full employment means, in practical effect, that workers cannot change jobs except pursuant to official order that permits no gap between one employment and the next.

8. Social control of wages

This being the manner of the determination of labor's compensation in the free market society, what shall we say of social control over that compensation? Proposals for various forms of such control are constantly being made.

We should first note that no social control can increase the maximum amount which the employer can pay. This maximum is the productivity of labor. No matter what formulas of control be adopted, income must still cover outgo, and controls cannot change the fact that productivity limits wages.

Most proponents of social control of wages recognize this, and do not contend that minimum wage laws, for example, can increase the top possibility of wages. Their contention is that without such laws employers do not pay to labor its full productivity but retain too much for themselves. As proof they point to what they say are excessive profits in the operation of enterprises. Let us look briefly at the level of entrepreneurial profit in its relation to wages.

There are three basic ways in which entrepreneurial profit can be raised above the amount normally required to induce the assumption of the risks of operating a business enterprise. One of them we have already noted; it is by improving the productivity of labor, i.e., the market value of the product per unit of labor. Since the going rate of wages rises only slowly, there occurs a longer or shorter period when the entrepreneur is able to retain more than a normal profit. This is frequently cited as a fault in the free market system. On the contrary, it is one of the great advantages of the free market system and it is largely because of it that increases in wages have occurred in the past and will continue to occur. If increases in labor's productivity were reflected immediately in corresponding increases in wages, there would be no incentive to the entrepreneur to effect increased productivity. It is because the businessman can reap a temporary profit from increasing the productivity of labor in his business that he seeks to accomplish such increase. Not only so, but such increase is impossible unless the entrepreneur temporarily profits. An increase in productivity is not accomplished by a wave of the hand but by difficult experimentation. For every successful experiment there are some costly failures. If the successful experiments cannot result in profit, the unsuccessful experiments cannot be financed; experimentation could result only in loss and would necessarily be abandoned.

But increases in labor's productivity per unit constitute the sole means of increasing the maximum possibility of wages. Any limitation on productivity is a limitation on wages. If improved ways of production are restricted or eliminated, increases in wages are restricted or eliminated.

Entrepreneurs, however, may also increase their profits by monopoly. In the free market, monopoly is either permitted and regulated or it is forbidden, on principles studied in the preceding chapter. Patents are an important form of permitted monopoly. Typically the inventions covered by patents involve improvements in production which increase labor's productivity. Accordingly such inventions would temporarily increase profit even if they were not patented. But the verdict of experience is that the increase in profit would be of such short duration in the absence of patent protection that it would not induce the costly research much invention requires. To encourage such research, therefore, the possibility of higher profit is increased by permitting a monopolistic use of patented inventions for a period of years. After the period of monopoly, competition among entrepreneurs results in higher wages because of the increased productivity due to the invention. Patent monopoly profit accordingly results in increased wages, as do the temporary profits from other improvements in production. Other forms of permitted monopoly, such as public utilities, affect wages only as they are economical forms of operation and to that extent increase labor's productivity.

Entrepreneurs may also acquire unusually high profits through monopsony, discussed in the preceding chapter. The principal instance affecting labor is the industrial plant which furnishes the only demand for labor within a given area. Such cases, however, are rare and they tend to lose their monopsonic character as facility of transportation improves. In theory, a minimum wage law could remove monopsonic profits by requiring a high enough wage to effect a distribution to labor of an amount equal to its entire productivity. In practice, however, this is made difficult by the impossibility of determining the exact amount of the production properly to be attributed to labor. The free market wage approximates labor's productivity, and the competition of entrepreneurs is always driving the wage toward its productivity; but an abstract computation apart from the free market is impossible. Accordingly it can never be known whether a wage minimum fixed by law is only eliminating monopsonic profit or is preventing employment.

Apart from its beneficial use in cases of monopsonic control of demand for labor, a minimum wage law can only work harm. At best it can be innocuous. At worst it can prevent employment and impede increases in wages. Most of our minimum wage laws have in fact been innocuous, because they have set a figure below the going wage for all classifications of labor. But if the minimum legal wage is raised above the free market wage, the result can be only an impairment of welfare. Telling an entrepreneur that he must pay a minimum does not make it financially possible for him to do so, and if it is financially impossible to pay such a wage it will not be paid.

As these lines are written, the minimum wage for goods sold in interstate commerce has been set by national law at $1 per hour. For most employment in the United States this minimum has no meaning. But there are unskilled and handicapped persons whose present wages are less than this minimum. The new law does not mean that all these unfortunates are now going to receive $1 an hour; some of them will do so, as employers are stimulated to make extra efforts to increase productivity; but many of them will find it impossible to obtain employment at the new wage, for no one can employ them at a rate below their productivity. For the same reason, the establishment of new plants in areas of unskilled labor will be slowed. The harm of the new law promises, nevertheless, to be of short duration. The phenomenal rate of increase in the productivity of labor at present being effected by businessmen, coupled with the steady inflation in the volume of our money, will soon make the $1 minimum harmless because it will have no practical application.

Wage controls must, from the nature of things, set minimum wages, maximum wages, or precise wages. Although maximum and precise wages by law have often been tried, no one at present urges them and it is unnecessary to discuss them.

But minimum wage controls, having the effect discussed above, show the result of all interference with wage rates set by the free market for labor. Those rates always are proceeding, and at a satisfactory speed, toward equality with labor's productivity as measured in the prices that consumers pay for the goods produced. Any interference with those rates must either cause unemployment by setting the rates above productivity, or cause a slowing in the rate of increase of productivity and wages by impairing the incentive and compensation to entrepreneurs for increasing productivity.

9. Labor monopoly

Labor monopoly consists in substantial control of the supply of labor for a particular industry or of a particular kind. For the past half century we have encouraged labor monopoly in this country and we now have many unions or combinations of unions which are monopolies.

The effects of a labor monopoly flow from the operation of the same principles that apply to other forms of monopoly. The effects of a labor monopoly are three: First, it defeats consumer preference; second, it reduces the number of workers in the kind of labor monopolized; and third, it produces a higher wage for workers in the labor monopoly than they would receive in a free market, and a lower wage for all other workers.

Since a labor monopoly controls the supply of labor for particular production, it thereby also controls the supply of the good produced. If the coal miners can exercise control over the supply of labor they can thereby also exercise control over the supply of coal. If they raise the price of labor above its free market price, which their monopolistic position enables them to do, they will thereby also raise the price of coal above its free market price. The quantity of coal produced and consumed must accordingly decline. This is a defeat of consumer preference and a consequent lowering in the standard of living for the community.

Coincident with the reduced production of the monopolized product there must be reduced employment for the labor in the monopoly. A labor monopoly, if it exercises its monopolistic position by putting its wage above the free market wage, must always also experience reduced employment.

The labor so displaced must seek employment in other lines. But the fact that the free market would direct its employment to the field of the monopoly, except for the existence of the monopoly, is proof that the monopolized field represents the area of highest productivity for the displaced labor, and that its employment anywhere else must be at a lower rate of productivity and consequently at a lower wage. Labor monopoly must always have this harmful effect upon workers outside the monopolized field. The workers in the monopoly are fewer than they otherwise would be, and they receive a higher wage than they otherwise would receive. The displaced labor and the labor which would otherwise be employed must find its employment in other fields. And since productivity as fixed by consumer preference is lower for this transferred labor in any other field, as proved by the fact that consumer preference would employ it in the monopolized field if it could, the wages of transferred labor are lowered. Thus labor monopoly always effects an aggrandizement in the welfare of the monopoly laborers at the expense of the welfare of others. Labor monopoly always destroys liberty, as do all other forms of monopoly.

10. Wages and collectivism

The theorists of communism and socialism, from Karl Marx to H. J. Lasky, have founded their argument upon the proposition that the owners of land and capital—the "capitalists"—are able by virtue of their ownership to pay such wages for labor as they choose. Being thus in control, they pay only enough wages to keep workers quiescent, retaining the rest for themselves. This theory was supported by Marx through recourse to the wages-fund theory, then recently developed by Adam Smith but now quite abandoned. Communists since Marx, however, have seldom thought it necessary to attempt any analytical foundation, but have insisted upon the control of the "capitalists" over wages as a self-evident proposition.

This power of the "capitalists" is said to arise from their ownership of the instruments of production—land and capital; and from this position communism evolves its principal argument for collective ownership of property. The argument is very simple. Ownership of land and capital is asserted to confer the power to fix wages. Therefore if land and capital are owned by only a part of the community, the wages of the non-owning portion of the community will be kept unfairly low and the non-owning portion will not receive its fair share of production. But if land and capital are owned by all the community, then all the community will join in fixing wages and therefore no portion of the community will be unfairly treated. The way to accomplish ownership by all, communism next asserts, is by placing ownership of land and capital in the state, for all citizens are members of the state and therefore if the state owns, all its citizens share in its ownership.

Let us examine the first part of this argument—that the owners of land and capital can fix the wages of labor and need make them no more than sufficient to keep labor from revolting.

Here, as so often in the criticisms of collectivists, the stricture leveled at the free market of individualism is in truth applicable only to the controlled market of collectivism. It is in the latter that the owners of land and capital—who in collectivism are the bureaucracy of the state— can closely control wages. They can do so because they have a monopoly of ownership of land and capital, and because of this monopoly they in turn occupy a monopsonic position with respect to the demand for labor. In Russia today there is no bargaining which the worker can do, no moving from one employer to another in a search for the best wage. There is only one employer, the state, and it realistically is composed of the state's bureaucracy.

But in the free market of individualism the owners of land and capital cannot arbitrarily fix wages because they, as well as workers, are in competition. In the free market society there are always entrepreneurs who are looking for opportunities to employ labor, and if an entrepreneur seeks to fix wages below labor's productivity, other entrepreneurs can be found who will offer more. And if one owner of land or capital seeks to obtain a part of labor's share of productivity, by charging more for the use of his land and capital in the productive process, he will soon find that his land or capital is going unused. It is only when monopolistic control, public or private, over land and capital is allowed that the owners of land and capital can also control wages. But monopoly is banned by individualism. In the free market of the individualistic society, therefore, entrepreneurs can be counted on to appear who will have access to natural resources and who will bid for labor to the extent that the wage offered will equal the productivity of labor.

The unparalleled increase in real wages in our own country during the past century is a complete refutation of the communist and socialist theory of wages. Under that theory the only explanation would be that American employers have been more kindhearted than those elsewhere in the world and also more kindhearted than in any similar period in history. But this dubious explanation the communists and socialists themselves would be the first to reject. The real explanation is that we have succeeded on the whole in maintaining, despite many deviations from sound individualistic theory, a free market. Monopoly of enterprise, and the consequent monopsonic conditions of demand for labor, have been substantially restricted. In consequence, new enterprises are continually appearing, with new bidding for labor by entrepreneurs, and workers are continually moving to new and better jobs.

"Americans are always moving on," said Benet in *Western Star*, and it is true; not only to new locations but also to new enterprises, new jobs, and new levels of material living. It is economic freedom that is to be credited for the strain of well-being in our history. We must maintain this freedom, in labor and employment as elsewhere.

PART III: THE LIBERTY OF CHILDREN

Chapter 23

THE LIBERTY OF CHILDREN

Social philosophy tends to speak exclusively of adults, without directing its regard to children. But a consideration of social philosophy in the light of the needs and experiences of childhood is clearly called for. Children comprise about one-third of the human community, and the application of social theory to this large group will both test the adequacy of theory and enable it to develop its thesis to a dimension commensurate with society.

Collectivism, however, encounters no difficulty in assimilating children to its program. The collectivized state always converges upon a planned program for its citizenry, as we have had occasion to note many times. Such a planned program being the necessary central core of all collectivistic practice, and the enforcement of adherence to it by the power of the state being its complement, no philosophical problem is discerned in including children as well as adults in the program's coercion. Children indeed are regarded as peculiarly suitable objects of the state's directive attention, since they can be molded by education, it is believed, to an acceptance of the collectivistic design for their lives.

With the philosophy of individualism, however, the case is far otherwise. Here, as in so much else, the comparatively simple conceptual structure of collectivism is replaced by a pattern of thought requiring careful consideration for its understanding.

1. The elements of the liberty of children

We do not ordinarily think of the experience of childhood as involving the problem of liberty, but rather the problem of training. What training shall we give our children? is the tenor of our concern. But if the individualistic philosophy is correct, training must be related to liberty, and in the relation liberty must be dominant. Is this position valid?

Liberty, we have said, is ethical imperative. The reason disclosed by our study was that life's purpose, good character, can be attained only by the practice of human decision, for which liberty is the indispensable environment.

But here we encounter a difficulty. For although the purpose of good character clearly applies to children as well as to adults, yet children may be incompetent to exercise decision. The newborn infant cannot decide to procure his own sustenance, and he will quickly die if he be simply given freedom to do so. The same incompetence to make meaningful economic decisions continues for many years; and throughout childhood economic freedom can have little or no value because the child is unable to make economic decisions that can have bearing upon his career. Not until adulthood is reached does the liberty of the free market have value for character development.

The case is the same with intellectual liberty. Religious freedom, cultural freedom, freedom of speech, and the other elements of intellectual liberty have at first no value at all for the child and acquire value only slowly as the child grows in competence to make meaningful decisions within the area of intellectual action. Freedom of speech is meaningless until the child has learned a language. Liberty of the press is of no value unless the child learns to read and write. There can be no meaningful decisions concerning religion before there has been some instruction concerning religion, or sufficient experience with living to bring religious questions to mind.

Thus freedom of decision in both the economic and intellectual areas becomes of significance only as the human being experiences physical development and as he acquires acquaintance with his environment. At the moment of birth, only the freedom of elementary muscular movement can have value; all other elements of freedom are valueless because of the child's incompetence to make use of them. But as time passes, the area within which the child is competent to make decisions slowly enlarges, until at adulthood he is competent to share in liberty with all other adults. Will's arena for the child may be likened to the space within the two arms of a V; the infant begins his career in the point of the V, where the area for choice is minimal; with the passage of time the area widens, until at adulthood the individual passes out of the V-area and becomes subject only to the equal restraints on freedom applicable to all adults. The arms of the V are the limits of the child's competence. Beyond the area of the expanding V the child's incompetence prevents him from making meaningful decisions.

Thus childhood is the experience of a growing competence to exercise freedom. Therefore the first element in the liberty of children is the right to an enlarging freedom that increases at equal pace with competence to make decisions. In this the liberty of children differs from the liberty of adults; for adults liberty is equal liberty; for children it is an enlarging liberty that approaches equal liberty as its goal. The child cannot have a right to equal liberty with adults because the child is not competent to exercise such large liberty. His right must be restricted by his incompetence, and accordingly must be allowed to extend only to such freedom of action as he is competent to exercise.

But, it may be said, if liberty is thus to be restricted for children, why should it not also be restricted for adults when they exhibit incompetence to exercise it? And if this be allowed, what becomes of the theory of equality in liberty? Here we must be alert to the semantic danger of shifting the sense of a word while retaining its form. The word "incompetence" can mean either a failure to make a wise decision or an inability to make any meaningful decision at all. With the wisdom of decisions the philosophy of liberty refrains from concerning itself, and accordingly it does not withdraw freedom from those whose incompetence consists only in a failure to be wise. But with the ability to make a meaningful decision, i.e., the ability to make what is really a decision, the philosophy of liberty is concerned, and it modifies equal freedom, or supplements the institutions of equal freedom with other devices, whenever incompetence, in the sense of such inability, makes its appearance either in children or adults. We saw an application of this principle in the case of persons unable to participate in the free market, who are incompetent to make meaningful decisions in the area of economic freedom; the philosophy of liberty indicates special institutions for their assistance as discussed in Chapter 19. Insane persons constitute another group of adults whose incompetence to make meaningful choices calls for a modification of equal liberty. In similar manner the incompetence of children is their inability to make meaningful decisions in certain areas of human action, and it is this incompetence which the application of liberty to childhood has regard to.

Therefore the liberty of children is not at all a repudiation of the theory of the equal liberty of individualism, but is an application of that theory to the particular facts of childhood.

One of these facts is that childhood terminates in adulthood as its goal. Childhood is thus a preparation for adulthood; consequently it is also a preparation for the equal liberty of adulthood. But although children cannot make good claim to equal liberty with adults, yet they can properly demand that they all have equal preparation for the challenge presented by the equal liberty of adulthood. Precisely the same reasons that teach us equality of opportunity for adults teach us also that there should be equal preparation for that equal opportunity. The merit of equal opportunity is lost if those to whom it is presented are unequally prepared to respond.

The second element, therefore, in the liberty of children is equal preparation for adulthood. Individualism thus teaches that all children have a right to receive, during the period of childhood, an equal opportunity to be prepared for the free intellectual and economic life they will enter upon as adults. Here again liberty differs slightly for adults and children; for adults it is equal opportunity to participate in free life, for children it is equal opportunity to prepare for participation.

The liberty of children consists, then, in the adjustment of freedom to an expanding competence and in equal opportunity for preparation for adulthood.

2. Adjusting freedom to expanding competence

A great art of the child's upbringing is to adjust the arena for the exercise of his will to his competence, that the arena may match his growing ability to exercise decision. If there be maladjustment, if his will's arena be too large or too small for his competence as it has been developed at a particular time, the child will be harmed.

In this great art, however, on which so much human welfare and happiness depend, there is but little room for social action. Most of the delineation of childhood's liberty must always be done by parents and teachers, who can be guided hardly at all by specific rule, and must in large part act pursuant to discretion addressed to particular situations. Only in exceptional circumstances can society through law control the extension of freedom to children in accordance with their competence. It can, for example, forbid violent physical treatment of children, and thereby seek to prevent the undue restriction of freedom which would result from physical harm. On the other hand it can establish curfew laws for children, in case of need, and thus prevent an undue extension of freedom to children by careless or indulgent parents. But the role of these and similar social enactments must nevertheless always remain comparatively small, leaving this vital matter largely to individual practice.

3. Childhood as preparation for adult liberty

If the social role in adjusting the child to his growing freedom must remain small, it nevertheless must become large in guiding his more deliberate preparation for the liberty of adulthood, which preparation constitutes the second element in the liberty of children.

The main factors in the preparation of children for adult liberty are four: emotional sympathy, physical sustenance, protection of health, and education.

The first two are supplied to the child primarily in the home. Emotional sympathy, or love, can scarcely be supplied outside a home. The protection of health and education, however, must be carried on primarily by institutions outside the home—by health services and schools.

The preparation of children for adult liberty therefore consists in supplying them with good homes and with health services and schools.

Whose responsibility is this preparation? It is the responsibility both of the parents and of society. But the content of the responsibility differs. The parents' duty is to supply an affectionate and adequate home, to do what can be done by the parents in protecting health and supplying education, and to join with other members of society in furnishing additional health protection and education. The duty of society is to see that parents do not neglect their responsibility, to assist parents when they are unable to discharge their responsibility, and to supply to all children an equal opportunity for health services and education.

In so far as society has responsibility, its responsibility falls upon all members of the community. Liberty is a common duty, an ethical imperative for all, as our analysis has heretofore shown. Therefore the liberty of children is also common duty, an ethical imperative for all. Included in the liberty of children is their equal preparation for adult liberty, and in consequence this equal preparation becomes common duty. Not all elements of this preparation can be supplied by social action, however; some can be supplied only by parental action. Obviously social duty does not extend to that which cannot be socially done. But it extends to all that which can be done socially, and therefore the duty of supplying to children an equal preparation for adulthood, in so

The Challenge of Liberty

far as that preparation can be supplied socially, applies to all members of society. In this regard the responsibility for children is not simply that of their parents but of all society and the obligation to carry out this responsibility is not one based on sympathy but one based on ethical imperative.

4. Home

The social duty is to see that parents supply a home for their children. Where this cannot be accomplished, society should arrange for substitute homes, through adoption and in orphanages. Under principles already examined, the supplying of substitute homes is preferably done through private philanthropy instead of state agencies.

Occasionally parents maintain a home for children, but fail to furnish them adequate sustenance. Should society intervene? Clearly it should, first by trying to compel the parents to supply adequate food and clothing, and failing in this, by supplying it to the children. Society's obligation is to its children, and its duty is not dependent upon the performance of the parents' duty.

On the same principle, society should furnish aid to widows with children to support and with inadequate means to maintain them in a suitable home. Likewise its aid to parents who, under the principles discussed in Chapter 19 are the appropriate recipients of public assistance, should include the means for supplying a home to their children.

5. Health

The social obligation is to furnish every child with an equal opportunity for good health. What society can do must depend on the state of medical science at particular times. The health a child will have upon reaching adulthood will depend in part upon natural endowment, in part upon the health services offered to him, and in part upon his response to the opportunity furnished by such services. The role of health services in accomplishing good health is therefore only partial, and consequently it is folly to suppose, as is frequently assumed under the influence of collectivistic theory, that everyone has a right to good health.

But although health services cannot assure good health, society has a duty to make them equally available to all its children. This is a large specification. What can be done to meet it must depend upon the wealth and knowledge of the community. The obligation is that of parents as well as of society, and the action of society should, in a sense, be supplemental. But the health services required outside the home and beyond the economic means of many parents to provide are large in scope, and consequently should be regarded as a normal part of social action.

In the good society, however, this social action will preferably be furnished by institutions of private philanthropy rather than through the machinery of the state. But private philanthropy failing, the state will intervene. The principles which lead to these conclusions we have discussed in Chapter 19.

6. Education

The obligation of society is to assure equality of education for its children, as part of their equal preparation for adulthood. In what does equality of education consist, and what are the means to the attainment of that equality?

Clearly equality in education does not mean that every child should have the same education. Sameness in human affairs is not equality, as we have had occasion to note many times. Therefore neither the extent nor kind of education should be the same for all. What liberty demands is equality of opportunity for education. Each child must have the same chance at an education, the same opportunity at acquiring the information, the skills, and the background that proceed from educational processes.

The technique of supplying such equal opportunity would take us into a discussion too large for the present study. We may note, however, that the concept of education as a form of equal opportunity has little currency at the present time. Nor has the concept that education is a preparation for the liberty of adulthood received much recognition. Currently educational methods seem to be under the dominance of two somewhat conflicting concepts. The one is that education is a process of self-expression, whereby learning is accomplished by experimentation. The other is that the object of education is to mold the child to a predetermined pattern, whereby he will acquire certain habits of thought deemed desirable. The methods of so-called progressive education have been developed under the influence of the first concept, and the attempt to inculcate attitudes of so-called social responsibility or cooperation are evidences of the second.

The implication of the doctrine of liberty is that each of these concepts, though not devoid of truth, is nevertheless incorrect. Education is an individual and social process. As individual process it is the individual's growing awareness of himself and of his universe. As social process it is aid in accomplishing this growing awareness. Its end, both as individual and social process, is the largest freedom of the spirit, and to this end all techniques should be adjusted. Therefore the essence of all techniques used in education should be explanation, and children should be required to learn these explanations as they are contained in science, history, and literature, and to acquire the skills—reading, writing, mathematics—necessary to deal with the explanations. Into the realm of propaganda educational processes should not go, because propaganda for the young defeats, rather than aids, the attainment of the educational goal.

Should the educational program be administered in private or public schools, in schools supported by private enterprise and philanthropy or in schools supported by taxes? In either one, replies the philosophy of individualism, as students and parents may decide. If, however, private enterprise and philanthropy do not provide schools for all children, then it is the duty of the state to do so. In practice this means that the state must furnish most of the school facilities for the earlier years of education, because the parents of younger children typically are unable to afford private school facilities of good quality. Accordingly the state, in fulfillment of the social obligation to supply equal educational opportunity, must furnish public schools. And because the state's activity in furnishing education in the younger years becomes large it also tends to become dominant.

It is sometimes supposed that public education is not only the obligation of the state, but is also the sole proper mode of education in a democratic society, that private education is undemocratic. Within the confines of the tenets of collectivism, this view is certainly correct; education, of all human activities, is most importantly placed within state control in the society devoted to collectivistic principles, because it bears so largely on the entire practice of conformity to common plan. But within the principles of individualism no such reasoning obtains. Not only does it permit private educational activity, so long as the obligation to furnish public education is not slighted or denied, but its whole position is such that it encourages the diversity represented by private schools operating alongside the public system. Through such diversity comes experimentation and improvement, and avoidance of the danger of adhering to a common mediocrity as standard.

Private schools have another reason for existence in the liberal society, in that they can properly supply the religious training which tax-supported schools must abstain from furnishing, for reasons heretofore examined. The principle of liberty therefore requires that parents and students desiring an educational process permeated by religion be permitted to support and attend private schools providing such educational facilities. Again, the exercise of this permission must not be accepted as a license to neglect the quality of the secular education of the public schools; the same principle which demands the allowance of the private religious school calls for the equal educational quality (barring the religious aspect) of the facilities furnished to children in public schools.

A proper understanding of the justification of the public school system within the philosophy of individualism is most important. In the first place, it makes clear the purpose of public education, that is, the presentation to all children of an equal opportunity of preparing for adulthood, and thereby indicates the appropriate extent of the effort of public education.

In the second place, an understanding of individualism's support of public education discloses the falsity of an argument commonly thought to support socialism. The argument runs thus: Education is an activity which is conducted in our society at present by the state, and as so conducted is generally approved. This public educational system is a demonstration of socialism, and in consequence is an example of successful and approved socialism. Since, therefore, we thus practice and endorse socialism in one way, why not try it in other ways, expanding the benefits obtainable from socialistic practices?

The defect in this point of view is its assumption that public education finds its justification only in the principles of collectivism, and in consequence is an example of collectivism, or, more particularly, of socialism. But a public school system is no more the product of collectivistic teaching than of individualistic teaching. Collectivism and individualism join in approving certain forms of communal action, e.g., courts of justice, police, and public schools; but their respective approvals proceed from diverse origins, even as their concepts of the good life, both individual and social, differ radically. In consequence, their respective uses of these forms differ radically. The fact that an individualistic society such as our own makes use of an institution approved by collectivism as well as by individualism, e.g., public schools, is no more evidence of its approval of collectivism than the fact that a collectivistic society such as Russia makes use of an institution approved by individualism as well as by collectivism, e.g., police, is evidence of its approval of individualism. We use our public schools for a different purpose from that followed in Russia, and Russia uses its police for a different purpose from that permitted here; and the differences in purpose are radical, because they stem from radically different social philosophies.

7. Economic opportunity

Children take but small part in the production of goods, mostly as assistants to their parents. Moreover, equality of economic opportunity can be of little meaning to children because they are unequipped by nature to respond to equal opportunity while childhood continues. If, therefore, the free society will devote adequate attention to supplying its children with homes, health, and education as above discussed, it will have small occasion to be concerned with the equality of the economic opportunity presented to them.

There is, further, little that the state can do toward assuring equality of economic opportunity for children other than what it does for adults in maintaining a free market. The unequal economic position of children arises not from social causes but from biological ones which the state cannot modify. The state should guard children against their own incompetence, by such things as limitations on employment, voidability of contracts, the appointment of guardians, and the like. But these provisions do not deal directly with economic opportunity, which must remain for children a closed area of activity for the most part.

But children as they pass into adulthood enter the area of economic action, sometimes abruptly, sometimes gradually, and when they do so they frequently feel that the doors of opportunity are closed against them. They come in contact with others who seem much better equipped by nature for the competition of economic action, or whose ownership of property makes their lot easier and their competitive position stronger. But the vagaries of natural endowment are beyond the reach of social action, which can do no more for those less generously gifted than to equalize their opportunity of action. And the principles which should prevail concerning property have already been examined by us in Chapter 18. When society, therefore, observes the principle of liberty in maintaining the equal opportunity of a free market, it grants to its children as they become adults the utmost in economic opportunity that can be given to them.

Primarily society's concern, as it seeks to accomplish equal preparation of all its children for adulthood, must be with their homes, their health, and their education.

PART IV: POLITICAL LIBERTY

Political action, as it appears in the stream of human process, is inseparably joined with all other forms of human action, particularly with economic action. Politics and economics should therefore pursue compatible goals, avoiding the confusion of conflicting purposes. If political and economic objectives out of harmony each with the other are adopted, the result must necessarily be inefficiency in action and perplexity in theory. Politics and economics must be harmonized in their procedures, moreover, as well as in their aims. A liberal political system will have difficulty surviving in a controlled market society, and free enterprise will almost certainly succumb to controls where the political system is illiberal.

Social theory, therefore, must include a synthesis of politics and economics, by which their respective aims and procedures can be harmonized. There must be established a common goal and standard of reference for all parts of political and economic theory. The departmentalization of learning is too much permitted to obscure this truth. Political theory is pursued without attention to economic values, and economic programs are proposed without consideration of political values.

It is the concept of liberty which furnishes the needed synthesis. The free society must build both its politics and its economics in the light of the ethical imperative of liberty, and accordingly liberty is the common goal and standard of reference for all political and economic theory and action. Thereby all conflict between politics and economics is removed and they are brought into complete harmony, with logical relation replacing confusion, and with integrity taking the place of disjunction. The goal of politics and economics becomes one, and their procedures join in attaining the common goal.

Chapter 24

LIBERTY AND REPRESENTATIVE GOVERNMENT

We live in an age which accepts without question the theory of representative government. We hold it to be self-evident that people should be governed by representatives of their own choosing. But upon what base of reasoned conviction does this belief rest? What principles lead to the conclusion that representative government is the best government? Certainly during most of human history no such persuasion has obtained in theory or been evidenced in practice; and if during the past two centuries the theory of representative government has won common acceptance, yet that acceptance was accomplished by theories of natural law, expounded by Locke and others, that are now entirely forgotten.

But a concept not understood cannot long be believed in. And signs of crumbling in the conviction have already begun to appear. Our officials increasingly attempt to assume authorities for which they have not been elected, and significant opposition does not arise. The Korean War was declared by the executive branch of our national government instead of by the legislative, as required by the Constitution, and to this momentous departure from the principles of representative government scarcely any objection was made.

If representative government is to endure in the western world it must be supported by an understanding of principles that demonstrate its validity. The philosophy of liberty furnishes that demonstration.

1. Government as means and end

Since liberty is the goal of politics, the role of government is to furnish the means to that end. Government is political action to attain equal intellectual and economic freedom for all citizens. The importance of government in the social order is accordingly derivative rather than primary. The primary element in society's goal is intellectual and economic liberty; the state as servitor to that end is no more than a secondary element. To the extent, accordingly, that the state accomplishes the end for which it is means, the state is good; but to the extent that it passes beyond this and becomes the support of pomp and power for their own sakes it is evil.

The liberty that is thus the end of political action is both present and future liberty, but as between the two it is present liberty that is paramount, both because it is the reality and because the future acquires worth only as it becomes the present. Yet how often have governments persuaded citizens to acquiesce in a sacrifice of present liberties by holding out the prospect of future liberties! The promise of a future gain in liberty in return for a present loss is always the mark of attempted tyranny. But within the philosophy of liberty the reality of present loss must be justified by the immediate prospect of the reality of a present larger gain.

Thus war, the great destroyer of human liberty, can be justified only when the present danger of loss of liberty through war is less than the present danger of loss of liberty without war. Our own history contains the clear example of the promise of present gain outweighing the promise of present loss. The revolutionaries did not resort to war until all institutions of self-government had been abolished in the colony of Massachusetts, supplanted by a military governor whose decrees, enforced by a foreign soldiery, were issued in the name of a monarch claiming the right to absolute rule. A similar destruction of liberty awaited the other colonies, whose choice was between submission to a tyrannous government and recourse to arms.

But government is not only the political means to liberty, it is also an end in itself, since it is human action, which always has as end its own good character. Government as end therefore must embody liberty; it must not only look to liberty, it must encompass it in its own processes. A want of freedom in the processes of government can accordingly never be excused on the ground that welfare is being served. Liberty is the ultimate welfare and must be preserved in politics as in all other parts of human action. Paternalism is never government's proper character, because government's character as end in itself is the protection of freedom of action by all citizens to seek their own welfare as they think best.

Both as means and as end, therefore, government has liberty as its proper goal.

2. Constitutional form

Current thought includes a heavy strain of impatience with the concept of constitutional form as a guide to political action. The urge to get things done is permitted to brush aside as irrelevant considerations of how things should be done.

In part this disregard for constitutional form is due to the wide, even if undetected, influence of the tenets of communism in modern thought. The state's importance, communism asserts, lies in the fact that in the dialectic of history the state is the means by which the proletarian revolution will be brought about; but when that revolution has been achieved and the ultimate communist society established, the state, communism believes, will wither away as a no longer needed institution. Thus the attitude of communism toward political action purports to be extremely practical. Any political procedure that assists in the promotion of communism is acceptable, particularly since it is regarded as more or less transitory, constituting only a step in the movement toward a stateless society. Current thought, though it may not acknowledge the correctness of this Marxian view, nevertheless is colored by it; a rather low value is placed on the constitutional form of political action.

This viewpoint is encouraged by the vogue of pragmatism, instrumentalism, and experimentalism, whose import is that validity is to be found only in the experience of practical desirabilities rather than in so-called abstract principles. Constitutional form is held to be an abstract principle of no great importance.

Under the influence of these attitudes, much modern political theory has chosen to disregard concepts of what governmental form ought to be. The law, it says, is what it happens to be at the present moment, and this positive law is the proper concern of intellectual activity. What the positive law will become tomorrow will be determined by the pragmatic solution of problems as they arise. And therefore construction of concepts of what the law ought to be, based on a consideration of the nature of man and the universe, is an unnecessary and indeed harmful intellectual exercise.

Within the philosophy of individualism this exaltation of momentary positive law and denial of timeless natural law is great error. Individualism, with its teaching of maximum equal liberty for all individuals as social ideal, is rooted in the conviction that knowable principles obtain in the human process and in the process of the universe, and that these principles can be ascertained in part at least by human reason.

These principles can accordingly be relied on to indicate the form of political action best suited to the purpose of human life. And even as that purpose is timeless, so the ideal of the best form of political action is timeless. The state is not a transitory pragmatism, but a permanent necessity in the preservation of liberty in human society. Since all social action has its ideal in the concept of equal freedom for all persons, political action has its ideal in the concept of the form of government which will best serve that equal freedom. Government therefore has its ideal constitutional form, which it is the task of men to identify and in so far as they can to realize in practice.

But the realization of the ideal of equal freedom must always occur in the environment of particular times and places; the ideal is complete and timeless, but the accomplishment is partial and conditioned by the circumstances of the times. Similarly the ideal form of constitutional government, though it is valid for all societies at all times and in all places, must nevertheless be achieved in practice in the circumstances, historical and cultural, in which particular societies find themselves.

Thus the elements which we shall identify in the ideal constitutional form must always be accomplished with the cultural materials that are available. A society, for example, whose culture has not progressed to the point of possessing a written language cannot make use of elections by secret written ballot. Similarly the current techniques of communication and transport must always bear on the political forms that can practically be realized in the effort to attain the ideal form.

These limitations of practicality occur as well in all human actions as in politics, but they deserve more careful attention in political action than elsewhere because so often in politics the practical limitation is used as an excuse for abandoning the ideal goal. A society may not be able at a given time in its history to employ a secret written ballot because of prevailing illiteracy, but it should nevertheless pursue the goal of being able to do so. The limitations of the times must never be allowed to obscure the nature of the timeless ideal, which in political action is the ideal constitutional form.

3. Government by the people

Government by the people, the first element in the ideal constitutional form, means that government should originate in the consent of the people governed and should continue subject to their control.

Why does the liberty of individualism demand that government be by the people? Why cannot a welfare state, run by wise rulers—philosopher kings—who do all things for the people's benefit, meet as well the specifications of liberty as the more inept accomplishments of people who govern themselves? These questions are being asked today, because they compose the conceptual background for many political changes which are being offered.

Government by the people follows necessarily from the nature of liberty. The liberty of individualism is for all persons. Therefore government, both as end and as means, should be by all persons.

As end, government is a mode of human action which should embody liberty, and to embody liberty government must extend to all citizens an equal opportunity to take part in political action. But the only government in which all citizens can be given an equal opportunity to participate in political action is a government by the people; for a government based upon the primacy of a single ruler or class is one in which, from its nature, most of the people are barred from taking an equal part.

As means, government must be by the people because only a government by all the people can have an interest in maintaining liberty for all the people. How can a government which denies equal opportunity for all persons in political action possibly direct its efforts toward accomplishing equal liberty for all persons in economic and intellectual action? The repudiation of liberty in politics is consistent only with its repudiation in economics and intellectual action. A government cannot long continue to support two basic positions diametrically opposed. A politically despotic government either will become despotic also in economics and intellectual action or will be overthrown. The only welfare state which will continue its interest in the people's welfare is the state whose welfare is achieved by political procedures consonant with the liberty of the people.

The constitutional form of liberty, therefore, must embody as its first element government by the people, who originate and control the government's authority.

4. The delegation of power

The second constitutional principle prescribed by equal liberty is that the people must delegate some portion of their governmental power to selected representatives.

Experience indicates beyond question that the town-meeting type of democracy cannot effectively protect liberty in any save a very small society. If public meetings of citizens could accomplish all the requirements of government, a solution to the entire problem of the form of government would at once be had. But even in Athens, where the citizens of that small city-state clung as tenaciously to the equality of the group meeting as any people in history, it was necessary to delegate some of the authority of the group to selected persons who thereby became public officers. It is interesting to note that the Athenians were so desirous of preserving equality of opportunity in political affairs and so anxious to prevent continuation of power in particular men that they selected most of their public officials by lot for short terms of office. But this very loathness to delegate power was in part the undoing of the Athenian community. For being confronted with the inescapable need of delegating power as the Athenian hegemony expanded, and possessing little reasoned machinery for guiding and controlling such delegation, the society became the victim of the assumption of power by strong men acting under the guise of necessity. A parallel development occurred later at Rome, where the inefficiency of government through meetings of citizens in the forum, though supplemented and in part overridden by an aristocratic senate, ended in the overthrow of all democratic government and the substitution of the absolute rule of an emperor.

The people, therefore, although they must continue to preserve in themselves the source of governmental power, must nevertheless delegate their power to representatives if they are to preserve their liberty. The broad diffusion of political power in the hands of all must be supplemented by a concentration of political power in the hands of a few agents for the specialized tasks of government. This concentration is not a repudiation of equal liberty, but constitutes rather a social tool needed for the maintenance of equal liberty. As we have repeatedly had occasion to observe, the maintenance of intellectual liberty, the free market, and private property requires social intervention, which from the nature of things must be accomplished by designated people performing assigned functions. The performance of these tasks, when in the hands of a government composed of representatives of the people, is not the repudiation of equal liberty but its affirmance.

Therefore the society of individualism is a society of representative government, wherein the specific tasks of government are carried on by persons to whom the people delegate segments of their political power. The authority of these representatives must be limited by the grant which creates it, and this is accomplished by the society's constitution. The constitution of a free society is its specification of the limited powers extended to its representatives in the task of governing.

The powers so conferred upon the people's representatives must be strictly limited to the object to be obtained—the maintenance of liberty in the human process. Such is the human bent to arrogance, and such the influence of the principle that power always tends to corrupt, that the danger of too large assumption of power never ceases to threaten. The art of constitutionalism consists, on the one hand, in granting sufficient authority to the people's representatives to enable them to maintain and protect liberty, and on the other hand in so restricting the same authority that it cannot be turned to the destruction of liberty.

5. Majority rule

The representatives upon whom these limited powers are conferred must be selected by majority vote, not because majority vote contains a promise that the wisest decisions will thereby be made, but because no other method of selection is compatible with the libertarian principle of government by the people. There must be decision if there is to be government; and where the decision must be by the people it must, in case of diversity, be either by the majority or by the minority. As between the two, the decision of the majority should as the general rule prevail, since in most cases more of freedom will be accomplished by realizing the will of the majority and defeating the will of the minority than otherwise.

This, however, is not invariably the case. There are occasions when the will of the majority may be more destructive of liberty than the will of the minority, for example, where the majority wills to enslave the minority or to deny it religious freedom—common instances in history. Recognizing this danger of illiberal action by a majority, the constitutions of free societies have sought to guard against it by adopting bills of rights, the most notable being the first ten amendments to our own federal constitution. Thus the liberal constitution, though of necessity adopting the principle of majority rule, yet must seek to curb the majority from illiberal action by the affirmation of basic principles of liberty which changeful majority decision cannot invade. But even as bills of rights can be adopted, so they can be repudiated or forgotten, and when this is suffered the only recourse of an oppressed minority is rebellion.

The specification of basic rights remains, nevertheless, the only method available for protecting individuals from the illiberal deeds of majorities and of officers in power. Adopted by the majority in calm consideration, the constitutional affirmation of the principles of liberty, of the natural rights of man, restrains that same majority in the irresponsible and cruel moods that undeniably can come upon it. A statement of such principles is an indispensable part of a liberal constitution.

6. Democracy

The word "democracy" has come to mean many things in the past fifty years, and by the very spreading of its coverage has lost much of its former significance. With this loss in specification has come a large increase in emotional aura. Anything described as democratic is thought thereby to be established as good, and democracy is assumed to be an unqualifiedly desirable condition.

But democracy, within any of the meanings ascribed to it, does not constitute the unconditioned goal of human association, since that goal is liberty. Democracy, rather, is a means for attaining the social goal. And although democracy, in the sense of government by the people, is the ideal constitutional form indicated by the principles of liberty, yet under particular times and places, and with regard to the particular institutions antecedently developed by a people, it may be less suitable as the immediate device for securing liberty than some other form. A group long nurtured in the totalitarianism of clan institutions cannot precipitately turn to the ways of democracy without suffering terrible disaster. Consider the experience, for example, of the American Indians, who were thrust out of tribalism and nomadism by historical events that offered them little in exchange except the chance to participate in a democracy for which they were in no wise prepared.

The tragic results that can flow from a failure to understand democracy's place as means rather than end are dramatically illustrated by the first World War. Our participation in that war and the impressment of our men to fight in foreign campaigns were justified on the ground that this was a war "to make the world safe for democracy." Initially considered, this seems a worthy and inspiring ideal, and so it appeared to the American people. But when the war was won and democratic institutions had been set up everywhere, the world was found to be little better than it had been before; indeed it was clear that in many respects it was worse; the millennium had not arrived simply with the advent of democracy. The cynicism and sense of frustration that characterized the ensuing decade had their beginning in the knowledge that somehow the ideal of the war had failed of realization. It failed of realization because it was an incorrect ideal, doomed to disappoint those who should entrust themselves to it. Democracy is not an ultimate goal, but only essential means. Consequently if democracy be striven for as ultimate goal, its acquisition must become a hollow achievement, for most of the problems of liberty will remain.

But democracy's limited role as means being recognized, it nevertheless constitutes, in the sense of government by the people through elected representatives, the ideal constitutional form of the liberty of individualism, toward which ideal all societies should aim their practical progress.

7. Local government

Since liberty means the largest equal freedom for all, this becomes, in political action, the largest equal opportunity for all citizens to take part in government. Liberty therefore demands self-government, which means an equal part for all citizens in governmental action.

But liberty also requires, through representation, that citizens relinquish some portion of their freedom of action to representatives of their choosing. This principle, however, since it is an intrusion upon equal freedom, should be extended in its application as little as possible. There are, indeed, some areas in government where representation need not be resorted to at all. The people themselves can decide, for example, whether there shall be a new bond issue to build a road; they need

not elect representatives to determine the question. Very commonly
matters of this kind are decided in our society by popular vote. In so
far as such popular action can be resorted to without loss of liberty as
discussed above, it should be adopted as superior, in preserving equality
of political action, to decision by representatives.

By the same logic, the authority of representatives should not be
extended over any larger segment of government than necessary for
discharge of the delegated governmental function. Consider, for example,
the administration of parks. Conceivably all the parks in the United
States, including all those in towns and cities, could be administered
by a national board, which would levy a nation-wide tax to support the
nation-wide park system. But the delegation of power to such a national
board would be far greater than that necessary to obtain good parks.
The people in a city desiring parks need not resort to a board with
nation-wide powers; they need only to create one with powers limited
to their own community. The board with only local authority is accordingly the one called for by the principle of equal liberty in political action.

This same analysis applies to all government. Equal liberty in political
action requires local government except where a larger coverage is
clearly called for by the nature of the governmental function.

The framers of our federal constitution recognized the validity of
the principle of local government and strove diligently to apply it.
Accordingly the powers of the national government were carefully
limited to those items, such as defense, coinage, tariffs, foreign relations, and similar matters, which seemed clearly to call for power in
the national representatives to act for the entire populace. But all other
segments of governmental power were reserved to the people of the
several states.

A society is always under a strong temptation to abandon the principle of local government. It is simpler, for example, to prescribe a
uniform system of good education for the entire United States, requiring local communities to meet the standards of such a system, than it is
to encourage each school district in the United States to reach a high
standard of schooling through its own efforts. But the local system
is the system of liberty. It may require more attention, but it will
produce better people. The national system would, like the Prussian
system, give the appearance of efficient operation and impressive accomplishment, but because it would impair freedom of action it would
lack the vitality of decision at the local level. It would impair char-

acter development by the people because it would transfer the function of decision—liberty—to a few.

Such concentration of power in a few representatives is to be resorted to only when it is clear that it is necessary to avoid a larger evil. Restricting the powers of political representatives to the smallest locale consistent with the function to be performed preserves equal liberty and builds the character of the nation's citizens.

8. Conservatism and radicalism

Is the philosophy of liberty essentially conservative or essentially radical in its attitude toward constitutional form?

In political speculation the antithetical positions of the conservative and radical have usually occupied a conspicuous place, and much of political thought has been oriented around the supposedly fixed points represented by these opposed positions.

But whatever descriptions be given to the conservative and radical viewpoints—and such descriptions are various—liberty is concerned with them not as permanent positions but as transitory vantage points to be used in movement to its ultimate goal of maximum equal liberty for all.

The central idea included in the concept of conservatism is the conservation of established institutions. The central idea included in the concept of radicalism is the excision of established institutions clean to the root if necessary to forward desired reforms. Because each point of view includes not only a reasoned concept but also an emotional response, each has frequently been regarded as an ultimate political position which particular political conviction should definitively accept or reject.

To individualism, however, the positions of conservatism and radicalism are but means to an end. Neither the conservation nor the destruction of established institutions is *per se* important; it all depends on what the established institutions are. If the established institutions are predominantly liberal, individualism adopts a conservative position, believing that in the given circumstances liberty will best be served by

A land of settled government,
. . .
Where freedom slowly broadens down
From precedent to precedent.

But if the established institutions are predominantly illiberal, individualism favors the radical attitude, with resort to the force of arms if that seems necessary to the accomplishment of the liberal purpose.

In the lexicon of individualism, accordingly, conservatism and radicalism do not indicate permanent points of view to be approved or disapproved, but only conceptual tools to be used or abandoned as the needs of liberty demand. They become good or bad, to be favored or disfavored, as liberty requires conservative progress or radical change in the constitutional form of a particular government.

Chapter 25

LIBERTY AND THE SEPARATION OF POWERS

1. The clash of principles

The society of liberty founds its governmental power in the people, who delegate precise and limited segments of that power to representatives exercising the force of the state as public officials. But since power always tends to corrupt, every delegation of power contains inescapably an impulsion toward the corrupt aggrandizement of that power by the holder of it, as we discussed in Chapter 10.

Thus arises a clash of principles. How can the free society grant power to its representatives and at the same time prevent the loss of its representative government through the corrupt growth of the power it has delegated? This question lies at the base of the problem of successful democracy. It is placed before us at the present time with particular urgency. Current thought runs much in terms of law as the solution to all problems; but more law means more power by officials of the state; and how can such enhanced power be limited? If we are unsuccessful in containing the power of our public officials there will certainly be an end to liberty in our society.

2. The theory of the separation of powers

Experience discloses only two principles available for the curbing of power. The first is the limited grant of power, whereby general grants are never made but only grants for specific and limited purposes. But this principle is not self-executing; unless supplemented by an additional principle looking to enforcement of the limitation, the limitation will soon come to be disregarded. This needed addition is supplied by the principle of the separation of powers, whereby checks are placed on the aggrandizement of power through the balancing of one power against another.

The device of dividing governmental power has been tried from time to time throughout history. It would seem that for the most part, however, there has been a failure to understand the general object of the separation of powers and in turn the particular forms such separation should assume. The separation of powers has not the purpose of efficiency, nor does it constitute simply an adjustment of the processes of government to natural or inevitable divisions. Rather its purpose is the protection of liberty from the threat of growth of power. The maintenance of liberty accordingly is the occasion and the aim of the separation of governmental powers.

This being true, it follows that the application of the principle, looking to the realization of the general purpose, must adopt those means of organization and process suitable to the end sought to be attained. And since the end is the containment of power within the limits set in its delegation, the means must be designed to achieve that containment.

Human experience thus far in history has disclosed but one mode of effecting a separation of power of such kind as will accomplish power's containment. Governmental power must be so divided that an attempted enlargement of the power and prerogative of one official or group of officials will threaten to encroach upon the power and prerogative of another official or group of officials. It may be that in the course of time, as the art of political government is developed, some other or better method of protecting liberty from the growth of power may be found; but certainly it must be admitted that no prospect of such a discovery can be seen at present, and we must accordingly build liberty with the tools that we now have. We must accordingly contain power by setting it against itself whenever it seeks its aggrandizement beyond its delegated limits.

The basic element in this is the division of power among different men and groups of men. There can be no protection to liberty without this initial division, because without such division no possibility can exist of turning segments of power one against the other for purposes of containment. The second element is the arrangement of the division in such manner that a transgression of an assigned boundary by one segment of power will bring it into the area of another segment of power, and thus will be restrained by it.

The theory of checks and balances through a division of powers is not infrequently attacked because of the inefficiency it assertedly leads to. An analogy is made with the management of a modern business corporation, where efficiency is obtained, it is said, through the concentration of authority in the hands of a few men. A considerable tendency, indeed, can be observed at the present time toward concentrating governmental power in few and unrestricted hands, apparently under the influence of the supposed example of modern business practice.

The analogy, however, breaks down under examination. The object of political organization differs radically from the object of business administration. Business management is concerned simply with profitable operation within the pattern for economic action fixed by the society's laws and customs. But the object of government is nothing less than the maintenance of human liberty in all its forms. It is true that the ultimate object of economic action as well as of political is the maintenance of equal liberty. But business management contributes to this ultimate object by directing production at a profit in a free market; its immediate object is profitable operation, which in turn serves liberty in a free market society. The object of governmental action, however, is broader, comprising not only the maintenance of the free market itself, but also the maintenance of liberty in intellectual and political action. The procedures suitable for business management are therefore not necessarily suitable for government, since the immediate objective is different in the two cases. The pattern of business management accordingly does not furnish a logical or safe guide for the organization of government, beyond its use in purely administrative procedures, and the current favor extended to business organization as a pattern for government should be cautiously regarded.

3. Legislative and executive powers

Since government operates through laws, a primary form of the separation of powers is with regard to the making and enforcing of laws. If the same men who make the laws are also charged with enforcing them, they will be constantly under a great temptation to twist the system of law to their own benefit, and there will be no one in power to oppose. But when one group of men enacts the laws and another enforces them the danger of corruption is much reduced. If the makers of laws attempt to enact laws for their own advantage, they will have to overcome the opposition of an independent executive; and if the enforcers of laws seek to administer laws in their own favor, they will face the difficulty of avoiding remedial legislation by an independent legislature.

Long experience has amply demonstrated the salutary results of this separation. It does not of course remove all occasions for the wrongful use of power, but it restrains the greatest ones. If either the executive or legislative branch seeks the expansion of its authority, it must encounter the jealous opposition of the other, whose area of power would be invaded by the attempted expansion.

A basic principle of governmental organization for the free society, therefore, is that the legislative and executive functions of government must be separated.

The exact mode of effecting such a separation is not important, provided that the basic logic of the separation always be observed. Indeed it will be better if the details are developed in accordance with the society's customs and cultural progress. But the details must always give effect to the proposition that the executive must not make laws and the legislature must not enforce laws. Any departure places liberty in danger.

Our own practice observes the separation of the executive and legislative branches in most respects. Nevertheless there are exceptions.

An important one is the issuance of executive decrees. Admittedly the line is not always easy to draw between those orders within the executive department which are necessary to its operation and those broader decrees which resemble general laws. But admittedly too there is a difference between the two categories. The former falls within the proper domain of the executive branch, but the latter without it. Our current practice, however, does not always attempt to observe this distinction, particularly where foreign relations are concerned. The agreements made by the executive at Yalta and Potsdam, for example, with the many decrees issued in implementation, controlled not only the operation of the executive department but also the acts and resources of our entire nation. Our Supreme Court has ruled that executive decrees, or at least some of them, have the force of law, which the citizen must obey.

Defenders of the procedures by which the Yalta and Potsdam agreements were reached and implemented by decree assert that the conduct of foreign relations, in the course of which these particular agreements were effected, is placed by our constitution in the executive department, and that therefore the agreements and decrees were a proper employment of the executive authority. The question for our present consideration, however, is not whether our constitution authorizes executive decrees with the force of general law, but whether it ought to do so.

Under the principles of liberty in political action, it is clear that it ought not to grant such authority to the executive. It gives the executive a power to which there is no effective check, with continuous expansion of the power the only prospect in the future, even as it has been the only experience of the past.

Our constitution ought to be amended to correct this violation of the principle of separating the executive and legislative. No doubt, as the executive will always contend, the efficiency of the executive department will be hampered by a change, but considerations of executive efficiency must not be allowed to obscure the danger to liberty of a grant to the executive of legislative power. No executive decree should be permitted to have any effect outside the executive department unless authorized by prior legislative action or affirmed by subsequent legislative action, and within the executive department such decrees should have effect only as they do not conflict with laws otherwise established.

4. The independent judiciary

The judicial function is anomalous in that it involves both the making and enforcing of law. Judges make law as they develop the body of rules that are employed in settling disputes, adapting those rules to changing circumstances. They also, in our legal system, pass on the validity of statutes enacted by the legislature, refusing to enforce statutes beyond the constitutional authority of the legislature to enact. But not only do judges thus make law, they also enforce it. The judgments of courts are carried out by the courts' officers, who are authorized by law to use such force as is necessary.

This is an enormous power thus vested in the judiciary, and it necessarily violates the principle of dividing the power to make and enforce laws. How is the corrupt aggrandizement of this power to be guarded against? By the application of three principles: first, the principle of non-autonomous action, by which the judiciary is prohibited from taking action on its own motion and is permitted to exercise its power only on the petition of an aggrieved party; second, the principle of the division of power between lower and upper courts, whereby judicial decision in the first instance is subject to review; third, the principle of the independence of the judiciary from the executive and legislative branches of government.

The constitutions of our national and state governments were framed with the independence of the judiciary in mind. To this independence is largely due the good record of our courts.

Experiments have occasionally been made with the exercise of an appointive power by judges, as, for example, the appointment of certain administrative officers by judges. This is extremely unwise because it impairs the independence of the judges, and though that impairment may be small, it must be expected to exercise only a deleterious influence upon the quality of the judiciary. The power of the judiciary should be firmly separated from all other governmental functions of whatever sort.

5. The federal system

The American federal system, as it was developed in the decisions of the Supreme Court during the first quarter-century of the republic's existence, was an implementation of the principle of local government, which, as we noted in the preceding chapter, was recognized in the national constitution. But the federal system did more than simply apply the principle of local government to the states; it did it in such manner as to separate the powers of the national government from the powers of the state governments, placing the national and state governmental powers in opposition so that an enlargement of power by either state or national government would be at the expense of the other. By this separation of powers each government was held within its assigned sphere.

An essential feature of this system was the recognition of two political communities, the state and the nation, each of which was a sovereignty in its own right, but each limited in the exercise of sovereignty by the other.

Thus far the Constitution was an adaptation of previously known political devices, for the Achaean League of the Greeks had embodied dual sovereignty of federal and local governments, with consequent dual citizenship. But the power of the Supreme Court to police the federal arrangement was an invention in political science of the first order, apparently without historical precedent. This power of the court was not conferred directly by the Constitution, but was built by the court itself through the rather simple expedient of refusing to enforce laws of the national and state governments which it held to be in transgression of their respective constitutional orbits. Thus the court developed by

Congressional Record

PROCEEDINGS AND DEBATES OF THE 85th CONGRESS, SECOND SESSION

The Challenge of Liberty

EXTENSION OF REMARKS

OF

HON. B. CARROLL REECE

OF TENNESSEE

IN THE HOUSE OF REPRESENTATIVES

Wednesday, June 11, 1958

Mr. REECE of Tennessee. Mr. Speaker, Americans who believe with Dr. Franklyn Bliss Snyder that liberty is the key to good life will be interested in a recent book, The Challenge of Liberty, which has been written on our concept of liberty. It is an interesting and challenging book and I would include in the RECORD the very excellent review of it by Dr. Franklyn Bliss Snyder, president emeritus of Northwestern University.

THE CHALLENGE OF LIBERTY

(Reviewed by Dr. Franklyn Bliss Snyder, president emeritus, Northwestern University)

Here is a book which should be in every library, and on the living room table of every intelligent citizen. It is an historical and philosophical analysis of our concept of liberty, and in the light of that analysis an examination of the role of government in human life. The scope is broad, the reasoning close and accurate, the application to major problems of the contemporary world interesting and stimulating. A good book. Once start reading it, and you'll finish it.

Most Americans believe that liberty is the key to good life, both for the individual and for society. They affirm their faith in this creed, and then passively watch as the Federal Government little by little filches their liberty from them and substitutes for it a paternalistic socialism. Mr. Jones makes

quite clear what is happening, and, more to the point, indicates what we should do about it.

The basic structure of the work is simple and effective. Book I: The Challenge to Understand Liberty, opens with what might be called an anticipatory summary of the entire volume:

"The challenge to the occidental world in our time is to maintain liberty, as individual freedom of action and as the social order providing such freedom. Our generation, the recipient of such a heritage of liberty as few other societies have ever obtained, has become oblivious to its riches by reason of their abundance. Careless of our inheritance, we now face the challenge of maintaining it, and the danger is great that it may be lost.

"If the loss occurs, it will come through the growth of collectivism, which continues to increase its influence throughout the Western World. We today devote much of our energy and wealth to preparation for possible war with Communist nations; nevertheless at the same time we continue to adopt additional collectivistic practices, not seeming to comprehend that by this course the ultimate victory of communism is insured. This anomalous policy, which opposes Communists but receives their teaching, is possible only because we presently fail to understand the nature of liberty and are not resolved upon its practice."

After thus showing the reader where he is headed, Mr. Jones turns historian and traces the development of liberty throughout the Western World. Too much praise cannot be given the brilliant summaries which sketch the rise and fall of old civilizations, and show that where liberty has been suppressed mankind has suffered and society has decayed.

470476—66843

2

Book II, the Challenge to Practice Liberty, examines such concepts as "religious liberty, cultural liberty, liberty of political thought, and freedom of speech and of press," and gives the reader what this reviewer considers the best discussion of academic freedom he has ever read. This second book concludes with a grim prophecy of what will happen unless present trends are reversed:

"Our National Government, released from the restraint of the rights of the States, will absorb segments of local government one after another. Its power to do this, through familiar devices of taxation, is irresistible, now that the constitutional limitations have been removed. The evidence of the trend is plain before us. In housing, roads, education, medicine—all fields which should be reserved to local government if liberty is to be preserved—the National Government is moving in. We are becoming ruled by a na-

470476—66843

tional bureaucracy over which we, the people, have and can have no control.

"The evil will grow until it is cured. There is only one cure—adherence to the principle of local government, made effective by the restoration of the Federal system. Let us hope that the restoration will be made in good time."

These are intelligible words, and we are grateful to Mr. Jones for having written them. He has plotted carefully and intelligibly the path down which the United States is now moving, has shown the socialistic and communistic influences that are operating on the Nation, and with effective restraint has called intelligent citizens to the defense of their own liberty. He has written a notably good book: timely, interesting, true, and well written. Buy it, read it, and do something about the situation which it presents.

stages its authority to hold laws unconstitutional, and by this authority it made effective the separation of federal and state powers envisaged by the Constitution.

But the same court which completed the edifice of the American federal system later tore it down. By a series of momentous decisions ending about 1940, reached apparently under the pressure of a misguided public opinion, the separation of powers between the nation and state was rapidly demolished. By these decisions, the power of the national government was given expansion until in reality all prior limitations on it were removed. Today there is no governmental function which the national government cannot exercise, if it chooses to do so, under the authority of some one or other of these decisions.

Doubtless the several states will indefinitely be permitted to exercise local government in many fields. But their activities will be by sufferance of the national government and not by right. State sovereignty was a reality when it had a tribunal in which it could assert its rights in opposition to national sovereignty; but that tribunal no longer being available, state sovereignty has become no more than a name. The hollow form of state sovereignty may long drag on, as the forms of republican Rome continued an obsolete existence after the arrival of the empire, but the reality of state sovereignty is gone.

The judgment of history will be wiser than ours, but we may hazard the opinion that the first American federal system terminated after about forty years of the twentieth century.

Can the federal system be restored? Certainly; the Constitution provides the manner of its amendment, and amendments can be adopted to give again to liberty the protection of the separation of powers inherent in the federal system. But that cannot easily or quickly be done. The institutions of liberty, though they may be demolished with ease, are constructed only with much art and time. Doubtless, too, a movement for the reconstruction of the federal system cannot succeed until the loss of liberty occasioned by its want has grown to dimensions more threatening than at present.

But that time is certain to arrive. Our national government, released from the restraint of the rights of the states, will absorb segments of local government one after another. Its power to do this, through familiar devices of taxation, is irresistible, now that the constitutional limitations have been removed. The evidence of the trend is plain before us. In housing, roads, education, medicine—all fields which should be reserved to local government if liberty is to be preserved—the national government is moving in. We are becoming ruled by a national bureaucracy over which we, the people, have and can have no control.

The evil will grow until it is cured. There is only one cure—adherence to the principle of local government, made effective by the restoration of the federal system. Let us hope that the restoration will be made in good time.

THE SUCCESS OF LIBERTY

The success of liberty depends only upon its being used. Liberty is not a way of social arrangement to be enjoyed merely when times are fair, but a way for all times, and a way through when times are at their worst.

Liberty cannot fail, because it serves the purpose of God in the universe, and whatever serves the purpose of the Creator of the universe cannot fail in the universe.

Finally, liberty always succeeds because it builds the best human character, and the best character that men can build is the only success available to them in the universal scheme.

INDEX

INDEX

A

Academic freedom, 175–188.
Achaean League, 77, 414.
Acton, John (Lord), 97, 105.
Admirable Crichton, The, 80.
American Revolution, 26.
Amoral aspect of collectivism, 139.
Anarchism, definition, 11; inequality in, 44; 89.
Antimonopoly laws, 340, 346, 352.
Aquinas, Thomas, 18, 21.
Aristotle, 15, 75.
Artistic activity, liberty of, 173.
Assistance, 285, 301, 302, 306–326; persons entitled to, 312; extent of, 313.
Athens, 67, 109, 174, 221, 402.

B

Browne, Robert, 20.

C

Calvin, John, 19.
Capital compensation, 266–276.
Capitalism, definition, 12.
Censorship, of religious communication, 159; of art, 173; of press, 211–214.
Central planning, place in collectivism, 41; controlled by a few, 41–44, 138.
Challenge, nature of present challenge, 3.
Character, development of as life's purpose, 46–52.

W

BIOGRAPHICAL SKETCH

Robert V. Jones

JONES, Robert Vernon, lawyer; born in Peterson, Iowa, September 16, 1901; son of Alonzo W. and Ada Marian (Dunn) J.; A.B. degree Northwestern University, 1923, J.D., 1926; married Elsie Pierce Brown, June 14, 1926; children—Richard Vernon, Nancy Gwendolyn, David Owen, Robert Alonzo. Lecturer in economics, Northwestern University 1924–26; admitted to Illinois Bar, 1926; law clerk with Foreman, Bluford, Steele and Schultz, Chicago, 1926–28; partner, Stearns and Jones, Chicago, 1928–42; in private law practice, 1942–45; with United States Group of Control Council for Germany, 1945. Professor at Northwestern University, teaching Business and Government, 1946–48. Member American, Illinois, and Chicago Bar Associations, Chicago Law Institute, American Economics Association, Northwestern University Associates, Phi Beta Kappa, Alpha Delta Phi, Phi Alpha Delta, Phi Mu Alpha, Order of the Coif. Clubs: Law, University (Chicago), University (Evanston), Glenview Club, Cliff Dwellers. Home: 1100 Lake Shore Drive, Chicago. Business: 8 S. Michigan Avenue, Chicago.

THE DESIGN

This book was designed and set by Country Life Press, Garden City, N. Y., in 10 Point Electra Linotype leaded 2 points. The chapter headings and subheadings are set in Futura Medium. It was printed and bound at the Doubleday plant in Hanover, Pennsylvania.